QuickBooks® 2006
The Official Guide

Custom Edition

QuickBooks® 2006
The Official Guide

Custom Edition

McGraw-Hill/Osborne
New York   Chicago   San Francisco
Lisbon   London   Madrid   Mexico City   Milan
New Delhi   San Juan   Seoul   Singapore   Sydney   Toronto

The *McGraw-Hill* Companies

McGraw-Hill/Osborne
2100 Powell Street, 10th Floor
Emeryville, California 94608
U.S.A.

To arrange bulk purchase discounts for sales promotions, premiums, or fund-raisers, please contact **McGraw-Hill**/Osborne at the above address.

QuickBooks® 2006 The Official Guide

1234567890 CUS CUS 0198765

QuickBooks® 2006 The Official Guide For Premier Edition Users, ISBN 0-07-226274-5
QuickBooks® 2006 The Official Guide For Enterprise Solutions 6.0 Users, ISBN 0-07-226275-3

Acquisitions Editor
  Megg Morin

Project/Copy Editor
  Mark Karmendy

Acquisitions Coordinator
  Agatha Kim

Proofreader
  Paul Tyler

Indexer
  Jack Lewis

Composition
  Apollo Publishing Services

Cover Design
  Pattie Lee

Series Design
  Peter F. Hancik

This book was composed with Corel VENTURA™ Publisher.

Contents at a Glance

Part Three
Tracking Time and Mileage

Part Four
Managing QuickBooks

Part Five
Appendices

Contents

Part Two
Bookkeeping

Part Four
Managing QuickBooks

Part Five

Appendices

Acknowledgments

The publisher would like to thank Dawn Hughan, Shane Hamby, and all the Project Managers at Intuit, Inc. for their assistance and cooperation.

Introduction

How to Use This Book

This book is organized with a certain amount of logic connected to the way you'll probably use your QuickBooks software. You can consult the table of contents, where you'll notice that the topics start with the tasks you perform immediately after installing the software, move on to the tasks you perform often, and then cover the tasks you perform less frequently.

The index guides you to specific tasks and features, so when you absolutely must know immediately how to do something, it's easy to find the instructions.

What's Provided in This Book to Help You

There are some special elements in this book that you'll find extremely useful:

- **Tips**   Give you some additional insight about a subject or a task. Sometimes they're shortcuts, and sometimes they're workarounds for QuickBooks restrictions.

- **Notes**   Provide extra information about a topic or a task. Sometimes they provide information about what happens behind the scenes when you perform a task, and sometimes they have additional information you might be curious about.

- **Cautions**   Are presented to help you avoid the traps you can fall into if a task has a danger zone.

- **Sidebars**   Are filled with facts you don't necessarily need to perform a task, but the information may be helpful. Some sidebars help you understand the way QuickBooks "thinks" (all software applications have a predictable thinking pattern); others are designed to point out the way certain procedures help you run your business.

You and Your Accountant

One of the advantages of double-entry bookkeeping software like QuickBooks is that a great many simple bookkeeping tasks are performed automatically. If you've been keeping manual books or using a check-writing program such as Quicken, your accountant will probably have less work to do now that you're using QuickBooks.

Many accountants visit clients regularly or ask that copies of checkbook registers be sent to the accountants' offices. Then, using the data from the transactions, a general ledger is created, along with a trial balance and other reports based on the general ledger (Profit & Loss Statements and Balance Sheets).

If you've had such a relationship with your accountant, it ends with QuickBooks. Your accountant will only have to provide tax advice and business-planning advice. All those bookkeeping chores are performed by QuickBooks, which keeps a general ledger and provides reports based on the data in the general ledger.

Throughout this book you'll find information about general ledger postings as you create transactions in QuickBooks, and you'll also find references to specific information that is going to be important to your accountant. Accountants tend to ask questions about how software handles certain issues (especially payroll, inventory, accounts receivable, and accounts payable). There are also a number of places in this book where you're advised to call your accountant before making a decision about how to handle a certain transaction.

Don't worry, your accountant won't complain about losing the bookkeeping tasks. Most accountants prefer to handle more professional chores, and they rarely protest when you tell them they no longer have to be bookkeepers. Their parents didn't spend all that money on their advanced, difficult educations for that.

Part One

Getting Started

Congratulations on deciding to use QuickBooks to track your business finances. Accounting software such as QuickBooks, however, has to be set up, configured, and carefully tweaked before you can begin using it. If you don't do the preliminary work, the software won't work properly.

Part One of this book has two chapters. In Chapter 1 you'll learn about the features that are unique to the Premier and Enterprise Solutions editions. Then, starting in Chapter 2, and continuing through all the other chapters in this book, you'll learn how to set up, configure, and use all the features in QuickBooks Pro. Those features are also available, of course, in your Premier or Enterprise Solutions edition.

Features Unique to QuickBooks 2006 Premier and Enterprise Solutions Editions

This chapter provides an overview of the features found only in Premier and Enterprise Solutions editions. The discussion starts with the Premier editions, and then covers Enterprise Solutions, describing the features and functions not available in other editions (QuickBooks Online/Pro).

In addition, this chapter presents an overview of the features and functions unique to the industry-specific versions of QuickBooks. Intuit, Inc. has wisely included many industry-specific features that are tailored to your needs.

QuickBooks Premier Edition

QuickBooks Premier Edition has powerful features and functions not found in QuickBooks Pro. All Premier Edition features are also available in all the industry-specific versions of QuickBooks Premier editions, and in all versions of QuickBooks Enterprise Solutions.

Advanced Options for General Journal Entries

QuickBooks Premier Edition offers additional functions you can use when you're creating a general journal entry (GJE). The additional power available in these functions makes it easier to create and track journal entries.

 TIP: See Chapter 14 to learn about creating general journal entries.

AutoFill Memos in General Journal Entries

When you're creating a GJE, any text you enter in the Memo field on the first line of the transaction can be automatically entered on all lines of the transaction. When you view the registers of any accounts involved in the journal entry, the memo text is available to help you remember or understand the reason for the transaction.

AutoFill is enabled by default in the Preferences dialog, in the My Preferences tab of the Accounting Preferences section (see Figure 1-1). If your memo text isn't repeated on the second line of your GJE, the feature has been disabled. Choose Edit | Preferences and enable it.

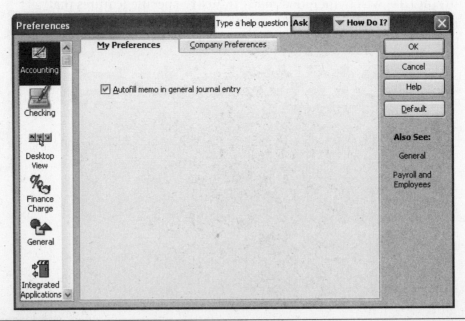

FIGURE 1-1   Make sure the AutoFill Memos option is enabled, to save yourself a lot of work.

When AutoFill is disabled, you have to enter (or copy and paste) the text in the memo field manually on each line of the general journal entry. If you enter text only in the Memo field on the first line of the transaction, then only the register for that account reveals the reason for the GJE. When you're examining account registers for other accounts involved in the transaction, you won't see an explanation for the transaction unless you open the original transaction. Think of the frustration and extra steps this feature saves!

AutoReverse General Journal Entries

Reversing general journal entries is a common transaction type. Frequently, your accountant makes the entry (or sends you instructions for creating the transaction yourself) at the end of the year. Many times, these entries adjust figures for the purpose of creating an accurate business tax return, and then are reversed so your reports provide the same view of your financial situation that you saw before the entry.

In QuickBooks Premier/Enterprise, you can automate the reversal process by clicking the Reverse icon at the top of the GJE window after you save the GJE. By default, when QuickBooks Premier/Enterprise creates the new, reversed GJE, it's dated the first day of the following month (the normal and usual method for reversing journal entries). However, if circumstances warrant, you can change the date.

Previous Bank Reconciliation Reports

Unlike QuickBooks Pro, which only saves the last bank reconciliation report, QuickBooks Premier/Enterprise Solutions editions save all bank reconciliation reports in your company file. This means you don't have to print a report each month, and file it away in case you have to refer to it later (usually because you have a problem reconciling the current month's statement). The previous reconciliation reports are available in two places:

- Choose Reports | Banking | Previous Reconciliation.
- In the Begin Reconciliation dialog box, click Locate Discrepancies, then click Previous Reports.

 TIP: See Chapter 12 for a detailed explanation of reconciling bank accounts.

Export Memorized Reports

If you customize a report that has absolutely everything you need, arranged in a beautifully logical order, you can memorize it. Then, it's available every time you need exactly that information, in exactly that format.

 TIP: Read Chapter 15 to learn about creating and running QuickBooks reports.

To add more power to this feature, QuickBooks Premier/Enterprise Solutions editions offer an Export function for memorized reports. If you're an accountant, this means that after you develop memorized reports that provide the information you need, exactly the way you need it, you can export those reports to a file, and e-mail the file to your clients. If you're a bookkeeper, you can travel to client sites with the memorized reports you've created on a floppy disk (the exported report files are quite small).

The real beauty of this feature is that all QuickBooks editions can import the exported memorized reports (only the export feature, not the import feature, is limited to Premier/Enterprise Solutions editions). Because the Import Memorize Report feature is a standard QuickBooks function, businesses running QuickBooks Pro (and, of course, Premier or Enterprise Solutions) can add these reports to their Memorized Reports list with the click of a mouse.

Memorized reports are templates, and contain no data, so each QuickBooks installation that imports your exported reports will produce reports that use local data, but are based on the format, filters, and sorting designs you memorized and exported.

 C A U T I O N :   When you're exporting a memorized report, you cannot use any custom fields you added to the company file that is open when you memorize the report. Those fields won't exist in other QuickBooks company files.

Closing Date Exception Report

Want to drive an accountant crazy? Create a report that shows opening balances for accounts as of the current year that don't match last year's closing balances for the same accounts. The rule is, "This year's opening balances must match last year's closing balances." When they don't match, accountants go into a frenzy, and sometimes they won't leave your office until they've found the reason for the discrepancy. They don't have an easy time in their quest for the answer to the question, "What changed, and why did it change?" The business owner is usually interested in the answer to the question, "Who changed it?"

It's almost impossible to find the cause of these mismatched balances, unless you happen to have a detailed report of every transaction that occurred last year (printed at the moment you recorded the closing balances), so you can compare each transaction to the transactions currently in the registers. This can take days, or weeks, and it's going to cost you a lot of money no matter how reasonable your accountant's fees seem to be.

 T I P :   Read Chapter 17 to learn about closing your books and setting a closing date.

QuickBooks Premier and Enterprise Solutions editions offer a Closing Date Exception Report, which lists all transactions that were added or changed after the closing date. (A transaction that was changed shows the date and amount of the modification, as well as the date and amount of the original transaction.) If your QuickBooks configuration includes user logins, the report displays the login name of the user who created the transaction.

To view the Closing Date Exception Report, choose Reports | Accountant & Taxes | Closing Date Exception Report. Any transactions that occurred after the closing date appear in the report.

Sales Orders

It's quite common for product-based businesses to receive an order from a customer that can't be filled and invoiced immediately. Sometimes you have to wait for the product to be built or received, and sometimes you have to wait for a manager to approve a price (which usually means the sales person taking the order has offered the customer a discount not available in the discounts you've configured for items).

 TIP: Chapter 3 is all about invoicing.

You have to record the transaction, but you can't let it affect the balances in your accounts, because no money is owed, nor is there a commitment to reduce inventory. The solution is a sales order. Users of QuickBooks Basic/Pro have to use post-it notes, a handwritten log, or a workaround for a normal invoice entry when they encounter this scenario, but you don't, because QuickBooks Premier and Enterprise Solutions editions offer the ability to create sales orders.

 TIP: If you're an accountant with clients using QuickBooks Pro, see Chapter 3 to learn about workarounds for sales orders, and pass the information along. Or, even better, update them to a QuickBooks Premier/ Enterprise Solutions edition.

 NOTE: To use sales orders, you must enable the feature in the Company Preferences tab of the Sales & Customers Preferences.

Creating Sales Orders

Sales orders are as easy to create as invoices, and, in fact, they resemble invoices. To create a sales order, choose Customers | Create Sales Orders to open the Create Sales Orders window seen in Figure 1-2.

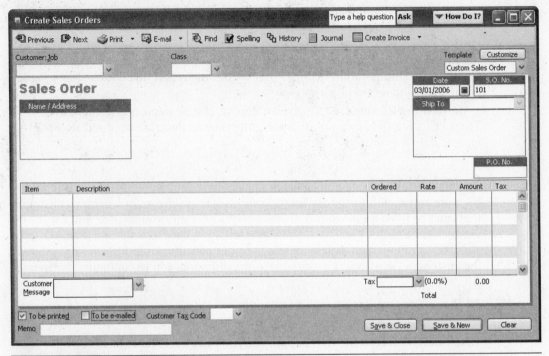

FIGURE 1-2   Sales orders have the "look and feel" of invoices, so you'll find it easy to work with them.

When you save a sales order, the transaction isn't posted to the normal accounts (A/R, Inventory, Income, Cost of Goods, etc.). Instead, QuickBooks posts the transaction to a special account named Sales Orders.

When you're ready to ship products, you can turn the sales order into an invoice automatically. Open the sales order and click the Create Invoice icon on the toolbar.

Sales Order Reports

QuickBooks Premier/Enterprise Solutions editions offer two useful reports for tracking sales orders (the names of the reports clearly indicate the contents):

- Open Sales Orders by Customer
- Open Sales Orders by Item

Both reports are available in the submenu you see when you choose Reports | Sales.

Generate Purchase Orders from Sales Orders Automatically

If you entered a sales order because you were out of product, you have to order the product. Instead of opening a blank purchase order transaction window, and filling in the data, you can tell QuickBooks Premier/Enterprise Solutions editions to generate the purchase order from the sales order. This saves a lot of time and effort,

and, perhaps more important, avoids the possibility of typing errors. To create the
purchase order, open the sales order transaction and click the arrow to the right of the
Create Invoice icon on the toolbar. Select Purchase Order from the drop-down menu.

 T I P :   QuickBooks Premier/Enterprise Solutions editions also offer the ability
to create purchase orders automatically from estimates.

Inventory Assemblies

Inventory assemblies are products that are assembled, or partially assembled, using
existing inventory parts. Only QuickBooks Premier and Enterprise Solutions editions
offer the software functions required for inventory assemblies.

 T I P :   You must enable inventory tracking in the Purchases & Vendors
category of the Preferences dialog to use the inventory assemblies feature.

In QuickBooks Premier/Enterprise Solutions editions you can create an item of the
type Assembly (an item type not available in QuickBooks Basic/Pro editions). The
New Item dialog for an Assembly item includes a components list (see Figure 1-3).
All you have to do is enter the existing components required to build this assembly.

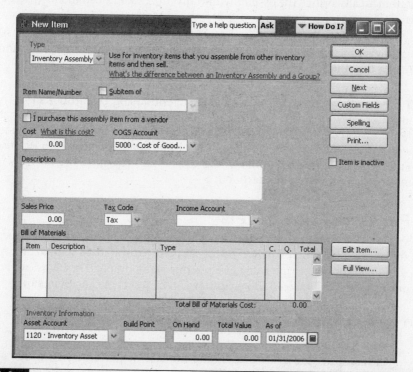

FIGURE 1-3   An Assembly item contains a list of the components required to build it.

TIP :   Chapter 10 covers everything you need to know about tracking inventory.

When you've built an assembly, you must receive it into inventory so you can sell it. QuickBooks Premier/Enterprise Solutions editions provide functions to automate this process. The Build Assemblies window provides an easy way to add your assembled items to your inventory, and automatically decrement your inventory of the components in the assembled items.

If you don't have enough components to build the number of assemblies you need, QuickBooks Premier/Enterprise Solutions editions accept the data, and mark the build as Pending. You can track current pending builds so you're sure you remember to order the components. Choose Reports | Inventory | Pending Builds to see a list of pending builds.

When the components needed for pending bills are received into inventory, you can finalize the appropriate pending bills. Choose Reports | Inventory | Pending Builds, and double-click the listing for the build you're ready to finalize. When the build's window opens, the new Quantity on Hand for the components is displayed automatically. If you have sufficient components to build the assemblies, click the Remove Pending Status button at the bottom of the window. QuickBooks automatically brings the assembly into inventory, and decrements the components from inventory.

If you over-build assemblies, or a customer cancels a built-to-order assembly, you can disassemble an assembly by deleting the build, and QuickBooks will automatically return the components to inventory. Cool!

 TIP :   If you're an accountant with clients using QuickBooks Pro that need inventory assemblies, read Chapter 10 for some workarounds that enable this feature. You can use this information to teach your clients how to use the workarounds. Of course, you can also urge them to upgrade to Premier/ Enterprise Solutions editions, where the feature is supported natively (always more efficient than a workaround).

Per Item Price Levels

While all versions of QuickBooks let you create discounts or markups by percentages, and apply them when you're creating an invoice, only the Premier/Enterprise Solutions editions permit price levels connected to items. The items can be services or products, and once established they can be linked to customers or jobs.

 TIP :   Chapter 2 has information on setting up price levels.

Per item price levels are prices (and can also be percentages), which gives you a great deal of flexibility in charging customers for products or services. You can use item price levels to set multiple prices for the same item; for example, assign a single item (a product or a service) prices of $50.00, $40.00, and $30.00.

You can assign a specific price for the item to a customer (or multiple customers), or to one or more jobs. In addition, if you wish, you can assign a specific price to an item when you're creating an invoice. If the invoice contains an item that has price levels assigned, a drop-down list containing all the price levels is available in the Rate column of the invoice. Just select the price you want to charge for this item, for this invoice.

Create a Business Plan

QuickBooks Premier/Enterprise Solutions editions include a robust software tool named Business Planner. You can use the software to create a detailed business plan, which is a way to predict, plan for, and control your company's future growth. You can create a business plan for your own business or, if you're an accounting professional, for a client's business. To access Business Planner, choose Company | Planning & Budgeting | Use Business Plan Tool.

Business Planner operates like the EasyStep Interview you used when you set up your QuickBooks company file, which is, of course, a wizard (anyone who uses Windows knows about wizards). You click Next to move through a series of windows, divided into sections (topics), answering questions and providing information in each window.

The software is extremely powerful, so the business plan it creates is extremely detailed. Don't plan on getting the entire plan written in one session; it takes a lot of time to do this right. Luckily, the Business Planner saves the information you enter, so whenever you go back to the software you can pick up where you left off.

The Business Planner uses existing data from your QuickBooks company file, and then asks a slew of questions about your expectations for the business. You don't need an MBA to answer the questions; they're simple and to the point. You know your own businesses well enough to answer these questions.

The Business Planner produces a pro forma balance sheet, a profit and loss statement, and a statement of cash flow for the next three years, based on the projections it makes from the data you enter. You can publish your plan in PDF format, which makes the document extremely portable—you can send it to anybody, regardless of the word processing software they use. Additionally, you can export the plan's financial projections to Microsoft Excel for those "what if" exercises that are always so valuable.

($) TIP: A good business plan is more than a blueprint you can use for growing your business; it's a useful tool for gaining investment funds or a line of credit. The format of the QuickBooks business plan matches the recommendations of the United States Small Business Administration for a loan application or a line of credit.

Forecasting

You can create a forecast for revenue and cash flow with the QuickBooks Set Up Forecast feature, available only in Premier and Enterprise Solutions editions. The process, the user interface, and the linked reports for the forecast feature all closely resemble the QuickBooks budget feature. Choose Company | Planning & Budgeting | Set Up Forecast to open the tool.

You can start your forecast with existing company data, and then use "what if" scenarios to manipulate that data so it more closely matches your expectations (or hopes) for the coming year. As with the budget feature, you can base your forecast on your P&L accounts, or narrow the scope of a forecast to one customer (or customer:job), or one class.

You can also create your forecast from scratch, ignoring the data in your company file. This is a good approach if you've changed your business substantially, or are planning to. Perhaps you're adding services or products, or hiring employees who bring a new, specialized expertise that will provide new sales opportunities and a new customer base. On the other hand, perhaps your current financials reflect losses and you've decided to remove the service or products that caused those losses.

After you create your forecast, you can generate reports on the forecast, including a "forecast vs. real figures" report.

 TIP: To learn how to create budgets and use the budget window, see Chapter 13.

Expert Analysis

Expert Analysis is a product of Sageworks, Inc., which you can read about at www.sageworksinc.com. The company's Expert Analysis product is offered without any fee (for one year) to users of all Premier editions.

Expert Analysis benchmarks your company's financial performance against past performance (if your company file has previous year data), and also against other companies in the same industry. The reports are incredibly comprehensive, which makes them a powerful resource for analyzing your company and planning for future growth.

Accountants can use Expert Analysis to examine and report on the performance of client companies, providing an opportunity for accountants to offer their clients a valuable professional service.

To create an Expert Analysis report on your company's financial condition, choose Company | Planning & Budgeting | Use Expert Analysis Tool. Using a wizard interface, Expert Analysis walks you through a series of windows in which you're asked to answer questions and enter information.

 CAUTION: If you're using the QuickBooks logins and permissions features, only a user with permission to access sensitive reports can use Expert Analysis.

Expert Analysis calculates period comparisons, and you can select monthly, quarterly, or yearly analysis periods. You can further refine the way the periods are analyzed. For example, if you select quarterly analysis, you can compare this quarter to the previous quarter, or this quarter to the same quarter last year.

In a wonderful concession to reality, the software lets you make adjustments for scenarios that are specific to your business environment. For example, you can tell Expert Analysis to put back a proprietor's salary (instead of making it an expense), since those amounts are really part of the profit for a proprietorship. You can also tell Expert Analysis to consider expenses you don't currently have but plan to incur in the future. For example, you may be planning to move your home-based business (no rent expense) to an office building, or you may be ready to hire somebody to replace the free labor you're getting from family members.

The reports you get from Expert Analysis are slick and professional. Every imaginable category is covered in detail (see Figure 1-4).

Remote Access

Remote Access lets you work on your QuickBooks files when you're not in the office. All you have to do is find a computer with Internet access, wherever you are, anywhere in the world. The computer you're working from doesn't need to have QuickBooks installed, because the QuickBooks software you'll be using is the software you installed on your own computer.

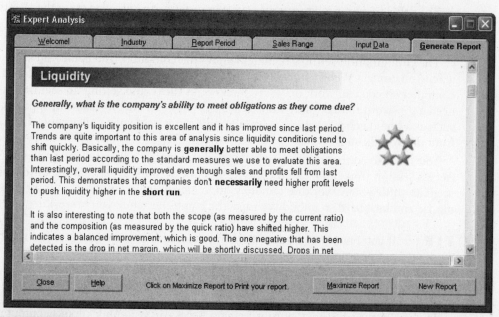

FIGURE 1-4   A detailed discussion of every phase of the business is available, along with a report card (the stars).

($) **NOTE:**   Premier/Enterprise Solutions Accountant editions have a version of Remote Access that works differently. Accountants can access client computers remotely, instead of their own computers.

When you use Remote Access to connect to the computer that holds your QuickBooks files from a remote computer, you're not making a direct connection between two computers. Instead, the two computers meet on the Internet, courtesy of WebEx, which is a third-party company. Both computers log into the same WebEx web site, and WebEx provides all the technology and security required.

The computer that holds your QuickBooks files must have an always-on, dedicated broadband Internet connection (DSL or cable service). If you didn't have an always-on service, you couldn't access your QuickBooks files at your convenience. (The computer you use at a remote location to connect to your QuickBooks files doesn't need an always-on connection.)

To use Remote Access you must have a Remote Access account, and you must install and configure the software that enables this feature on the computer that holds your QuickBooks files.

To sign up for an account, open QuickBooks, and choose File | Utilities | Remote Access. QuickBooks may display a message telling you it must open your Internet browser, so click OK. The account is free for a year. WebEx provides this free year of services to purchasers of QuickBooks Premier and Enterprise Solutions editions. If you find the service useful, you can continue to use it at a reasonable monthly cost.

The software you need to set up your computer is downloaded from the WebEx web site. After you download the software package, install it, and then configure the settings for the computer that holds your QuickBooks files.

The configuration settings include naming the computer (the name you see when you contact WebEx from a remote computer and ask to be admitted to your computer so you can work on your QuickBooks files), and setting up security. You need a password to make sure nobody except you (and anyone else you appoint, such as a bookkeeper who works from home) can access your QuickBooks files from the WebEx site.

You can also configure the way your office computer behaves during a Remote Access session. You can make the monitor blank, so nobody back at the office can see data while you're working remotely, and you can lock the office computer's mouse and keyboard so nobody can use the computer while you're working.

($) **TIP:**   If you have a multi-user QuickBooks installation, while you're working from a remote location other users can continue to access the QuickBooks file from their computers just as if you were in the office working at your QuickBooks computer.

By default, the software that runs Remote Access on your QuickBooks computer loads when Windows starts. It rests quietly in the background, waiting for WebEx to wake it up with an announcement that somebody on the Internet wants to authenticate his or her name and begin working in QuickBooks. QuickBooks doesn't have to be open on the computer in order to use your files from a remote location. One of the tools available at WebEx is the ability to open QuickBooks remotely.

 CAUTION: If you change the default behavior of the Remote Access software so it doesn't start whenever Windows starts, remember to start the software manually whenever you leave the office, and, of course, don't shut down the computer.

From a remote location, you can work on your QuickBooks files by logging into the WebEx site and entering your Remote Access user name and password. Once you're authenticated by WebEx, your personal web page appears, showing the name of the office computer that you set up when you configured your Remote Access account. Click the computer name, enter the authenticating password for this computer, and go to work.

Premier Accountant Edition

QuickBooks Premier Accountant Edition includes additional features that are specifically designed for accountants. In addition, you'll find a duplication of many of the features contained in other industry-specific versions of QuickBooks Premier, to help you support your clients who purchased those products.

In addition to the features unique to the Premier Accountant Edition that I discuss in this section, this edition of QuickBooks includes two major programs that are covered separately in the appendices for this book:

- Fixed Asset Manager (see Appendix A)
- Financial Statement Designer (see Appendix B)

Special Features for General Journal Entries

The Premier Accountant Edition includes several features that provide more power and functionality as you create journal entries.

GJE Adjusting Entries

Frequently, a GJE is an adjustment, made to correct a problem, or "clean up" an account. However, when you examine account registers and see a GJE, you have to rely on your memory for the reason behind the entry. Sometimes, even the text you put into the Memo field doesn't jog your memory sufficiently—it made sense when you wrote it, but not anymore. If you can't remember, you have to use all those extra keystrokes to open the original transaction window, and even then, you may not find enough information to determine the reason for the transaction.

Some GJEs are easy to figure out later; an entry in a fixed asset is almost certainly a depreciation or amortization entry. You don't even have to bother opening the original transaction window, because you know you'll find a depreciation expense account among the listings.

But what if the entry affects an income or expense account? Was this an adjustment, or did it represent some major change in the way books are kept? Most accountants want to know (and an auditor definitely wants to know).

In the Premier Accountant Edition you can specifically mark a GJE as an adjusting entry, via a check box available at the top of the GJE window. In fact, the Adjusting Entry check box has a check mark in it by default (because the majority of GJEs are created to make an adjustment).

To make this feature even more efficient, the Premier Accountant Edition has a report named Adjusting Journal Entries in the Accountant & Tax Reports submenu. As you'd expect, it's a display of the adjusting GJEs you created.

GJE Reports in the Transaction Window

When you open a GJE transaction window in the Accountant Edition, the bottom of the window displays existing GJEs. By default, the window displays the previous month's transactions, but you can change the selection to match your needs (last year, this quarter, and so on). This provides access to earlier GJEs without the need to click the Previous button multiple times.

If you don't want to see the previous transactions, click Hide List Of Entries (the button's name changes to Show List Of Entries so you can reverse your decision).

 TIP: Hiding the previous transactions enlarges the transaction window you're working on, which makes it easier to see all your entry lines when you're creating a large GJE.

Billing Rate Levels

Premier Accountant Edition offers billing rate levels. This feature lets you assign a billing rate to a person performing a specific service. For example, on a given job, your senior partners may be billable at one rate, while your bookkeepers generate a different rate.

The billing rates are a list, accessible from the Lists menu. When you create a billing rate, you link the rate to a name (the person providing the service) and a service. The service provider can exist in your Employee list, Vendor list, or Other Name list. When you create a billing rate, you can use the same hourly rate for all service items performed by people with this billing rate level, or you can create a service-specific rate for people at a particular billing level. To track services for each name and billing rate, the service providers must use the QuickBooks Timesheet feature.

 TIP: See Chapter 18 to learn about using Timesheets.

When you invoice your customers, the appropriate billing rates are automatically added to the invoice from the Time And Costs dialog that's available on the Invoice window. You can also apply any customer's percentage price level (usually a discount) to the billing rate invoice items.

Customized Reports for Multiple Industries

All of the industry-specific Premier and Enterprise Solutions editions contain customized reports that are designed to be specific to that industry or type of business. The Accountant Edition includes most of those reports, which makes it easier for you to ask your clients who use Premier or Enterprise Solutions edition to send specific reports.

To see the customized reports, choose Reports | Industry Specific, and point to one of the industry-specific categories to display its submenu of customized reports. Then select the report you want to view.

 TIP: You can further customize any of the industry-specific reports, memorize it, and export it to your clients.

Premier Contractor Edition

Intuit has created the Premier Contractor Edition with a view to making it easier for contractors to get up and running quickly with QuickBooks, as well as provide special features that contractors need to run and grow their businesses.

Change Order Tracking

Change orders are a fact of life in the construction industry, and the QuickBooks Premier Contractor Edition provides a way to create and track change orders. When you modify an estimate you'd created for a job, QuickBooks offers you the opportunity to track the changes instead of overwriting them.

You can track the items that changed (services or products), the dollar amount of each change, and the net dollar change to the estimate. Change order data is added to the description field after the last item on the estimate (see Figure 1-5).

Billing Rate Levels

New in 2005, the Premier Contractor Edition offers billing rate levels. This feature lets you assign a billing rate to a person performing a specific service. For example, on a given job, your operating engineers may be billable at one rate, while your carpenters generate a different rate. The billing rates are a list, accessible from the Lists menu.

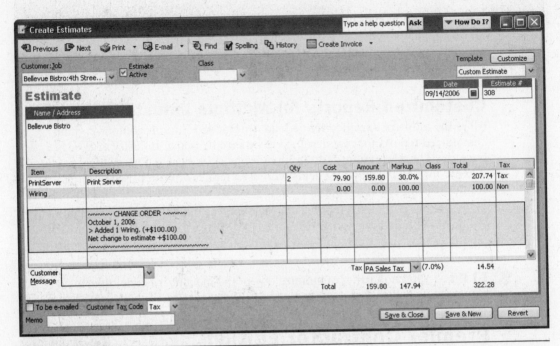

FIGURE 1-5   You can track changes you make to an estimate.

When you create a billing rate, you link the rate to a name (the person providing the service) and a service. The service provider can exist in your Employee list, Vendor list, or Other Name list. When you create a billing rate, you can use the same hourly rate for all service items performed by people with this billing rate level, or you can create a service-specific rate for people at a particular billing level. To track services for each name and billing rate, the service providers must use the QuickBooks Timesheet feature.

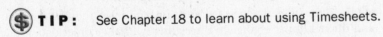**TIP:**   See Chapter 18 to learn about using Timesheets.

When you invoice your customers, the appropriate billing rates are automatically added to the invoice from the Time And Costs dialog that's available on the Invoice window. You can also apply any customer's percentage price level (usually a discount) to the billing rate invoice items.

Customized Reports

Premier Contractor Edition contains a wide variety of reports that have been customized for your business:

- Job Costs by Vendor
- Job Costs Detail
- Job Costs by Vendor & Job
- Job Cost-to-Complete
- Unpaid Bills by Job
- Unpaid Job Bills by Vendor
- Expenses Not Assigned to Jobs
- Billed/Unbilled Hours by Person
- Billed/Unbilled Hours by Person and Job
- Billed/Unbilled Hours by Person and Activity
- Open Purchase Orders by Vendor
- Open Purchase Orders by Vendor Detail
- Certified Payroll - Box 1 Employee Information
- Vendor Account Information
- Customer Account Information

Premier Manufacturing & Wholesale Edition

The Premier Manufacturing & Wholesale Edition has some nifty built-in features
that make it easy to track your business accurately and efficiently.

Customized Reports

The experts at QuickBooks have customized some reports that are particularly
useful for manufacturing and wholesale businesses. These reports help you
track the state of your business, your customers, and the products you make
or distribute.

- Sales by Rep Detail
- Sales by Product
- Sales by Customer Type
- Sales Volume by Customer
- Sales by Class and Item Type
- Profitability by Product
- Open Sales Orders by Item
- Open Purchase Orders by Item
- Open Sales Orders by Customer
- Inventory Reorder Report by Vendor

Forms

Premier Manufacturing & Wholesale Edition provides some extremely useful forms. The forms are Microsoft Word documents (so you need Microsoft Word installed on your computer to use them). The following forms are included:

- Customer Return Materials Authorization Forms
- Non-conforming Material Report
- Damaged Goods Log

 TIP: These forms aren't transactions; they don't post amounts to accounts, and they don't interact directly with your QuickBooks company file.

Customer RMA Forms

You probably follow the common rule that you won't issue a credit for returned merchandise unless there's an RMA (sometimes called RA) number, assigned by you, attached to the package. The Customer RMA form built into the Premier Manufacturing & Wholesale Edition is useful for documenting RMAs.

Non-conforming Material Report (Vendor RMA Form)

If you have to return a product to a vendor, after you get your RMA number, you can track the details about the returned merchandise with the Non-conforming Material Report. After you fill out the information, you can print a copy of this form and use it as a packing slip.

Damaged Goods Log

It's a good idea to log inventory products that can't be sold because they're damaged (or missing). QuickBooks provides a Damaged Goods Log to record the details when this happens in your warehouse. You can use the information in the Damaged Goods Log to enter inventory adjustments.

Premier Nonprofit Edition

The Premier Nonprofit Edition contains several important and useful features that make record keeping much easier for nonprofit organizations.

Unified Chart of Accounts (UCOA)

The Premier Nonprofit Edition includes the Unified Chart of Accounts (UCOA), which was developed by the California Association of Nonprofits and the National Center for Charitable Statistics (NCCS). The UCOA provides a comprehensive set of accounts for you to use as you track your nonprofit organization's financial records.

Customized Reports

The Premier Nonprofit Edition provides a number of essential reports that have customized and memorized for this QuickBooks edition:

- Biggest Donors/Grants
- Budget vs. Actual by Donors/Grants
- Budget vs. Actual by Program/Projects
- Donors/Grants Report
- Programs/Projects Report
- Statement of Financial Income and Expense
- Statement of Financial Position
- Statement of Functional Expenses (990)

Transaction Templates

QuickBooks Premier Nonprofit Edition provides special transaction templates that work better than standard business templates, because they use terminology that's appropriate for nonprofit organizations.

Pledge Template for Invoicing

The Pledge template makes it easy to send invoices to donors who have pledged money to your organization. QuickBooks treats the transaction as an A/R invoice, and posts the amount to the appropriate A/R and income accounts.

Donor Receipt for Cash Receipts

When you receive a spontaneous donation (the income arrived without any invoice or pledge sent from your organization), QuickBooks has a template you can use to record the transaction and send a printed copy to the donor as a receipt. Essentially, this template is a Cash Receipt (a cash sale in the business world), and is posted as such. However, the template uses the term Donor Receipt, which is more appropriate.

Forms and Letters

QuickBooks builds in some boilerplate documents you can use to send letters to your donors and potential donors. You can edit the letters to match your specific needs, and then use the Mail Merge feature in Microsoft Word to send the letters to customers (or people in your Other Names list). The following letters are included in the QuickBooks Letter subfolder:

- Nonprofit Fund Raising Letter
- Nonprofit Thank You Letter

TIP: After you've filled out a Pledge form, click the Letters icon on the transaction window to automatically merge the data in the transaction to one of the predefined letters. This is a good way to thank a donor who has made a pledge, or to remind the donor to honor the pledge.

Premier Professional Services Edition

QuickBooks' well-known and well-regarded innate strength in managing service businesses is made even more powerful by the additional features built into the Premier Professional Services Edition.

Billing Rate Levels

The Premier Professional Services Edition offers billing rate levels. This feature lets you assign a billing rate to a person performing a specific service. For example, your senior partners may be billable at one rate, while your staff members generate a different rate. The billing rates are a list, accessible from the Lists menu.

You link a billing rate to a name (the person providing the service) and a service. The service provider can exist in your Employee list, Vendor list, or Other Names list. When you create a billing rate, you can use the same hourly rate for all service items performed by people with this billing rate level, or you can create a service-specific rate for people at a particular billing level. To track services for each name and billing rate, the service providers must use the QuickBooks Timesheet feature.

 TIP: See Chapter 18 to learn about using Timesheets.

When you invoice your customers, the appropriate billing rates are automatically added to the invoice from the Time And Costs dialog box that's available on the Invoice window. If you wish, you can apply any customer's percentage price level (usually a discount) to the billing rate invoice items.

Customized Reports

The precustomized reports, designed to be useful for professional service businesses, will help you learn the things you need to know about the health of your business:

- Project Cost Detail
- Unbilled Expenses by Projects
- Billed vs. Proposal by Project
- Billed/Unbilled Hours by Person
- Billed/Unbilled Hours by Person and Project
- Billed/Unbilled Hours by Person and Activity

- Open Balances by Customer/Project
- A/R Aging Detail by Class
- Project Status
- Project Contact List
- Expenses Not Assigned to Projects
- Job Costs by Vendor and Job Summary
- Job Costs by Vendor and Job Detail
- Cost to Complete by Job Summary
- Cost to Complete by Job Detail

Premier Retail Edition

QuickBooks Premier Retail Edition is specifically designed for retailers to help you manage your business more effectively. You'll find plenty of customized features to help you set up, configure, and run your business finances.

Customized Reports

Retailers have some special reporting needs, and the Premier/Enterprise Retail Edition provides customized reports for retailers that you'll find useful:

- Profit & Loss Monthly Comparison
- Balance Sheet Monthly Comparison
- Gross Margin by Inventory Item
- Estimates by Customer
- Monthly Sales by Customer
- Accounts Payable Graph
- Bills by Due Date
- Purchase volume by vendor
- Vendor Returns Summary
- Vendor Returns Detail
- Open Purchase Orders by Vendor
- Sales Tax Liability

Track Individual Customers—or Not

You can track sales on a customer-by-customer basis, which is a good idea if you don't run a standard busy retail sales counter, and an especially good idea if you provide services for your products (such as repairs).

If your retail business has a counter with a cash register or a POS system, and you have no particular reason to keep running records on the names of the customers who buy products, QuickBooks Retail Edition provides a way to enter your sales transactions in summary form. Choose the Daily Sales Summary template (see Figure 1-6), that has been customized for this purpose.

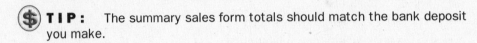

TIP: The summary sales form totals should match the bank deposit you make.

You can customize the summary sales form to add or remove columns, and many retailers add data to match the data they get from their cash register or point of sale system reports (the more powerful those front-end systems are, the more information you can track).

TIP: See Chapter 4 for detailed information on cash sales, including the way to set up your system to manage cash register over/short amounts.

Integrating with QuickBooks POS

If you use QuickBooks POS software for your retail business, your POS software handles the front end, and can transfer financial data to your QuickBooks company file.

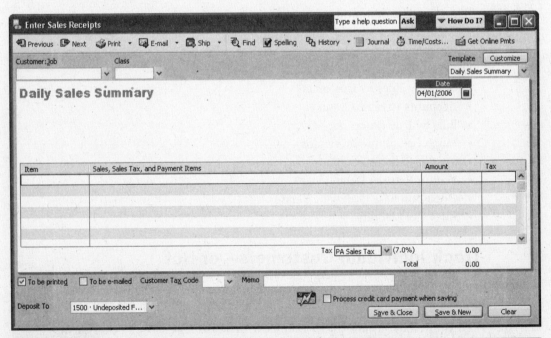

FIGURE 1-6   Enter the total sales for the day instead of creating a transaction for each sale.

If you're not using QuickBooks POS, you should investigate it because it provides a robust way to manage point of sale transactions and post totals to your QuickBooks general ledger. You can learn more about this software by visiting www.QuickBooks.com, and following the links to the products.

 TIP: A number of third-party developers have created POS applications that integrate with QuickBooks. You can get more information on the QuickBooks web site.

QuickBooks Enterprise Solutions

If you purchased a QuickBooks Enterprise Solutions edition, you've gained two important advantages in one fell swoop:

- You have an accounting software package that is so efficient and easy-to-use that it will be easy to grow your business.
- The additional power of Enterprise Solutions means that as your business grows, you won't outgrow your accounting software.

All of the features, functions, and additional power described earlier in this chapter for the QuickBooks Premier editions are available to you in your Enterprise Solutions software.

If you have an industry-specific edition of Enterprise Solutions, the industry-specific features described for Premier editions earlier in this chapter are yours as well.

But wait, there's more. Besides giving you all the power of Premier editions, Enterprise Solutions delivers additional powerful features that I'll describe in the following sections. In addition, be sure to read about two features that are covered separately:

- Fixed Asset Manager (see Appendix A)
- Financial Statement Designer (see Appendix B)

Increased Power for Lists

Your day-to-day work in QuickBooks revolves around lists—if you're not creating or editing a list entry, you're using a drop-down list in a transaction window. The Enterprise Solutions editions have attached more power to these important QuickBooks components.

More Capacity for Lists

Enterprise Solutions has twice the list capacity of the other versions of QuickBooks for the following lists:

- Names lists total (29,000 vs. 14,500)
- Items (29,000 vs. 14,500)
- Memorized transactions (29,000 vs. 14,500)

- Memorized reports (29,000 vs. 14,500)
- Sales Reps (29,000 vs. 14,500)

Powerful List Search Tools

So, now you have this enormous list capacity, and you can keep an incredible amount of information in your QuickBooks files. Of course, as files become large, it becomes difficult to find information, and even search functions take a long time.

In Enterprise Solutions, you can search lists, which is a terrific advantage. But, it doesn't stop there—you can define and refine the search process, selecting the field (or multiple fields) you want to search. You can even drill down by searching the results of the first search, which means you'll be able to find whatever you need.

This search tool is handy when you need to find information in a hurry (such as those times when a customer or vendor calls to discuss balances), and it's especially useful for companies who enter product part numbers in the Item Name/Number field.

 NOTE: The search list feature works in the Item, Customer, and Vendor lists.

More Powerful Multi-user Features

QuickBooks Enterprise Solutions is designed for growing companies, so it isn't surprising that many companies using this edition of QuickBooks have more users accessing the QuickBooks file than smaller companies do. Intuit provides extra multi-user and networking features for Enterprise Solutions.

More Simultaneous Users

Your Enterprise Solutions software permits ten simultaneous users, which is double the number for Premier and Pro multi-user editions.

Fewer Single-user Mode Activities

All QuickBooks versions that support multi-user mode require you to enter single-user mode when you perform certain tasks. This means you must notify the other users and wait for them to finish their tasks and close QuickBooks, before you can perform your task.

In Enterprise Solutions, some of the common tasks that require a switch to single-user mode in other versions of QuickBooks can be performed in multi-user mode:

- Adjusting inventory quantity/value on hand
- Deleting list entries, such as customers, vendors, items, etc.
- Changing sales tax rates

Improved Multi-user Performance

QuickBooks Enterprise Solutions offers a way to customize the software's performance when multiple users are performing a variety of tasks (frequently, some users are running reports while other users are entering transactions).

The Company Preferences tab in the General category of the Preferences dialog offers configuration options you can use to tweak performance. You can optimize the system for report generation, or for data entry.

Terminal Server Support

If you're running a Windows 2000 or Windows 2003 Windows domain (instead of a peer-to-peer network), you can run Enterprise Solutions in the built-in Terminal Server program that's available on Windows 2000/2003 Server editions.

After you install Enterprise Solutions on the Terminal Server, users can access the software via the Windows Client Terminal Services software. This brings you some significant advantages:

- Client users do not have to have Enterprise Solutions installed on their computers.
- You don't have to install special software to let users in remote locations access your QuickBooks computer.
- You can use less expensive thin clients.

 N O T E :   To use Terminal Server, you must purchase client licenses from Microsoft Corp., and set up a TS License Server as required for Windows domains.

User Roles

Enterprise Solutions offers "roles" so you can set up users and define permissions by assigning roles to them. Enterprise Solutions comes with 14 predefined roles. You can use them as is, or modify them to match your needs. You can even copy an existing role, change the permissions, and give it a new name to create your own new role. The following predefined roles are built into Enterprise Solutions:

- Accountant
- Accounts Payable
- Accounts Receivable
- Admin
- Banking
- Finance

- Full Access
- Inventory
- Payroll Manager
- Payroll Processor
- Purchasing
- Sales
- Time Tracking
- View-Only

Roles provide tighter security levels, which is necessary as companies grow and have employees in more specialized roles. It's important to be able to limit users' access to only the areas they need to perform their job. The increased permissions granularity in the Roles feature gives you much more control over customized access levels for each employee, because you can specify distinct access levels (view, create, modify, delete, print, and so on). For example, a user could be given create and print access to sales orders, but view-only access to invoices. You can use roles to control access to individual bank accounts (for example, a user could be given access to the operating account but not the payroll account).

The roles concept, which provides predefined roles, makes it much easier to set up and maintain permissions for a larger number of users. Users can be assigned multiple roles to make sure their permissions match their tasks, and a single role can be assigned to multiple users to reduce the effort of defining permissions.

Consolidated Reports for Multiple Companies

If you have separate QuickBooks company files for multiple companies, or for multiple locations, divisions, etc., use the Combine Reports feature to get a consolidated view of all the data files. You can create the following consolidated reports:

- Balance Sheet Standard
- Balance Sheet Summary
- Profit & Loss Standard
- Statement of Cash Flows
- Trial Balance

The configuration of the consolidated reports is completed in QuickBooks (selecting the companies, and selecting the report types). However, the data is sent to Microsoft Excel for consolidation, so you must have Excel installed on your computer to use this feature.

 N O T E :   See Chapter 15 to learn about creating financial reports.

Employee Organizer

Sold separately for other versions of QuickBooks, the Employee Organizer is included with Enterprise Solutions, and takes the worry out of even the most complex human resources and compliance tasks. Use Employee Organizer to streamline the management of employee information, and employment laws and regulations. This software tool integrates employee information with payroll information in QuickBooks, making it easy to access, update, and generate reports about employee information.

Stay on Top of Employment Regulations

Employee Organizer includes an Employment Regulations Update Service, which gives you access to current federal and state employment laws and regulations.

Employment-related Processes Are Easier

Employee Organizer provides guidance as you wend your way through employment-related processes. Make sure your processes are always consistent by using the Employee Organizer's step-by-step guidelines for the following processes:

- Recruiting
- Interviewing
- Hiring
- Raises
- Promotions
- Termination
- Leaves of absence

Forms and Templates with a Click of a Mouse

Employee Organizer includes federal and state government forms, as well as a selection of templates for letters, other employment-related documents, and employee management forms, including the following:

- INS Form I-9
- COBRA Notification
- Federal Form W-4
- Independent Contractor Agreement
- Job Descriptions Form
- Reference Check Form
- Driving Record Check Form

Expert Help and Advice

Send specific employment questions by e-mail. You'll receive answers including the text of relevant government policies, laws, and regulations on average within two business days. Answers are provided by CCH Incorporated, a leading provider of tax and business law information since 1913.

N O T E :   See Chapter 8 to learn about setting up payroll.

Enterprise Solution Industry-specific Editions

The following Enterprise Solutions industry-specific editions are available:

- QuickBooks Enterprise Solutions: Accountant Edition
- QuickBooks Enterprise Solutions: Contractor Edition
- QuickBooks Enterprise Solutions: Manufacturing & Wholesale Edition
- QuickBooks Enterprise Solutions: Nonprofit Edition
- QuickBooks Enterprise Solutions: Professional Services Edition
- QuickBooks Enterprise Solutions: Retail Edition

Each industry-specific edition contains the customized features that are discussed earlier in this chapter for the Premier industry-specific editions. If your business matches one of these industries, you can add even more power to your accounting software with the appropriate edition.

Setting Up Your Lists

Chapter 2

In this chapter:

- Create a full chart of accounts

- Enter data in lists

- Invent your own fields to make your lists more useful

In this chapter, I'm going to cover a lot of basic chores. They aren't terribly exciting or creative, but if you don't do them now, you'll regret it later. That's because every time you enter a transaction or fill out a form, you'll have to enter some basic data at the same time. Talk about annoying! So take the time now to get the basic data into the system. This is the preparation stuff, the work that makes future work faster and more efficient.

TIP: QuickBooks has a spell checker, and some of the List windows contain a Spelling button. Click it to check the text you entered. Then you won't have to worry about spelling errors in transactions (for instance, invoices) because you've prechecked the elements.

When you view the items in a list, you can sort the list by any column in the window. Just click the column heading to sort the list by the category of that column.

Creating a Full Chart of Accounts

The first priority is your chart of accounts. QuickBooks created some accounts for you during the initial setup of your company, but most people need lots of additional accounts in order to keep books accurately. You do the chart of accounts first because some of the other lists you create require you to link the items in the list to accounts. For example, the items you sell are linked to income accounts.

Using Numbers for Accounts

As you go through the entry of accounts, remember that I'm using numbers as the primary element in my chart of accounts. There's a title attached to the number, but the primary method of sorting my account list is by number (see the sidebar "How QuickBooks Sorts Accounts"). Even though the QuickBooks default is to use names, it's a simple matter to change the default and use numbers. Your accountant will be grateful, and you'll find you have far fewer mistakes in posting to the general ledger. If you prefer to stick to names, see the next section for some hints about creating account names.

To switch to a number format for your accounts, you just need to spend a couple of seconds changing the QuickBooks preferences:

1. Choose Edit | Preferences from the menu bar to open the Preferences dialog.
2. Select the Accounting icon from the scroll bar in the left pane.
3. Click the Company Preferences tab.
4. Select the Use Account Numbers check box (see Figure 2-1).

If you chose a prebuilt chart of accounts during the EasyStep Interview, those accounts are switched to numbered accounts automatically. You may want to change some of the numbers, and you can do so by editing the accounts (see "Editing

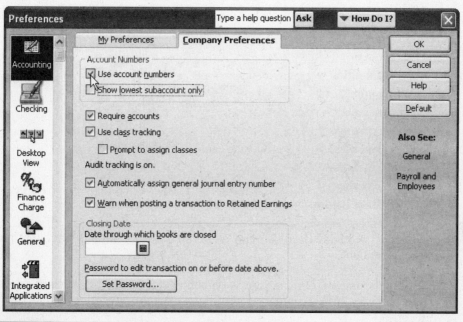

FIGURE 2-1   Enable numbers for your chart of accounts.

Accounts" later in this chapter). Some accounts (those you added yourself during or after the interview) have to be edited manually to turn them into numbered accounts; QuickBooks doesn't automatically number them.

When you select the option to use account numbers, the option Show Lowest Subaccount Only becomes accessible (it's grayed out if you haven't opted for account numbers). This option tells QuickBooks to display only the subaccount on transaction windows instead of both the parent account and the subaccount, making it easier to see precisely which account is receiving the posting. (Subaccounts, and details about this feature to display them alone, are discussed later in the section "Using Subaccounts.")

If all your accounts aren't numbered and you select Show Lowest Subaccount Only, when you click OK QuickBooks displays an error message that you cannot enable this option until all your accounts have numbers assigned. After you've edited existing accounts that need numbers (any accounts that QuickBooks didn't automatically number for you), you can return to this preferences window and enable the subaccount option.

After you've set up numbered accounts, you have a more efficient chart of accounts, so you, your bookkeeper, and your accountant will have an easier time. Numbers give you a quick clue about the type of account you're working with. As you enter the accounts, you must use the numbers intelligently, assigning ranges of numbers to account types. You should check with your accountant before finalizing the way you use the numbers, but the example I present here (and use in my own company) is a common approach. I use four-digit numbers, and the starting digit represents the beginning of a range:

- 1xxx Assets
- 2xxx Liabilities
- 3xxx Equity
- 4xxx Income
- 5xxx Expenses
- 6xxx Expenses
- 7xxx Expenses
- 8xxx Expenses
- 9xxx Other Income and Expenses

 NOTE: You can have as many as seven numbers (plus the account name) for each account.

Notice the amount of room (unused numbers) for further breakdowns, especially in the expenses. (Most companies need more expense categories than income categories.)

You can, if you wish, have a variety of expense types and reserve the starting number for specific types. Many companies, for example, use 5xxx for sales expenses (they even separate the payroll postings between the sales people and the rest of the employees), then use 6000 through 7999 for general operating expenses, and 8xxx for other specific expenses that should appear together in reports (such as taxes).

Some companies use one range of expense accounts, such as 7000 through 7999 for expenses that fall into the "overhead" category. This is useful if you bid on work and need to know the total overhead expenses so you can apportion them to appropriate categories as you prepare your bid.

If you have inventory and you track cost of sales, you can reserve a section of the chart of accounts for those account types. Some companies use 4300 through 4999 for cost of sales; other companies use the numbers in the 5000 range.

Also, think about the breakdown of assets. You might use 1000 through 1099 for cash accounts and 1100 through 1199 for receivables and other current assets, and then use 1200 through 1299 for tracking fixed assets such as equipment, furniture, and so on. Follow the same pattern for liabilities, starting with current liabilities and moving to long term. It's also a good idea to keep all the payroll withholding liabilities together.

Usually, you should add accounts by increasing the previous account number by ten, so that if your first bank account is 1000, the next bank account is 1010, and so on. For expenses (where you'll have many accounts), you might want to enter the accounts in intervals of five. This gives you room to squeeze in additional accounts that belong in the same general area of your chart of accounts when they need to be added later.

➡➡ FYI

How QuickBooks Sorts Accounts

You have to create a numbering scheme that conforms to the QuickBooks account types because QuickBooks sorts your chart of accounts by account type. If you have contiguous numbers that vary by account type, your reports won't appear in numerical order. QuickBooks uses the following sort order for the chart of accounts:

- Assets
  - Bank
  - Accounts Receivable
  - Other Current Asset
  - Fixed Asset
  - Other Asset
- Liabilities
  - Accounts Payable
  - Credit Card
  - Other Current Liability
  - Long-Term Liability
- Equity
- Income
- Cost Of Goods Sold
- Expense
- Other Income
- Other Expense
- Nonposting Accounts

(Nonposting accounts are created automatically by QuickBooks when you enable features that use those account types, such as Estimates and Purchase Orders.)

Naming Accounts

Even if you enable account numbers, you have to give each account a name. Here's an important rule about naming accounts: memorize it, print it out in big letters, and post it all over the office: **Follow The Company Protocol For Naming And Using Accounts**.

The company protocol is a system you invent for naming accounts. Your protocol must be clear, so that when everyone follows the rules, the account naming convention is consistent. Why is this important? Because when I visit clients who haven't invented and enforced protocols, I find accounts with names such as the following:

- Telephone Exp
- Exps-Telephone
- Tele Expense
- Telephone
- Tele

You get the idea, and I'll bet you're not shocked to hear that every one of those accounts had amounts posted to them. That's because users "guess" at account names and point and click on whatever they see that seems remotely related. If they don't find the account the way they would have entered the name, they invent a new account (using a name that seems logical to them). Avoid all of those errors by establishing protocols about creating account names, and then make sure everyone searches the account list before applying a transaction.

Here are a few suggested protocols—you can amend them to fit your own situation or invent different protocols that you're more comfortable with. The important thing is consistency, absolute consistency.

- Avoid apostrophes.
- Set the number of characters for abbreviations. For example, if you permit four characters, telephone is abbreviated "tele"; a three-character rule produces "tel."
- Decide whether to use the ampersand (&) or a hyphen. For example, is it "repairs & maintenance" or "repairs-maintenance"?
- Make a rule about whether spaces are allowed. For example, would you have "repairs & maintenance" or "repairs&maintenance"?

Using Subaccounts

Subaccounts provide a way to post transactions more precisely using subcategories for main account categories. For example, if you create an expense account for insurance expenses, you may want to have subaccounts for vehicle insurance, liability insurance, equipment insurance, and so on. Post transactions only to the subaccounts, never to the parent account. When you create reports, QuickBooks displays the individual totals for the subaccounts, along with the grand total for the parent account. To create a subaccount, you must first create the parent account, as described in the section, "Creating Subaccounts," later in this chapter.

If you're using numbered accounts, when you set up your main (parent) accounts, be sure to leave enough open numbers to be able to fit in all the subaccounts you'll need. If necessary, use more than four digits to make sure you have a logical hierarchy for your account structure. For example, suppose you have the following parent accounts:

- 6010 Insurance
- 6020 Utilities
- 6030 Travel

You can create the following subaccounts:

- 6011 Insurance:Vehicles
- 6012 Insurance:Liability
- 6013 Insurance:Equipment
- 6021 Utilities:Heat
- 6022 Utilities:Electric
- 6031 Travel:Sales
- 6032 Travel:Seminars and Meetings

The colon in the account names listed here is added automatically by QuickBooks to indicate a parentaccount:subaccount relationship—you only have to create the subaccount name and number.

Adding Accounts

After you've done your homework, made your decisions, invented your protocols, and checked with your accountant, adding accounts is a piece of cake.

Follow these steps:

1. Press CTRL-A (or click the Chart Of Accounts icon on the Home page) to open the Chart Of Accounts window.
2. Press CTRL-N to enter a new account. The New Account dialog opens so you can begin entering information.
3. Click the down arrow to the right of the Type box and select an account type from the drop-down list.

The dialog for entering a new account changes its appearance depending on the account type because different types of accounts require different information. In addition, if you've opted to use numbers for your accounts, there's a field for the account number. Figure 2-2 shows a blank New Account dialog for an Expense account.

The Description field is optional, and I've found that unless there's a compelling reason to explain the account, descriptions only make your account lists busier and harder to read. The Note field, which only appears on some account types, is also optional, and I've never come up with a good reason to use it.

If you're not currently using an account, or you don't want anyone to post transactions to the account at the moment, you can select the Account Is Inactive option, which means the account won't be available for posting amounts while you're entering transactions. (Inactive accounts don't appear on the account drop-down list when you're filling out transaction windows.)

Some account types (for example, accounts connected to banks) have a field for an opening balance. Do *not* enter data in that field when you're creating an account, because it causes complications that your accountant won't appreciate.

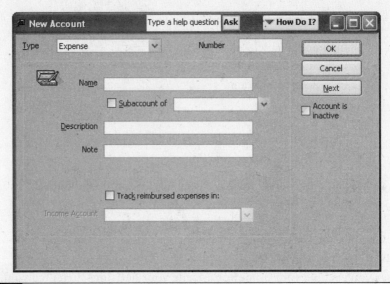

FIGURE 2-2   The only required entry for an account is a name, unless you've enabled account numbers.

As you finish entering each account, click Next to move to another blank New Account dialog. When you're finished entering accounts, click OK, and then close the Chart Of Accounts window by clicking the X in the upper-right corner.

Editing Accounts

If you need to make changes to any account information (including adding a number after you enable numbered accounts), select the account's listing in the Chart Of Accounts list, and press CTRL-E. The Edit Account dialog appears, which looks like the account card you just filled out. Make your changes and click OK to save them.

Creating Subaccounts

To create a subaccount, you must have already created the parent account.

Now take these steps:

❶ Open the Chart Of Accounts list.
❷ Press CTRL-N to create a new account.
❸ Select the appropriate account type.
❹ Enter a number (if you're using numbered accounts).
❺ Name the account.
❻ Click the Subaccount check box to place a check mark in it.
❼ In the drop-down box next to the check box, select the parent account.
❽ Click OK.

You can have multiple levels of subaccounts. For example, you may want to track income in the following manner:

Income
    Income:Consulting
        Income:Consulting:Engineering
        Income:Consulting:Training
    Income:Products
        Income:Products:Technical
        Income:Products:Accessories

Creating the sub-subaccounts is as easy as creating the first level; just make sure you've already created the first-level subaccounts (which are the parents of the sub-subaccounts). When you fill in the New Account dialog, after you check the Subaccount check box, select the appropriate subaccount to act as the parent account.

When you view the Chart Of Accounts list, subaccounts appear under their parent accounts, and they're indented. When you view a subaccount in a transaction window, it appears in the format: *ParentAccount:Subaccount* or *ParentAccount:Subaccount:Subaccount*.

For example, if you create a parent account named Income with a subaccount Consulting, the Account field in transaction windows shows Income:Consulting. If you've used numbers, the Account field shows 4000-Income:4001-Consulting. Because many of the fields in transaction windows are small, you may not be able to see the subaccount names without scrolling through each account. This can be annoying, and it's much easier to work if only the subaccount name is displayed. That's the point of enabling the preference Show Lowest Subaccount Only, discussed earlier in the section "Creating a Full Chart of Accounts." When you enable that option, you see only the subaccounts when you're working in a transaction window, which makes it much easier to find the accounts you need.

Merging Accounts

Sometimes you have two accounts that should be one. For instance, you may have accidentally created two accounts for the same purpose. As I discussed earlier in this chapter, I've been to client sites that had accounts named Telephone and Tele, with transactions posted to both accounts. Those accounts badly need merging. Accounts must be of the same account type in order to be merged.

Take the following steps to merge two accounts:

1. Open the Chart Of Accounts List window.
2. Select (highlight) the account that has the name you *do not* want to use.
3. Press CTRL-E to open the Edit Account dialog.
4. Change the account name and number to match the account you want to keep.
5. Click OK.
6. QuickBooks displays a dialog telling you that the account number or name you've entered already exists for another account and asks if you want to merge the accounts. Click Yes to confirm that you want to merge the two accounts.

Customers and Jobs

In QuickBooks, customers and jobs are handled together. You can create a customer and consider anything and everything you invoice to that customer a single job, or you can have multiple jobs for the same customer.

Some businesses don't worry about jobs; it's just the customer that's tracked. But if you're a building contractor or subcontractor, an interior decorator, a consultant, or some other kind of service provider who usually bills by the job instead of at an hourly rate for an ongoing service, you should track jobs.

Jobs don't stand alone as an entity; they are attached to customers, and you can attach as many jobs to a single customer as you need to. If you are going to track jobs, it's a good idea to enter all the customers first (now), and then attach the jobs second (later).

If you enter your existing customers now, when you're first starting to use QuickBooks, all the other work connected to the customer is much easier. It's bothersome to have to stop in the middle of every invoice you enter to create a new customer record.

The Customers & Jobs List

If you've been using QuickBooks, you're used to the fact that the list that holds your customer names is called the Customer:Job List, and it's available on the Lists menu. With the release of QuickBooks 2006, the name of the list has changed, and it no longer appears on the Lists menu or on the Customers menu. The new location of the list, now called Customers & Jobs, is the Customer Center.

(The same new paradigm has been adopted for the Vendor List and the Employee List, both of which have disappeared from their respective menus, as well as the Lists menu, and have been relocated to the Vendor Center and the Employee Center.)

However, in transaction windows and dialogs, any field that requires the entry of a customer or job is still labeled Customer:Job.

To access the Customers & Jobs List, you must open the Customer Center (seen in Figure 2-3).

You have several ways to get to the Customer Center:

- Click the Customer Center icon on the QuickBooks toolbar.
- Click the Customers icon on the left side of the Home page.
- Press CTRL-J.

Entering a New Customer

Putting all your existing customers into the system takes very little effort:

1. Open the Customer Center and select the Customers & Jobs tab to display your list of customers.
2. Press CTRL-N (or click the New Customer button above the Customers & Jobs tab) to open the New Customer window (see Figure 2-4), and fill in the information.

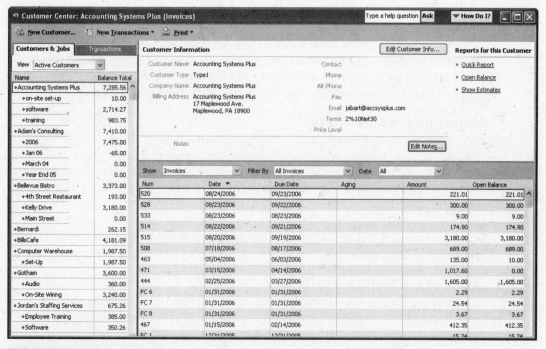

FIGURE 2-3 The Customers & Jobs List is part of the Customer Center.

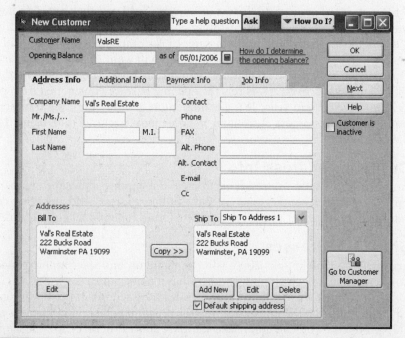

FIGURE 2-4 The customer record holds quite a lot of information.

Address Info Tab

The New Customer window opens with the Address Info tab in the foreground. The first field to enter information in is the Customer Name field. Consider this field a code rather than a customer name. It doesn't appear on your invoices or other sales transactions. (The transactions use the data in the Company Name field.)

Customer Name Field

You must invent a protocol for this Customer Name field so that you'll enter every customer in the same manner. Notice the Customer Name field in Figure 2-4. This customer code entry has no apostrophe or space, even though the customer name contains both. Avoiding punctuation and spaces in codes is a good protocol for filling in code fields.

Each customer must have a unique entry in this field, so if you have a lot of customers named Jack Johnson, you may want to enter them as JohnsonJack001, JohnsonJack002, and so on.

Opening Balance Field

QuickBooks makes an Opening Balance field available, along with the date for which this balance applies (by default, the current date is inserted). The field is designed to hold the amount this customer currently owes (if an open balance exists for the customer).

Don't use this field. If you enter an amount, you'll have no detailed records on how the customer arrived at this balance, which makes it difficult to accept payments against specific invoices. It's better to skip this field and then enter an invoice or multiple invoices to post this customer's balance to your books. In addition, QuickBooks posts the amount you enter to Accounts Receivable, into an account named Opening Bal Equity. Your accountant will want to get rid of the balance in Opening Bal Equity, and sometimes that's a difficult job because it's hard to tell how the balance was arrived at—is this the opening balance you entered from past years? Is it from the current year? Is it a combination of both? Entering transactions that represent the customer's current status is far more accurate than using the Opening Balance field.

Customer Address Info

In the Company and Addresses sections of the window, enter the company name, optionally enter a contact, and enter the billing address. Add any other contact information you want to track for this customer (telephone, e-mail, and so on).

Ship To Addresses

Starting with QuickBooks 2006, you can maintain multiple shipping addresses for your customers. Each shipping address has a name (title), so you can select it from a drop-down list when you're entering sales transactions. If the shipping address isn't different from the billing address (or if you have a service business and never ship products), you can ignore the shipping address field, or use the Copy button to copy the address block data.

To create a shipping address, click the Add New button under the Ship To address block to open the Add Ship To Address Information dialog.

Give this Ship To address a name, and enter the address information. QuickBooks enters the name Ship To Address 1, but that's merely a placeholder. Replace that text with a name that reminds you of the address location, to make it easier to select this address from a drop-down list when you have to ship goods to this address.

Specify whether this address should be the default Ship To address, and click OK. Then, if necessary, enter another Ship To address for this customer.

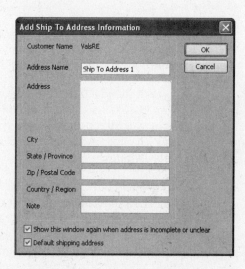

Additional Info Tab

The information you enter in the Additional Info tab of a customer card (see Figure 2-5) ranges from essential to convenient. Prepopulating the fields with information makes your work go faster when you're filling out transaction windows, and it makes it easier to create in-depth reports. It's worth spending the time to design some rules for the way data is entered. (Remember, making rules ensures consistency, without which you'll have difficulty getting the reports you want.)

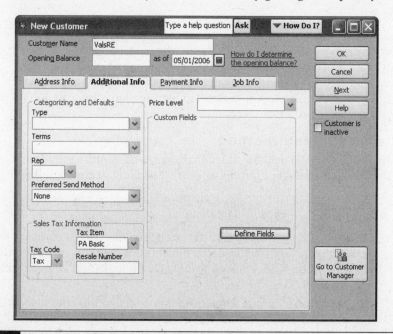

FIGURE 2-5 Entering additional information makes your work in QuickBooks go faster.

NOTE: The fields you see on the Additional Info tab may not be the same as the fields shown in Figure 2-5. The preferences you configure (for example, whether you track sales tax) determine the available fields.

Let's spend a minute going over the fields in this tab. Most of the fields are also QuickBooks lists, and if you haven't already entered items in those lists, you can do so as you fill out the fields in the customer card. Each field that is also a list has an entry named <Add New>, and selecting that entry opens the appropriate new blank entry window.

Type

Use the Type field to sort your customers by a type you find important (or convenient) when you create reports. QuickBooks maintains a Type list (see the section "Customer Type List" later in this chapter). For example, you may want to consider wholesale and retail customers as your customer types. To use the field, click the arrow to select a type that you already entered, or create a new type.

Terms

Terms, of course, refers to payment terms. Click the arrow to the right of the text box to see the terms that QuickBooks already defined, or choose <Add New> to define a new one.

The terms in the Terms List are for both customers and vendors, and you may need additional terms to meet your customers' and vendors' needs. See the section "Terms List" later in this chapter to learn how to create different types of terms.

Rep

This field is the place to track a sales representative, and it's useful whether you pay commissions or you just want to know who is in charge of this customer. Sales reps can be employees, vendors, or "other names" (which means the name is entered in the Other Names List). Select a rep from the list of reps or add a new rep by choosing <Add New>. See the section "Sales Rep List" for more information on populating this list.

Preferred Send Method

This field stores the default value for the way you want to send invoices, statements, or estimates to this customer. The choices are the following:

- None, which means no special features are used to send the documents. You print them and you mail them (the old-fashioned way).
- E-Mail, which means you e-mail the documents. This feature lets you attach the documents as PDF files to an e-mail message. The processes involved are managed within QuickBooks, using a QuickBooks server for sending the e-mail. Chapter 3 has the details.
- Mail, which lets you use a QuickBooks service to mail the invoices. The data is reproduced on a form that has a tear-off your customers enclose with their payment. See Appendix B for information about this QuickBooks service.

Regardless of the method you choose as your default, you can use any send method when you're creating a transaction.

 NOTE: The Preferred Send Method does not have an <Add New> entry, because it doesn't exist as a QuickBooks list.

Sales Tax Information

If you've configured QuickBooks to collect sales tax, the sales tax information uses several fields. If the customer is liable for sales tax, select the appropriate sales tax item for this customer, or create a new sales tax item. If the customer does not pay sales tax, select Non and enter the Resale Number provided by the customer (this is handy to have when the state tax investigators pop in for a surprise audit). See Chapter 7 for a complete discussion of sales tax codes and sales tax items.

Price Level

Price levels are a pricing scheme, usually involving special discounts that you want to use for this customer's purchases. Select an existing price level or create a new one. See the section "Price Level List" to learn about creating and assigning price levels.

Custom Fields

Custom fields provide an opportunity to invent fields for sorting and arranging your QuickBooks lists. See the section "Using Custom Fields" later in this chapter.

Payment Info Tab

This tab (see Figure 2-6) puts all the important information about customer finances in one place.

Account No.

This is an optional field you can use if you assign account numbers to your customers.

Credit Limit

A *credit limit* is a way to set a threshold for the amount of money you'll extend to a customer's credit. If a customer places an order, and the new order combined with any unpaid invoices exceeds the threshold, QuickBooks displays a warning. QuickBooks won't prevent you from continuing to sell to and invoice the customer, but you should consider rejecting the order (or shipping it COD).

 TIP: If you aren't going to enforce the credit limit, don't bother to use the field.

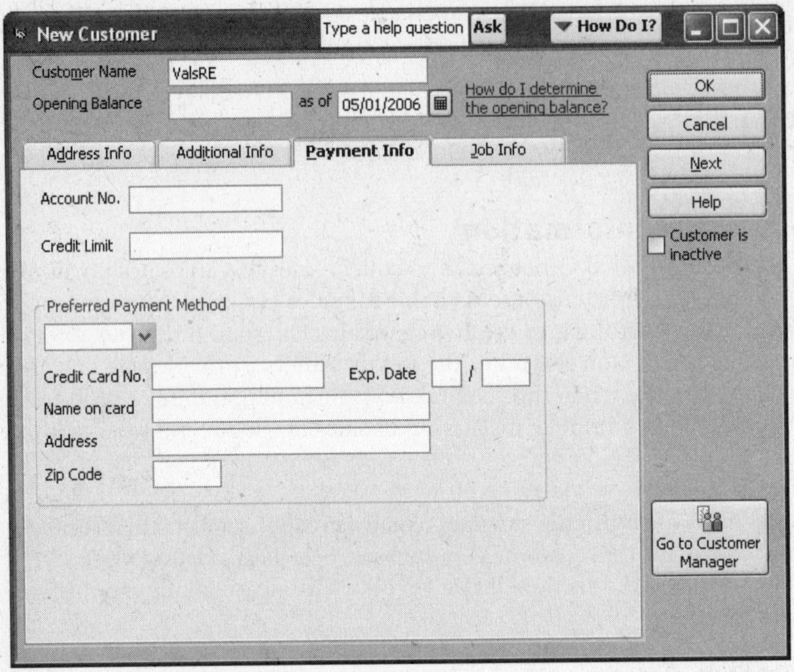

FIGURE 2-6   Use the Payment Info tab to track details needed for this customer's transactions.

Preferred Payment Method

This means the customer's preferred method for payments, and a list of payment methods is offered in the drop-down list. You can select the appropriate item from the list or add a new one by selecting <Add New>. See the section "Payment Method List" later in this chapter for more information.

TIP: The payment method you select automatically appears on the Receive Payments window when you are using this customer in the transaction. You can change the payment method at that time, if necessary.

Credit Card No.

This field is intended to contain this customer's credit card number, if that's the customer's preferred payment method. Don't fill it in unless your computer and your QuickBooks file are protected with all sorts of security. In fact, the laws (both government and merchant-card providers) about keeping credit card numbers on file are changing, and it's probably illegal for you to keep anything more than the last four or five digits of the card number on file.

When you have finished filling out the fields (I'm skipping the Job Info tab because there's a full discussion on entering jobs later in this chapter), choose Next to move to another blank customer card so you can enter the next customer. When you have finished entering all of your customers, click OK.

Editing Customer Records

You can make changes to the information in a customer record quite easily. Open the Customers & Jobs List (using the steps described earlier) and select the customer record you want to change. Double-click the customer's listing (or select the listing and click the Edit Customer Info button, or press CTRL-E), to open the customer card in Edit mode.

When you open the customer card, you can change any information or fill in data you didn't have when you first created the customer entry. In fact, you can fill in data you *did* have but didn't bother to enter. (Some people find it's faster to enter just the customer name and company name when they're creating their customer lists and then fill in the rest at their leisure or the first time they invoice the customer.)

However, there are several things I want you to note about editing the customer card:

- Don't mess with the Customer Name field.
- There's a Notes button on the right side of the customer card.
- You can't enter an opening balance.

Unless you've reinvented the protocol you're using to enter data in the Customer Name field, don't change this data. Many high-end (translate that as "expensive and incredibly powerful") accounting software applications lock this field and never permit changes. QuickBooks lets you change it, so you have to impose controls on yourself.

Click the Notes button to open a Notepad window that's dedicated to this customer, as shown in Figure 2-7. This is a useful feature, and I bet you'll use it frequently.

The Notepad is a great marketing tool because you can use it to follow up on a promised order, track a customer's special preferences, and notify the customer when something special is available. When you view the Customers & Jobs List, an Edit Notes icon appears in the pane of the Customer Center. You can open the Notepad for the selected customer by double-clicking the icon; you don't have to open the customer record to get to the note.

Vendors

The vendors you purchase goods and services from have to be entered into your QuickBooks system, and it's far easier to do it now. Otherwise, you'll have to go through the process of establishing the vendor and entering all the important information when you want to enter a vendor bill or write a check.

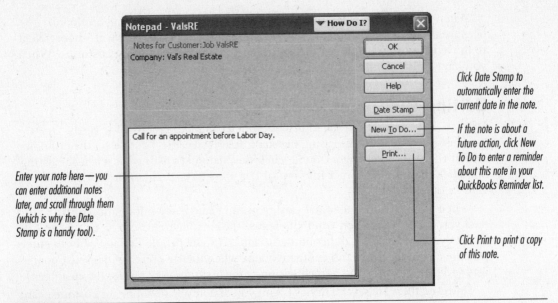

Click Date Stamp to automatically enter the current date in the note.

If the note is about a future action, click New To Do to enter a reminder about this note in your QuickBooks Reminder list.

Enter your note here—you can enter additional notes later, and scroll through them (which is why the Date Stamp is a handy tool).

Click Print to print a copy of this note.

FIGURE 2-7   Each customer has a notepad.

To get to the Vendors List, open the Vendor Center by clicking its icon on the toolbar, or by clicking the Vendors icon on the left side of the Home page. Click the Vendors tab to display the list. Press CTRL-N (or click the New Vendor button above the list) to open a New Vendor card and fill out the fields (see Figure 2-8).

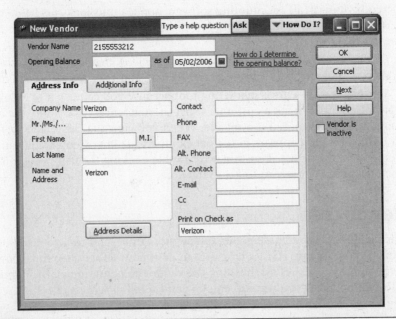

FIGURE 2-8   Vendor records are less complicated than customer records.

As with customers, you should have a set of rules about entering the information in the Vendor Name field. This field doesn't appear on checks or purchase orders; it's used to sort and select vendors when you need a list or a report. Think of it as a code. Notice that in Figure 2-8, the vendor code is a telephone number, but the vendor is the telephone company. This is how I create separate checks for each telephone bill I receive.

Skip the Opening Balance field, and enter an invoice (or multiple invoices) to represent the current open balance, so you have details about the transaction(s).

The Name And Address block is important if you're planning to print checks and the vendor doesn't enclose a return envelope, making it necessary for you to put the address on the check. You can purchase window envelopes, and when you insert the check in the envelope, the vendor name and address block are in the right spots.

The Additional Info tab (see Figure 2-9) for vendors has several important categories:

- **Account No.**   Enter your account number with this vendor (to the vendor, it's your customer number), and the number will appear in the memo field of printed checks.
- **Type**   Select a type or create one. This optional field is handy if you want to sort vendors by type, which makes reports more efficient. For example, you can create vendor types for inventory suppliers, tax authorities, and so on.
- **Terms**   Enter the terms for payment this vendor has assigned to you.

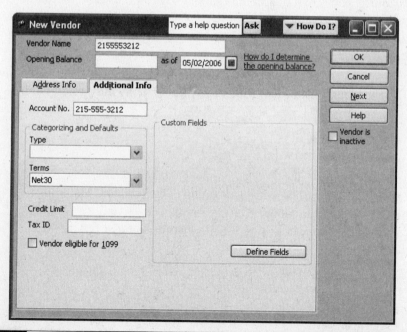

FIGURE 2-9   Add data to this tab to make it easier to print checks and produce detailed reports.

- **Credit Limit**   Enter the credit limit this vendor has given you.
- **Tax ID**   Use this field to enter the social security number or EIN if this vendor receives a Form 1099.
- **1099 status**   If appropriate, select the check box for Vendor Eligible For 1099.
- **Custom Fields**   As with customers, you can create custom fields for vendors (see the section "Using Custom Fields" later in this chapter).

After you fill in the information, choose Next to move to the next blank card and enter the next vendor. When you're finished, click OK.

When you view or edit a vendor card by selecting the vendor's listing and pressing CTRL-E, you'll find a Notes button just like the one in the customer card. You can use it in the same way.

Payroll Lists

If you plan to use QuickBooks for payroll, you must enter all of your employees, including their pertinent tax information. To do that, you have to define the tax information, which requires you to define the items that make up the payroll check. This means you have two lists to create—the payroll items and the employees.

I'm assuming all the vendors who receive checks from the payroll system have been entered into your Vendor List (the IRS, the state and local tax authorities, the medical insurance companies, pension providers, and so on). Of course, your chart of accounts should have all the accounts you need in order to post payroll items.

Entering Payroll Items

The number of individual elements that go into a paycheck may be more than you thought. Consider this list, which is typical of many businesses:

- Salaries
- Wages (hourly)
- Overtime
- Double-time
- Federal tax withholdings (including FIT, FICA, and Medicare)
- State tax withholdings
- State unemployment and disability withholdings
- Local tax withholdings
- Pension plan deductions
- Medical insurance deductions
- Life insurance deductions
- Garnishes

- Union dues
- Reimbursement for auto expenses
- Bonuses
- Commissions
- Vacation pay
- Sick pay
- Advanced Earned Income Credit

Whew! And don't forget that you also have to track company-paid payroll items, such as matching FICA and Medicare, employer contributions to unemployment (both state and federal), state disability funds, pension and medical benefit plans, and more!

Each payroll item has to be defined and linked to the chart of accounts. The vendors who receive payments (for example, the government and insurance companies) have to be entered and linked to the payroll item.

You cannot create payroll items until you've enabled, and signed up for, the payroll service (covered in Chapter 8). Once you've completed enrollment, create payroll items by choosing Employees | Payroll Item List from the menu bar to display the Payroll Item List seen in Figure 2-10. Some payroll items were added to the list automatically when you enabled payroll services.

If anything is missing (for example, state and local taxes, medical benefits deductions, and other payroll items may not be listed), add a new item by pressing CTRL-N to open the Add New Payroll Item Wizard shown in Figure 2-11.

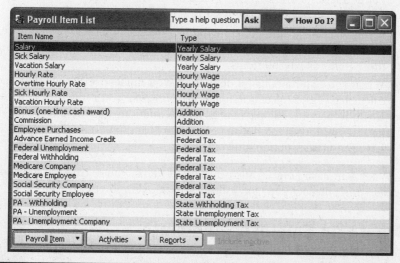

FIGURE 2-10   The payroll items created automatically may not include everything you need.

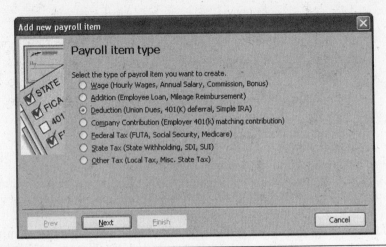

FIGURE 2-11   This wizard helps you create a payroll item.

Step through the wizard, making selections and answering questions. Use the following guidelines as you enter payroll items:

- Check everything with your accountant.
- QuickBooks already has information on many state taxes, so check for your state before you add the information manually.
- You'll probably have to enter your local (city or township) taxes manually, because QuickBooks only has built-in information on a few cities.
- For deductions, the wizard will ask about the vendor who receives this money. (It's called an *agency* in the wizard window, but it's a vendor.)
- If you want the employer contributions to pension, health insurance, life insurance, and so on to appear on the payroll check stubs, you must enter those items as payroll items.
- When you enter a pension deduction, you must specify the taxes that are *not* calculated (I said *calculated*, not *deducted*) before you deduct the new payroll item. If you forget one, the paychecks and deductions may be incorrect. Some plans permit employees to choose between pre- and post-tax deductions. Some states have pre-tax deduction allowances.

When you have entered all your payroll items, you're ready to move on to the next step in entering your payroll information: employees.

Create an Employee Template

There is a great deal of information to fill out for each employee, and some of it is probably the same for all or most of your employees. For example, you may have many employees who share the same hourly wage or the same deductions for medical insurance.

To avoid entering the same information over and over, you can create a template and then apply the information to all the employees who match that data. You'll save yourself lots of time, even if some employees require you to edit one or two entries that differ from the template.

To get to the template, you have to start with the Employees List, which is in the Employee Center. To open the Employee Center, click its icon on the toolbar, or choose Employees | Employee Center from the menu bar.

Click the Related Activities button at the top of the window, and choose Employee Defaults from the menu that appears. This opens the Employee Defaults window, where you can enter the data that applies to most or all of your employees.

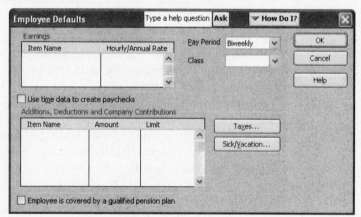

The information you put into the template is used on the Payroll Info tab for each employee record you create (discussed in the next section, "Entering Employees").

- Click in the Item Name column of the Earnings box, and then click the arrow to see a list of earnings types that you've defined in your Payroll Items. Select the one that is suitable for a template.

- In the Hourly/Annual Rate column, enter a wage or salary figure if there's one that applies to most of your employees. If there's not, just skip it and enter each employee's rate on the individual employee card later.

- Use the arrow to the right of the Pay Period field to see a list of choices and select your payroll frequency. The available choices are Daily, Weekly, Biweekly, Semimonthly, Monthly, Quarterly, and Yearly.

- Use the Class field if you've enabled classes to track data. (See Chapter 20 for information on using classes.)

- If you're using QuickBooks' time-tracking features to pay employees, you also see a check box labeled Use Time Data To Create Paychecks. Put a check mark in the check box to enable the feature. (See Chapter 19 to learn how to transfer time tracking into your payroll records.)

- If all or most of your employees have the same additional adjustments (such as insurance deductions, 401(k) deductions, or reimbursement for car expenses), click in the Item Name column in the Additions, Deductions And Company Contributions box, and then click the arrow to select the appropriate adjustments.

- Click the Taxes button to open the Taxes Defaults dialog, and select those taxes that are common and therefore suited for the template (usually all or most of them).

- Click the Sick/Vacation button to set the terms for accruing sick time and vacation time if your policy is similar enough among employees to include it in the template.

When you are finished filling out the template, click OK to save it.

Entering Employees

Finally, you're ready to tell QuickBooks about your list of employees. Select the Employees tab in the Employee Center, and press CTRL-N to bring up a New Employee form (see Figure 2-12).

The New Employee form opens with the Personal Info tab selected in the Change Tabs drop-down list at the top of the form. This selection displays three tabs: Personal, Address And Contact, and Additional Info. Additional tab sets exist, and you use the drop-down list in the Change Tabs field at the top of the window to access them. The following tab categories are available in the drop-down list:

- **Personal Info**   A three-tab dialog where you enter personal information about the employee (the three tabs shown in Figure 2-12).

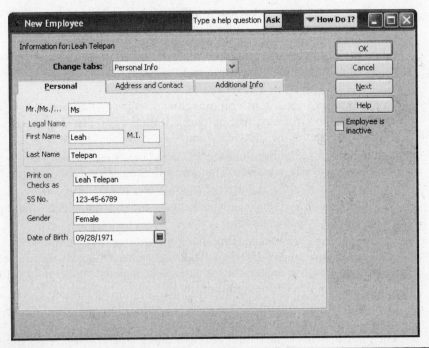

- **Payroll And Compensation Info**   Where you enter information about earnings, taxes, deductions, and other financial data.
- **Employment Info**   Where you enter information about the employee's hiring date and other employment history.
- **Workers Compensation**   Only available if you signed up for Enhanced Payroll. If so, workers comp is automatically enabled (you can disable it in the Payroll & Employees category of the Preferences dialog).

I'll discuss all of these tabs in this section.

Personal Info Tab Set

The Personal Info tab set is the place to record personal information about this employee. It's really three tabs, because the information is divided into three categories.

Personal Tab   Enter the employee's name, social security number, and the way the name should be printed on paychecks. QuickBooks automatically inserts the data from the name fields, which is usually the way paychecks are written, but you may want to make a change (for instance, omitting the middle initial).

Enter the Gender and/or Date Of Birth if you have a company policy of recording this information, or if any tax or benefits agency requires it. For example, your state unemployment form may require you to note the gender of all employees; your medical or life insurance carrier may require the date of birth.

Address And Contact Tab   Use this tab to record the employee's address, as well as information about contacting the employee (phone number, e-mail, fax, and so on).

Additional Info Tab   Use this tab to enter the employee number (if your company uses employee numbers). This tab also contains a Define Fields button, so you can create custom fields for employee records (covered in the section "Using Custom Fields" later in this chapter).

Payroll And Compensation Info Tab Set

This tab set has only one tab, and it contains the information QuickBooks needs to pay employees (Figure 2-13). Where the employee's payroll items and amounts match information already filled in from the default template, just accept the items. Otherwise, make additions and changes as necessary for this employee.

If the amount of the earnings or the deduction is the same every week, enter an amount. If it differs from week to week, don't enter an amount on the employee card. Instead, you'll enter that information when you create the payroll check.

Employee Tax Information   Click the Taxes button to open the Taxes dialog, which starts with Federal tax information, as seen in Figure 2-14. Fill in any data that wasn't automatically filled in from the Employee Template, and modify data that is different for this employee.

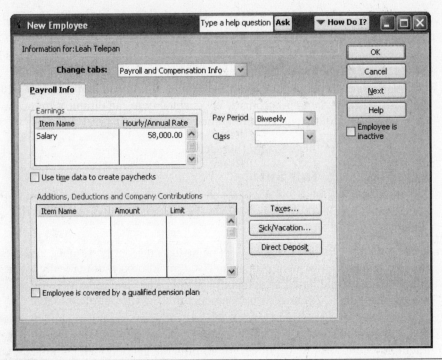

FIGURE 2-13   Enter information about this employee's compensation and deductions (excluding tax deduction).

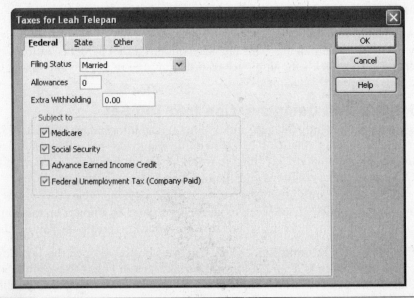

FIGURE 2-14   Configure the employee's tax information.

Move to the State tab and configure the employee's status for the state. This varies from state to state, of course, and you should check with your accountant if you aren't sure of something you find there.

 NOTE: QuickBooks has built in a great deal of state information. Depending on the state, you should see the appropriate withholdings and company-paid items. For example, states that don't deduct SUI from employees have a check box for SUI (Company Paid); states that collect disability funds will display the appropriate check box.

In the Other tab, apply any local payroll tax that applies to this employee. If you haven't already configured that tax in the Payroll Item List, you can click <Add New> to enter it now.

Click OK to save the tax status information and return to the Payroll Info tab.

Sick and Vacation Pay Information   Click the Sick/Vacation button and enter the configuration for this employee (which may include data from the Employee Template). When you are finished, click OK to return to the employee card.

Direct Deposit   The Payroll Info tab has a Direct Deposit button, which you can use to establish direct deposit of the employee's paycheck to his or her bank account. If you haven't signed up for direct deposit, the dialog that opens offers the chance to enroll. See Chapter 8 to learn how to use direct deposit.

Employment Info Tab Set

Select Employment Info in the Change Tabs drop-down list to see the Employment tab, which lets you track the following information about the employee:

- Hire date
- Release date (fill this in when an employee leaves your company)
- Employee type

For more information on employee types, see the next section.

Workers Compensation Tab Set

(For Enhanced Payroll subscribers.) If you haven't disabled workers comp tracking in the Payroll & Employees category of the Preferences dialog, choose Workers Compensation from the Change Tabs drop-down list. Assign the workers comp code that applies to the employee, or select Exempt.

Understanding Employee Types

The Type field on the Employment Info tab offers four choices, which are explained in this section. The selection you make has an impact on the way your tax returns are prepared. You must check with your accountant if you have any questions about the type you should assign to any employee.

Regular Employee

A *Regular employee* is exactly what it seems to be: a person you hired for whom you deduct withholdings, issue a W-2, and so on. It's important to have every employee fill out a W-4 form every year (don't accept "I did that last year, nothing has changed").

 TIP: If you need extra W-4 forms, you can download them from the IRS at www.irs.ustreas.gov. Go to the forms section, select W-4, and print or download the form. Then make as many copies as you need.

Officer Employee

An *Officer* is someone who is an officer of a corporation. If your business isn't incorporated, you have no officers. On federal corporate tax returns, you are required to report payroll for officers of the corporation separately from the regular payroll amounts. Selecting Officer as the type has no impact on running your payroll (calculations, check printing, and so on); it only affects reports.

Statutory Employee

A *Statutory employee* is someone who works for you that the IRS has decided qualifies as an employee instead of as an independent contractor. The list of the job types that the rules cover isn't very long, and the definition of *independent contractor* is the subject of much debate (especially in IRS audit hearings). The IRS has a list of criteria that must be met in order to qualify as an independent contractor (which means you don't have to put that person on your payroll, you don't have to withhold taxes, and you don't have to pay employer taxes). The rules that govern this change frequently, so it's important to check the rules in Circular E or with your accountant.

Owner Employee

Owner and *Employee* are mutually exclusive terms to the IRS. If you own a company, that means the company is a proprietorship; it's not a corporation (a corporation doesn't have owners; it has officers and directors). The same thing is true of a partnership, which has multiple owners. You cannot put yourself on the payroll; you must draw regular checks and post the amounts against a Draw account in the Equity section of your accounts.

QuickBooks puts this type in the list in case it's too late and you have already listed yourself or a partner in the Employee List. The QuickBooks payroll program won't perform payroll tasks for any employee of this type. If you did add your name to the Employee List, delete it rather than assign this type.

Entering Items

If you are a service business, this is going to be a snap. If you sell a few items, it'll still be pretty easy. But if you have a large inventory, get a cup of coffee or a soda or take a bathroom break, because this is going to take some time.

Understanding Items

Items are the things that appear on your invoices when you send an invoice to a customer. If you think about it, that's a bit more complicated than it might appear. Do you charge sales tax? If you do, that's an item. Do you subtotal sections of your invoices? That subtotal is an item. Do you show prepayments or discounts? They're items, too.

While you can issue an invoice that says "Net amount due for services rendered" or "Net amount due for items delivered" and enter one total in the invoice, your customers aren't going to be very happy with the lack of detail. More important, when you try to analyze your business to see where you're making lots of money and where you're making less money, you won't have enough information to determine the facts.

This is another setup chore that requires some planning. Each of your items must have a code, a unique identification (QuickBooks calls that the Item Name/Number). Try to create a system that has some logic to it so your codes are recognizable when you see them listed.

Understanding Item Types

It isn't always clear how and when some of the item types are used (or why you must define them). Here are some guidelines you can use as you plan to enter your items:

Service   A service you provide to a customer. You can create services that are charged by the job or by the hour.

Inventory Part   A product you buy for the purpose of reselling. This item type isn't available if you haven't enabled inventory during the EasyStep Interview or activated inventory in the Purchases & Vendors section of the Preferences dialog.

Non-Inventory Part   A product you sell but don't track as inventory.

Other Charge   You'll need this item type for things like shipping charges, or other line items that appear on your invoices.

Subtotal   This item type adds up everything that comes before it. It provides a subtotal before you add shipping charges or subtract any discounts or prepayments.

Group   This item type is a clever device. You can use it to enter a group of items (all of which must exist in your Item List) all at once. For example, if you frequently have a shipping charge accompanying another type of charge, you can create a group item that includes those two items.

Discount   You can't give a customer a discount as a line item if this item type doesn't exist. You may have more than one item that falls within this item type—for example, a discount for wholesale customers and a discount for a volume purchase. When you enter the item, you can indicate a flat rate or percentage.

Payment   If you receive a prepayment (either a total payment or a partial payment as a deposit), you must indicate it as a line item, using this item type.

Sales Tax Item   Create one of these item types for each sales tax authority for which you collect (available if sales tax is enabled).

Sales Tax Group   This is for multiple sales taxes that appear on the same invoice (available if sales tax is enabled).

 TIP: I've described all of the item types in terms of their use on your invoices, but many of them are used on your purchase orders too.

Entering the Data for Items

To put your items into the system, choose Lists | Item List from the menu bar. When the Item List window opens, any items that were created during your EasyStep Interview are listed.

To create a new item, press CTRL-N. The New Item window opens, displaying a list of item types, as described in the previous paragraphs. Select an item type to display the appropriate fields in the blank New Item window.

Figure 2-15 shows a blank New Item window for an Inventory Part. Other item types (such as Service items) have fewer fields.

The Item Name/Number field is the place to insert a unique identifying code for the item. When you are filling out invoices (or purchase orders), this is the listing you see in the drop-down list.

 NOTE: After you've created an item, you can create subitems. For example, if you sell shoes as an item, you can create subitems for dress shoes, sneakers, boots, and so on. Or use subitems for a parent item that comes in a variety of colors. Not all item types provide subitems.

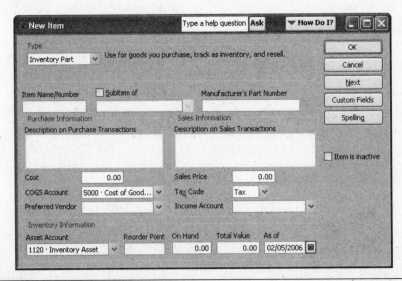

FIGURE 2-15   The fields in the New Item dialog hold the information you need to use the item, post it correctly to your general ledger, and produce accurate reports.

Many of the rest of the fields in the New Item window change depending on the item type you select. Most of them are self-explanatory, but some are important enough to merit discussion:

- If you're entering an inventory item, fill in the cost of the item and enter the account to which you post the cost of goods (COG). Optionally, fill in the name of the vendor from whom you purchase the item.
- In the Sales Price field, you can enter a rate for those items that you've priced; leave the rate at zero for the items you want to price when you are preparing the invoice. Don't worry—nothing is etched in stone. You can change any rate that appears automatically when you're filling out an invoice.
- In the Income Account field, link the item to an income account in your chart of accounts and indicate whether the item is taxable (choose Tax) or not (choose Non). (The tax option is only available if you've configured your company to collect sales tax.)

When you complete the window, choose Next to move to the next blank New Item window. When you finish entering items, click OK.

Entering Jobs

If you plan to track jobs, you can enter the ones you know about during your QuickBooks setup phase, or enter them as they're needed in transactions. Jobs are attached to customers; they can't stand alone. To create a job, press CTRL-J to open the Customer Center (or click the Customer Center icon on the toolbar) and select the Customers & Jobs tab.

Right-click the listing of the customer for whom you're creating a job, and choose Add Job to open the New Job window, shown in Figure 2-16.

Create a name for the job (you can use up to 41 characters) and make it descriptive enough for both you and your customer to understand.

If this job requires you to bill the customer at an address that's different from the address you entered for this customer, or to ship goods to a different shipping address than the one that's entered, make the appropriate changes. QuickBooks maintains this information only for this job and won't change the original shipping address in the customer record.

The Additional Info tab and the Payment Info tab are related to the customer rather than the job, so you can skip them.

Move to the Job Info tab (see Figure 2-17) to begin configuring this job. All of the information on the Job Info tab is optional; the job may not require this data.

The Job Status drop-down list offers choices that you can change as the progress of the job moves along. You can change the text that describes each progress level to suit your own business.

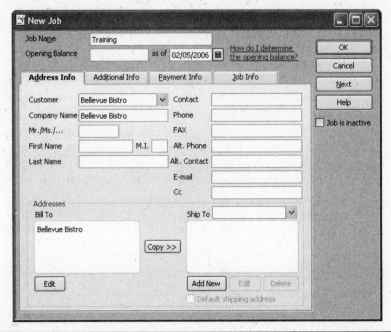

FIGURE 2-16   To create a new job, enter the job name—all the basic information about the customer is already filled in.

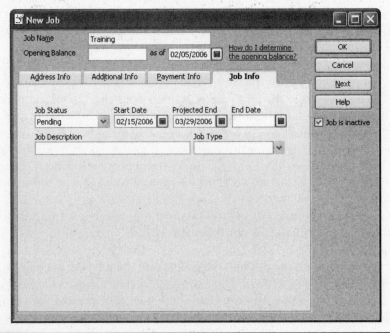

FIGURE 2-17   Track job details on the Job Info tab.

To accomplish this, follow these steps:

① Choose Edit | Preferences to open the Preferences dialog.

② Click the Jobs & Estimates icon in the left pane.

③ Click the Company Preferences tab in the right pane to see the current descriptive text for each status level (see Figure 2-18).

④ Change the text of any status levels if you have a descriptive phrase you like better. For example, you may prefer "Working" to "In Progress."

⑤ Click OK.

The new text is used on every job in your system.

When you finish entering all the data about this job, choose Next to create another job for the same customer. Otherwise, click OK to close the New Job window and return to the Customers & Jobs List. The jobs you create for a customer become part of the customer listing.

Entering Other Lists

There are a few items in the Lists menu that I haven't covered in detail. They don't require extensive amounts of data, and you may or may not choose to use them. If you do plan to use them, here's an overview of the things you need to know.

Some of these items are in the Lists menu, and some of them are in a submenu of the Lists menu called Customer & Vendor Profile Lists.

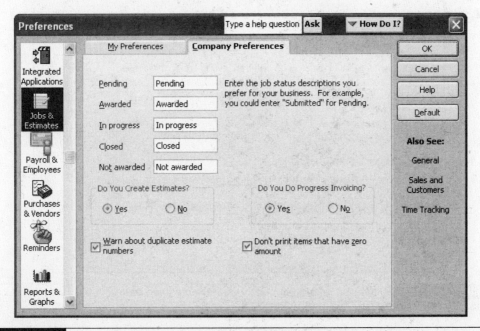

FIGURE 2-18   Customize the text to match the jargon you use in your business.

N O T E :   One item in the Lists menu, Templates, isn't covered here. These are the lists of invoice, purchase order, sales receipt, and other forms you use in transactions. Working with and customizing those templates are discussed throughout this book in the appropriate chapters.

Fixed Asset Item List

Use the Fixed Asset Item List to store information about fixed assets. This list is meant to track data about the assets you depreciate. As you can see in Figure 2-19, each asset's record includes detailed information and even has fields to track the sale of a depreciated asset.

This is an inert list that doesn't provide any method for calculating depreciation, nor does it link to any depreciation feature in QuickBooks. It's designed to let you use QuickBooks to track your fixed assets as a QuickBooks list instead of whatever list you're keeping outside of QuickBooks.

QuickBooks has a tool named Depreciate Your Assets, and you can use it to determine depreciation rates in QuickBooks, but it doesn't open the Fixed Asset

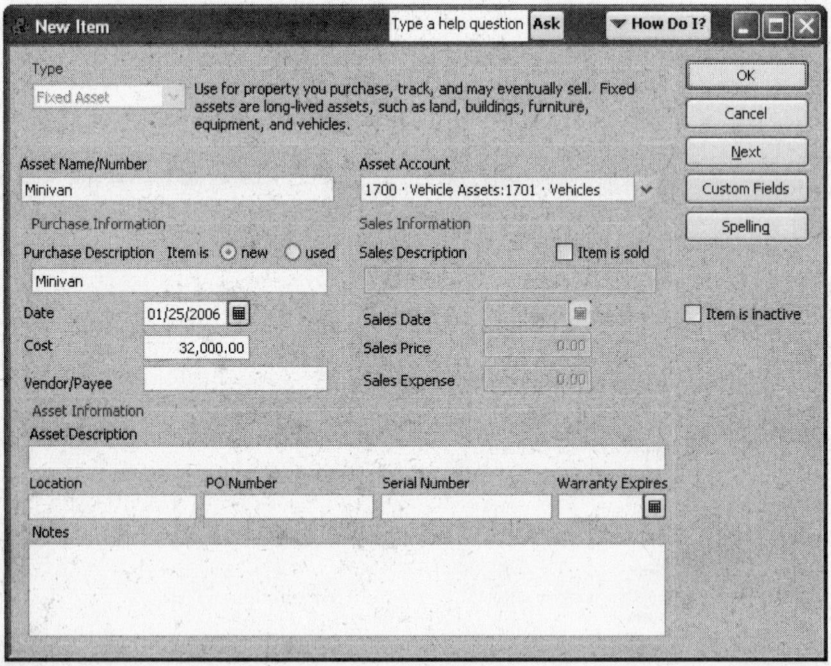

FIGURE 2-19   Keep detailed information about depreciable fixed assets in the Fixed Asset Item List.

Item List—instead, you have to enter asset information to use the tool (the same data you typed in the Fixed Asset Item List). Depreciate Your Assets is a planning tool, and it does not perform depreciation tasks. You have to depreciate your assets in regular QuickBooks transaction windows. You can learn about the Depreciate Your Assets tool in Chapter 13.

However, QuickBooks Premier Accountant Edition contains a program called Fixed Asset Manager, which uses the Fixed Asset Item List to populate the data needed to generate depreciation as part of the tax preparation chores for your company.

If tracking depreciation is an important financial task, consider upgrading to QuickBooks Premier Accountant Edition. At the very least, make sure your accountant is using QuickBooks Premier Accountant Edition, because the depreciation processes can take place more quickly (which will probably reduce your accounting fees expense).

To learn more about Fixed Asset Manager and the other advanced tools in QuickBooks Premier Accountant Edition, look for *Running QuickBooks 2006 Premier Editions* from CPA911 Publishing (www.cpa911publishing.com). You can buy the book at your favorite bookstore.

Price Level List

This list is only available if Price Levels are enabled in the Sales & Customers section of your Preferences (choose Edit | Preferences). The Price Level List is a nifty, easy way to connect special pricing to customers and jobs. Each price level has two components: a name and a formula. The name can be anything you wish, and the formula is based on the already-entered price of items (the formula increases or reduces that price by a percentage).

For example, you may want to give your favorite customers an excellent discount. Name the price level something like "Special" or "StarCustomer". Then enter a healthy percentage by which to reduce the price of items purchased by this customer. Or you may want to create a discount price level for customers that are nonprofit organizations.

On the other hand, you may want to keep your regular prices steady (assuming they're competitive) and increase them for certain customers (perhaps customers who don't pay in a timely fashion). It's probably politically incorrect to name the price level "Deadbeat", so choose something innocuous such as "DB", or "StandardPrice". You could also use numbers for the price-level names, perhaps making the highest numbers the highest prices.

After you create price levels, you can apply a price level to customers. Open the Customers & Jobs List and select a customer. Press CTRL-E to edit the customer card and select a price level on the Additional Info tab.

TIP: QuickBooks Premier editions have a price-level feature that's more robust—you can apply price levels to items in addition to customers, which makes it easier to provide discounts (or increases) while you're creating invoices. These per-item price levels let you set custom prices (using either a specific amount or a percentage) for items. If you've purchased a Premier edition of QuickBooks or are considering upgrading to a Premier edition, you can learn how to use price levels (and other Premier-only features) in *Running QuickBooks 2006 Premier Editions* from CPA911 Publishing (www.cpa911publishing.com). You can buy the book at your favorite bookstore.

Sales Tax Code List

This list is available if you configured your business to collect sales tax. Most businesses only need the two built-in sales tax codes: Tax and Non (meaning taxable and nontaxable). You can learn more about using sales tax codes effectively in Chapter 7.

Class List

The Class List appears in the Lists menu only if you've enabled the classes feature (in the Accounting category of the Preferences dialog). Classes provide a method of organizing your activities (income and disbursement activities) to produce reports that you need. Many times, a well-designed chart of accounts will eliminate the need for classes, but if you do want to use them, you can create them ahead of time through the Lists menu.

Some business owners find it's a good idea to work with QuickBooks for a while and then, if they feel they need a report that can only be produced with the use of classes, they can create the class at that point. Chapter 20 covers the use of classes.

Workers Comp List

This list, which appears if you're using QuickBooks Enhanced Payroll and have enabled workers comp tracking, contains the workers comp codes you create. Enter a code, optionally enter a description, and specify the rate per $100.00 of gross wages. Also specify a start date for using the code.

Other Names List

QuickBooks provides a list called Other Names, which is the list of people whose names come up in transactions but whose activity you don't want to track. This list will appear when you write checks, but the names are unavailable for invoices, purchase orders, and any other QuickBooks transaction type.

If your business is a proprietorship, put yourself on the list to make sure your name is listed when you write your draw check. If there are several partners in your business, use this list for the checks you write to the partners' draws.

When you press CTRL-N to open a New Name window, there are fields for the address (handy for printing checks), telephone numbers, and other contact information.

 TIP: Many people overuse this category and end up having to move these names to the Vendor List because they do need to track the activity. Unless you're a proprietor or partner, it's totally possible to use QuickBooks efficiently for years without using this list.

Memorized Transaction List

This list (which isn't really a list, but rather a collection of transactions) is built as you memorize transactions. You can tell QuickBooks to memorize any transaction at the time you create it, which adds the transaction to this list. You can learn how to memorize specific types of transactions throughout this book in the chapters devoted to creating transactions.

Sales Rep List

(This list appears in the submenu of Customer & Vendor Profile Lists.) By common definition, a *sales rep* is a person who is connected to a customer, usually because he or she receives a commission on sales to that customer. However, it's frequently advantageous to track sales reps for other reasons: to know which noncommissioned person is attached to a customer (some people call this a *service rep*) or to track the source of referrals.

To enter a new sales rep, press CTRL-N to open a New Sales Rep form and select the person's name from the drop-down list. If that name doesn't already exist as an employee, vendor, or other name, QuickBooks asks you to add the name to one of those lists.

Customer Type List

(This list appears in the submenu of Customer & Vendor Profile Lists.) When you create your customer list, you may decide to use the Customer Type field as a way to categorize the customer. This gives you the opportunity to sort and select customers in reports, perhaps to view the total income from specific types of customers.

You can predetermine the customer types you want to track by opening this list item and creating the types you need during setup. (Oops, it's too late if you've followed this chapter in order.) Or you can create them as you enter customers.

Vendor Type List

(This list appears in the submenu of Customer & Vendor Profile Lists.) See the two preceding paragraphs and substitute the word "vendor" for the word "customer."

Job Type List

(This list appears in the submenu of Customer & Vendor Profile Lists.) Use this list to set up categories for jobs by creating job types. For example, if you're a plumber, you may want to separate new construction from repairs.

Terms List

(This list appears in the submenu of Customer & Vendor Profile Lists.) QuickBooks keeps both customer and vendor payment terms in one list, so the terms you need are all available whether you're creating an invoice, entering a vendor bill, or creating a purchase order. To create a terms listing, open the Terms List window and press CTRL-N to open the New Terms window.

Use the Standard section to create terms that are due at some elapsed time after the invoice date:

- Net Due is the number of days allowed for payment after the invoice date.
- To create a discount for early payment, enter the discount percentage and the number of days after the invoice date that the discount is in effect. For example, if 30 days are allowed for payment, enter a discount percentage that is in effect for 10 days after the invoice date.

Use the Date Driven section to describe terms that are due on a particular date, regardless of the invoice date:

- Enter the day of the month the invoice payment is due.
- Enter the number of days before the due date that invoices are considered payable on the following month (but it's not fair to insist that invoices be paid on the 10th of the month if you mail them to customers on the 8th of the month).
- To create a discount for early payment, enter the discount percentage and the day of the month at which the discount period ends. For example, if the standard due date is the 15th of the month, you may want to extend a discount to any customer who pays by the 8th of the month.

 T I P :   Date-driven terms are commonly used by companies that send invoices monthly, usually on the last day of the month. If you send invoices constantly, as soon as a sale is completed, it's very difficult to track and enforce date-driven terms.

Customer Message List

(This list appears in the submenu of Customer & Vendor Profile Lists.) If you like to write messages to your customers when you're creating an invoice, you can enter a bunch of appropriate messages ahead of time and then just select the one you want to use. For example, you may want to insert the message "Thanks for doing business with us" or "Pay on time or else."

Press CTRL-N to enter a new message to add to the list. You just have to write the text (which can't be longer than 101 characters, counting spaces)—this is one of the easier lists to create.

Payment Method List

(This list appears in the submenu of Customer & Vendor Profile Lists.) You can track the way payments arrive from customers. This not only provides some detail (in case you're having a conversation with a customer about invoices and payments), but also allows you to print reports on payments that are subtotaled by the method of payment, such as credit card, check, cash, and so on. (Your bank may use the same subtotaling method, which makes it easier to reconcile the bank account.)

QuickBooks prepopulates the payment methods with common payment types. If you have a payment method that isn't listed, you can add that method to the list. To do so, press CTRL-N to open the New Payment Method window. Name the payment method and select the appropriate payment type.

Ship Via List

(This list appears in the submenu of Customer & Vendor Profile Lists.) You can describe the way you ship goods on your invoices (in the field named Via), which many customers appreciate. QuickBooks prepopulates the list with a variety of shipment methods, but you may need to add a shipping method. To do so, press CTRL-N to add a new Ship Via entry to the list. All you need to do is enter the name, for example Our Truck, or Sam's Delivery Service.

If you use one shipping method more than any other, you can select a default Ship Via entry, which appears automatically on your invoices (you can change it when the shipping method is different).

To perform this task, follow these steps:

1. Choose Edit | Preferences.
2. Select the Sales & Customers icon.
3. Select the Company Preferences tab.
4. In the Usual Shipping Method field, click the drop-down list and select the Ship Via entry you want to make the default. (Select <Add New> if you want to enter a new shipping method for the default.)
5. Enter the FOB site you want to appear on invoices, if you wish to display this information.

FOB (Free On Board) is the site from which an order is shipped and is also the point at which transportation and other costs are the buyer's responsibility. (There are no accounting implications for FOB—it's merely informational.)

Vehicle List

(This list appears in the submenu of Customer & Vendor Profile Lists.) The Vehicle List lets you track mileage for vehicles used in your business. You can use the mileage information for tax deductions for your vehicles and to bill customers for mileage expenses. However, even if you don't bill customers for mileage or your accountant uses a formula for tax deductions, the Vehicle List is a handy way to track information about the vehicles (yours or your employees) used for business purposes.

To add a vehicle to the list, press CTRL-N to open a New Vehicle dialog. The box has two fields:

- Vehicle, in which you enter a name or code for a specific vehicle. For example, you could enter BlueTruck, MikesToyota, FordMustangConvertible, or any other recognizable name.
- Description, in which you enter descriptive information about the vehicle.

While the Description field is handy for standard description terms (such as black, or blue/white truck), take advantage of the field by entering information you really need. For example, the VIN, the license plate number, the expiration date for the plate, the insurance policy number, or other "official" information are good candidates for inclusion. You can enter up to 256 characters in the field. You can learn how to track mileage and bill customers for mileage in Chapter 6.

Using Custom Fields

You can add your own fields to the Customer, Vendor, Employee, and Item records. Custom fields are useful if there's information you just have to track but QuickBooks doesn't provide a field for it. For example, if it's imperative for you to know what color eyes your employees have, add an Eye Color field. Or perhaps you have two offices and you want to attach your customers to the office that services them. Add an Office field to the customer card. If you maintain multiple warehouses, you can create a field for items to indicate which warehouse stocks any particular item (you can do the same thing to track bins).

Adding a Custom Field for Names

To add one or more custom fields to names, open one of the names lists (Customers & Jobs, Vendor, or Employee).

Now follow these steps:

1. Select any name on the list.
2. Press CTRL-E to edit the name.
3. Move to the Additional Info tab.

④ Click the Define Fields button.

⑤ When the Define Fields dialog opens, name the field and indicate the list for which you want to use the new field (see Figure 2-20).

That's all there is to it, except you must click OK to save the information. When you do, QuickBooks flashes a message reminding you that if you customize your templates (forms for transactions, such as invoices), you can add these fields. (Instructions for adding fields to transaction windows are found throughout this book in chapters covering invoices, estimates, purchase orders, and so on.) Click OK to make the message disappear (and select the option to stop showing you the message, if you wish). The Additional Info tab for every name in the list now shows those fields.

To add data to the custom fields for each name on the list, select the name and press CTRL-E to edit the name. Then add the appropriate data to the custom field.

Adding a Custom Field for Items

You can add custom fields to your items (except subtotal items and sales tax items) in much the same manner as you do for names.

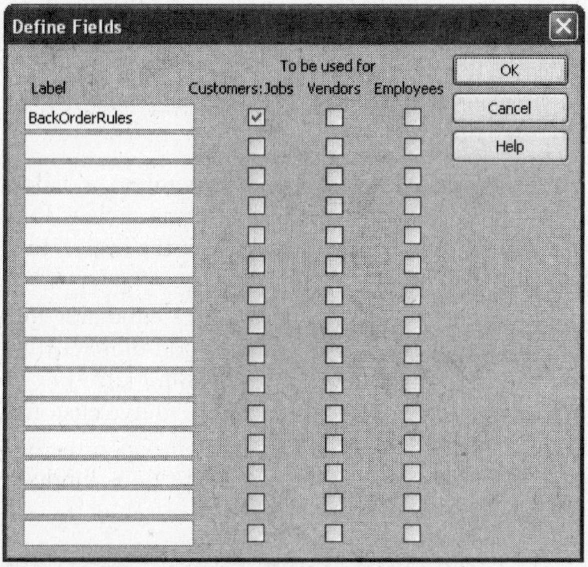

FIGURE 2-20 Custom fields appear on the records of the list you indicate, so it's easy to add appropriate fields.

Use the following steps:

1. Open the Item List and select any item.
2. Press CTRL-E to edit the item.
3. Click the Custom Fields button.
4. When a message appears telling you that there are no custom fields yet defined, click OK.
5. When the Custom Fields dialog appears, it has no fields on it (yet). Choose Define Fields.
6. When the Define Custom Fields For Items dialog opens, enter a name for each field you want to add. You can add fields that fit services, inventory items, and so on, and use the appropriate field for the item type when you enter data in an item's record.

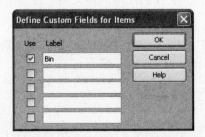

7. Click the Use box to use the field. (You can deselect the box later if you don't want to use the field anymore.)
8. Click OK.

The first time you enter a custom field on an item, a dialog appears to tell you that you can use these fields on templates (forms such as Invoices, Purchase Orders, or Packing Slips). Click OK and select the option to stop displaying this message in the future.

When you click Custom Fields on the Edit Item dialog for any item, your existing custom fields appear. If you want to add more custom fields, click the Define Fields button to open the Define Custom Fields For Items dialog and add the additional custom field. You can create up to five custom fields for items.

To enter data for the custom fields in an item, open the item from the Item List and click the Custom Fields button on the Edit Item window. Then enter the appropriate data.

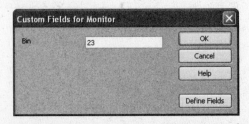

Merging Entries in Lists

After you've been working in QuickBooks for a while, you may find that some lists have entries that should be combined. For example, a vendor was entered twice (with different spellings), or you realize that several items in your chart of accounts are covering similar expenses and should be merged. One common scenario is an Item List that's far too large and complicated. For example, I've seen inventory items such as the following:

- Cable-cut to 2ft long
- Cable-cut to 3ft long
- Cable-cut to 4ft long

This makes the Item List too long and invites careless errors such as users clicking the wrong item (because they all look alike at first glance). It would be easier and smarter to have one item, named Cable, and then enter the length as a quantity (in the Qty field) or in the Description field. You can only merge entries from the following lists:

- Chart of Accounts
- Item
- Customers & Jobs
- Vendor
- Other Names

Performing a Merge Operation

To merge entries within a list, take the following steps:

1. Select the list entry you want to get rid of and press CTRL-E to open the entry in Edit mode.
2. Change the entry's name to match the name of the entry you want to keep.
3. Click OK.
4. QuickBooks opens a message box to tell you the name is already in use and asks if you want to merge them. Click Yes.

All the information, including transaction data, is merged into the entry you're keeping.

Guidelines and Restrictions for Merging List Entries

Bear the following information in mind when you decide to merge entries:

- You cannot "unmerge"—the process is not reversible.
- For accounts and items, you cannot merge entries that have subentries. Change the subentries to parent entries by removing the Subaccount Of or Subitem Of

check mark. Merge the parent entries and then reapply the Subaccount Of or Subitem Of check mark (all of which will now be subentries of the new single, merged, parent entry).

- You can merge subentries of the same parent (which is in fact the most common type of merge).
- You can merge jobs that are subentries of the same customer.

Now that all your lists exist and they're fine-tuned, you can work quickly and easily in QuickBooks transaction windows. The following chapters walk you through those tasks.

Additional Features for Premier and Enterprise Editions

If you're running QuickBooks Premier Edition or QuickBooks Enterprise Solutions, you may have some additional features available, above and beyond the features covered in this chapter. (Not all features are in all Premier or Enterprise versions.)

Billing Rate Levels List

In addition to the lists covered in this chapter, Contractor, Professional Services, and Accountant Editions also have the ability to create a Billing Rate Levels List. This feature lets you assign a billing rate to a person performing a specific service. For example, on a given job, your senior partners may be billable at one rate, while your bookkeepers generate a different rate.

When you create a billing rate, you link the rate to a name (the person providing the service) and a service. The service provider can exist in your Employee List, Vendor List, or Other Names List. To track services for each name and billing rate, use the QuickBooks Timesheet feature.

 TIP: See Chapter 18 to learn about using Timesheets.

When you invoice your customers, the appropriate billing rate levels are automatically added to the invoice from the Time and Costs dialog that's available in the Invoice window. You can also apply any customer's percentage price level (usually a discount) to the billing rate invoice items.

Per Item Price Levels

In addition to the price levels explained in this chapter, all Premier/Enterprise editions offer per item price levels. *Per item price levels* are prices, not percentages, which gives you a great deal of flexibility in charging customers for products or services. You can use item price levels to set multiple prices for the same item; for example, assign a single item (a product or a service) prices of $50.00, $40.00, and $30.00.

You can assign a specific price for the item to a customer (or multiple customers), or to one or more jobs. In addition, if you wish, you can assign a specific price to an item when you're creating an invoice. If the invoice contains an item that has price levels assigned, a drop-down list containing all the price levels is available in the Rate column of the invoice. Just select the price you want to charge for this item, for this invoice.

Part Two

Bookkeeping

Part Two contains chapters about the day-to-day bookkeeping chores you'll be performing in QuickBooks. The chapters are filled with instructions, tips, and explanations. There's even a lot of information that you can pass along to your accountant, who will want to know how QuickBooks and you are performing tasks.

The chapters in Part Two take you through everything you need to know about sending invoices to your customers and collecting the money they send back as a result. You'll learn how to track and pay the bills you receive from vendors. There's plenty of information about dealing with inventory—buying it, selling it, and counting it—and keeping QuickBooks up to date on those figures. Payroll is also discussed, both in-house payroll systems and outside services.

All the reports you can generate to analyze the state of your business are covered in Part Two. So are the reports you run for your accountant—and for the government (tax time is less of a nightmare with QuickBooks).

Finally, you'll learn about budgets, general ledger adjustments, and all the other once-in-a-while tasks you need to know how to accomplish to keep your accounting records finely tuned.

Invoicing

In this chapter:

- Create and edit invoices
- Create and edit credit memos
- Print invoices and credit memos
- Use invoices for sales orders
- Create pick lists and packing slips
- Work with estimates
- Customize invoice forms

For many businesses, the only way to get money is to send an invoice to a customer (the exception is retail, of course). Creating an invoice in QuickBooks is easy once you understand what all the parts of the invoice do and why they're there. In addition to invoices, you often have to create credits, packing slips, estimates, and other business financial documents.

In this chapter, I'll go over all those transaction documents, and after I've explained how to create them, I'll move on to describe the choices you have for getting those documents to your customers.

Creating Standard Invoices

QuickBooks offers several ways to open the Create Invoices window. You can select Customers | Create Invoices from the menu bar, press CTRL-I, or click the Invoice icon in the Customer section of the Home page (there are additional methods, but three choices should be enough). Any of those actions opens the Create Invoices window, which is a blank invoice form (see Figure 3-1).

There are several invoice templates built into QuickBooks, and you can use any of them (as well as create your own, which is covered later in this chapter in the section "Customizing Templates"). The first thing to do is decide whether or not the displayed template suits you. You should probably look at the other templates

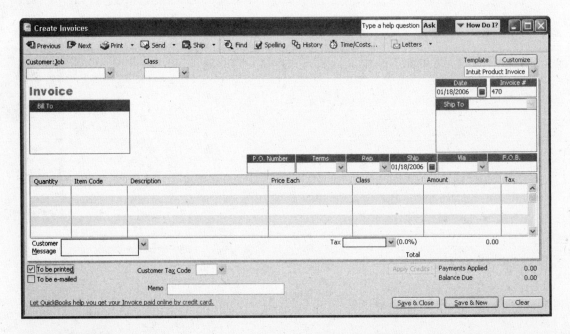

FIGURE 3-1   The Create Invoices window has all the fields you need to track sales.

before settling on the one you want to use. To do that, click the arrow next to the Template field and select another invoice template from the drop-down list:

- The Professional and Service templates are almost identical. There's a difference in the order of the columns, and the Service template has a field for a purchase order number.

- The Product template has more fields and different columns because it contains information about the items in your inventory.

- The Progress template, which is covered later in this chapter in the "Creating Progress Billing Invoices" section, is designed specifically for progress billing against a job estimate. It doesn't appear in the Template list unless you have specified Progress Invoicing in the Company Preferences tab of the Jobs & Estimates category of the Preferences dialog.

- The Finance Charge template appears if you enable finance charges in the Finance Charge category of the Preferences dialog. Information about finance charges is in Chapter 5.

- The Packing Slip template is discussed in the section "Printing Packing Slips" later in this chapter.

NOTE: The Template drop-down list includes the item Download Templates. This choice takes you to the QuickBooks web page that has templates you can use to design your own templates. The list also includes the item Customize, which opens the same window you see if you click the Customize button above the Template list field.

For this discussion, I'll use the Product template, because it's the most complicated. If you're using any other template, you'll still be able to follow along, even though your invoice form lacks some of the fields related to products.

The top portion of the invoice is for the basic information and is called the *invoice heading*. The middle section, where the billing items are placed, is called the *line item* section. The bottom section holds the totals and other details (such as customer messages). Each section of the invoice has fields into which you must enter data.

Entering Heading Information

To create an invoice, start with the customer or the job. Click the arrow to the right of the Customer:Job field to see a list of all your customers. If you've attached jobs to any customers, those jobs are listed under the customer name. Select the customer or job for this invoice. If the customer isn't in the system, choose <Add New> to open a new customer window and enter all the data required for setting up a customer. Read Chapter 2 for information on adding new customers.

If you've charged reimbursable expenses or time charges to this customer, QuickBooks displays a message reminding you to add those charges to this invoice. You can learn how to do that in Chapter 6.

In the Date field, the current date is showing, which usually suffices. If you want to change the date, you can either type in a new date, or click the calendar icon at the right side of the field to select a date.

If you change the date, the new date appears automatically in each invoice you create during this session of QuickBooks (the current date returns after you close, and then reopen the software).

The first time you enter an invoice, fill in the invoice number you want to use as a starting point. Hereafter, QuickBooks will increment that number for each ensuing invoice.

The Bill To address is taken from the customer record, as is the Ship To address that's available on the Product Invoice template. You can select another Ship To address from the drop-down list, or add a new Ship To address by choosing <Add New> from the list.

If you have a purchase order from this customer, enter it into the P.O. Number field (not available on the Professional template).

The Terms field is filled in automatically with the terms you entered for this customer when you created the customer record. You can change the terms for this invoice if you wish. If terms don't automatically appear, it means you didn't enter that information in the customer record. If you enter it now, when you save the invoice, QuickBooks offers to make the entry the new default for this customer by adding it to the customer record.

($) **TIP:**   If you enter or change any information about the customer while you're creating an invoice, QuickBooks offers to add the information to the customer record when you save the invoice. If the change is permanent, click the Yes button in the dialog that displays the offer. This saves you the trouble of going back to the customer record to make the changes. If the change is only for this invoice, click the No button.

The Rep field (only in the Product template) is for the salesperson attached to this customer. If you didn't indicate a salesperson when you filled out the customer record, you can click the arrow next to the field and choose a name from the drop-down list.

The Ship field (only in the Product template) is for the ship date, and the data defaults to the invoice date.

The Via field (only in the Product template) is for the method of shipping. Click the arrow next to the field to see the available shipping choices. (See Chapter 2 for information about adding to this list.)

The F.O.B. field (only in the Product template) is used by some companies to indicate the point at which the shipping costs are transferred to the buyer and the assumption of a completed sale takes place. (That means if it breaks or gets lost, the customer owns it.) If you use FOB terms, you can enter the applicable data in the field; it has no impact on your QuickBooks financial records and is there for your convenience only.

 N O T E :   FOB stands for Free On Board, and I'm sure there's some meaningful reason for the term, but I suspect it's been lost in history.

Entering Line Items

Now you can begin to enter the items for which you are billing this customer. Click in the first column of the line item section.

If you're using the Product invoice template, that column is Quantity. (If you're using the Professional or Service invoice template, the first column is Item.) Enter the quantity of the first item you're billing for.

In the Item Code column, an arrow appears on the right edge of the column—click it to see a list of the items you sell. (See Chapter 2 to learn how to enter items.) Select the item you need. The description and price are filled in automatically, using the information you provided when you created the item. If you didn't include the information when you created the item, you can enter it manually now.

QuickBooks does the math, and the Amount column displays the total of the quantity times the price. If the item and the customer are both liable for tax, the Tax column displays "Tax."

Repeat this process to add all the items that should be on this invoice. You can add as many rows of items as you need; if you run out of room, QuickBooks automatically adds pages to your invoice.

Applying Price Levels

If you've created items in your Price Levels List (explained in Chapter 2), you can change the amount of any line item by applying a price level. Most of the time, your price levels are a percentage by which to lower (discount) the price, but you may also have created price levels that increase the price.

When your cursor is in the Price Each column, an arrow appears to the right of the price that's entered for the item on this line. Click the arrow to see a list of price level items, and select the one you want to apply to this item. As you can see in Figure 3-2, QuickBooks has already performed the math, so you not only see the name of your price level, you also see the resulting item price for each price level.

After you select a price level, QuickBooks changes the amount you're charging the customer for the item and adjusts the amount of the total for this item (if the quantity is more than 1).

The customer sees only the price on the invoice; there's no indication that you've adjusted the price. This is different from applying a discount to a price (covered in the next section), where a discrete line item exists to announce the discount.

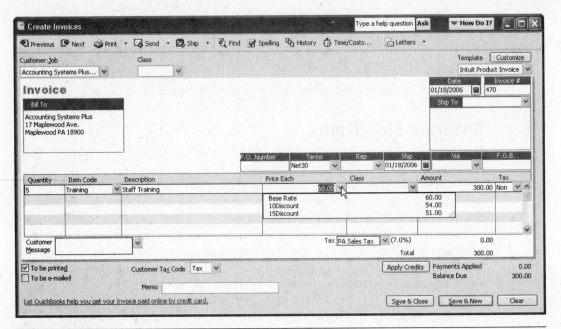

FIGURE 3-2   Assign a predefined price level to the price of any item.

NOTE: You can apply price levels as you enter a line item, or finish all the line items and then return to the Price Each column for the items you want to change with a price level. QuickBooks adjusts line totals and the final total as you apply the price levels.

Entering Discounts

You can also adjust the invoice by applying discounts. Discounts are entered as line items, so the discount has to exist as an item in your Items List.

When you enter a discount, its amount (usually a percentage) is applied based on the line item immediately above it. For example, let's suppose you have already entered line items as follows:

- Qty of 1 for Some Item with a price of $100.00 for a total line item price of $100.00
- Qty of 2 for Some Other Item with a price of $40.00 for a total line item price of $80.00

Now you want to give the customer a 10 percent discount (you created a 10 percent discount item in your Items List). If you enter that item on the next line, QuickBooks will calculate its value as 10 percent of the last line you entered—an $8.00 discount.

If you want to apply the discount against all the line items, you must first enter a line item that subtotals those lines. To do this, use a subtotal item type that you've created in your Items List. Then enter the discount item as the next line item, and when the discount is applied to the previous amount, that previous amount is the amount of the subtotal. The discount is based on the subtotal.

You can use the same approach to discount some line items but not others. Simply follow these steps:

1 Enter all the items you're planning to discount.

2 Enter a subtotal item.

3 Enter a discount item.

4 Enter the remaining items (the items you're not discounting).

This method makes your discounts and your discount policies very clear to the customer.

Checking the Invoice

When you're finished entering all the line items, you'll see that QuickBooks has kept a running total, including taxes (see Figure 3-3).

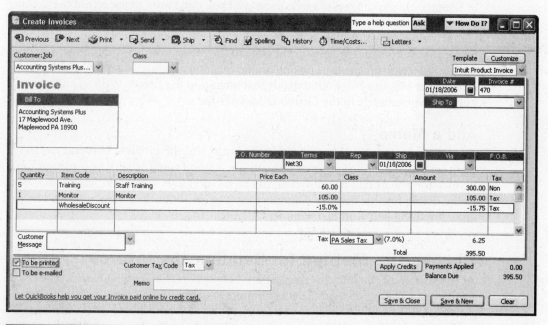

FIGURE 3-3 The invoice is complete, and there are no math errors because computers never make math errors.

Check Spelling

Click the Spelling icon on the toolbar of the Create Invoices window to run the QuickBooks spell checker. If the spell checker finds any word in your invoice form that isn't in the QuickBooks dictionary, that word is displayed. You can change the spelling, add the word to the QuickBooks dictionary (if it's spelled correctly), or tell the spell checker to ignore the word.

($) TIP: If you check the spelling each time you create an item, you eliminate the need to worry about spelling on an invoice—everything is prechecked before you insert the items in the invoice form. (The spell check ignores the data in the heading section of the invoice.)

($) NOTE: The spell checker is turned on by default, which I find annoying. If you want to control the spell checker, remove its automatic behavior in the Spelling section of the Preferences dialog.

Add a Message

If you want to add a message, click the arrow in the Customer Message field to see all the available messages (which you created in the Customer Message List, as described in Chapter 2). You can create a new message if you don't want to use any of the existing notes. To do so, choose <Add New> from the message drop-down list and enter your text in the New Customer Message window. Click OK to enter the message in the invoice and automatically save the message in the Message list so you can use it again. You can also type the message directly in the Customer Message window, which opens a Customer Message Not Found dialog that offers you the chance to do a QuickAdd to put your new message in the Customer Message list.

Add a Memo

You can add text to the Memo field at the bottom of the invoice. This text doesn't print on the invoice—it appears only on the screen (you'll see it if you reopen this invoice to view or edit it). However, the memo text *does* appear on statements, next to the listing for this invoice. Therefore, be careful about the text you use—don't enter anything you wouldn't want the customer to see.

Choose the Method for Sending the Invoice

At the bottom of the invoice template are two options for sending the invoice: To Be Printed and To Be E-mailed. Select the appropriate method if you're going to print or e-mail all your invoices after you finish entering them. (If you select the e-mail option, you have to provide more information, all of which is covered in the section "Sending Invoices and Credit Memos" later in this chapter.)

The QuickBooks Save Options for Invoices—Annoying and Dangerous

QuickBooks' inability to save an invoice and keep it in the Create Invoices window is a paradigm I find annoying. However, the ability to print an invoice without saving it is more than annoying, it's dangerous.

The removal of an invoice from the Create Invoices window when you save the invoice is annoying because you can't easily save and keep working. You have to select Save & New, and then click the Previous icon to return to the invoice. When I train users in other accounting software applications, I always teach them to save the invoice as they work. If they're entering a long list of line items, and the computer freezes or the network goes down after they've entered the fifteenth item, they have to start all over (talk about annoying!).

As to danger, all accounting software should force you to save an invoice before you can print it (or before you can print a packing slip or a pick slip). Every time I've worked with a client to investigate suspected embezzlements or stolen inventory, we've uncovered schemes involving fake invoices with payments directed to the miscreant, or fake customers (friends of the employee-thief) who are shipped products by a warehouse crew that was given a printed invoice. With any accounting software except QuickBooks, these schemes are difficult to hide, and almost always come to light rather quickly.

With QuickBooks, however, the lack of the rule that forces users to save invoices before printing, along with the ability to delete transactions, combine to make this software an embezzler's best friend. You can protect yourself from the side effects of transactions that were deleted for nefarious reasons by examining the Audit Trail (discussed in Chapter 21). You have no protection against fake invoices that are never saved, but are printed and sent with shipments.

You can also print or e-mail each invoice as you complete it. All of the options for printing and sending invoices are explained later in this chapter, in the section "Sending Invoices and Credit Memos."

Save the Invoice

Choose Save & New to save this invoice and move on to the next blank invoice form. If this is the last invoice you're creating, click Save & Close to save this invoice and close the Create Invoices window.

You're ready to send the invoices to your customers, which is discussed later, in the section "Sending Invoices and Credit Memos."

Creating Progress Billing Invoices

If you've enabled estimates and progress billing in the Jobs & Estimates category of the Edit | Preferences dialog, you can use the Progress invoice template to invoice your customers as each invoicing plateau arrives. See the section "Using Estimates" later in this chapter to learn how to create the estimates.

Choosing the Estimated Job

Progress invoices are just regular invoices that are connected to estimates. Open the Create Invoices window, select Progress Invoice from the Template drop-down list,

and choose the customer or job for which you're creating the Progress invoice. Because you've enabled estimates in your QuickBooks preferences, the system always checks the customer record to see if you've recorded any estimates for this job, and if so, presents them.

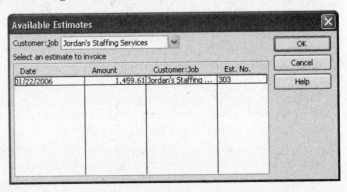

Select the estimate you're invoicing against and click OK. QuickBooks then asks you to specify what to include on the invoice:

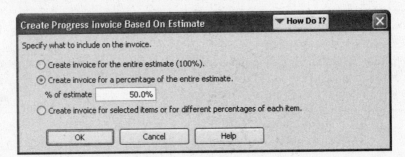

Fill out the dialog, using the following guidelines:

- You can bill for the whole job, 100 percent of the estimate. When the line items appear, you can edit any individual items.
- You can create an invoice for a specific percentage of the estimate. The percentage usually depends upon the agreement you have with your customer. For example, you could have an agreement that you'll invoice the job in a certain number of equal installments, or you could invoice a percentage that's equal to the percentage of the work that's been finished.

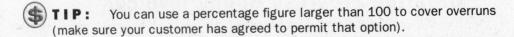 **TIP:** You can use a percentage figure larger than 100 to cover overruns (make sure your customer has agreed to permit that option).

- You can create an invoice that covers only certain items on the estimate, or you can create an invoice that has a different percentage for each item on the estimate. This is the approach to use if you're billing for completed work on a job that has a number of distinct tasks. Some of the work listed on the estimate may be finished, other work not started, and the various items listed on the estimate may be at different points of completion.

After you've created the first progress billing invoice for an estimate, a new option is available for subsequent invoices. That option is to bill for all remaining amounts in the estimate (it replaces the Enter Estimate (100%) option). This is generally reserved for your last invoice, and it saves you the trouble of figuring out which percentages of which items have been invoiced previously.

As far as QuickBooks is concerned, the items and prices in the estimate are not etched in stone; you can change any amounts or quantities you wish while you're creating the invoice. Your customer, however, may not be quite so lenient, and your ability to invoice for amounts that differ from the estimate depends on your agreement with the customer.

Entering Line Items

After you choose your progress billing method and click OK, QuickBooks automatically fills in the line item section of the invoice based on the approach you selected. For example, in Figure 3-4, I opted to create a progress bill for 50 percent of the estimate (because half the work was done).

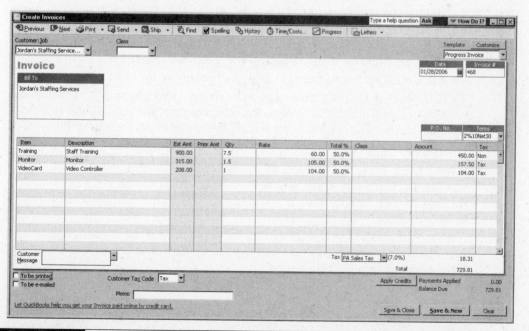

FIGURE 3-4   Progress invoices are automatically filled in, using the information in the estimate.

Changing Line Items

If you chose to invoice for a percentage of the estimate's total, the amount of every line item on the estimate reflects that percentage. This doesn't work terribly well for those lines that have products (it's hard to sell a percentage of a physical product). You can leave the invoice as is, because the customer will probably understand that this is a progress invoice. Or, you can make changes to the invoice.

In addition to strange or inaccurate line items for products, the line items for services rendered may not be totally accurate. For example, some of the line items may contain service categories that aren't at the same percentage of completion as others.

To change the invoice and keep a history of the changes against the estimate, click the Progress icon on the toolbar of the Create Invoices window. This opens a dialog (see Figure 3-5) that allows reconfiguration of the line items.

You can change the quantity, rate, or percentage of completion for any individual line item. Here's how to make changes:

1. Select Show Quantity And Rate. The columns in the dialog change to display the columns from the estimate, and you can make changes to any of them.
2. Click the Qty column for any line item to highlight the default number that's been used to calculate the invoice.
3. Replace the number with the amount you want to use for the invoice. You can also change the rate, but generally that's not cricket unless there are some circumstances that warrant it (which you and the customer have agreed upon).
4. Select Show Percentage to display the column that has the percentage of completion for this and previous billings. The percentages compare the dollar amounts for invoices against the estimated total.
5. Click the Curr % column to change the percentage for any line item.
6. Select both options if you need to make changes to one type of progress on one line item and another type of progress on another line item. All the columns (and all the history from previous billings, if any exists) appear in the window.

Click OK when you have finished making your adjustments. You return to the invoice form, where the amounts on the line items have changed to match the adjustments you made. Click Save & New to save this invoice and move on to the next invoice, or click Save & Close to save this invoice and close the Create Invoices window.

Using this method to change a line item keeps the history of your estimate and invoices intact (as opposed to making changes in the amounts directly on the invoice form, which does not create a good history).

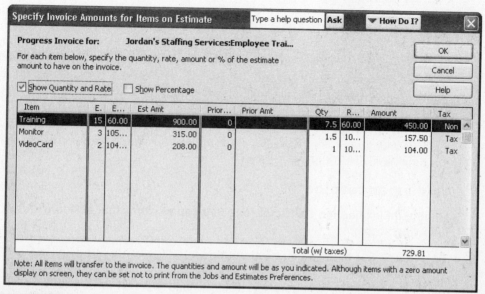

FIGURE 3-5   You can make changes to the data that QuickBooks automatically inserted in the invoice.

Editing Invoices

If you want to correct an invoice (perhaps you charged the wrong amount or forgot you'd promised a different amount to a particular customer), you can do so quite easily.

Editing the Current Invoice

Editing the invoice that's currently on the screen is quite easy. Click in the field or column that requires changing and make the changes (you probably figured this out).

Editing a Previously Entered Invoice

You can open the Create Invoices window (or perhaps you're still working there) and click the Previous button to move back through all the invoices in your system. However, if you have a great many invoices, it's faster to use the QuickBooks Find feature (covered in Chapter 22). Use the following guidelines when you're editing a previously entered invoice:

- If a previously entered invoice has been paid, you cannot edit the amount, date, or items. However, you can edit the memo field.
- If a previously entered invoice has not been paid, but has been mailed, you shouldn't edit anything, although it's probably safe to enter or modify text in the memo field if necessary.
- If the previously entered invoice has not yet been sent to the customer, you can make any changes you wish.

When you click Save & Close, QuickBooks displays a message dialog asking whether you want to save the changes you made. Click Yes.

Voiding and Deleting Invoices

There's an enormous difference between voiding and deleting an invoice. Voiding an invoice makes the invoice nonexistent to your accounting and customer balances. However, the invoice number continues to exist (it's marked "VOID") so you can account for it—missing invoice numbers are just as frustrating as missing check numbers.

Deleting an invoice, on the other hand, removes all traces of it from your transaction registers and reports. It's a dangerous act (unless you're an embezzler, in which case the ability to delete an invoice is a gift).

Voiding an Invoice

Voiding an invoice isn't difficult, and you can perform this action with the following steps:

1 Press CTRL-A or click the Accnt button on the toolbar to bring up the Chart Of Accounts list.

2 Double-click the Accounts Receivable account to open the register.

3 Find the invoice you want to void and click anywhere on the row to select it.

4 Right-click and choose Void Invoice from the shortcut menu. The word "VOID" appears in the Description field in the register. (If you'd entered memo text in the invoice, the word "VOID" is placed in front of your text.)

5 Click Record to save your action.

6 Close the register by clicking the X in the top-right corner.

You can also use the Find feature (to locate the invoice instead of scrolling through the Accounts Receivable account register. Open the invoice and choose Edit | Void Invoice from the menu bar.

 NOTE: When you void an invoice, QuickBooks marks the status of the invoice as Paid. This means nothing more than the fact that the invoice isn't "open," but QuickBooks should have thought of a different word (like maybe, "void"?). It's a bit startling to see that notation.

Deleting an Invoice

Don't delete invoices; in fact, don't delete anything, because it's a bad bookkeeping habit. Voiding transactions performs almost the same action (except you can see what you did). I've never seen another accounting software application that lets users delete transactions.

If you choose to ignore my advice, and you feel you must delete an invoice, follow steps 1 through 3 in the preceding section, then press CTRL-D. You'll have to confirm the deletion.

 CAUTION: Never delete an invoice to which a customer payment has been attached. Straightening out that mess is a nightmare.

Understanding the Postings for Invoices

It's important to understand what QuickBooks is doing behind the scenes, because everything you do has an impact on your financial reports. Let's look at the postings for an imaginary invoice that has these line items:

- $500.00 for services rendered
- $30.00 for sales tax

Because QuickBooks is a full, double-entry bookkeeping program, there is a balanced posting made to the general ledger. For this invoice, the following postings are made to the general ledger:

Account	Debit	Credit
Accounts Receivable	530.00	
Sales Tax		30.00
Income—Services		500.00

If the invoice includes inventory items, the postings are a bit more complicated. Let's post an invoice that sold ten widgets to a customer. The widgets cost you $50.00 each and you sold them for $100.00 each. This customer was shipped ten widgets, and was also charged tax and shipping.

Account	Debit	Credit
Accounts Receivable	1,077.00	
Income—Sales of Items		1,000.00
Sales Tax		70.00
Shipping		7.00
Cost of Sales	500.00	
Inventory		500.00

There are some things to think about as you look at these postings. To keep accurate books, you should fill out the cost of your inventory items when you create the items. As you purchase replacement items, QuickBooks updates the cost (from the vendor bill). This is the only way to get a correct posting to the cost of sales and the balancing decrement in the value of your inventory.

You don't have to separate your income accounts (one for services, one for inventory items, and so on) to have accurate books. Income is income. However, you may decide to create accounts for each type of income so you can analyze where your revenue is coming from.

There are two theories on posting shipping:

- Separate your own shipping costs (an expense) from the shipping you collect from your customers (revenue)
- Post everything to the shipping expense

To use the first method, create an income account for shipping and link that account to the shipping item you created to use in invoices.

If you use the latter method, don't be surprised at the end of the year if you find your shipping expense is reported as a negative number, meaning that you collected more than you spent for shipping. You won't have a shipping expense to deduct from your revenue at tax time, but who cares—you made money.

Issuing Credits and Refunds

Sometimes you have to give money to a customer. You can do this in the form of a credit against current or future balances, or you can write a check and refund money you received from the customer. Neither is a lot of fun, but it's a fact of business life.

Creating Credit Memos

A credit memo reduces a customer balance. This is necessary if a customer returns goods, has been billed for goods that were lost or damaged in shipment, or wins an argument about the price of a service you provided.

The credit memo itself is usually sent to the customer to let the customer know the details about the credit that's being applied. The totals are posted to your accounting records just as the invoice totals are posted, except there's an inherent minus sign next to the number. (Information about applying the credit memo against the customer's account is in Chapter 4.)

Creating a credit memo is similar to creating an invoice:

1. Click the Refunds & Credits icon on the Home page (or choose Customers | Create Credit Memos/Refunds from the menu bar) to open a blank Create Credit Memos/Refunds form (see Figure 3-6).
2. Select a customer or job, and then fill out the rest of the heading.
3. Move to the line item section and enter the item, the quantity, and the rate for the items in this credit memo. Don't use a minus sign—QuickBooks knows what a credit is.
4. Remember to insert all the special items you need to give credit for, such as shipping.
5. You can use the Customer Message field to add any short explanation that's necessary.
6. Click Save & Close to save the credit memo (unless you have more credit memos to create—in which case, click Save & New).

When you save the credit memo, QuickBooks asks you to specify the way you want to apply the credit amount. (See the next section, "Applying Credit Memos.")

See the section "Sending Invoices and Credit Memos" later in this chapter to learn about delivering your credit memos.

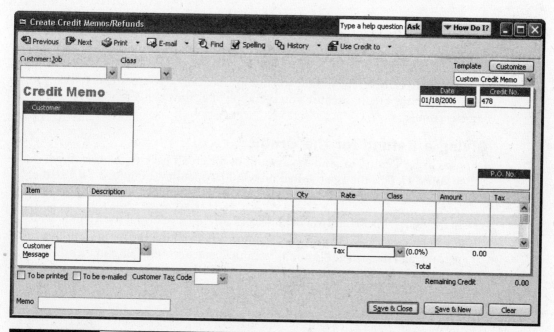

FIGURE 3-6 The Credit Memo template has all the fields needed to provide information to the customer about the credit.

$ TIP: By default, the credit memo number is the next available invoice number. If you change the number because you want a different numbering system for credit memos, you'll have to keep track of numbers manually. QuickBooks will use the next number (the one after this credit memo) for your next invoice. Therefore, it's easier to use the default procedure of having one set of continuous numbers for invoices and credit memos.

Applying Credit Memos

When you save the credit memo, QuickBooks displays a dialog where you can choose the way to apply this credit.

Retaining the Credit

Choose Retain As An Available Credit to let the credit amount stay with the customer. You can apply the credit to a future invoice, or apply it to an open invoice later (depending on what the customer wants to do). When you create invoices, or apply customer payments to existing invoices, the credit is available.

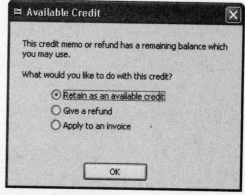

TIP: The jargon for a credit that is not yet applied to an invoice is *floating credit.*

If the credit is for a job, and the job doesn't have any outstanding invoices, you should retain the credit, because you can apply it against a different job for the same customer.

Giving a Refund for the Credit

Choose Give A Refund to send the amount of the credit back to the customer. When you click OK, the Issue A Refund window opens (see Figure 3-7). Use the following guidelines to configure the Issue A Refund window:

- In the Issue This Refund Via field, select Cash or Check from the drop-down list.
- If you choose Cash, QuickBooks assumes you're taking the money out of a cash register, and deducts the amount from the bank account. (Be sure to select the appropriate bank account in the Account field.)
- If you choose Check, the dialog adds an option labeled To Be Printed, which is selected by default.
- If you print checks, leave the check mark in the check box and click OK. The check is added to the list of checks to be printed when you choose File | Print Forms | Check. (The check also appears in the bank account register with the notation "To Print".)
- If you write checks manually, deselect the check mark in the To Be Printed check box, and click OK. The check is added to your bank account register, using the next available check number. Don't forget to write, and send, the check.

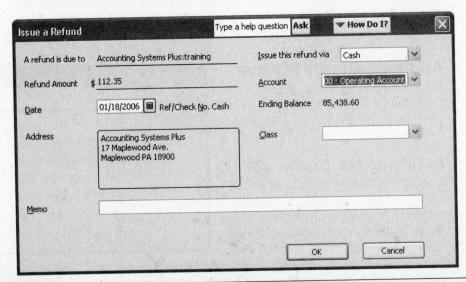

FIGURE 3-7   Tell QuickBooks how to manage the refund you want to send to the customer.

Applying the Credit to an Invoice

Choose Apply To An Invoice to apply the credit to a current invoice. When you click OK, QuickBooks displays a list of open invoices for this customer (or job, if the credit is for a job), and automatically applies the credit against the oldest invoice.

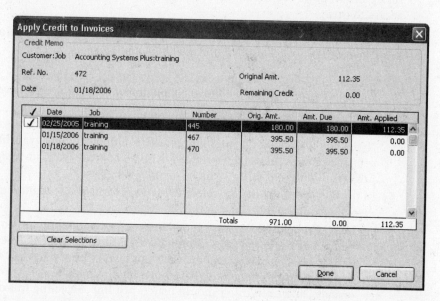

If the credit is larger than the oldest invoice, QuickBooks applies the remaining amount of the credit to the next oldest invoice. If there are no additional invoices, the remaining amount of the credit is held in the customer's record, and is treated as a retained credit. Click Done to close the window.

Sending Invoices and Credit Memos

You have several choices about the method you use to send invoices and credit memos. You can print and mail them, or send them via e-mail—and within those options are other options, which I discuss in this section.

For those of you who print invoices, insert them in envelopes, and put them in the mail, I'll start with instructions for printing. Then I'll explain how to e-mail invoices.

Printing Invoices and Credit Memos

You can print invoices and credit memos on blank paper, preprinted forms on a single sheet of paper, preprinted multipart forms, or on your company letterhead. You have to set up your printer for invoices and credit memos, but once you complete this task you don't have to do it again. There are several steps involved in setting up a printer, but they're not terribly difficult.

Setting Up the Printer for Forms

If you have multiple printers attached to your computer or accessible through a network, you have to designate one of them as the invoice printer. If you use multipart forms, you should have a dot matrix printer. Your printers are already set up in Windows (or should be), so QuickBooks, like all Windows software, has access to them.

Now you have to tell QuickBooks about the printer and the way you want to print invoices:

❶ Choose File | Printer Setup from the menu bar to open the Printer Setup dialog and select Invoice from the Form Name drop-down list (you'll have to perform these steps again for credit memos).

❷ In the Printer Setup dialog (see Figure 3-8), click the arrow next to the Printer Name box to choose a printer if you have multiple printers available. This printer becomes the default printer for Invoice forms (you can assign different printers to different forms, which is a nifty time-saver).

❸ In the bottom of the dialog, select the type of form you're planning to use for invoices from the following options:

- **Intuit Preprinted Forms** Templates with all your company information, field names, and row and column dividers already printed. These forms need to be aligned to match the way your invoice prints. You can also purchase the forms from a company that knows about QuickBooks' invoice printing formats, and everything should match just fine. Selecting this option tells QuickBooks that only the data needs to be sent to the printer because the fields are already printed.

- **Blank Paper** Selecting this option tells QuickBooks that everything, including your company name and address, field names, etc., must be sent to the printer. This is easiest, but it may not look as pretty as a printed form. Some of us don't care about pretty—we just want to ship invoices and collect the payments. But if you care about image this may not be a great choice.

- **Letterhead** This means you print your invoices on paper that has your company name and address (and perhaps a logo) preprinted. Selecting this option tells QuickBooks not to print the company information when it prints the invoice.

💲 **TIP:** It's a good idea to print lines around each field to make sure the information is printed in a way that's easy to read. To accomplish that, make sure the option titled Do Not Print Lines Around Each Field is disabled (not selected).

Setting Up Form Alignment

You have to test the QuickBooks output against the paper in your printer to make sure everything prints in the right place. To accomplish this, click the Align button in the Printer Setup dialog, select the invoice template you're using (e.g., Service,

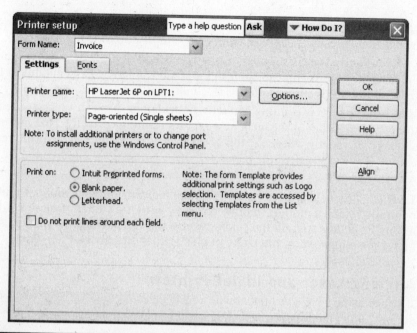

| FIGURE 3-8 | Specify the type of paper you want to use when you print invoices.

Product, etc.), and then click OK. The dialog you see to set up alignment differs, depending on the type of printer you've selected.

Aligning Dot Matrix Printers

If you're using a continuous-feed printer (dot matrix using paper with sprocket holes), you'll see a dialog that lets you perform both coarse and fine adjustments. This is necessary because you must set the placement of the top of the page, which you don't have to do with a page printer (laser, inkjet).

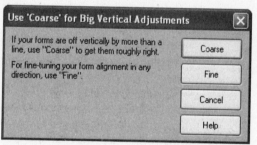

Start by clicking the Coarse button. A dialog appears telling you that a sample form is about to be printed and warning you not to make any physical adjustments to your printer after the sample has printed. QuickBooks provides another dialog where you can make any necessary adjustments. Make sure the appropriate preprinted form, letterhead, or blank paper is loaded in the printer. Click OK.

The sample form prints to your dot matrix printer and QuickBooks displays a dialog asking you to enter pointer line position. You can see the pointer line at the top of the printed sample. Enter the line it's on in the dialog and click OK (the printout numbers the lines). Continue to follow the instructions as QuickBooks takes you through any adjustments that might be needed. (I can't give specific instructions because I can't see what your sample output looks like.)

If you want to tweak the alignment a bit further, choose Fine. (See the information on using the Fine Alignment dialog in the section "Aligning Laser and Inkjet Printers" that follows this section.) Otherwise, choose OK.

When the form is printing correctly, QuickBooks displays a message telling you to note the position of the form now that it's printing correctly. That means you should note exactly where the top of the page is in relation to the print head and the bar that leans against the paper.

 TIP: The best way to note the position of the forms in your dot matrix printer is to use a marker to draw an arrow with the word "invoice" (or the letter "I") at the spot on the printer where the top of the form should be. I have mine marked on the piece of plastic that sits above the roller.

Aligning Laser and Inkjet Printers

If you're using a page printer, you'll see only this Fine Alignment dialog:

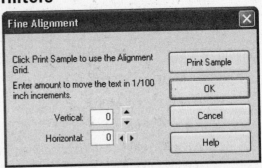

Click Print Sample to send output to your printer. Then, with the printed page in your hand, make adjustments to the alignment in the dialog. Use the arrows next to the Vertical and Horizontal boxes to move the positions at which printing occurs.

Click OK, and then click OK in the Printer Setup dialog. Your settings are saved, and you don't have to go through this again for printing invoices.

Repeat all these steps to create settings for credit memos.

Batch Printing

If you didn't print each invoice or credit memo as you created it, and you made sure that the To Be Printed check box was selected on each invoice you created, you're ready to start a print run.

Place the correct paper in your printer and, if it's continuous paper in a dot matrix printer, position it properly.

Use the following steps to print your invoices:

1. Choose File | Print Forms | Invoices.
2. In the Select Invoices To Print window, all your unprinted invoices are selected with a check mark.
3. If there are any invoices you don't want to print at this time, click the check marks to remove them.

④ If you want to print mailing labels for these invoices, you must print them first (see the next section).

⑤ Click OK to print your invoices.

The Print Invoices dialog appears, where you can change or select printing options. Click Print to begin printing. Repeat the steps to print your credit memos.

Printing Mailing Labels

If you need mailing labels, QuickBooks will print them for you. You must print the mailing labels before you print the invoices.

In the Select Invoices To Print window, click the Print Labels button to bring up the Select Labels To Print dialog.

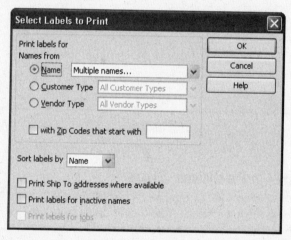

The options have been preselected to match a label run for multiple customers, and the customers selected are those customers who have invoices waiting to be printed. Click OK to open the Print Labels dialog (see Figure 3-9).

QuickBooks assumes you've loaded Avery labels into your printer. Select the appropriate printer, specify the label format you use (if you purchased preprinted labels from QuickBooks, they're in the drop-down list), and click Print.

After the labels are printed, you're returned to the Select Invoices To Print dialog. Choose OK to open the Print Invoices dialog and begin printing your invoices.

After you've finished printing invoices, check the print job to make sure nothing went wrong (the printer jammed, you had the wrong paper in the printer, whatever). If anything went amiss, you can reprint the forms you need when the following dialog appears. (Use the invoice number as the form number.)

If everything is hunky-dory, click OK.

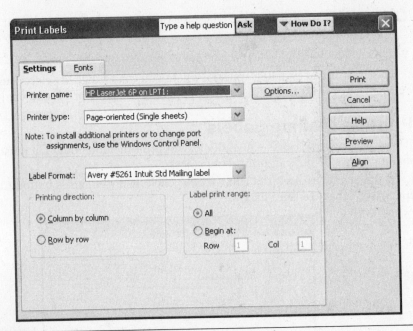

FIGURE 3-9   Configure the label printing options you need.

Printing Packing Slips

QuickBooks provides a template for a packing slip, which is basically an invoice that doesn't display prices. The theory behind packing slips is that for the warehouse personnel who manage and pack products, the cost of those products falls under the category "none of your business."

Print the Default Packing Slip

To print the default packing slip, complete the invoice. Then click the arrow next to the Print icon at the top of the Create Invoices window and select Print Packing Slip from the drop-down list. The Print Packing Slip dialog opens so you can select your printing options (which are the same as the options described earlier for printing invoices).

Change the Default Packing Slip

If you create your own customized packing slip template, you can select it each time you print a packing slip.

You can also make that new form the default packing slip by following these steps:

❶ Choose Edit | Preferences to open the Preferences dialog.
❷ Go to the Sales & Customers section and click the Company Preferences tab.

③ In the Choose Template For Invoice Packing Slip field, select your new packing slip form from the drop-down list.

④ Click OK.

If you have multiple packing slips, you can choose any of them for printing. With the completed invoice in the Create Invoices window, instead of selecting Print Packing Slip from the Print button's drop-down list, select a packing slip template from the drop-down list in the Template field. The Create Invoices window changes to display the packing slip, as shown in Figure 3-10.

I know I just told you that a packing slip doesn't display any amounts, and there they are! Well, no they're not. Confused? Don't be—the packing slip in Figure 3-10 is the Intuit Packing Slip, which has one set of configuration options for the screen and another set for the printed version. This is true for any packing slip template you create, and it's a handy feature, as you'll learn when you read the section on customizing templates later in this chapter.

To see what the printed version of the packing slip looks like, click the arrow next to the Print icon on the Create Invoices window toolbar and choose Preview. Satisfied? Close the Preview window and return to the Create Invoices window. Now you can print the packing slip.

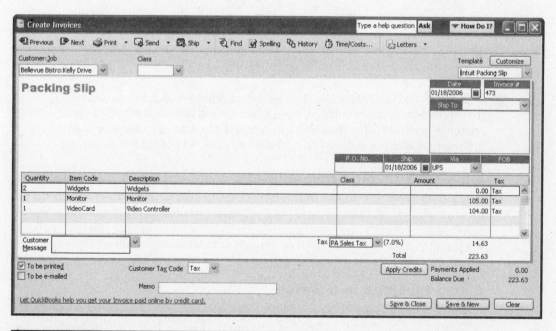

FIGURE 3-10 View a packing slip before you print it.

E-mailing Invoices and Credit Memos

QuickBooks provides a way to e-mail invoices and credit memos to customers. (From here on I'll refer to invoices in the discussion, but all the same instructions apply to credit memos and other customer forms.)

To e-mail an invoice, make sure the completed invoice is in the Create Invoices window. (If you saved the invoice previously, open the Create Invoices window and use the Previous button to move backward through saved invoices.)

Now follow these steps:

1. Click the arrow to the right of the Send icon on the Create Invoices window toolbar and select E-mail Invoice to save the invoice and open the Send Invoice dialog box.

2. In the Send Invoice dialog (see Figure 3-11), select E-mail, and make sure the e-mail addresses in the To and From fields are correct (they're taken from the data you entered for your company and your customers). If you didn't enter e-mail address data for your company or your customer, enter the e-mail address manually.

3. If you want to send a copy of the invoice to another recipient, enter the e-mail address in the CC field. For multiple recipients, separate each address with a comma.

4. Make any needed changes to the text of the e-mail message (the invoice itself is an attachment).

5. Click Send Now to e-mail the invoice immediately, or click Send Later to save the invoice and mail it (with other invoices) in a batch.

 NOTE: If you manually enter an e-mail address, QuickBooks notifies you that the address doesn't match the current stored data and offers to update the customer's record. This almost always means the data is missing (you didn't fill in the e-mail address field on the customer record), so accept the offer.

E-mail the Invoice Immediately

If you click Send Now to e-mail this invoice immediately, QuickBooks opens a browser window and takes you to the Business Services section. Your regular e-mail software doesn't open; this is all done by QuickBooks through the Internet. Follow the prompts to complete the sign up process (the service is free). When your e-mail is sent, QuickBooks issues a success message.

E-mail Invoices in a Batch

If you click Send Later, QuickBooks saves the message, along with any others you save, until you're ready to send all of them.

When you want to e-mail all the invoices, choose File | Send Forms to open the Select Forms To Send dialog as shown in Figure 3-12. (You can also open this dialog by selecting Send Batch from the Send icon drop-down list in the Create Invoices window.)

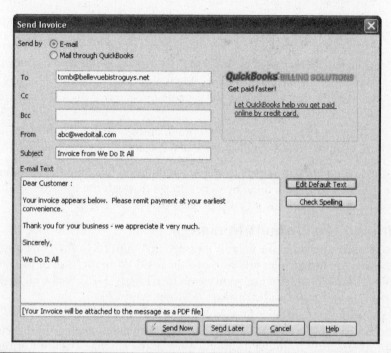

Be sure the information is correct before you send the invoice.

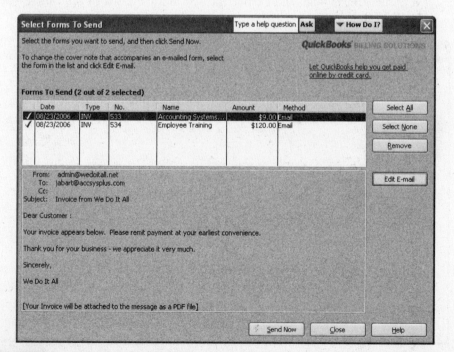

E-mail all your transactions at once.

Here are some guidelines for working with the Select Forms To Send dialog:

- By default, all e-mails are selected. Deselect an e-mail by clicking the check mark in the leftmost column of its listing. Click again to put the check mark back.
- You can delete any item by selecting it and clicking Remove. You're not deleting the invoice, you're deleting the e-mail. You can return to the invoice and send it anytime.
- To edit the message text of any e-mail, double-click its listing, or highlight it and click the Edit E-mail button. Make your changes and click OK.

Click Send Now to e-mail all the selected items. Your regular e-mail software doesn't open; this is all done by QuickBooks through the Internet. Follow the prompts to complete the sign-up process (the service is free).

Change the Default Message

If you want to change the default message that appears in the e-mail message, choose Edit | Preferences and move to the Send Forms section of the Preferences dialog. In the Company Preferences tab (see Figure 3-13), make changes to any part of the message header or text.

You can use this dialog to customize the e-mail for all QuickBooks forms that can be sent by e-mail (look at the list; it's amazingly complete). Select the appropriate form from the drop-down list in the Change Default For field.

You can change the way the salutations are inserted in the message, change the text of the Subject field, and change the text in the message. (You can also perform a spell check.)

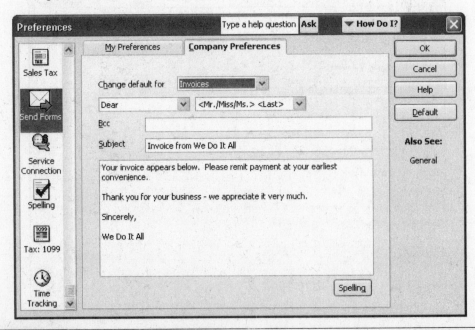

FIGURE 3-13   Customize your e-mail forms.

The Customer-side of E-mailed Invoices

When the customer receives your e-mail invoice, the invoice is a PDF attachment. In addition to the message text you sent, below your signature, the e-mail message includes a statement that the recipient needs Acrobat Reader to open the attached invoice file.

Dear Customer :

Your invoice appears below. Please remit payment at your earliest convenience.

Thank you for your business - we appreciate it very much.

Sincerely,

We Do It All

To view your invoice
Open the attached PDF file. You must have Acrobat® Reader® installed to view the attachment.

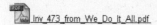 Inv_473_from_We_Do_It_All.pdf

If your customer doesn't have Acrobat Reader (now called Adobe Reader) installed, clicking the link (the words "Acrobat Reader" are a link) sends your customer to the Adobe web site, where the software is available for downloading (and it's free).

Additional Send Features for Forms

The Send drop-down list on the invoice form (and other forms) includes a choice named Mail Invoice. This refers to a feature you can sign up for (for a fee) to let QuickBooks print and mail your invoices. The printed form has a tear-off remittance slip, a return envelope, and other features.

You can also add power to your e-mail delivery options by adding a "pay online" feature for customers, available (for a fee) from QuickBooks.

Information about both additional services is available on the QuickBooks web site (www.quickbooks.com).

Creating Sales Orders

Many inventory-based businesses use sales orders as the first step in selling products to a customer. A *sales order* is a tentative document, on hold until there is sufficient inventory to fill it or until prices and discounts are approved by management. Some companies don't want to consider a sale as a final step until the items are packed, weighed, and on the truck. Other companies don't want an invoice processed until a sales manager approves the prices (especially if the salesperson has the right to give discounts to favorite customers). Nothing on a sales order is posted to the general ledger.

QuickBooks Pro doesn't include the sales order feature. However, you can imitate this protocol if you need it. I discovered I could set up sales order processing in QuickBooks Pro by using a little imagination and a couple of keystrokes.

N O T E :   QuickBooks Premier editions provide sales orders. To learn how to use them, read *Running QuickBooks 2006 Premier Editions* from CPA911 Publishing (www.cpa911publishing.com). The book is available at your favorite bookstore.

In more robust (and more expensive) accounting software, the sales order is a separate form and a separate menu choice. It's frequently printed along with a *pick list* (a document that's printed for the warehouse personnel, listing the items in bin order and omitting prices); then there's a menu item that converts sales orders to invoices. When the sales order is converted, shipping costs are added (because the shipment has been packed and weighed by now) and a packing slip is printed. I found it easy to duplicate all the steps I needed for small businesses that wanted sales order and pick list functions in their QuickBooks software. Creating a sales order is just a matter of creating an invoice and then taking the additional step of configuring the invoice so it's not really a sale.

Here's how:

1. Create an invoice as described earlier in this chapter.
2. Choose Edit | Mark Invoice As Pending from the QuickBooks menu bar (or right-click anywhere in the Invoice window and choose Mark Invoice As Pending from the shortcut menu). The Pending notice is placed on the invoice (see Figure 3-14).
3. Print the invoice and send it to a supervisor to approve the pricing (and send a packing slip to the warehouse as a pick list).
4. When the order is through the system, bring the invoice back to the window and add the shipping costs.
5. Choose Edit | Mark Invoice As Final. Now you have a regular invoice and you can proceed accordingly.

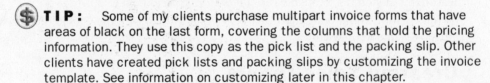 **T I P :**   Some of my clients purchase multipart invoice forms that have areas of black on the last form, covering the columns that hold the pricing information. They use this copy as the pick list and the packing slip. Other clients have created pick lists and packing slips by customizing the invoice template. See information on customizing later in this chapter.

If you have a service business, the sales order protocol can be handy for tracking specific jobs or tasks that customers request. It's a good first step, even before the estimating process (if you use estimates).

Creating Backorders

If you're selling inventory, there's nothing more frustrating than getting a big order when you're out of some or all of the products being ordered. You can ship the items you do have in stock and consider the rest of the items a backorder. The problem is that there's no backorder button on a QuickBooks invoice, nor is there a backorder form.

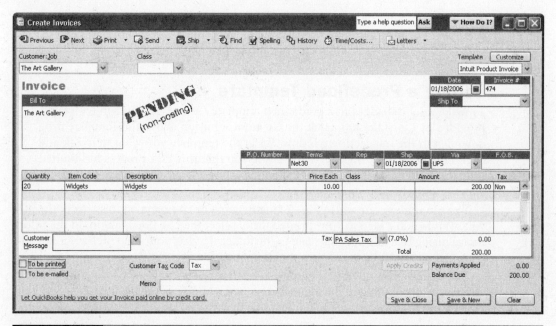

FIGURE 3-14   There's no mistaking the fact that this invoice isn't a real sale.

Instead of a backorder form, use the Pending Invoice feature described in the previous section. Here are some guidelines for making that feature work for backorders:

- As the items arrive in your warehouse from the vendor, remove them from the pending invoice (and save the invoice again if any backordered items remain) and place them in a regular invoice form.
- Use the Notes feature on customer records to indicate whether this customer accepts backorders, automatically cancels the portion of the order that must be backordered, or wants you to hold the shipment until the entire order can be sent.
- Check with the vendor of a backordered item regarding delivery date, and then create a QuickBooks reminder. The reminder tells you to grab the products as they arrive, so nobody puts them onto the shelves without remembering to fill the backorder.

NOTE: QuickBooks Premier editions support backorders. To learn how to use them, read *Running QuickBooks 2006 Premier Editions* from CPA911 Publishing (www.cpa911publishing.com). The book is available at your favorite bookstore.

Customizing Templates

QuickBooks makes it very easy to customize the forms you use to create transactions. Forms, such as invoices, purchase orders, statements, and so on, are called *templates* in QuickBooks. An existing template can be used as the basis of a new template, copying what you like, changing what you don't like, and eliminating what you don't need. In the following discussion, I'm using invoice templates, but you can customize other transaction forms just as easily.

Editing a Predefined Template

To make minor changes to a predefined template (one of the built-in templates provided by QuickBooks), click the Customize button above the Template drop-down list in the transaction window. Select the template you want to tweak and click Edit. After a message appears telling you that this Edit process has limited features (remember, I said it was for minor changes), the Customize Invoice dialog appears with the Edit mode options.

You can remove (or add) your company name or company address (or both). If you want to add a logo to your printed form, select the Use Logo option. In the Select Image dialog that appears, navigate to the folder that has your logo file, select it, and click Open. Click OK to confirm the use of this file.

The logo is positioned in the upper-left corner of your invoice form. You cannot change the positioning of the logo when you're working in Edit mode. See the section "Designing the Layout" to learn how to change the location of your logo on your invoices.

 TIP: By default, QuickBooks assumes your logo file is in the same folder in which you've installed QuickBooks. If it's not, after you locate the file in the Select Image dialog, QuickBooks asks if it's okay to copy the file to the folder in which you installed QuickBooks.

Designing a New Template

If you want to add, remove, or reposition elements in your invoice, you have to design a new template. This is also the way to add any custom fields you may have created for any of your lists to the transaction form.

To begin, click the Customize button above the Template drop-down list. Select the template you want to use as the basis of this new template and choose New in the Customize Template dialog. The Customize Invoice dialog opens with a whole raft of choices (see Figure 3-15).

You must give the template a name to create a new form. Enter a name for the form—something that reminds you of the format. Then move through the tabs to make changes, using the guidelines presented in this section.

Changing the Header

On the Header tab, you can change the information that appears. For example, you can add or remove the Ship To block, or change the word Invoice to something else (e.g., Services Rendered).

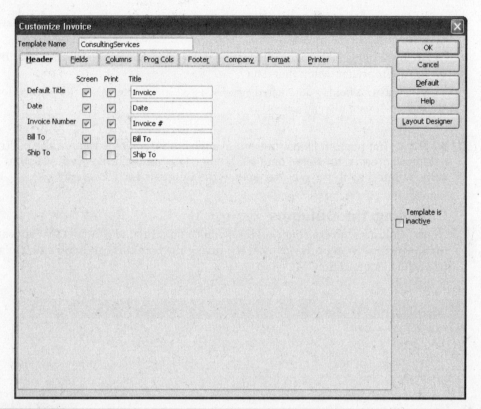

FIGURE 3-15   Start by giving your new template its own name.

Changing the Fields

On the Fields tab, you can make changes to the screen copy of the form, the printed copy of the form, or both. For example, as you can see in Figure 3-16, the custom field that was created for customer records to track backorder preferences has been added to the on-screen version of the invoice (the custom field is named BackorderRules, the invoice form will display the label BO, meaning Backorder). This data needs to be tracked for internal purposes, to let the user who is creating the invoice know whether to create a backorder if goods are not in the warehouse. The field is of no interest to the customer who receives the printed invoice.

Following are some of the common changes made in the Fields tab:

- Add a field that is displayed on the screen copy of the form to the printed copy (if you want the customer to see the new field and its information).
- Add a field to the screen copy to display data not currently displayed on the screen (a way to provide information to the person who is entering the data).

- Add a field to both the printed form and the screen display if it's appropriate for everybody to see the data.
- Remove fields from the printed copy of the form, the screen display, or both, if it's appropriate to skip that data.
- Add custom fields you created (as discussed in Chapter 2) to the printed form, the on-screen display, or both.

 TIP: The custom fields that are available on the Fields tab are the custom fields you created for Name lists (Customer:Job, Vendor, Employee). Custom fields created for items are available in the Columns tab (covered next).

Changing the Columns

On the Columns tab (see Figure 3-17), you can modify the columns that appear in the line item section of the invoice. Modifying the columns can be an efficient and powerful customization.

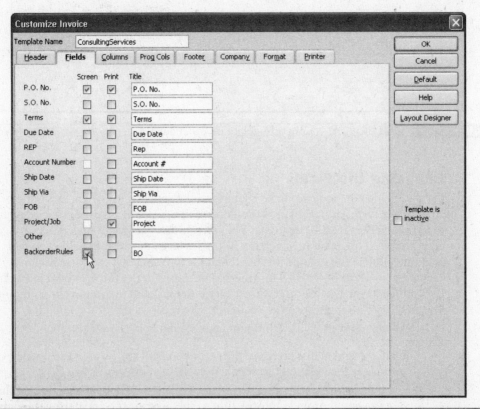

FIGURE 3-16   You can add a custom field to the invoice; in this case, only the data entry person sees the field.

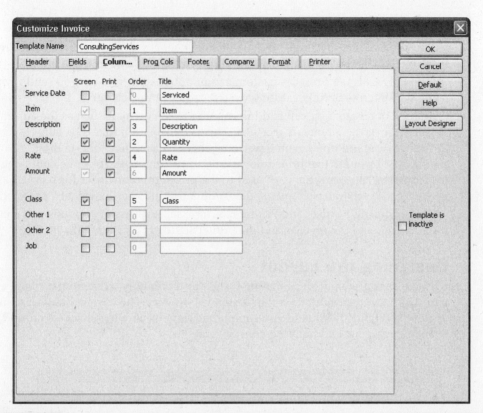

The Job column is a custom field created for the Items list, and can be added to the invoice so the customer knows which job each line item applies to.

You can add or remove columns from the screen or printed version of the form (or both). You can also change the order of columns (the numbers displayed in the Order boxes determine the left to right position on the form, with 1 as the leftmost column).

 N O T E :   Some fields can only be removed from the printed version of the form, not the on-screen display.

QuickBooks provides two extra columns for your use, Other 1 and Other 2. To add the columns to the screen or print version of the invoice (or both), put a check mark in the appropriate box. Then enter the text for the Label that appears at the top of the column. For example, you may want to add a column for Backordered, in which you enter the number of items you're not shipping with this order. The number of items you're shipping is in the Quantity column, and in this case you could change the text for the Quantity column to Qty Shipped.

Changing Data in the Other Tabs

Go through all the tabs on the dialog, making changes as needed. Following are some guidelines for changing the data and formats available in those tabs.

The Prog Cols tab provides customization options for invoices you send if you're using the Progress Billing feature (covered earlier in this chapter).

In the Footer tab, you can add information to the invoice, such as the current balance due or the payments received. This is information that is usually reserved for statements, and unless you have some cogent reason to avoid sending statements, I wouldn't add this information to each invoice. It can be confusing to customers, most of whom are used to the paradigm of invoices for services and products, and separate statements that summarize invoices, payments, and credits.

The Company, Format, and Printer tabs have self-explanatory options that control the appearance of the invoice, and the printer settings for printing the invoice.

Designing the Layout

If you're comfortable with designing forms (or if you like to live on the edge), click the Layout Designer button on the Customize window. The Layout Designer window opens (see Figure 3-18), and you can plunge right in, moving elements around, changing margins, and building your own layout.

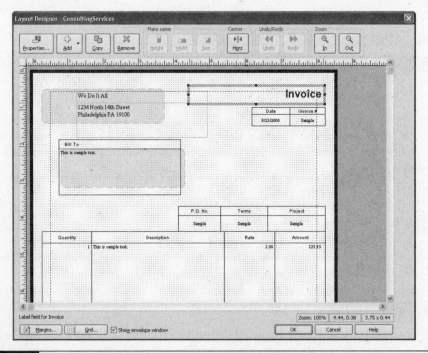

FIGURE 3-18   Move components around to create your own design.

N O T E :   If you've added custom fields to the template, the Layout Designer issues a message warning you that these fields may overlap existing fields. You can tell the system to re-layout the design by clicking Relayout, or click the Skip button to move any fields that overlap manually. After you make your choice, the Layout Designer window opens.

If you use window envelopes to mail your invoices, select the Show Envelope Window option at the bottom of the Layout Designer before you start. The area of the form that will appear in the envelope windows is highlighted in green. This helps you avoid moving any fields into that area.

Select any element to put a frame around it. Now you can perform an action on the frame, as follows:

- To change the size of the element, position your pointer on one of the sizing handles on the frame, then drag the handle to resize the element.
- To move an element, position your pointer inside the frame and, when your pointer turns into a four-headed arrow, drag the frame to a different location on the form.
- Double-click an element's frame to see a Properties dialog that permits all sorts of option changes for the selected element.
- To change the margin measurements, click the Margins button at the bottom of the Layout Designer.
- Click the Grid button to eliminate the dotted-line grid from the screen, to change the spacing between grid lines, or to turn off the Snap To Grid option (automatically aligns objects to the nearest point on the grid).
- Use the toolbar buttons to align, resize, and zoom into the selected elements. There's also an Undo/ Redo choice, thank goodness. When you finish with the Layout Designer, click OK to move back to the Customize Invoice window.

Once everything is just the way you want it, save your new template by clicking OK. This new template name appears on the drop-down list when you create invoices.

 T I P :   You can also use this new template as the basis for other customizations.

Duplicating a Template

You can duplicate existing templates, which is a good idea. You're not messing around with the original (always a safe way to approach making changes), and after you make changes to a duplicate template, you have a new starting place for additional changes (creating duplicates of duplicates). This is a good way to experiment with template configuration, because you can always return to the last version if the latest set of changes proves to be inefficient when you're entering transactions.

To duplicate a template, open the Templates list by choosing Lists | Templates from the QuickBooks menu bar. Right-click the listing for the template you want to clone and choose Duplicate from the shortcut menu to open the Select Template Type dialog.

Select a template type for the duplicate you're creating, which doesn't have to be the same as the original template type. The duplicate template is saved in the Template list, with the name DUP:*original template name*, along with a notation of its type. This means you can have a template name that doesn't match the template type, or two templates with similar names.

To eliminate any confusion, you should change the name of a duplicated template, as follows:

1 Double-click the listing of the duplicate template to open the Customize Invoice dialog, with the template name selected (highlighted).

2 Enter a new name for this template.

3 Click OK.

 N O T E :   The name of the dialog changes to match the type of template you're editing.

Notice that when you select Edit for a duplicate template, you don't see the same Edit dialog you see when you edit a built-in template. Instead, you see the same dialog you'd see if you selected New as your edit mode. That's because it's okay to make sweeping changes to duplicate templates; it's not as dangerous as making changes to the basic, built-in templates.

Using Memorized Invoices

If you have a recurring invoice (most common if you have a retainer agreement with a customer), you can automate the process of creating it. Recurring invoices are those that are sent out at regular intervals, usually for the same amount.

Create the first invoice, filling out all the fields. If there are any fields that will change each time you send the invoice, leave those fields blank and fill them out each time you send the invoice. Then press CTRL-M to open the Memorize Transaction dialog.

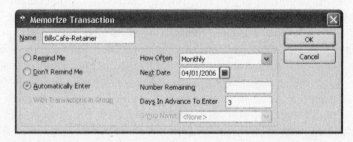

Fill in the fields using the following guidelines:

- Change the title in the Name box to reflect what you've done. It's easiest to add a word or phrase to the default title (which is the customer or job name), such as Retainer. You can use up to 32 characters, including spaces, in the Name box.
- Choose Remind Me and specify how and when you want to be reminded in the How Often and Next Date fields. The reminder will appear in the automatic QuickBooks Reminder window.
- Choose Don't Remind Me if you have a great memory, or if you only use this memorized invoice for special occasions.
- Choose Automatically Enter if you want QuickBooks to issue this invoice automatically. If you opt for automatic issuing of this invoice, you must fill in the fields so that QuickBooks performs the task accurately, as follows:
  - The How Often field is where you specify the interval for this invoice, such as monthly, weekly, or so on. Click the arrow to see the drop-down list and choose the option you need.
  - The Next Date field is the place to note the next instance of this invoice.
  - The Number Remaining field is a place to start a countdown for a specified number of invoices. This is useful if you're billing a customer for a finite number of months because you only have a one-year contract.
  - The Days In Advance To Enter field is for specifying the number of days in advance of the next date you want QuickBooks to create the invoice.

Click OK when you have finished filling out the dialog. Then click Save & Close in the Invoice window to save the transaction. Later, if you want to view, edit, or remove the transaction, you can select it from the Memorized Transaction List by pressing CTRL-T.

Using Estimates

For certain customers or certain types of jobs, it may be advantageous to create estimates. An estimate isn't an invoice, but it can be the basis of an invoice (you can create multiple invoices to reflect the progression of the job).

Creating an Estimate

The first (and most important) thing to understand is that creating an estimate doesn't impact your financial records. When you indicate that you use estimates in your QuickBooks preferences, a nonposting account named Estimates is added to your Chart Of Accounts. The amount of the estimate is posted to this account (invoices, on the other hand, are posted to the Accounts Receivable account).

To create an estimate, click the Estimates icon on the Home page, or choose Customers | Create Estimates from the menu bar. Either action opens the Create Estimates form. As you can see in Figure 3-19, the form is very much like an invoice form. Fill out the fields in the same manner you use for invoices.

Estimates permit you to invoice customers with a markup over cost. This is often the approach used for time and materials on bids. Just enter the cost and indicate the markup in dollars or percentage. Incidentally, if you decide to change the total of the item, QuickBooks will change the markup to make sure your math is correct.

Creating Multiple Estimates for a Job

You can create multiple estimates for a customer or a job, which is an extremely handy feature. You can create an estimate for each phase of the job or create multiple estimates with different prices. Of course, that means each estimate has different contents.

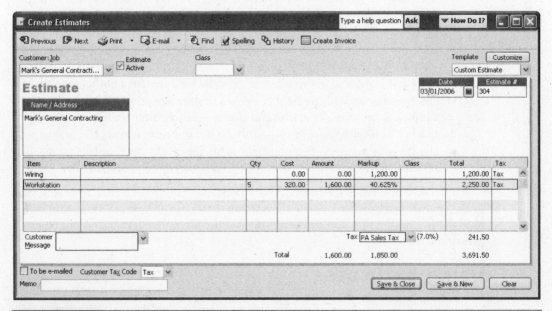

FIGURE 3-19   Estimates provide a way to track a job.

When you create multiple estimates for the same job, the Estimate Active option is checked by default. If a customer rejects any estimates, you can either delete them or deselect the Estimate Active option (effectively closing the estimate).

Duplicating Estimates

You can also duplicate an estimate, which provides a quick way to create multiple estimates with slightly different contents. Choose Edit | Duplicate Estimate while the estimate is displayed in your QuickBooks window (or right-click anywhere in the estimate form and choose Duplicate Estimate from the shortcut menu). The Estimate # field changes to the next number, while everything else remains the same. Make the required changes, and then click Save & Close.

Memorizing Estimates

If you frequently present the same estimated items to multiple customers, you can use the Memorize Estimate feature to create boilerplate estimates for future use. Memorized estimates do not contain the customer name (QuickBooks removes the name when memorizing the document).

Follow these steps:

1. Create an estimate, filling in the items that belong on this type of estimate. Don't fill in amounts (quantities, prices, or both) that usually change.
2. Press CTRL-M to memorize the estimate.
3. Give the estimate a name that reminds you of its contents.
4. Select the option Don't Remind Me.
5. Click OK.

To use the boilerplate estimate, press CTRL-T, or choose Lists | Memorized Transaction List. Double-click the estimate, fill in the Customer:Job information, and save it. The memorized estimate isn't changed; only the new estimate is saved.

This chapter covered a great deal of information about invoices, and that reflects the importance of your invoicing procedures. The more details you put in your invoices, the fewer questions you'll have from your customers. This increases the likelihood that your customers will send checks right away.

Additional Features for Premier and Enterprise Solutions Editions

If you're running QuickBooks Premier Edition or QuickBooks Enterprise Solutions, you may have some additional features available, above and beyond the features covered in this chapter. (Not all features are in all Premier or Enterprise versions.)

Sales Orders

Instead of the Sales Order workaround described in this chapter, all versions of QuickBooks Premier/Enterprise support sales orders. Sales orders are as easy to create as invoices, and, in fact, they resemble invoices. To create a sales order, choose Customers | Create Sales Orders to open the Create Sales Orders window.

When you save a sales order, the transaction isn't posted to the normal accounts (A/R, Inventory, Income, Cost of Goods, etc.). Instead, QuickBooks posts the transaction to a special account named Sales Orders.

When you're ready to ship product, you can turn the sales order into an invoice automatically. Open the sales order and click the Create Invoice icon on the toolbar.

Sales Order Reports

QuickBooks Premier/Enterprise editions offer two useful reports for tracking sales orders (the names of the reports clearly indicate the contents):

- Open Sales Orders by Customer
- Open Sales Orders by Item

Both reports are available in the submenu you see when you choose Reports | Sales.

Generate Purchase Orders from Sales Orders Automatically

If you entered a sales order because you were out of product, you have to order the product. Instead of opening a blank purchase order transaction window, and filling in the data, you can tell QuickBooks Premier/Enterprise editions to generate the purchase order from the sales order. This saves a lot of time and effort, and, perhaps more importantly, avoids the possibility of typing errors. To create the purchase order, open the sales order transaction and click the arrow to the right of the Create Invoice icon on the toolbar. Then select Purchase Order from the drop-down menu.

 TIP: QuickBooks Premier/Enterprise editions also offer the ability to create purchase orders automatically from estimates.

Receiving Payments

*I*n this chapter:

- Apply customer payments

- Apply credits and discounts to invoices

- Handle cash sales

- Deposit payments and cash sales into your bank account

The best part of accounts receivable chores is receiving the payments. However, you need to make sure you apply customer payments correctly so that you and your customers have the same information in your records.

Receiving Invoice Payments

As you create invoices and send them to your customers, there's an expectation that money will eventually arrive to pay off those invoices. And, in fact, it almost always works that way. In accounting, there are two ways to apply the receipts that pay off invoices:

Balance Forward   This is a system in which you consider the total of all the outstanding invoices as the amount due from the customer, and you apply payments against that total. It doesn't matter which particular invoice is being paid because it's a running total of payments against a running total of invoices.

Open Item   This is a system in which payments you receive are applied to specific invoices. Most of the time, the customer either sends a copy of the invoice along with the check or notes the invoice number that is being paid on the check stub to make sure your records agree with the customer's records.

QuickBooks assumes you're using a balance forward system, but you can override that default easily. In fact, changing the system so you apply payments directly to specific invoices is just a matter of a mouse click or two.

 N O T E :   QuickBooks refers to the process of handling invoice payments from customers as "receive payments." The common bookkeeping jargon for this process is "cash receipts." You'll find I use that term frequently throughout this chapter (it's just habit).

Recording the Payment

When a check arrives from a customer, follow these steps to apply the payment:

1 Click the Receive Payments icon on the Home page (or choose Customers | Receive Payments from the menu bar), to bring up a blank Receive Payments window, as shown in Figure 4-1.

2 Click the arrow to the right of the Received From field and select the customer or job from the drop-down list as follows:

- If the payment is from a customer for whom you're not tracking jobs (or for an invoice that wasn't related to a job), select the customer. The current balance for this customer automatically appears in the Customer Balance field.

- If the payment is for a job, select the job. The current balance for this job automatically appears in the Customer Balance field.

- If the payment covers multiple jobs, select the customer to see all invoices for all jobs. The current balance for this customer automatically appears in the Customer Balance field.

3 In the Amount field, enter the amount of this payment. (You can omit this step and let QuickBooks calculate the amount of the payment—see the section "Calculating the Payment.")

4 Click the arrow to the right of the Pmt. Method field and select the payment method:

- If the payment method is a credit card, complete the Card No. and Exp. Date fields. If you have a merchant account with the QuickBooks Merchant Account Service, click the option Process *<credit card name>* Payment When Saving.
- If the payment method is a check, enter the check number in the Check # field.

5 The Memo field is optional, and I've never come across a reason to use it, but if there's some important memorandum you feel you must attach to this payment record, feel free.

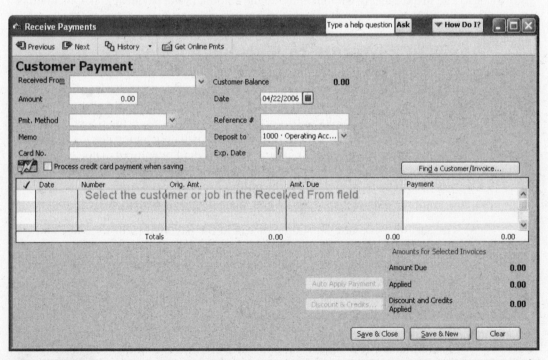

| FIGURE 4-1 | The Customer Payment form has all the fields needed to apply payments accurately. |

In the Deposit To field (if it exists), select the bank account for depositing the payment, or select Undeposited Funds if you're using that account to receive payments (see the section "Turning Payments into Bank Deposits," later in this chapter). If the Deposit To field doesn't exist, you've set your Sales & Customers Preferences to deposit payments to the Undeposited Funds account.

 N O T E :   You can add any additional payment methods you need by choosing <Add New> in the Pmt. Method drop-down list (see Chapter 2 to learn about adding items to QuickBooks lists).

Calculating the Payment

If you've enabled the Automatically Calculate Payments option in the Sales & Customers category of the Preferences dialog, you can omit data entry in the Amount field and head directly for the list of invoices in the Receive Payments window. As you select each invoice for payment, QuickBooks calculates the total and places it in the Amount field. For some reason, when you click the first invoice listing, QuickBooks opens a dialog asking you if you'd like to turn off this option.

If you haven't enabled the option to calculate payments automatically, and you select an invoice listing without entering the amount of the payment first, QuickBooks issues an error message.

Applying Payments to Invoices

Now you have to apply the payment against the customer invoices. By default, QuickBooks automatically applies the payment to the oldest invoice (see Figure 4-2), unless the amount of the payment exactly matches the amount of another invoice.

You can force QuickBooks to let you apply payments to specific invoices instead of automatically heading for the oldest invoice, or matching an invoice for an amount equal to the payment, by changing the options in the Preferences dialog. Choose Edit | Preferences and click the Sales & Customers icon in the left pane. On the Company Preferences tab, deselect the option Automatically Apply Payments.

You could face several scenarios when receiving customer payments:

- The customer has one unpaid invoice, and the payment is for the same amount as that invoice.
- The customer has several unpaid invoices, and the payment is for the amount of one of those invoices.
- The customer has one or more unpaid invoices, and the payment is for an amount lower than any single invoice.
- The customer has several unpaid invoices, and the payment is for an amount greater than any one invoice but not large enough to cover two invoices.
- The customer has one or more unpaid invoices, and the payment is for a lesser amount than the current balance. However, the customer has a credit equal to the difference between the payment and the customer balance.

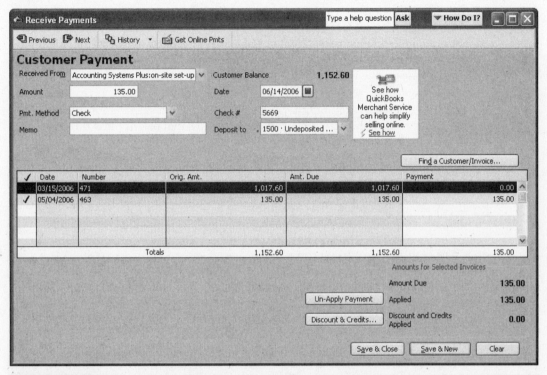

FIGURE 4-2 QuickBooks has applied the payment in a logical manner.

You have a variety of choices for handling any of these scenarios, but for situations in which the customer's intention isn't clear, the smart thing to do is call the customer and ask how the payment should be applied. You can manually enter the amount you're applying against an invoice in the Payment column. You must, of course, apply the entire amount of the customer's check.

If you are not tracking invoices and are instead using a balance forward system, just let QuickBooks continue to apply payments against the oldest invoices.

If the customer sent a copy of the invoice with the payment or indicated the invoice number on the check or stub, always apply the payment to that invoice, even if it means an older invoice remains unpaid. Customers sometimes do this deliberately, usually because there's a problem with the older invoice. The rule of thumb is "apply payments according to the customer's wishes." Otherwise, when you and the customer have a conversation about the current open balance, your bookkeeping records won't match.

If the customer payment doesn't match the amount of any invoice, check to see whether the customer indicated a specific invoice number for the payment. If so, apply the payment against that invoice; if not, let the automatic selection of the oldest invoice stand.

Handling Underpayments

After you apply the customer's payment, if it isn't sufficient to pay off an existing invoice, the Receive Payments window displays a message that asks whether you want to leave the underpaid amount as an underpayment, or write it off (see Figure 4-3).

If you opt to retain the underpayment, the invoice you selected for payment remains as a receivable, with a new balance (the original balance less the payment you applied). When you click Save & Close (or Save & New if you're entering more customer payments), QuickBooks makes the appropriate postings.

If you select the option to write off the underpayment, when you click Save & Close or Save & New, QuickBooks opens the Write Off Amount dialog so you can choose the posting account, and, if applicable, apply a class to the transaction.

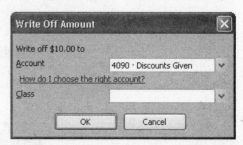

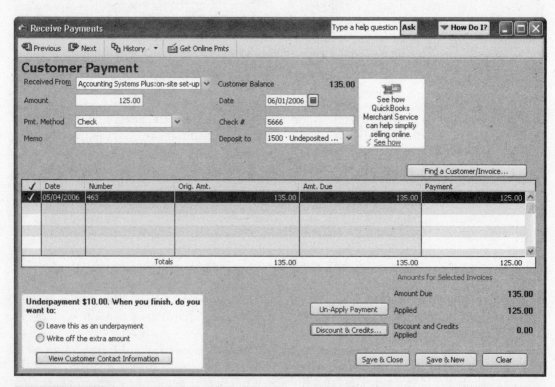

FIGURE 4-3   You must decide how to handle the underpayment.

Discuss the account to use for a write off with your accountant. You can create an Income or Expense account for this purpose, depending on the way your accountant wants to track receivables you've decided to forgive. Do not use this feature as a "bad debt" solution, because writing off bad debts for tax purposes is a more complicated function than merely deciding, "Oh, what the heck, I'll let this slide."

Applying Credits to Invoices

You can apply any existing credits to an open invoice, in addition to applying the payment that arrived. If credits exist, customers usually let you know how they want credits applied, and it's not unusual to find a note written on the copy of the invoice that the customer sent along with the check. To apply a credit balance to an invoice, click the Discount & Credits button on the Customer Payment window, which opens the Discount And Credits dialog.

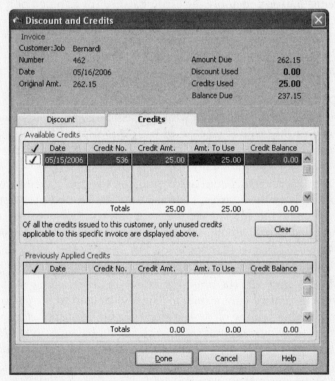

Select the credit you want to apply. Depending on the circumstances, here's how QuickBooks handles the credits:

The Credit Total Is Equal to or Less Than the Unpaid Amount of the Oldest Invoice   This reduces the balance due on that invoice. If the customer sent a payment that reflects a deduction for the amount of his or her credits (a common scenario), so that the credit total is equal to the unpaid amount, the invoice has no remaining balance.

If applying the existing credit along with the payment doesn't pay off the invoice, the balance due on the invoice is reduced by the total of the payment and the credit.

The amount of the credit is added to the postings for the invoice. Don't worry—this change only affects the invoice balance and the accounts receivable posting; it doesn't change the amount of the payment that's posted to your bank account.

The Credit Total Is Larger Than the Amount Required to Pay Off an Invoice

If the customer payment is smaller than the amount of the invoice, but the amount of credit is larger than the amount needed to pay off the invoice, the balance of the credit is available for posting to another invoice.

To apply the unapplied credit balance to another invoice, click Done and select the next invoice in the Receive Payments window. Then click the Discount & Credits button and apply the credit balance (or as much of it as you need) against the invoice. Any unused credits remain for the future.

You should send a statement to the customer to reflect the current, new invoice balances as a result of applying the payments and the credits (even though the customer's accounting software probably reflects the facts accurately).

Applying Credits to a Different Job

You may have a situation in which a customer has already paid the invoices for a job when the credit is created, or has paid for part of the job, exceeding the amount of the credit. If the customer tells you to apply the credit balance to another job or to float the credit and apply it against the next job, you have a problem.

Sigh! QuickBooks does not permit you to apply a credit from one job to another job. You have the same problem if you created a credit for a customer that has one or more jobs but you applied the credit directly to the customer instead of a job. You can't use the credit amount against an invoice payment for one of that customer's jobs.

However, as a workaround, you can unapply and reapply credits, and you have a couple of methods to choose from, as described here.

Wash (zero out) the original credit with an invoice against the same job (or the same customer if you mistakenly applied a credit to the customer name instead of the job name). If the credit is a partial credit (you applied some of it against its job), make the invoice amount equal to the credit balance. In the Description column, enter **Offset to CM** *xxx*, where *xxx* is the original credit memo number, so you can mail the invoice to the customer to explain what you're doing. Then create a new credit for an equal amount and apply it to the other job.

There are some minor problems (well, *irritations...*) with this approach, due to the fact that QuickBooks does not have an element called a *debit memo* (traditionally used by most accounting software to offset and correct credit memos). Therefore, when your customer gets a statement at the end of the month, an invoice is listed that makes no sense to the customer. I solve this for my clients by instructing them to use the letters "DM" in front of the invoice number in the Invoice # field. Then they customize their Statement template to add a footer that explains the DM invoices. (See Chapter 5 to learn how to customize Statement forms.) Of course, if you use this approach, you have to remember to remove the DM from the Invoice # field when you next open the Create Invoices window.

Another technique is to wash the credit with a debit via a journal entry. To do this, you need to have a "wash" account. For my clients, I create an account named "Exchanges" with an account type of Other Expense.

Then I take the following steps:

1. Choose Company | Make General Journal Entries to open the Make General Journal Entries window.
2. In the Account column, select the Accounts Receivable account and press TAB.
3. In the Debit column, enter the amount of the credit.
4. Optionally, enter a note to yourself in the Memo column (e.g., **Moving CM # xxx**) and press TAB.
5. In the Name column, select the Customer:Job listing from which you are *removing* the credit and press TAB to move to the next line.
6. In the Account column, select the "wash" account. QuickBooks automatically puts the correct amount in the Credit column.
7. Click Save & New to open a new, blank General Journal Entry window.
8. In the Account column, select the Accounts Receivable account and press TAB twice to move to the Credit column.
9. In the Credit column, enter the amount of the credit and press TAB.
10. Optionally, write a note to yourself in the Memo column (e.g., **Moving CM # xxx**) and press TAB.
11. In the Name column, select the Customer:Job listing to which you are *applying* the credit and press TAB.
12. In the Account column, enter the "wash" account. QuickBooks automatically puts the correct amount in the Debit column.
13. Click Save & Close.

Now, before you send me an e-mail to ask (sarcastically) why I didn't put all four lines on the same journal entry, I'll explain. QuickBooks, unlike other accounting software programs, does not permit you to use the A/R or A/P account multiple times in the same journal entry. There are lots of situations that arise during the course of business bookkeeping activities that would be much easier if you could have multiple entries to A/R or A/P, but QuickBooks has had this restriction forever.

Also annoying is the fact that QuickBooks doesn't permit you to put both an A/R and A/P entry on the same journal entry (making entering opening trial balances a real pain). Further, you can't post anything to A/R or A/P in a journal entry without charging the amount to a specific customer or a specific vendor, which is frequently a bother. I can't explain their reasons for imposing these restrictions; I can only explain the ramifications.

Both of my workarounds create an audit trail that you can understand in the future and that your accountant will approve of. However, even though I continuously rail against the practice of deleting transactions, I know that many of you will have figured out that merely deleting the credit memo and creating a new one for the right job is easy (and that's what you'll do). The math works, but you're not following good accounting/bookkeeping practices.

Applying Discounts for Timely Payments

If you offer your customers terms that include a discount if they pay their bills promptly (for instance, 2% 10 Net 30), you must apply the discount to the payment if it's applicable.

Figure 4-4 shows the Receive Payments window for a customer who has been offered a discount for timely payment and has taken it by reducing the amount of the payment. The only clue you have to explain the difference between the payment amount and the invoice amount is the fact that the Disc. Date column shows the date by which the invoice must be paid to receive the discount. For customers or invoices without discount terms, that column is blank in the Receive Payments window.

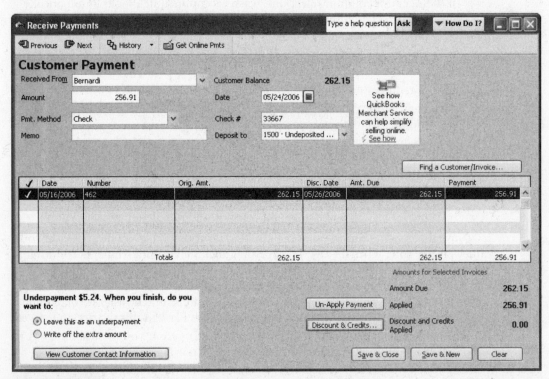

FIGURE 4-4   A discount date appears for invoices that have terms offering discounts.

QuickBooks doesn't apply the discount automatically, for instance, by offering a column with the discount amount and selecting that amount as part of the payment. Instead, you must select the invoice (unless QuickBooks automatically selected it in order to apply the payment) and click the Discount & Credits button to see the Discount And Credits dialog connected to this invoice.

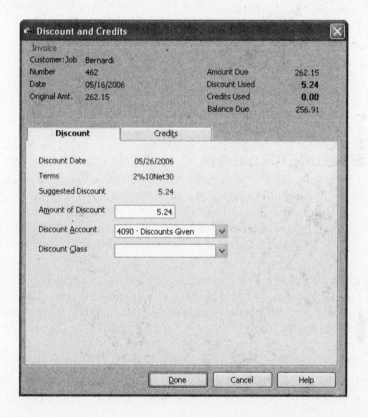

If the payment arrived by the discount date, QuickBooks inserts the amount of the discount to use. Accept the amount of discount and enter a Discount Account (see "Posting Discounts" later in this section). If you're tracking classes, enter the class, and then click Done.

You can change the amount of the discount, which you may want to do if the customer only made a partial payment (less than is required to pay off the invoice after the discount is applied) and you want to give a proportionately smaller discount.

When you return to the Receive Payments window, you'll see that QuickBooks has changed the Amt. Due column to reflect the discount. If the Amt. Due figure and the customer payment amount are the same, the invoice is now paid off.

Applying Discounts for Untimely Payments

Sometimes customers take the discount even if the payment arrives after the discount date. (It's probably more accurate to say that customers *always* take the discount even if the payment arrives later than the terms permit.) You can apply the payment to the invoice and leave a balance due for the discount amount that was deducted by the customer, if you wish. However, most companies give the customer the discount even if the payment is late, as part of "good will."

When you click the Discount Info button in that case, QuickBooks does not automatically fill in the discount amount—it's too late, and accounting software is not forgiving, generous, or aware of the need to humor customers to preserve good will. Simply enter the amount manually and then click Done to apply the discount to the invoice.

Posting Discounts

To track the amount of money you've given away with discounts, you should create a specific account in your chart of accounts. You could post discounts to your standard income account(s), which will be reduced every time you apply a discount. The math is right, but the absence of an audit trail bothers me (and bothers many accountants). It's better to create an Income account (I call mine "Discounts Given").

 CAUTION: If there's an account named "Discounts" in the part of your chart of accounts that's devoted to expenses or cost of goods, don't use that account for your customer discounts, because it's there to track the discounts you take with your vendors.

Turning Payments into Bank Deposits

Use the Deposit To field in the Receive Payments window to select an account for depositing the payments. You can select a bank account or select the Undeposited Funds account.

If you don't see the Deposit To field, it means you set your configuration options to post cash automatically to the Undeposited Funds account. (The option is in the Preferences dialog in the Sales & Customers category.)

Depositing Cash Receipts into the Undeposited Funds Account

When you enable automatic use of the Undeposited Funds account (or manually select that account in the transaction window), each payment you receive is entered into the account named Undeposited Funds (QuickBooks establishes this account automatically). It's an account type of Other Current Asset. When you finish applying customer payments in QuickBooks, and you're ready to make your bank deposit, you move the money from the Undeposited Funds account into a bank account by clicking the Record Deposits icon on the Home page (or by choosing

Banking | Make Deposits from the menu bar). See the section "Depositing Income" later in this chapter for the rest of the details.

While the Undeposited Funds account shows each individual payment you received, the bank account shows only the total amount of each bank deposit. This matches the bank statement that shows up each month, making it easier to reconcile the account.

Depositing Cash Receipts into a Bank Account

Depositing each payment directly to the bank means you don't have to take the extra step involved in moving cash receipts from the Undeposited Funds account into the bank account. However, each payment you receive appears as a separate entry when you reconcile your bank account. If you receive six payments totaling $10,450.25 and take the checks to the bank that day, your bank statement shows that amount as the deposit. When you reconcile the bank statement, each deposit you made (for each individual payment you received) is listed in your bank register. You'll have to select each payment individually, mark it as cleared, and make sure it matches the day's deposits on the bank statement. (See Chapter 12 for detailed instructions on reconciling bank accounts.)

Understanding Customer Payment Postings

When you receive money in payment for customer invoices, QuickBooks automatically posts all the amounts to your general ledger. Following are the postings if you select the Undeposited Funds account:

Account	Debit	Credit
Undeposited Funds	Total of cash receipts	
Accounts Receivable		Total of cash receipts

When you make the actual deposit, using the Make Deposits window, QuickBooks automatically posts the following transaction:

Account	Debit	Credit
Bank	Total of deposit	
Undeposited Funds or Bank Account		Total of deposit

Here are the postings for a sale to a customer who has terms that permit a 1% discount. Let's assume the sale was for $100.00. The original invoice posted the following amounts:

Account	Debit	Credit
Accounts Receivable	$100.00	
Income		$100.00

Notice that the postings are unconcerned with the discount amount. You don't have to account for the discount until it occurs.

When the customer's payment arrived, the 1% discount was deducted from the invoice total. When you enter the customer payment, which is in the amount of $99.00, the following postings occur:

Account	Debit	Credit
Undeposited Funds or Bank Account	$99.00	
Accounts Receivable		$100.00
Discounts Given	$1.00	

Handling Cash Sales

A *cash sale* is a sale for which you haven't created an invoice, because the exchange of product and payment occurred simultaneously, or you received money for an order you'll ship to the customer.

Cash sales are the same as invoiced sales insofar as an exchange of money for goods or services occurs. The difference is that there's no period of time during which you have money "on the street." You can have a cash sale for either a service or a product, although it's far more common to sell products for cash. Most service companies use invoices.

 NOTE: QuickBooks uses the term *sales receipt* instead of *cash sale*. However, the term *cash sale* is the common jargon (a *sales receipt* is a piece of paper a cash customer receives).

I'm assuming that a cash sale is not your normal method of doing business (you're not running a candy store). If you *are* running a retail store, the cash sale feature in QuickBooks isn't an efficient way to handle your cash flow. You should either have specialized retail software (that even takes care of opening the cash register drawer automatically and also tracks inventory) or use QuickBooks to record your daily totals of bank deposits as a journal entry. You might want to look at the QuickBooks Point of Sale product, which is designed for retailers. More information is available on the QuickBooks web site, www.quickbooks.com.

 NOTE: Don't take the word "cash" literally, because a cash sale can involve a check or a credit card.

There are two methods for handling cash sales in QuickBooks:

- Record each cash sale as a discrete record. This is useful for tracking sales of products or services to customers. It provides a way to maintain records about those customers in addition to tracking income and inventory.

• Record sales in batches (usually one batch for each business day). This method tracks income and inventory when you have no desire to maintain information about each customer that pays cash.

To record a cash sale, click the Create Sales Receipts icon on the Home page (or choose Customers | Enter Sales Receipts from the menu bar) to open the Enter Sales Receipts window shown in Figure 4-5.

Entering Cash Sale Data

If you want to track customer information, enter a name in the Customer:Job field or select the name from the drop-down list. If the customer doesn't exist, you can add a new customer by choosing <Add New>.

TIP: If you track customers who always pay at the time of the sale, you might want to consider creating a customer type for this group ("Cash" seems an appropriate name for the type). You can separate this group for reports or for marketing and advertising campaigns.

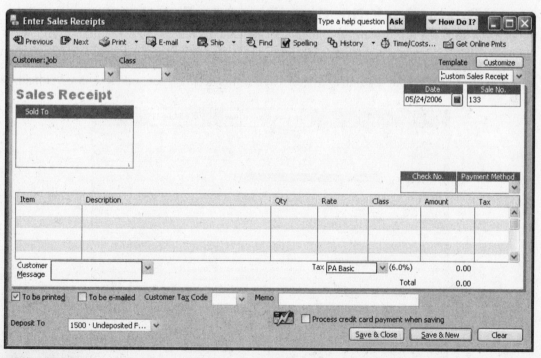

FIGURE 4-5   A Sales Receipt form is like an invoice, a receive payment form, and a printable customer receipt, all rolled into one transaction window.

If you're not tracking customers, invent a customer for cash sales (I named the customer "Cash Sale," which seemed appropriate, if not creative).

(\$) TIP: Even if you don't track individual cash customers, you can put the customer's name and address in the Ship To box. After you print and save the transaction, QuickBooks asks if you want to change the Ship To information in the customer record of your generic cash customer. Click No. In the future, as you view the transactions for that generic customer, the name and address of the specific customer for each cash sale remain in the box.

Every field in the Enter Sales Receipts window works exactly the way it works for invoices and payments—just fill in the information. To save the record, click Save & New to bring up a new blank record, or click Save & Close if you're finished.

Printing a Receipt for a Cash Sale

Some cash customers want a receipt. Click the Print button in the Enter Sales Receipts window to open the Print One Sales Receipt window, shown in Figure 4-6. If you're not printing to a dot matrix printer with multipart paper and you want a copy of the receipt for your files, be sure to change the specification in the Number Of Copies box.

Customizing the Cash Receipts Template

I think a lot is missing from the QuickBooks cash receipts template. For example, there's no place for a sales rep, which is needed if you're paying commissions on cash sales, or you just want to track the person who made the sale. There's no Ship To address if the customer pays cash and wants delivery, nor is there a Ship Via field.

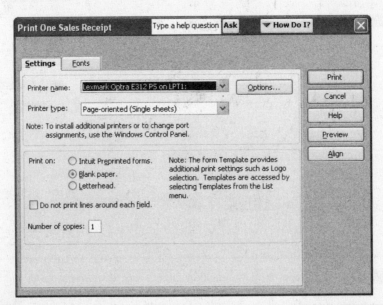

FIGURE 4-6   Choose the options you need to print a receipt for the customer.

The solution is to customize the Custom Sales Receipts form. Here's how to do that:

1 Click the Customize button on top of the Template box in the upper-right corner of the form to open the Customize Template dialog. There aren't multiple forms to use as a basis for the new form, so Custom Sales Receipts is selected.

2 Click New to open the Customize Sales Receipt window.

3 Give the form a name in the Template Name box.

Following are some suggestions and guidelines for customizing this template.

Change the Options in the Header Tab

Depending on your needs, you should consider one or more of the following suggestions for making changes in the Header tab:

- If you wish, change the Default Title. You might prefer the term Cash Receipt, or just Receipt.
- If you ever ship products to cash customers, select the Ship To field for both the Screen and the Print forms.

Change the Options in the Fields Tab

In the Fields tab, you can add any fields you need. If you're tracking salespersons (either for commission or just to know who made the sale), add the REP field. You can add the field to the screen version and omit it from the print version.

If you ship products to cash customers, add the Ship Date and Ship Via fields to the template.

Change the Options in the Columns Tab

Use the Columns tab to add or remove columns in the line item section of the form. You can also change the order in which the columns appear. (For instance, perhaps you'd rather have Qty in the first column instead of the Item number.)

After you finish making the changes you need, click OK. You're returned to the Enter Sales Receipts window, and your new form is ready to use.

Handling Batches of Cash Sales

If you sell products or services and receive instant payment on a more frequent basis, you might want to consider batching the transactions. This works only if you don't care about maintaining information about the customers and no customer expects a receipt. This technique also works if you have a business in which sales and service personnel return to the office each day with customer payments in hand.

Create a customized form using the steps described in the previous section, with the following guidelines:

- Name the form appropriately (for example, "Batch Sales" or "Sales Batch").
- On the Header tab, keep only the Date and Sale Number fields in the heading.

- On the Fields tab, deselect all the optional fields.
- On the Footer tab, remove the Message field.

To batch-process cash sales, use the Enter Sales Receipts window with the following procedures:

- Use a customer named "Cash" or "CashSale."
- In the line item section, use a new line for each sale, regardless of whether the same customer is purchasing each item, each item is purchased by a different customer, or there's a combination of both events.
- Use the Save & Close button at the end of the day. If you need to close the window during the day (perhaps you'd like to get some other work done in QuickBooks), open the Enter Sales Receipts window and click the Previous button to find your previous sales.

Understanding the Cash Sale Postings

Accounting standards treat cash sales in the simplest, most logical manner. If you've sold a service instead of an inventory item for cash (perhaps a service call for a one-time customer you don't want to invoice), the postings are very straightforward:

Account	Debit	Credit
Undeposited Funds or Bank Account	Total cash sales	
Revenue		Total cash sales

If the cash sale involved inventory items, here are the postings:

Account	Debit	Credit
Undeposited Funds or Bank Account	Total cash sales	
Income		Total cash sales
Cost of Sales	Total cost of items sold	
Inventory Asset		Total cost of items sold

Now I'm going to suggest you make it a bit more complicated, but don't panic, because it's not difficult. In the long run, these suggestions will make your bookkeeping chores easier. There's also a chance you'll make your accountant happier.

If you haven't enabled the automatic posting of received funds to the Undeposited Funds account (in the Sales & Customers category of the Preferences dialog), you can choose any bank account you wish. If you use a regular bank account, your sales won't appear in the Payments To Deposit window when you tell QuickBooks you're taking your cash receipts to the bank. (See the section "Depositing Income" later in this chapter.) In fact, your bank account will be incremented by the amount of cash you post to it from cash sales, even though the money isn't really there until you make the trip to the bank. There are two other ways to track receipts from cash sales separate from customer payments; pick the one that appeals to you:

- Opt to post the receipts to the Undeposited Funds account, but make those deposits separately when you work in the QuickBooks Payments To Deposit window.
- Opt to post the receipts to a new account called "Undeposited Till" (or something similar) and move the money into your bank account with a journal entry.

The advantage of having a "Till" account is that you can match the contents of the physical till to the posting account. Create an account of the type Other Current Asset to represent the cash till, and select it as the account when you use the Enter Sales Receipts window.

If you deal in real cash and have a cash register, you need to fill the till to make change. Cash a check from your operating account and post the amount to the new account (which I call "Undeposited Till"). Then put the cash (small bills and change) into your physical till. This produces the following posting (assuming $100.00 was the amount of the check):

Account	Debit	Credit
Checking		$100.00
Undeposited Till	$100.00	

When it's time to go to the bank, leave the original startup money (in this example, $100.00) in the till, count the rest of the money, and deposit that money into your checking account. When you return from the bank, make the following journal entry:

Account	Debit	Credit
Checking	Amt. of deposit	
Undeposited Till		Amt. of deposit

In a perfect world, after you make the deposit and the journal entry, you can open the register for the Undeposited Till account and see a balance equal to your original startup cash. The world isn't perfect, however, and sometimes the actual amount you were able to deposit doesn't equal the amount collected in the Enter Sales Receipts transaction window. To resolve this, see the section "Handling the Over and Short Problem" later in this chapter.

Incidentally, if you want to raise or lower the amount you leave in the till for change, you don't have to do anything special. Just deposit less or more money, and the remainder (in the register for the Undeposited Till account and also in the physical till) just becomes the new base.

Depositing Income

If you use the Undeposited Funds account, when it's time to go to the bank you have to tell QuickBooks about your bank deposit. Otherwise, when it's time to reconcile your checkbook, you'll have a nervous breakdown.

Choosing the Payments to Deposit

As you've been filling out the payment and cash sales forms, QuickBooks has been keeping a list in the Undeposited Funds account. That list remains designated as Undeposited Funds until you clear it by depositing them. (If you've been depositing every payment and cash receipt to a specific bank account, this section doesn't apply.)

To tell QuickBooks to make a deposit, click the Record Deposits icon on the Home page (or choose Banking | Make Deposits from the menu bar), which brings up the Payments To Deposit window, shown in Figure 4-7.

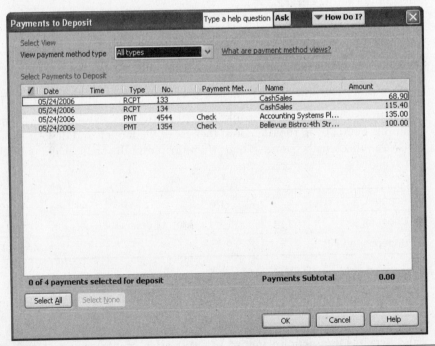

FIGURE 4-7   All the income you've collected since the last bank deposit is waiting to be deposited.

NOTE: You may have other deposits to make, perhaps refunds, loan proceeds, capital infusion, or some other type of deposit. Don't worry—you can tell QuickBooks about them in the next transaction window. This window is only displaying the cash receipts you've entered into QuickBooks through the Payments and Sales Receipts transaction windows.

Notice the following about the Payments To Deposit window:

- The Type column displays information about the payment type for each transaction—PMT for payment of an invoice and RCPT for a cash sale.
- The Payment Method column displays the specific payment method for each transaction, such as cash, check, a specific credit card, and so on.

This information is important because you should match it to the way your bank records deposits; otherwise, bank reconciliation becomes much more complicated. For example, your bank probably lists credit card deposits separately from a deposit total for cash and checks, even if all the money was deposited the same day. That's because your credit card deposits are probably made directly to your bank account by your merchant account bank. Even if you take deposit slips for credit card transactions to the bank and hand them to the teller along with your regular (cash/checks) deposit slip, the credit card deposits are probably listed separately on your bank statement.

Select Deposit Items

If you only have a few transactions to deposit, select those you just deposited (when you went to the bank) by clicking their listings to place a check mark in the left column. Click Select All if you want to select all the payments for deposit.

Separate Deposit Items by Payment Method

If you have many individual deposits, separate your deposits by payment method to make it easier to work with this window. Select a payment method from the drop-down list at the top of the Payments To Deposit window.

Choose Selected Types to open the Select Payment Types list and choose multiple payment types to include in the same deposit. For example, you may use the Other category to signify a money order or a traveler's check.

The listings on the Payments To Deposit window change to include only the deposits that match the selected payment method.

Separate Cash from Checks

QuickBooks doesn't provide separate payment methods for cash and checks. However, if you turn in a cash bag, select only the checks and deposit them; then start the process over to select only the cash (or do it the other way around). This is a common practice when depositing cash, because sometimes the bank notifies you that their automatic counting machine produced a different total from the total on your deposit slip (you probably don't own counting machines for coins and paper money). If that happens, you can edit the cash sales deposit item in your bank register, and the cause of the edit will be obvious. (I'm a stickler for good audit trails.)

Separate Deposits by Bank Account

If you're depositing money into multiple bank accounts, select only the transactions that go into the first account. After you complete the deposit, start this process again and deposit the remaining transactions into the appropriate account.

Credit Card Deposits

You can't deposit credit card payments until your merchant bank notifies you that the funds have been placed in your account.

- If you have QuickBooks online banking, the deposit shows up in the QuickReport (see Chapter 16 to learn about managing online banking transactions).
- If you have online access to your merchant card account, the transfer will appear on the activities report on the web site.
- If you don't have any form of online access, you'll have to wait for the monthly statement to arrive (or contact the bank periodically to see if anything showed up in your account).

If your merchant bank deducts fees before transferring funds, learn how to deposit the net amount in the section "Calculating Merchant Card Fees," later in this chapter.

Deselect Items to Delay Their Deposit

If you want to hold back the deposit of any income, deselect it by clicking its listing (the check mark is a toggle). Only the items that have a check mark will be cleared from the undeposited payments list. There are several reasons to deselect deposit items:

- You received a payment in advance from a customer and don't want to deposit it until you're sure you can fill the order.
- You've accepted a postdated check and it cannot yet be deposited.

After you make your selections, click OK.

Filling Out the Deposit Slip

Clicking OK in the Payments To Deposit window brings up the Make Deposits window, shown in Figure 4-8.

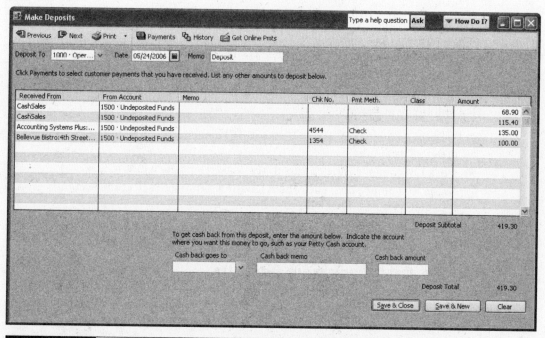

FIGURE 4-8 The Make Deposits form is a virtual bank deposit slip.

Select the bank account you're using for this deposit. Then make sure the date matches the day you're physically depositing the money.

Adding Items to the Deposit

If you want to add deposit items that weren't in the Payments To Deposit window, click anywhere in the Received From column to make it accessible and select an existing name by clicking the arrow, or click <Add New> to enter a name that isn't in your system. If the source of the check is a bank or yourself or any other entity that isn't a customer or vendor, use the Other Name classification for the type of name.

Press TAB to move to the From Account column and enter the account to which you're posting this transaction. For example, if the check you're depositing represents a bank loan, use the liability account for that bank loan (you can create it here by choosing <Add New> if you didn't think to set up the account earlier). If the check you're depositing represents an infusion of capital from you, use the owner's capital account in the Equity section of your chart of accounts. If the check is a refund for an expense (perhaps you overpaid someone, and they're returning money to you), use the vendor's name, and post the deposit to that expense. Use the TAB key to move through the rest of the columns, which are self-explanatory.

Calculating Merchant Card Fees

If your merchant card bank deposits the gross amount of each transaction and charges your bank account for the total fees due at the end of the month, you don't have to do anything special to deposit credit card payments. You can deal with the fees when you reconcile your bank account.

If your merchant card bank deducts fees from transactions and deposits the net proceeds to your account, you can track credit card transactions and deposit the correct amount.

Use the following steps:

1. Select the credit card transactions in the Payments To Deposit window. These are gross amounts.
2. Click OK to move the deposits to the Make Deposits window.
3. In the first empty line, click the Account column and select the account to which you post merchant card fees.
4. Move to the Amount column and enter the fee as a negative number.
5. The net matches the amount that is deposited in the bank.

Getting Cash Back from Deposits

If you're getting cash back from your deposit, you can tell QuickBooks about it right on the virtual deposit slip, instead of making a journal entry to adjust the total of collected payments against the total of the bank deposit.

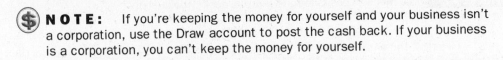 **N O T E :**   If you're keeping the money for yourself and your business isn't a corporation, use the Draw account to post the cash back. If your business is a corporation, you can't keep the money for yourself.

Enter the account to which you're posting the cash (usually a petty-cash account), and enter the amount of cash you want back from this deposit. Even though you can put the cash in your pocket, you must account for it, because these are business funds. As you spend the cash for business expenses, post the expense against a petty-cash account with a journal entry.

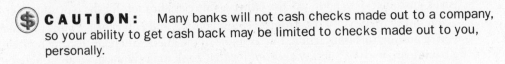 **C A U T I O N :**   Many banks will not cash checks made out to a company, so your ability to get cash back may be limited to checks made out to you, personally.

Printing Deposit Slips

If you want to print a deposit slip or a deposit summary, click the Print button in the Make Deposits window. QuickBooks asks whether you want to print a deposit slip and summary, or just a deposit summary.

If you want to print a deposit slip that your bank will accept, you must order printable deposit slips from QuickBooks. Visit their web site, which is at www .quickbooks.com/services/supplies/.

The QuickBooks deposit slips are guaranteed to be acceptable to your bank. You must have a laser printer or inkjet printer to use them. When you print the deposit slip, there's a tear-off section at the bottom of the page that has a deposit summary. Keep that section for your own records and take the rest of the page to the bank along with your money.

If you don't have QuickBooks deposit slips, select Deposit Summary Only and fill out your bank deposit slip manually. Be sure to fill out the payment method field (cash or check), or QuickBooks won't print the deposit slip. A Print dialog appears so you can change printers, adjust margins, or even print in color. Choose Print to send the deposit information to the printer. When you return to the Make Deposits window, click Save & Close to save the deposit.

Handling the Over and Short Problem

If you literally take cash for cash sales, when you count the money in the till at the end of the day, you may find that the recorded income doesn't match the cash you expected to find in the till. Or you may find that the money you posted to deposit to the bank doesn't match the amount of money you put into the little brown bag you took to the bank.

This is a common problem with cash, and, in fact, it's an occasional problem in regular accrual bookkeeping. One of the ensuing problems you face is how to handle this in your bookkeeping system. QuickBooks is a double-entry bookkeeping system, which means the left side of the ledger has to be equal to the right side of the ledger. If you post $100.00 in cash sales but only have $99.50 to take to the bank, how do you handle the missing 50 cents? You can't just post $100.00 to your bank account (well, you could, but your bank reconciliation won't work and, more importantly, you're not practicing good bookkeeping).

The solution to the Over/Short dilemma is to acknowledge it in your bookkeeping procedures. Track it. You'll be amazed by how much it balances itself out—short one day, over another. (Of course, if you're short every day, and the shortages are growing, you have an entirely different problem, and the first place to look is at the person who stands in front of the cash register.) To track Over/Short, you need to have some place to post the discrepancies, which means you have to create some new accounts in your chart of accounts.

Create two new accounts as follows:

❶ Click the Chart Of Accounts icon on the Home page (or press CTRL-A) to open the Chart Of Accounts list.

❷ Press CTRL-N to create a new account.

❸ In the New Account window, select an account type of Income.

❹ If you're using numbered accounts, choose a number that's on the next level from your regular Income accounts; for example, choose 4290 if your regular Income accounts are 4000, 4010, and so on.

⑤ Name the account "Over."

⑥ Click Next and repeat the processes, using the next number and naming the account "Short."

If you want to see a net number for Over/Short (a good idea), create three accounts: name the first account (the parent account) Over-Short, and then make the Over and Short accounts subaccounts of Over-Short.

In addition, you need items to use for your overages and shortages (remember, you need items for everything that's connected with entering invoices and cash sales).

Create these new items as follows:

① Click the Items & Services icon on the Home page, or choose Lists | Item List to open the Item List.

② Press CTRL-N to create a new item.

③ Create a non-inventory part item named Overage.

④ Don't assign a price.

⑤ Make it nontaxable.

⑥ Link it to the account (or subaccount) named Over that you just created.

⑦ Click Next to create another new, non-inventory part item.

⑧ Name this item Short and link it to the account (or subaccount) named Short.

⑨ Click OK to close the Item List window.

Now that you have the necessary accounts and items, use the Over and Short items right in the Enter Sales Receipts window to adjust the difference between the amount of money you've accumulated in the cash-sale transactions and the amount of money you're actually depositing to the bank. It's your last transaction of the day. Remember to use a minus sign before the figure if you're using the Short item.

Tracking Accounts Receivable

Chapter 5

Collecting the money owed to you is one of the largest headaches in running a business. You have to track what's owed and who owes it, and then expend time and effort to collect it. All of the effort you spend on the money your customers owe you is called *tracking accounts receivable* (or, more commonly, *tracking A/R*).

You can use finance charges as an incentive for your customers to pay on time, and you can track overdue invoices and then remind your customers, in gentle or not-so-gentle ways, to pay. In this chapter I go over the tools and features QuickBooks provides to help you track and collect the money your customers owe you.

Using Finance Charges

One way to speed up collections is to impose finance charges for late payments. Incidentally, this isn't "found money"; it probably doesn't cover its own cost. The amount of time spent tracking, analyzing, and chasing receivables is substantial, and in all businesses "time is money."

Configuring Finance Charges

To use finance charges, you have to establish the rate and circumstances under which they're assessed. Your company's finance charges are configured as part of your company preferences. Choose Edit | Preferences to open the Preferences window. Then click the Finance Charge icon in the left pane and select the Company Preferences tab (see Figure 5-1).

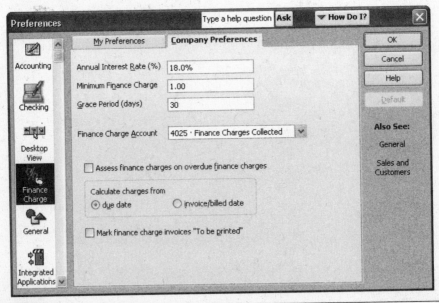

FIGURE 5-1   Configure the way in which you'll impose finance charges on overdue balances.

Here are some guidelines for filling out this window:

- In the Annual Interest Rate field, replacing the default data (0.00%) with any positive number enables the Finance Charges feature. The dialog does not have an "Enable" check box.

- Notice that the interest rate is annual. If you want to charge 1.5 percent a month, enter **18%** in the Annual Interest Rate field.

- You can assess a minimum finance charge for overdue balances. QuickBooks will calculate the finance charge, and if it's less than the minimum, the amount will be rolled up to the minimum charge you specify here.

- Use the Grace Period field to enter the number of days of lateness you permit before finance charges are assessed.

- During setup, QuickBooks probably created an account for finance charges. If so, select it. If not, enter (or create) the account you want to use to post finance charges (this is an income account).

- The issue of assessing finance charges on overdue finance charges is a sticky one. The practice is illegal in many states. Selecting this option means that a customer who owed $100.00 last month and had a finance charge assessed of $2.00 now owes $102.00. As a result, the next finance charge is assessed on a balance of $102.00 (instead of on the original overdue balance of $100.00). Regardless of state law, the fact is that very few businesses opt to use this calculation method.

- Specify whether to calculate the finance charge from the due date or the invoice date.

- QuickBooks creates an invoice automatically when finance charges are assessed in order to have a permanent record of the transaction. By default, these invoices aren't printed; they're just accumulated along with the overdue invoices so they'll print as a line item on a monthly statement. You can opt to have the finance charge invoices printed, which you should do only if you're planning to mail them to nudge your customers for payment.

Click OK to save your settings after you've filled out the window.

Assessing Finance Charges

You should assess finance charges just before you calculate and print customer statements. Click the Finance Charges icon on the Home page (QuickBooks adds the icon when you turn on the feature), or choose Customers | Assess Finance Charges from the menu bar. The Assess Finance Charges window opens (see Figure 5-2) with a list of all the customers with overdue balances.

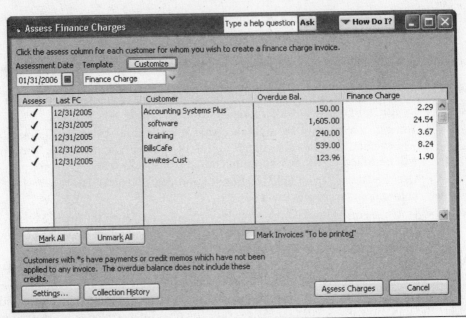

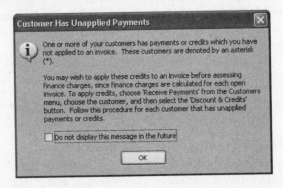

FIGURE 5-2   QuickBooks automatically assesses finance charges as of the assessment date you specify.

Before you see the window, if you have any customers that have made payments that you haven't yet applied to an invoice, or if any customers have credits that you haven't yet applied to an invoice, QuickBooks displays a message to that effect.

This message is not necessarily connected to the customers who are due to have finance charges assessed; it's a general statement that somewhere in your system there's an unapplied payment or credit. When the Assess Finance Charges window opens, if any customer has an asterisk next to the customer or job name, you have to pay attention to the message about unapplied payments or credits because the asterisk indicates an affected customer. Close the Assess Finance Charges window and correct the situation, then return to this window.

Choosing the Assessment Date

Change the Assessment Date field (which displays the current date) to the date on which you want the finance charge to appear on customer statements. It's common to assess finance charges on the last day of the month. When you press TAB to move out of the date field, the finance charges are recalculated to reflect the new date.

Selecting the Customers

You can eliminate a customer from the process by clicking in the Assess column to remove the check mark. QuickBooks, unlike many other accounting software packages, does not have a finance-charge assessment option on each customer record. Therefore, all customers with overdue balances are included when you assess finance charges.

 N O T E : Some customers on the list may display a zero balance. These customers have an A/R balance, but the balance isn't older than the grace period you specified when you configured finance charges. QuickBooks' automatic selection (check marks) excludes these customers.

It can be time-consuming to deselect each customer, so if you have only a few customers for whom you reserve this process, choose Unmark All, then reselect the customers you want to include. Of course, this means you have to know off the top of your head which customers are liable for finances charges and which aren't—or you have to keep a list near your desk.

Changing the Amounts

You can change the calculated total if you wish (a good idea if there are credit memos floating around that you're not ready to apply against any invoices). Just click the amount displayed in the Finance Charge column to activate that column for that customer. Then enter a new finance charge amount. If you need to calculate the new figure (perhaps you're giving credit for a floating credit memo), press the equal sign (=) on your keyboard to use the built-in calculator.

Checking the History

To make sure you don't assess a charge that isn't really due, you can double-check by viewing a customer's history from the Assess Finance Charges window. Select a customer and click the Collection History button to see a Collections Report for the selected customer (see Figure 5-3). Your mouse pointer turns into a magnifying glass with the letter "z" (for "zoom") in it when you position it over a line item. Double-click any line item to display the original transaction window if you need to examine the details.

Saving the Finance Charge Invoices

Click Assess Charges in the Assess Finance Charges window when all the figures are correct. When you create your customer statements, the finance charges will appear. If you've opted to skip printing, there's nothing more to do. (If you chose to print the finance charges, see the next paragraph.)

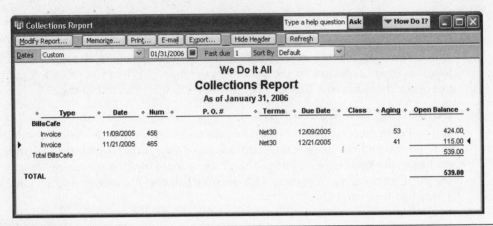

FIGURE 5-3   You can check a customer's history to make sure the finance charges are legitimate.

Selecting Printing Options

If you want to print the finance charge invoices (they really are invoices because they add charges to the customer balance), be sure to select the Mark Invoices "To Be Printed" check box in the Assess Finance Charges window. You can send the printed copies to your customers as a nagging reminder. If you just want the customer to see the finance charge on the monthly statement (the common method for most businesses), deselect the printing option.

To print the finance charge invoices, choose File | Print Forms | Invoices. The list of unprinted invoices appears, and unless you have regular invoices you didn't print yet, the list includes only the finance charge invoices. If the list is correct, click OK to continue on to the printing process. Chapter 3 has detailed information about printing invoices.

Sending Statements

On a periodic basis, you should send statements to your customers. (Most businesses send statements monthly.) They serve a couple of purposes: they remind customers of outstanding balances, and they ensure that your records and your customers' records reflect the same information.

If you're coming to QuickBooks from a manual system, or a system in which you tracked invoices and payments in a spreadsheet, statements will seem like a miraculous tool. Creating statements from manual customer cards, or cells in a spreadsheet, is a nightmare. As a result, companies without real accounting software generally don't even bother to try.

Entering Statement Charges

Before creating statements, you should create any transactions that should appear on the statements. Invoices and payments appear automatically, but you may want to add statement charges. A *statement charge* is a charge you want to pass to a customer for which you don't create an invoice. You can use statement charges for special charges for certain customers, such as a general overhead charge, or a charge you apply instead of using reimbursements for expenses incurred on behalf of the customer.

You can also use statement charges for discounts for certain customers, such as reducing the total due by a specific amount, instead of creating and applying discount rates or price levels. Some companies use statement charges instead of invoices for invoicing regular retainer payments.

You must add statement charges before you create the statements (or else the charges won't show up on the statements). Statement charges use items from your Item List, but you cannot use any of the following types of items:

- Items that are taxable, because the statement charge can't apply the tax
- Items that have percentage discounts, because the statement charge can't look up the discount percentage (and therefore can't apply it)
- Items that represent a payment transaction, because those are negative charges, which a statement charge doesn't understand

Statement charges are recorded directly in a customer's register or in the register for a specific job. You can reach the register to enter a statement charge in either of two ways:

- Click the Statement Charges icon on the Home page (or choose Customers | Enter Statement Charges from the menu bar), and then select the customer or job in the Customer:Job field at the top of the register that opens. (By default, QuickBooks opens the register for the first customer in your Customer:Job list.)
- Press CTRL-J to open the Customer Center, right-click the appropriate listing on the Customers & Jobs tab, and choose Enter Statement Charges from the shortcut menu. QuickBooks opens the register for the selected customer.

When the Customer:Job register opens, it looks like Figure 5-4.

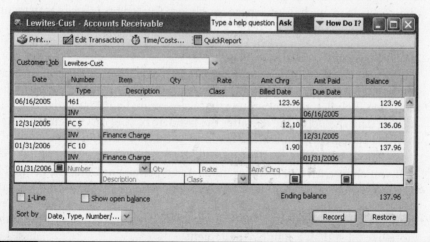

FIGURE 5-4   Statement charges are entered directly in a customer or job register.

Use the TAB key to move through the register line as you perform the following steps:

1 Select the item for the statement charge from the Item drop-down list (or use <Add New> to create a new item).

2 Enter a quantity in the Qty field if the item is invoiced by quantity.

3 Enter a rate (or accept the default rate if one exists) if you're using the Qty field.

4 Enter the amount charged if the Qty and Rate fields aren't used (if they are, the total amount is entered automatically).

5 Optionally, edit the item description.

6 Enter the billed date, which does not have to match the transaction date in the first column of the register. Postdating or predating this field determines which statement it appears on.

7 Enter the due date, which affects your aging reports and your finance charge calculations.

8 Click Record to save the transaction.

If your statement charges are recurring charges, you can memorize them to have QuickBooks automatically create them. After you create the charge, right-click its listing in the register and select Memorize Stmt Charge from the shortcut menu. This works exactly like memorized invoices (covered in Chapter 3).

Creating Statements

Before you start creating your statements, be sure that all the transactions that should be included on the statements have been entered into the system. Did you forget anything? Applying credit memos? Applying payments? Assessing finance charges? Entering statement charges? When all customer accounts are up-to-date, click the Statements icon on the Home page (or choose Customers | Create Statements from the menu bar) to open the Create Statements window, shown in Figure 5-5.

Selecting the Date Range

The statement date range determines which transactions appear on the statement. The printed statement displays the previous balance (the total due before the "From" date) and includes all transactions that were created within the date range. The starting date should be the day after the last date of your last statement run. If you do monthly statements, choose the first and last days of the current month; if you send statements quarterly, enter the first and last dates of the current quarter—and so on.

If you choose All Open Transactions As Of Statement Date, the printed statement just shows unpaid invoices and charges and unapplied credits. You can narrow the criteria by selecting the option to include only transactions overdue by a certain number of days (which you specify). However, this makes the printed statement more like a list than a standard statement.

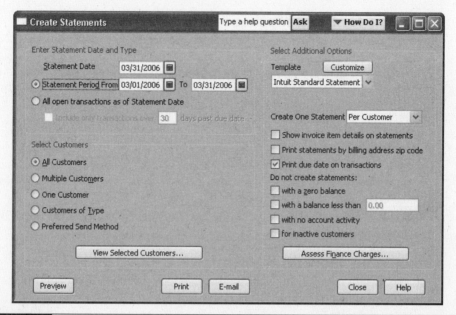

FIGURE 5-5   Configure the specifications for selecting customers who receive statements.

Selecting the Customers

It's normal procedure to send statements to all customers, but if that's not the plan, you can change the default selection.

If you want to send statements to a group of customers, click the Multiple Customers option to display the Choose button next to it. Then click the Choose button to bring up a list of customers and select each customer you want to include. You can manually select each customer, or select Automatic and then enter text to tell QuickBooks to match that text against all customer names and select the matching customers. (The automatic match option isn't efficient for multiple customers because it only matches exact text, not partial text, and therefore only matches one customer at a time.)

Click OK when all the appropriate customers are selected.

If you're sending a statement to one customer only, select One Customer, and then click the arrow next to the text box to scroll through the list of your customers and select the one you want.

To send statements to customers who are designated with a specific customer type, select the Customers Of Type option, and then select the customer type you want to include from the drop-down list. This works, of course, only if you created customer types as part of your QuickBooks setup.

TIP: If you want to send statements to certain customers only, that's a good reason in itself to create a customer type for statement recipients (name the type "Stmnts").

Filtering for Send Methods

If your customers vary in the way you send them statements (the option selected in the Preferred Send Method field of the customer record), you can opt to handle your statement delivery in batches, using one delivery method per batch. To do this, select the Preferred Send Method option, and then select the send method for this batch from the drop-down list that appears:

- **E-mail**   Sends the statements by e-mail, using the QuickBooks e-mail services feature.
- **Mail**   Sends the statements to QuickBooks services, where the invoice is created with a tear-off slip that the customer can use to pay the invoice. QuickBooks mails the invoice. (This is a fee-based service.)
- **None**   Means no special handling. You print the statements, put them in envelopes, and mail them.

Specifying the Printing Options

You can specify the way you want the statements to print using the following criteria and options in the Select Additional Options section:

- You can print one statement for each customer, which lists all transactions for all that customer's jobs, or you can print a separate statement for each job.
- You can opt to show invoice item details instead of just listing the invoice on the statement. If your invoices have a lot of line items, this could make your statements very long (possibly too many pages to get away with a single postage stamp). I don't see any particular reason to select this option, because most customers have copies of the original invoices—if they don't, they'll call you with questions and you can look up the invoice number and provide details (or reprint the invoice and send it).
- Printing statements in order by ZIP code is handy if you're printing labels that are sorted by ZIP code. This option is also important if you have a bulk mail permit, because the post office requires bulk mail to be sorted by ZIP code.
- By default, the original due date for each transaction listed on the statement is displayed on the statement. If you have some reason to hide this information from your customers (I can't think of a good reason), you can deselect the option.

Specifying the Statements to Skip

You may want to skip statement creation for customers who meet the criteria you set in the Do Not Create Statements section of the dialog. If statements are the only documents you send to customers (you don't send the individual invoices and credits you create), selecting any of these options makes sense.

If, however, you use statements to make sure you and your customers have matching accounting records, you should create statements for all customers except inactive customers.

Last Call for Finance Charges

If you haven't assessed finance charges and you want them to appear on the statements, click the Assess Finance Charges button. The Assess Finance Charges window opens, showing customers who have been selected for finance charges.

If you've already assessed finance charges, QuickBooks will warn you that finance charges have already been assessed as of the selected date. Unfortunately, if you ignore the message, QuickBooks is perfectly willing to add another round of finance charges (and you'll have a lot of angry and distrustful customers). Therefore, this window is useful only if you don't assess finance charges as described earlier in this chapter.

Previewing the Statements

Before you commit the statements to paper, you can click the Preview button to get an advance look (see Figure 5-6). This is not just to see what the printed output will look like; it's also a way to look at the customer records and to make sure that all the customers you selected are included.

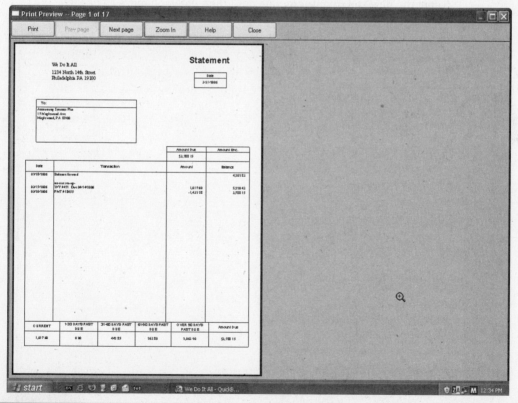

FIGURE 5-6 Look at all the statements in the Preview window, to make sure all selected customers are included.

Use the Zoom In button to see the statement and its contents close up. Click the Next Page button to move through all the statements. Click Close to return to the Create Statements window.

Printing the Statements

When everything is just the way it should be, print the statements by clicking the Print button in either the Print Preview window or the Create Statements window. If you click Close in the Preview window, you return to the Create Statements window—click Print to open the Print Statement(s) window. Then, change the printing options as needed.

Customizing Statements

You don't have to use the standard statement form—you can design your own. To accomplish this, in the original Create Statements window, click the Customize button to open the Customize Template window. Choose New in that window to open the Customize Statement window shown in Figure 5-7.

Name the new statement template, and then make changes as needed.

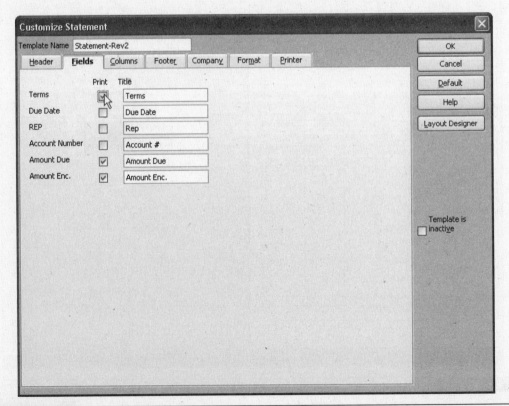

FIGURE 5-7   You can customize the statement form to make sure it matches your needs.

On the Fields tab, think about changing the following fields:

Terms   It's a good idea to select the Terms column (which is not selected by default). It doesn't seem fair to tell a customer of amounts past due without reminding the customer of the terms.

Amount Due   This field isn't really necessary because the same field and its data are positioned at the bottom of the statement page.

Amount Enc   If you use statements as bills or expect payment for the amount of the statement, this field is supposed to contain an amount filled in by the customer. (The amount is supposed to match the amount of the check that's returned with the statement.) If you mail invoices and use statements as reminders (and your customers never send checks attached to the statements), deselect this field.

On the Footer tab, you can add text if you think there's anything to explain about the items on the statement. For example, if you create and list debit memos, you may want to explain what they are.

Click OK when you're finished.

Running Aging Reports

Aging reports are lists of the money owed you by your customers, and they're available in quite a few formats. They're for you, not for your customers. You run them whenever you need to know the extent of your receivables. Many companies run an aging report every morning, just to keep an eye on the amount of money on the street ("on the street" is business jargon for uncollected receivables).

➡ **FYI**

A/R Totals

The total amount of A/R is the value of your A/R asset. It can be an important asset, and, in fact, banks give lines of credit and loans using the A/R balance as part of the collateral.

When your accountant visits, you can bet one of the things he or she will ask to see is this report. When your accountant asks for an aging report, another safe bet is that you'll receive a request to see the amount posted to A/R in your general ledger. The general ledger A/R balance and the total on the aging report must be the same (for the same date)—not close, not almost, but *exactly* the same. If the figures are not identical, your general ledger isn't "proved" (jargon for, "I'm sorry, we can't trust your general ledger figures because they don't audit properly").

If your A/R account balance doesn't prove to your A/R report, you've messed up some transactions. Most of the time, this means you used the A/R account in a journal entry, and that's a no-no. You or your accountant, or both of you, must find the bad entry and correct it, because your A/R report total must match the A/R account balance.

A couple of aging reports are available in QuickBooks, and you can also customize any built-in reports so they report data exactly the way you want it. To see an aging report, choose Reports | Customers & Receivables, and then choose either A/R Aging Summary or A/R Aging Detail (these reports are explained next).

Using Aging Summary Reports

The quickest way to see how much money is owed to you is to select A/R Aging Summary, which produces a listing of customer balances (see Figure 5-8).

Using Aging Detail Reports

If you choose Aging Detail from the Accounts Receivable reports menu, you see a much more comprehensive report, such as the one seen in Figure 5-9. The report is sorted by aging interval, showing individual transactions, including finance charges, for each aging period.

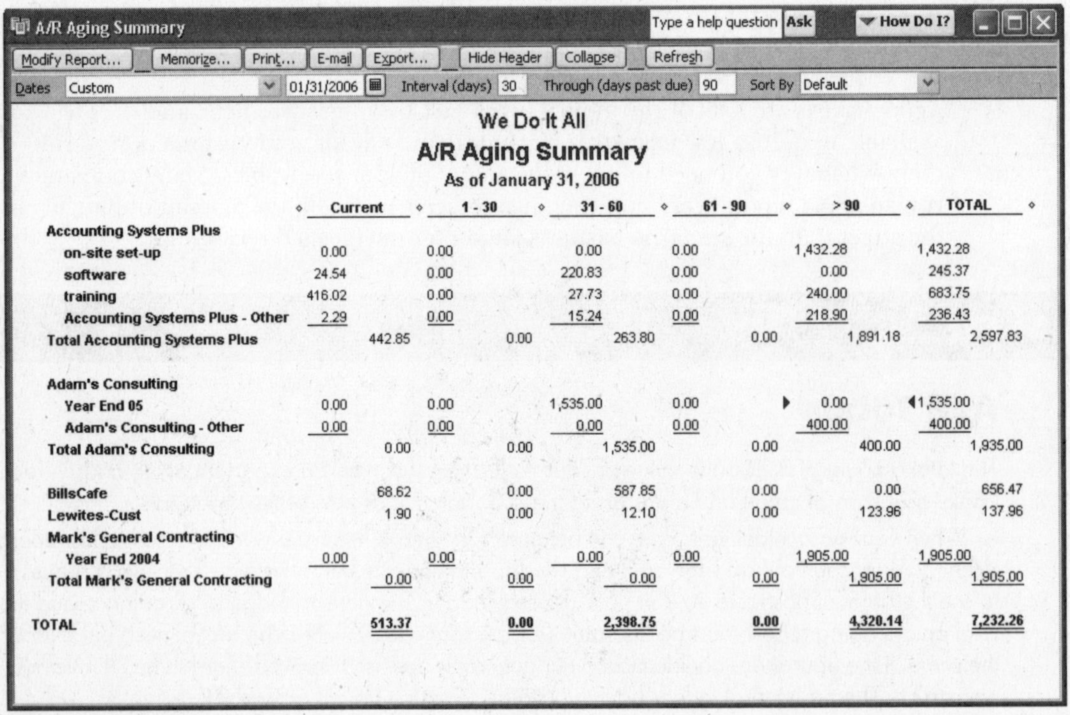

We Do It All
A/R Aging Summary
As of January 31, 2006

	Current	1 - 30	31 - 60	61 - 90	> 90	TOTAL
Accounting Systems Plus						
on-site set-up	0.00	0.00	0.00	0.00	1,432.28	1,432.28
software	24.54	0.00	220.83	0.00	0.00	245.37
training	416.02	0.00	27.73	0.00	240.00	683.75
Accounting Systems Plus - Other	2.29	0.00	15.24	0.00	218.90	236.43
Total Accounting Systems Plus	442.85	0.00	263.80	0.00	1,891.18	2,597.83
Adam's Consulting						
Year End 05	0.00	0.00	1,535.00	0.00	0.00	1,535.00
Adam's Consulting - Other	0.00	0.00	0.00	0.00	400.00	400.00
Total Adam's Consulting	0.00	0.00	1,535.00	0.00	400.00	1,935.00
BillsCafe	68.62	0.00	587.85	0.00	0.00	656.47
Lewites-Cust	1.90	0.00	12.10	0.00	123.96	137.96
Mark's General Contracting						
Year End 2004	0.00	0.00	0.00	0.00	1,905.00	1,905.00
Total Mark's General Contracting	0.00	0.00	0.00	0.00	1,905.00	1,905.00
TOTAL	513.37	0.00	2,398.75	0.00	4,320.14	7,232.26

FIGURE 5-8 A summary report provides totals for each customer, broken down by aging periods.

| | A/R Aging Detail | | | | | | | Type a help question | Ask | ▼ How Do I? | |

| Modify Report... | Memorize... | Print... | E-mail | Export... | Hide Header | Refresh |

| Dates | Custom | | 02/28/2006 | Interval (days) | 30 | Through (days past due) | 90 | Sort By | Default | |

We Do It All

A/R Aging Detail

As of February 28, 2006

Type	Date	Num	P. O. #	Name	Terms	Due Date	Class	Aging	Open Balance
Current									
▶ Invoice	02/25/2006	444		Accounting System...	Net30	03/27/2006			1,605.00 ◀
Total Current									1,605.00
1 - 30									
Invoice	01/31/2006	FC 6		Accounting System...		01/31/2006		28	2.29
Invoice	01/31/2006	FC 7		Accounting System...		01/31/2006		28	24.54
Invoice	01/31/2006	FC 8		Accounting System...		01/31/2006		28	3.67
Invoice	01/31/2006	FC 9		BillsCafe		01/31/2006		28	8.24
Invoice	01/31/2006	FC 10		Lewites-Cust		01/31/2006		28	1.90
Invoice	01/15/2006	467		Accounting System...	Net30	02/14/2006		14	412.35
Invoice	01/18/2006	466		BillsCafe	Net30	02/17/2006		11	60.38
Total 1 - 30									513.37
31 - 60									
Invoice	12/31/2005	FC 1		Accounting System...		12/31/2005		59	15.24
Invoice	12/31/2005	FC 2		Accounting System...		12/31/2005		59	220.83
Invoice	12/31/2005	FC 3		Accounting System...		12/31/2005		59	27.73
Invoice	12/31/2005	FC 4		BillsCafe		12/31/2005		59	48.85
Invoice	12/31/2005	FC 5		Lewites-Cust		12/31/2005		59	12.10
Total 31 - 60									324.75
61 - 90									
Invoice	11/09/2005	456		BillsCafe	Net30	12/09/2005		81	424.00
Invoice	11/21/2005	439		Adam's Consulting...	Net30	12/21/2005		69	1,535.00
Invoice	11/21/2005	465		BillsCafe	Net30	12/21/2005		69	115.00
Total 61 - 90									2,074.00

FIGURE 5-9   Detail reports display information about every transaction that's involved in each customer's A/R balance.

Customizing Aging Reports

If you don't use (or care about) all of the columns in the aging detail report, or you'd prefer to see the information displayed in a different manner, you can customize the report. Start by clicking the Modify Report button on the report to see the Modify Report window shown in Figure 5-10.

Customizing the Columns

The most common customization is to get rid of any column you don't care about. For example, if you use the classes feature but don't care about that information in your aging report, get rid of the column. Or you might want to get rid of the Terms column since it doesn't impact the totals. To remove a column, scroll through the Columns list and click to remove the check mark. The column disappears from the report.

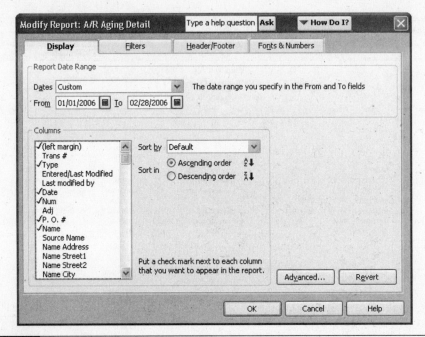

FIGURE 5-10   Customize aging reports to get exactly the information you need.

While you're looking at the list of column names, you may find a column heading that's not currently selected but that contains information you'd like to include in your report. If so, click that column listing to place a check mark next to it. The column appears on the report and the data linked to it is displayed.

Filtering Information

If you want to produce an aging report for a special purpose, you can easily filter the information so it meets criteria important to you. To filter your aging report, click the Filters tab (see Figure 5-11).

Select a filter and then set the conditions for it. (Each filter has its own specific type of criteria.) For example, you can use this feature if you want to see only those customers with receivables higher than a certain figure or older than a certain aging period.

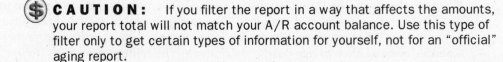

CAUTION: If you filter the report in a way that affects the amounts, your report total will not match your A/R account balance. Use this type of filter only to get certain types of information for yourself, not for an "official" aging report.

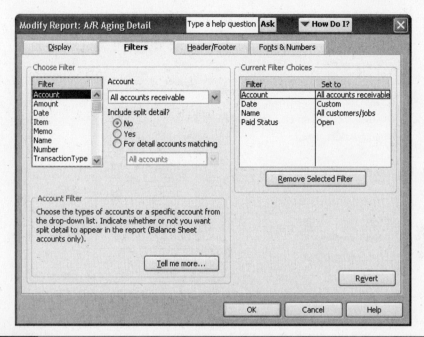

Filters let you specify criteria for displaying data.

Configuring Header/Footer Data

You can customize the text that appears in the header and footer of the report by making changes in the Header/Footer tab shown in Figure 5-12.

You'll probably find that your decisions about the contents of the header and footer depend on whether you're viewing the report or printing it. And, if you're printing it, some stuff is more important if an outsider (a banker or your accountant) will be the recipient of the report, rather than your credit manager.

For example, the date and time of preparation is more important for outsiders than for you. Incidentally, on the Header/Footer tab, the Date Prepared field has a meaningless date—don't panic, your computer hasn't lost track of the date. That date is a format, not today's date. Click the arrow to the right of the field to see the other formats for inserting the date. The Page Number field also has a variety of formats to choose from.

You can eliminate a Header/Footer field by removing the check mark from the field's check box. For fields you want to print, you can change the text. You can also change the layout by choosing a different Alignment option from the drop-down list.

Customizing the Appearance

Click the Fonts & Numbers tab (see Figure 5-13) to change the format of the report.

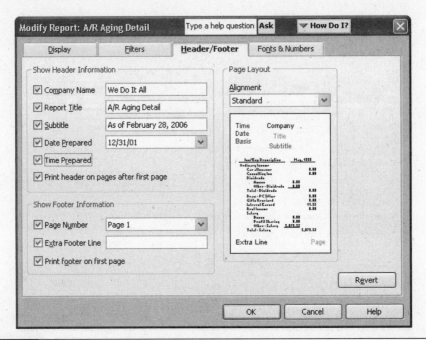

FIGURE 5-12   Specify the text you want to display on the top and bottom of the report.

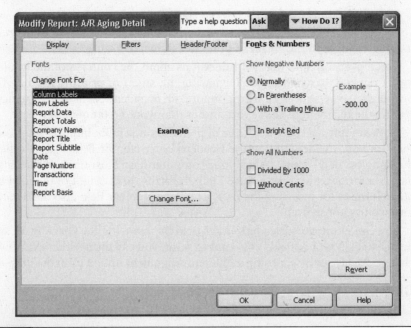

FIGURE 5-13   Change the look of the report by modifying the options in the Fonts & Numbers tab.

You can change the way negative numbers are displayed, and you can change the fonts for any or all the individual elements in the report.

When you close the report window, QuickBooks may ask if you want to memorize the report with the changes you made (if you told QuickBooks to stop asking, you won't see the message). Click Yes so you don't have to go through all the modifications again. If QuickBooks doesn't ask, memorize the report using the instructions in the next section.

Memorizing Aging Reports

If you've customized a report and have the columns, data, and formatting you need, there's no reason to reinvent the wheel the next time you need the same information. Instead of going through the customization process again next month, memorize the report as you designed it. Then you can fetch it whenever you need it.

Click the Memorize button in the report window. When the Memorize Report window appears, enter a new name for the report, optionally save it within a report group, and click OK.

From now on, this report name will be on the list of memorized reports you can select from when you choose Reports | Memorized Reports from the menu bar.

 N O T E :   When you use a memorized report, only the criteria and formatting are memorized. Each time you open the report, the data is generated from the QuickBooks transaction records, so you get current, accurate information.

Importing Memorized Reports

If you're using a Premier edition of QuickBooks, you can export a memorized report (all versions of QuickBooks can import a memorized report). If you're an accountant using a Premier edition, this means you can create and memorize a report that has exactly what you need, laid out exactly the way you need it. Then, send the memorized report to your client. You can open the report when you visit the client or have the client open the report, and then export the contents to Excel and send it to you. When you export a memorized report, the exported document is called a template. The template can be imported into any edition of QuickBooks. Detailed information about exporting memorized reports is available in *Running QuickBooks 2006 Premier Editions* from CPA911 Publishing (www.cpa911publishing .com). The book is available at your favorite bookstore or online bookseller.

If you receive an exported report template, the process of importing it converts the template into a memorized report that's added to the currently open company file.

To import a template, use the following steps:

❶ Choose Reports | Memorized Reports | Memorized Report List.
❷ Click the Memorized Report button at the bottom of the window, and select Import Template to open the Select File To Import dialog.

③ Navigate to the drive or folder that contains the template file you received, and double-click its listing.

④ In the Memorize Report dialog, enter a name for the report or accept the displayed name (which is the name used by the person who exported the template).

Printing Reports

Whether you're using the standard format or one you've customized, you'll probably want to print the report. When you're in a report window, click the Print button at the top of the window to bring up the Print Reports window. If the report is wide, use the Margins tab to set new margins, and use the options on the Settings tab to customize other printing options.

Running Customer and Job Reports

Customer and job reports are like aging reports, but they're designed to give you information about the selected customers/jobs instead of providing information on the totals for your business. There are plenty of customer reports available from the menu that appears when you choose Reports | Customers & Receivables:

- **Customer Balance Summary Report**   Lists current total balance owed for each customer.
- **Customer Balance Detail Report**   Lists every transaction for each customer with a net subtotal for each customer.
- **Open Invoices Report**   Lists all unpaid invoices, sorted and subtotaled by customer and job.
- **Collections Report**   A nifty report for nagging. Includes the contact name and telephone number, along with details about invoices with balances due. You're all set to call the customer and have a conversation, and you can answer any questions about invoice details.
- **Accounts Receivable Graph**   Shows a graphic representation of the accounts receivable. For a quick impression, there's nothing like a graph.
- **Unbilled Costs By Job**   Tracks job expenses you haven't invoiced.
- **Transaction List By Customer**   Displays individual transactions of all types for each customer.
- **Online Received Payments**   Shows payments received from customers who pay you online (if you've signed up for online payments).
- **Customer Phone List**   Displays an alphabetical list of customers along with the telephone number for each (if you entered the telephone number in the customer record).
- **Customer Contact List**   Displays an alphabetical list of customers along with the telephone number, billing address, and current open balance for each. Give this list to the person in charge of collections.
- **Item Price List**   Lists all your items with their prices and preferred vendors.

Customer Center

QuickBooks provides a Customer Center that displays data about your customers, their balances, and other important information. To open the Customer Center, take any of the following actions:

- Click the Customer Center icon on the toolbar.
- Click the Customers icon on the left side of the Home page.
- Press CTRL-J.
- Choose Customers | Customer Center from the menu bar.

As you can see in Figure 5-14, the layout of the Customer Center window is easy to understand and navigate. In this section, I'll give you a quick overview of the Customer Center functions.

$ SECURITY NOTE: Users who do not have access permissions for customer information do not see financial information when they open the Customer Center window.

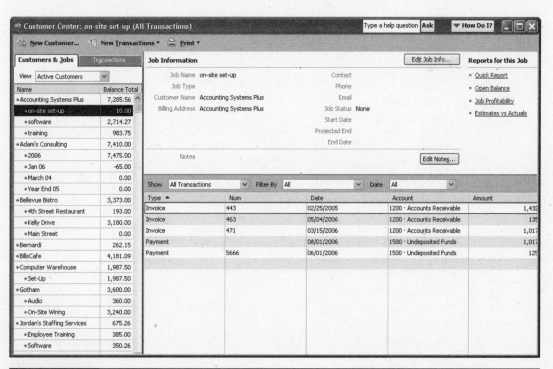

FIGURE 5-14 The Customer Center contains everything you need to know about your customers.

If you've been using QuickBooks (you updated to QuickBooks 2006 from a previous version), you'll find that the functions in the Customer Center replace functions that were previously available in the menu system. It won't take long to get used to the new interface, but to start, it's very important to note that neither the Lists menu nor the Customers menu contains the menu command Customer:Job List. The list is only available in the Customer Center, in the Customers & Jobs tab.

The left pane of the Customer Center has two tabs: Customers & Jobs, and Transactions. A customer is always selected in the Customers & Jobs tab (by default, the first customer in the list), and the right pane of the Customer Center displays information about the selected customer or job. The financial information in the right pane can be filtered by choosing a different category in the drop-down lists, and sorted by selecting a column heading.

The Transactions tab lists all your sales transactions (Invoices, Sales Receipts, and so on). Selecting a transaction type displays the current transactions of that type in the right pane. The display can be manipulated and filtered by choosing categories and sorting by column.

You can use the toolbar icons on the Customer Center window, and the links in the right pane to perform tasks and produce reports.

Entering Accounts Payable Bills

n this chapter:

- Enter vendor bills

- Track reimbursable expenses

- Enter inventory item purchases

- Use purchase orders

- Enter vendor credit memos

- Enter recurring bills

- Manage mileage costs

Entering your bills into QuickBooks, and then paying them in a separate transaction, is accrual accounting. That means an expense is posted to your Profit & Loss statement when you enter the bill, not when you actually pay the bill. The total of unpaid bills is the amount posted to the Accounts Payable account.

However, if your taxes are filed on a cash basis (which means an expense isn't posted until you actually pay the bill), be assured (and assure your accountant) that QuickBooks understands how to report your financial figures on a cash basis. (See Chapter 15 for information on financial reports.)

Recording Vendor Bills

When the mail arrives, after you open all the envelopes that contain checks from customers (I always do that first), you should tell QuickBooks about the bills that arrived. Don't worry—QuickBooks doesn't automatically pay them. You decide when to do that.

To enter your bills, click Enter Bills on the Home page (in the Vendor section of the page), click the Bill icon on the Icon Bar, or choose Vendors | Enter Bills from the menu bar. When the Enter Bills window opens (see Figure 6-1), you can fill out the information from the bill you received.

The window has two sections: the heading section, which contains information about the vendor and the bill, and the details section, which records the data related to your general ledger accounts. The details section has two tabs: Expenses and

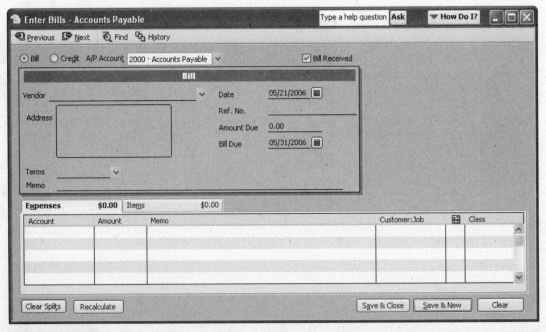

FIGURE 6-1   The Enter Bills window has a heading section and a details section.

Items. In this section, I'll cover bills that are posted to Expenses; entering Items is covered later in this chapter when I discuss the purchase of inventory items.

($) **N O T E :**   The A/P Account field (and accompanying drop-down list) appears at the top of the Enter Bills window only if you have multiple Accounts Payable accounts.

Depending on the bill, you may be able to assign the entire bill to one expense account, or you may have to split the bill among multiple expense accounts. For example, your utility bills are usually posted to the appropriate utility account (electric, heat, and so on). However, credit card bills may be split among numerous expenses, and loan repayments are split between interest (an expense account) and principal (a liability account).

Easy One-account Posting

In the Vendor field, click the arrow to choose this vendor from the list that appears. If the vendor isn't on the list, choose <Add New> to add this vendor to your QuickBooks vendor list.

Now fill out the rest of the bill as follows:

1. Enter the bill date. The due date then fills in automatically, depending on the terms you have with this vendor. You can change this date if you wish. (If you didn't set up terms for this vendor, the due date is automatically filled out using the default number of days for paying bills. QuickBooks sets this at ten days, but you can change the default by choosing Edit | Preferences and going to the Purchases & Vendors section.)

2. Enter the vendor's invoice number in the Ref. No. field.

3. Enter the amount due.

4. In the Terms field, click the arrow to display a list of terms, and select the one you need. If the terms you have with this vendor aren't available, choose <Add New> to create a new Terms entry. The due date changes to reflect the terms.

5. To enter the posting accounts, click in the Account column, and then click the arrow to display your chart of accounts. Select the account to which this bill should be assigned. QuickBooks automatically assigns the amount you entered in the Amount Due field to the Amount column.

6. If you wish, enter a note in the Memo column.

7. In the Customer:Job column, enter a customer or job if you're paying a bill that you want to track for job costing, or if this bill is a reimbursable expense. See the discussions on tracking and charging customers for reimbursable expenses later in this chapter.

8. If you're tracking classes, a Class column appears; enter the appropriate class.

9. When you're finished, click Save & New to save this bill and bring up another blank Enter Bills window. When you've entered all your bills, click Save & Close.

Splitting Expenses Among Multiple Accounts

Some bills aren't neatly assigned to one account in your general ledger; instead, they're split among multiple accounts. The most common example is a credit card bill.

Here's how to split a bill among multiple general ledger accounts:

1. Follow the first four steps in the instructions for entering bills in the previous section.
2. Click in the Account column to display the arrow you use to see your chart of accounts.
3. Select the first account to which you want to assign some portion of this bill.
4. If you've entered an amount in the Amount Due field in the heading section of the bill, QuickBooks automatically applies the entire amount of the bill in the Amount column. Replace that data with the amount you want to assign to the account you selected.
5. Click in the Account column to select the next account and enter the appropriate amount in the Amount column.

As you add each additional account to the column, QuickBooks assumes that the unallocated amount is assigned to that account (see Figure 6-2). Repeat the process of changing the amount and adding another account until the split transaction is completely entered.

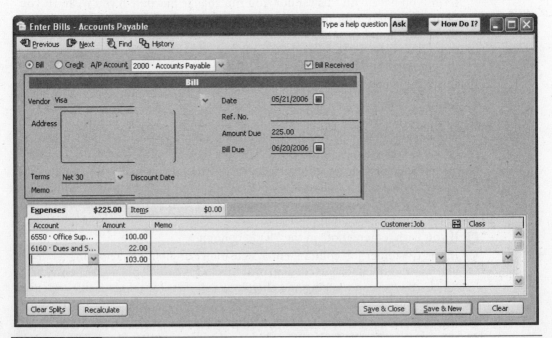

FIGURE 6-2   QuickBooks keeps recalculating, so the last account posting entry automatically has the correct amount.

Reimbursable Expenses

A reimbursable expense is one that you incurred on behalf of a customer. Even though you pay the vendor bill, there's an agreement with your customer that you'll send an invoice to recover your costs. There are two common types of reimbursable expenses:

- General expenses, such as long-distance telephone charges, parking and tolls, and other incidental expenses, are incurred on behalf of a client. Those portions of the vendor bill that apply to customer agreements for reimbursement are split out when you enter the bill.
- Specific goods or services are purchased on behalf of the customer.

Options for Managing Reimbursable Expenses

You have two ways to manage reimbursable expenses:

- Pay the bill, post it to an expense, and then let QuickBooks automatically post the customer's reimbursement to the same expense account. This cancels the original expense and reduces the expense total in your Profit & Loss statements.
- Pay the bill and then let QuickBooks automatically post the customer's reimbursement to an income account that's created for posting reimbursements. This lets you track totals for both the original expense and the reimbursement.

You may want to discuss these choices with your accountant. Many businesses prefer the second option—tracking the expenses and reimbursements separately—just because it's more accurate when you're analyzing your expenses and income. I'll therefore go over the steps you have to take to configure reimbursement tracking. You can ignore the instructions if you prefer to reduce your expense totals by posting reimbursements to the expense account you used when you entered the vendor's bill.

Configuring Reimbursement Tracking

To track reimbursed costs from customers, you need to enable reimbursement tracking in QuickBooks, and you must also create income accounts that are used for collecting reimbursements.

Enable Reimbursement Tracking

To tell QuickBooks that you want to track reimbursable costs, you must enable the feature in the Preferences dialog box.

Use the following steps:

1. Choose Edit | Preferences to open the Preferences dialog.
2. Select the Sales & Customers icon in the left pane.
3. Click the Company Preferences tab.
4. Click the check box next to the option labeled Track Reimbursed Expenses As Income to put a check mark in the box.
5. Click OK.

NOTE: You'll notice a field to enter a markup percentage right below the option to Track Reimbursed Expenses As Income. See the section "Marking Up Reimbursable Expenses" later in this chapter to learn about the markup feature.

As a result of enabling this option, QuickBooks adds a new field to the dialog you use when you create or edit an expense account. As you can see in Figure 6-3, you can configure an expense account to post reimbursements to an income account. Whenever you post a vendor expense to this account and also indicate that the expense is reimbursable, the amount you charge to the customer when you create an invoice for that customer is automatically posted to the income account that's linked to this expense account.

Set Up Income Accounts for Reimbursement

You may have numerous expense accounts that you want to use for reimbursable expenses; in fact, that's the common scenario. Portions of telephone bills, travel expenses, subcontractor expenses, and so on are frequently passed on to customers for reimbursement.

The easiest way to manage all of this is to enable those expense accounts to track reimbursements and post the income from customers to one account. After all, it's only important to know how much of your total income was a result of reimbursements (separating that income from the income you generate as the result of sales).

Alas, QuickBooks doesn't approach this with the logic inherent in this paradigm. Instead, the software insists on a one-to-one relationship between a reimbursable expense and the reimbursement income from that expense. As a result, if you have multiple expense accounts for which you may receive reimbursement (a highly likely scenario), you must also create multiple income accounts for accepting reimbursed expenses.

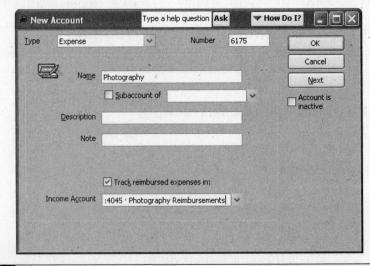

FIGURE 6-3   You can configure an expense account to post reimbursements to an income account.

This is a one-time chore, however, so when you've finished setting up the accounts, you can just enter transactions, knowing QuickBooks will automatically post reimbursed expenses to your new income accounts.

Because you probably only care about totals for income received as reimbursement, the best way to set up the income accounts you'll need is to use subaccounts. That way, your reports will show the total amount of income due to reimbursed expenses, and you can ignore the individual account totals unless you have some reason to audit a number.

Depending on the company type you selected during the EasyStep Interview, QuickBooks may have already created a Reimbursed Expenses account in the Income section of your chart of accounts. If so, you already have a parent account, and you can skip this section on setting up the account and move directly to the instructions for creating subaccounts.

Here's the most efficient way to set up your income accounts to track reimbursements:

1. Open the chart of accounts by clicking the Accnt icon on the toolbar, or by pressing CTRL-A.
2. Press CTRL-N to open a New Account window.
3. Select Income as the account type.
4. Enter an account number (if you use numbers) and name the account Reimbursed Expenses (or something similar).
5. Click OK.

You've created the parent account—now create the subaccounts as follows:

1. Press CTRL-N to open the New Account window.
2. Select Income as the account type.
3. If you're using numbered accounts, use the next sequential number after the number you used for the parent account. Also enter a name for the account, such as **Telephone Reimbursements**.
4. Select the Subaccount check box and link it to the parent account you created.
5. Click Next to create the next account.

Repeat this process as many times as necessary (click OK instead of Next when you're finished). For example, my chart of accounts has the following accounts for this purpose:

- 4040 Reimbursed Expenses
- 4041 Equip Rental Reimbursements
- 4042 Telephone Reimbursements
- 4043 Travel Reimbursements
- 4044 Subcontractor Reimbursements

My reports show the individual account postings as well as a total for all postings for the parent account (which is the only number I really look at).

Don't forget to edit your existing expense accounts if you'll be invoicing customers for reimbursements for those accounts. Select the check box to track reimbursed expenses and enter the appropriate income account.

Recording Reimbursable Expenses

If you want to be reimbursed by customers for expenses you incurred on their behalf, you must enter the appropriate data while you're filling out the vendor's bill. After you enter the account and the amount, click the arrow in the Customer:Job column and select the appropriate customer or job from the drop-down list.

Entering data in the Customer:Job column automatically places the strange-looking icon that appears to the right of the Customer:Job column in the column. The icon represents an invoice, and its appearance means you're tracking this expense in order to invoice the customer for reimbursement.

You can click the icon to put an X atop it if you don't want to bill the customer for the expense but you do want to track what you're spending for the customer. This disables the reimbursement feature, but the expense is still associated with the customer (which is how you track job costing).

Sometimes, a vendor's bill is for an amount that's not entirely chargeable to a customer. Some of the amount may be your own responsibility, and it may also be that multiple customers owe you reimbursement for the amount. (This is often the case with telephone expenses when your customers reimburse you for long-distance charges.)

Here's how to enter the transaction:

1. Select the expense account, and then enter the portion of the bill that is your own responsibility.
2. In the next line, select the same account, and then enter the portion of the bill you are charging back to a customer.
3. Enter an explanation of the charge in the Memo column. (When you create the invoice, the text in the Memo column is the only description the customer sees.)
4. In the Customer:Job column, choose the appropriate customer or job.
5. If you're only tracking expenses and don't want to include the amount in your invoice to this customer, click the invoice icon to place an X on it.
6. Repeat steps 2 through 5 to include any additional customers for this expense account.

When you're finished, the total amount entered should match the amount on the vendor's bill (see Figure 6-4).

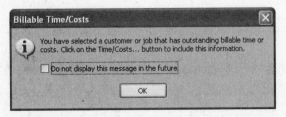

FIGURE 6-4   Charge portions of an expense to one or more customers by splitting the total expense among customers when you enter the vendor bill.

Invoicing Customers for Reimbursable Expenses

When you save the vendor bill, the amounts you linked to a customer are saved in the customer file. If you placed an Invoice icon in the column next to the Customer:Job column on the vendor bill, you can collect the money by adding those amounts to the next invoice you create. In fact, you're free to create an invoice specifically for the purpose of collecting reimbursable expenses.

Chapter 3 has complete information about creating invoices for customers, but in this section I'll discuss the particular steps you take when you want to create an invoice that includes costs for which you're seeking reimbursement.

As soon as you select a customer in the Invoice window, QuickBooks checks to see if that customer has any outstanding billable time or costs. If so, you're notified of that fact.

The alert message contains an option to stop showing this reminder when you're creating invoices, but I can't think of any reason to stop this handy reminder from appearing. (Tracking time for customer billing is covered in Chapter 18.)

Use the following steps to collect reimbursement for costs the customer has agreed to pay:

1 Fill in the data in the invoice heading (and line items if you're invoicing this customer for goods or services in addition to reimbursable costs).

2 Click the Time/Costs icon at the top of the Create Invoices window to open the Choose Billable Time And Costs window.

3 Move to the Expenses tab, which displays the reimbursable amounts you posted for this customer when you entered vendor bills.

4 Click in the Use column to place a check mark next to the expense(s) you want to include on the invoice you're currently creating (see Figure 6-5).

5 Click OK to move the item(s) to the invoice, to join any other invoice items you're entering.

If you selected multiple reimbursable costs, QuickBooks enters an item called Reimb Group, lists the individual items, and enters the total for the reimbursable items (see Figure 6-6).

Notice that the description of the reimbursable items is taken from the text you entered in the Memo column when you entered the vendor's bill. If you don't use

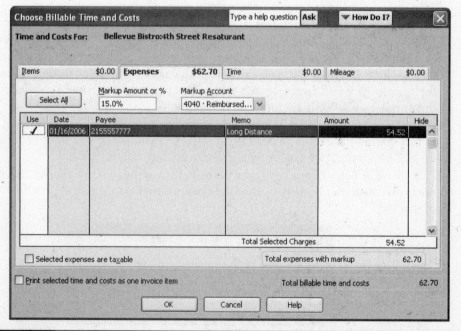

FIGURE 6-5   Select the reimbursable expenses you want to add to the invoice you're preparing.

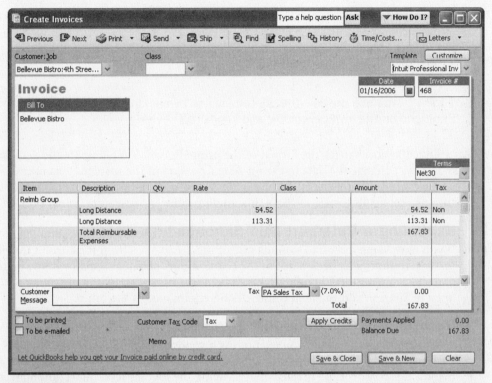

FIGURE 6-6 QuickBooks creates a group item for reimbursable charges and displays the total on the invoice.

that Memo column, you'll have to enter text manually in the Description column of the invoice (which is a real test of your memory). Otherwise, the customer sees only an amount and no explanation of what it's for.

Adding Taxes to Reimbursable Expenses

If an item is taxable and the customer is not tax exempt, choose the option Selected Expenses Are Taxable. When the items are passed to the invoice, the appropriate taxes are applied. If you select the taxable option and the customer is tax exempt, QuickBooks won't add the sales tax to the invoice.

If some items are taxable and others aren't, you have to separate the process of moving items to the invoice. First, deselect each nontaxable item by clicking its check mark to remove it (it's a toggle). Click OK to put those items on the invoice. Then return to the Choose Billable Time And Costs window, put a check mark next to each nontaxable item, deselect the Selected Expenses Are Taxable option, and click OK.

Omitting the Details on the Invoice

If you have multiple reimbursable items, you can combine all of them into a single line item on the invoice. Choose the option Print Selected Time And Costs As One Invoice Item. When you click OK and view the results in the invoice, you still see each individual item. Don't panic—you're not losing your mind. The screen version of the invoice continues to display the individual items. However, when you print the invoice, you'll see a line item named Total Reimbursable Expenses with the correct total in the Amount column.

 TIP: You can preview the printed invoice by clicking the arrow next to the Print icon on the invoice window and choosing Preview.

QuickBooks changes the format of the printed invoice to eliminate the details but doesn't change the data in the on-screen version of the invoice. This means you can open the invoice later and see the detailed items, which is handy when the customer calls to ask, "What's this reimbursable expense item on my bill?"

Excluding a Reimbursable Expense

If you have some reason to exclude one or more expenses from the current invoice, just avoid putting a check mark in the Use column. The item remains in the system and shows up on the Choose Billable Time And Costs window the next time you open it. You can add the item to the customer's invoice in the future.

Removing a Reimbursable Expense from the List

As explained earlier, when you're entering a vendor's bill and assigning expenses to customers and jobs, you can track the expense but not invoice the customer for it by putting an X over the invoice icon. Leaving the invoice icon intact automatically moves the expense to the category "reimbursable."

But suppose when it's time to invoice the customer, you decide that you don't want to ask the customer to pay this expense; you've changed your mind. The Choose Billable Time And Costs window has no Delete button and no method of selecting an item and choosing a delete function. You could deselect the check mark in the Use column, but afterwards, every time you open the window, the item is still there—it's like a haunting.

The solution lies in the Hide column. If you place a check mark in the Hide column, the item is effectively deleted from the list of reimbursable expenses that you see when you're preparing invoices (but the amount is still in your system). This means you won't accidentally invoice the customer for the item, but the link to this expense for this customer continues to appear in reports about this customer's activity (which is helpful for job costing).

Changing the Amount of a Reimbursable Expense

You're free to change the amount of a reimbursable expense. To accomplish this, select (highlight) the amount in the Amount column of the Billable Time And Costs window and enter the new figure.

If you reduce the amount, QuickBooks does not keep the remaining amount on the Billable Time And Costs window. You won't see it again, because QuickBooks makes the assumption you're not planning to pass the remaining amount to your customer in the future.

You may want to increase the charge for some reason (perhaps to cover overhead), but if you're increasing all the charges, it's easier to apply a markup (covered next) than to change each individual item.

Marking Up Reimbursable Expenses

You can mark up any expenses you're invoicing, which many companies do to cover any additional costs incurred such as handling, time, or general aggravation. To apply a markup, select the items you want to mark up by placing a check mark in the Use column in the Choose Billable Time And Costs window. Then enter a markup in the Markup Amount or % field in either of the following ways:

- Enter an amount.
- Enter a percentage (a number followed by the percent sign).

Specify the account to which you're posting markups. You can create an account specifically for markups (which is what I do because I'm slightly obsessive about analyzing the source of all income) or use an existing income account.

The item amounts and the total of the selected charges don't change when you apply the markup; the change is reflected in the amounts for Total Expenses With Markup and Total Billable Time And Costs.

When you click OK to transfer the reimbursable expenses to the customer's invoice, you'll see the reimbursable expenses and the markup as separate items (see Figure 6-7).

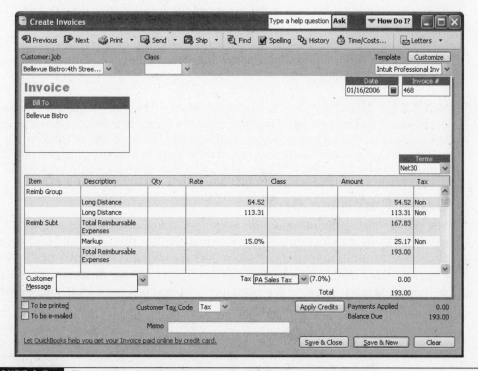

FIGURE 6-7   The markup is clearly indicated—it has its own line item.

Although it would be unusual for you to be marking up items without having discussed this with your customer, if you don't want your customer to see the markup amounts, select the Print Selected Time And Costs As One Invoice Item option. You'll see the breakdown on the screen version of the invoice, but the printed invoice will contain only the grand total.

One big difference between using the markup function and just changing the amount of the reimbursable expense in the Amount column is the way the amounts are posted to your general ledger. If you use the markup function, the difference between the actual expense and the charge to your customer is posted to the markup account. If you change the amount of the expense, the entire amount is posted to the income account you linked to the reimbursable expense account.

Managing Inventory Item Purchases

If the vendor bill you're recording is for inventory items, you need to take a different approach, because the accounting issues (the way you post amounts) are different. Two transactions are involved when you buy items for your inventory:

- You receive the inventory products.
- You receive the bill for the inventory products.

Once in a while, the bill comes before the products, and sometimes both events occur at the same time. (In fact, you may find the bill pasted to the carton or included inside the carton.) In this section, I'll go over all the available scenarios, including how to track purchase orders.

To use the Inventory and Purchase Order features, you must enable them in the Purchases & Vendors category of Preferences (choose Edit | Preferences to open the Preferences dialog box).

 NOTE: QuickBooks Premier editions can automatically create a purchase order when you create a sales order or estimate involving inventory items. If you think this is useful for your company, consider upgrading to one of the Premier editions. You can learn how to use this nifty feature in *Running QuickBooks 2006 Premier Editions* from CPA911 Publishing, available at your favorite bookstore.

Using Purchase Orders

You can use purchase orders to order inventory items from your suppliers. It's not a great idea to use purchase orders for goods that aren't in your inventory, such as office supplies or consulting services—that's not what purchase orders are intended for.

Creating and saving a purchase order has no effect on your financials. No amounts are posted, because purchase orders exist only to help you track what you've ordered against what you've received.

TIP: When you enable the Inventory and Purchase Order features, QuickBooks creates a nonposting account named Purchase Orders. You can double-click the account's listing to view and drill down into the purchase orders you've entered, but the data in the register has no effect on your finances and doesn't appear in financial reports.

Here's how to create a purchase order:

❶ Choose Purchase Orders on the Home page, or choose Vendors | Create Purchase Orders from the menu bar, to open a blank Create Purchase Orders window.

❷ Fill in the purchase order fields, which are easy and self-explanatory (see Figure 6-8).

❸ Click Save & New to save the purchase order and move on to the next blank purchase order form, or click Save & Close if you have created all the purchase orders you need right now.

TIP: If you're purchasing something on behalf of the customer, you can use the Customer column to treat the purchase as a reimbursable transaction when you enter the vendor's bill for this purchase.

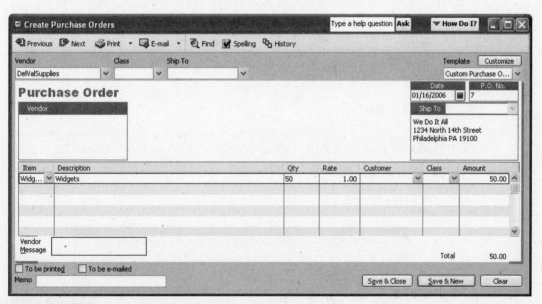

FIGURE 6-8 A purchase order looks like a vendor bill, but you don't incur any accounts payable liability.

You can print the purchase orders as you create them by clicking the Print button as soon as each purchase order is completed. If you'd prefer, you can print them all in a batch by clicking the arrow to the right of the Print button on the last purchase order window and selecting Print Batch. If you want to print them later, be sure the option To Be Printed is selected on each PO. When you're ready to print, choose File | Print Forms | Purchase Orders.

You can also e-mail the purchase orders as you create them, or e-mail them as a batch by selecting Send Batch from the drop-down list next to the E-mail icon on the transaction window's toolbar.

 T I P :   Many companies don't send purchase orders; instead, they notify the vendor of the purchase order number when they place the order over the telephone, via e-mail, or by logging into the vendor's Internet-based order system.

When the inventory items and the bill for them are received, you can use the purchase order to automate the receiving and vendor bill entry processes.

Receiving Inventory Items

Since this chapter is about accounts payable, we must cover the steps involved in paying for the inventory items. However, you don't pay for items you haven't received, so the processes involved in receiving the items also merit attention.

If the inventory items arrive before you receive a bill from the vendor, you must tell QuickBooks about the new inventory, so the items can be brought into the inventory asset account and become available for sales.

Follow these steps:

1 Choose Vendors | Receive Items from the menu bar (or choose Receive Inventory | Receive Inventory Without Bill on the Home page) to open a blank Create Item Receipts window (see Figure 6-9).

2 Enter the vendor name, and if open purchase orders exist for this vendor, QuickBooks notifies you:

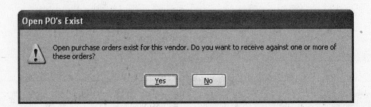

3 If you know there isn't a purchase order for this particular shipment, click No, and just fill out the Create Item Receipts window manually.

④ If you know a purchase order exists for this shipment, or if you're not sure, click Yes. QuickBooks displays all the open purchase orders for this vendor so you can put a check mark next to the appropriate PO (or multiple POs if the shipment that arrived covers more than one PO). If no PO for this shipment is listed on the Open Purchase Orders list for this vendor, click Cancel on the Open Purchase Orders window to return to the receipts window and fill in the data manually.

⑤ If a PO exists, QuickBooks fills out the Create Item Receipts window using the information in the PO (see Figure 6-10). Check the shipment against the PO and change any quantities that don't match.

⑥ Click Save & New to receive the next shipment into inventory, or click Save & Close if this takes care of all the receipts of goods.

QuickBooks posts the amounts in the purchase order to your Accounts Payable account. This is not the standard, Generally Accepted Accounting Procedure (GAAP) method for handling receipt of goods, and if your accountant notices this QuickBooks action, you can stop the screaming by explaining that QuickBooks has a workaround for this (see the section "Understanding the Postings" later in this chapter).

I'll take a moment here to explain why your accountant might start screaming: First, an accounts payable liability should only be connected to a bill. When a bill

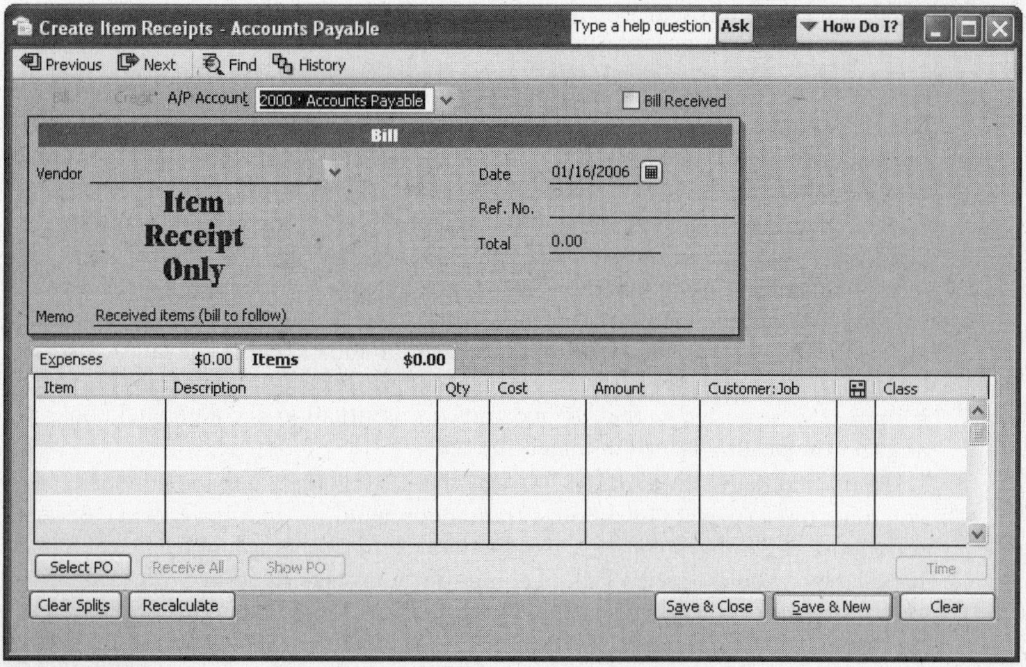

FIGURE 6-9   Receive items into inventory so you can sell them.

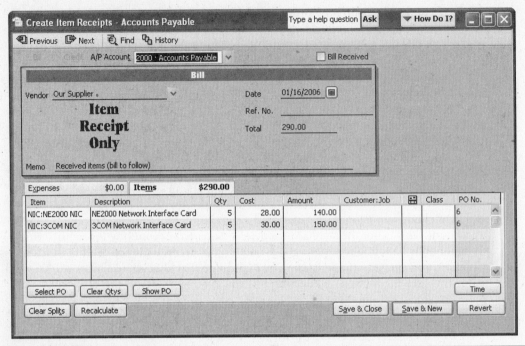

FIGURE 6-10   Line items are auto-filled from the data in the PO, and the Memo field automatically reminds you that the bill hasn't arrived yet.

comes, you owe the money. While it's safe to assume that if the goods showed up, the bill will follow, and you'll owe the money in the end; technically you don't incur the A/P liability until you have a bill.

Second, costs on the PO may not be the current costs for the items, and the vendor bill that shows up may have different amounts. The PO amounts you filled in were taken from your inventory records or by your own manual entry (perhaps using an out-of-date price list from the vendor). It's not uncommon for purchasing agents to fill out a PO without calling the vendor and checking the latest cost. The bill that arrives will have the correct costs, and those costs are the amounts that are supposed to be posted to the A/P account. If this situation occurs, QuickBooks changes the posting to A/P to match the bill.

Third, in order to avoid double-posting the A/P liability when the bill does arrive, you must use a special QuickBooks transaction window (discussed next). Because warehouse personnel frequently handle the receipt of goods, and receipt of bills is handled by a bookkeeper, a lack of communication may interfere with using the correct transaction methods. QuickBooks prevents this problem by alerting the data-entry person of a possible error. If the bookkeeper uses the standard Enter Bills transaction window, as soon as the vendor is entered in the window, QuickBooks displays a message stating that a receipt of goods record exists for this vendor and the bill should not be recorded with the standard Enter Bills window.

Recording Bills for Received Items

After you receive the items, eventually the bill comes from the vendor.

To enter the bill, do *not* use the regular Enter Bills icon in the Vendors Navigator window, which would cause another posting to Accounts Payable.

Instead, do the following:

1 Choose Vendors | Enter Bill For Received Items (or click the Enter Bills Against Inventory icon on the Home page) to open the Select Item Receipt window. Choose the vendor, and you see the current items receipt information for that vendor.

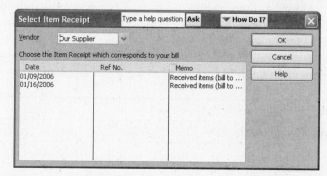

2 Select the appropriate listing and click OK to open an Enter Bills window. The information from the items receipt is used to fill in the bill information.

3 Change anything that needs to be changed: a different cost per unit, taxes and shipping costs that were added, and so on. If you make any changes, you must click the Recalculate button so QuickBooks can match the total in the Amount Due field to the changed line item data.

4 Click Save & Close.

Whether or not you've made changes to the amounts, QuickBooks displays a message warning you that the transaction is linked to other transactions and asking if you're sure you want to save the changes. Say Yes. Even if you didn't make changes to the line items, you've changed the transaction from a receipt of goods transaction to a vendor bill transaction, and QuickBooks replaces the original posting to Accounts Payable that was made when you received the items.

Receiving Items and Bills Simultaneously

If the items and the bill arrive at the same time (sometimes the bill is in the shipping carton), you must tell QuickBooks about those events simultaneously. To do this, choose Vendors | Receive Items And Enter Bill, or click the Enter Bills icon on the Home page. This opens the standard Enter Bills window, and when you enter the vendor's name you see a message telling you an open PO exists for the vendor. The message dialog asks if you want to receive these goods (and the bill) against an open PO.

Click Yes to see the open POs for this vendor and select the appropriate PO. The line items on the bill are filled in automatically, and you can correct any quantity or price difference between your original PO and the actuals. When you save the transaction, QuickBooks receives the items into inventory in addition to posting the bill to A/P.

Understanding the Postings

You need to explain to your accountant (or warn your accountant) about the way QuickBooks posts the receipt of goods and the bills for inventory items. It seems a bit different from standard practices if you're a purist about accounting procedures, but as long as you remember to use the correct commands for receiving items and bills (as described in the preceding paragraphs), it works fine.

QuickBooks makes the same postings no matter how, or in what order, you receive the items and the bill. Let's look at what happens when you receive $400.00 worth of items and fill out the Receive Items window:

Account	Debit	Credit
Accounts Payable		$400.00
Inventory	$400.00	

Notice that the amount is posted to Accounts Payable, even if the bill hasn't been received. The entry in the Accounts Payable register is noted as a receipt of items with a transaction type ITEM RCPT.

When the vendor bill arrives, as long as you remember to use Vendors | Enter Bill For Received Items, the amount isn't charged to Accounts Payable again; instead, the A/P register entry is changed to reflect the fact that it is now a bill (the item type changes to BILL). If you made changes to any amounts, the new amounts are posted, replacing the original amounts.

It's that "replacing" approach that is bothersome to many accountants, because when you overwrite one transaction (the receipt of goods) with another transaction (the receipt of the vendor bill), you have an incomplete audit trail. This is especially bothersome if amounts are changed during the replacement.

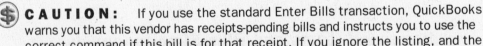 **CAUTION:**   If you use the standard Enter Bills transaction, QuickBooks warns you that this vendor has receipts-pending bills and instructs you to use the correct command if this bill is for that receipt. If you ignore the listing, and the bill is indeed for items already received into QuickBooks, you'll have double entries for the same amount in your Accounts Payable account.

In many accounting software applications, the receipt of items and the vendor bill are posted as separate transactions to a liability account called a receipts holding account. Because the postings to the receipts holding account are washed between the receipt of goods and the receipt of the bill, the bottom-line effect to your general ledger is the same when QuickBooks does it.

However, the QuickBooks approach denies you the ability to look at the amount currently posted to the receipts holding account to see where you stand in terms of items in but bills not received (or vice versa).

In terms of bottom-line financials, however, as long as you use the correct commands on the Vendor menu to enter these transactions, all the arithmetic works and you won't have a problem.

Recording Vendor Credits

If you receive a credit from a vendor, you must record it in QuickBooks. Then, you can apply it against an open vendor bill or let it float until your next order from the vendor. (See Chapter 7 for information about paying bills, which includes applying vendor credits to bills.)

QuickBooks doesn't provide a discrete credit form for accounts payable; instead, you can change a vendor bill form to a credit form with a click of the mouse.

Follow these steps:

1. Click the Enter Bills icon on the Home page, (or the Bill icon on the QuickBooks toolbar) or choose Vendors | Enter Bills from the menu bar to open the Enter Bills window.
2. Select the Credit option, which automatically deselects Bill and changes the available fields in the form (see Figure 6-11).
3. Choose the vendor from the drop-down list that appears when you click the arrow in the Vendor field.
4. Enter the date of the credit memo.
5. In the Ref. No. field, enter the vendor's credit memo number.
6. Enter the amount of the credit memo.
7. If the credit is not for inventory items, use the Expenses tab to assign an account and amount to this credit.
8. If the credit is for inventory items, use the Items tab to enter the items, along with the quantity and cost, for which you are receiving this credit.
9. Click Save & Close to save the credit (unless you have more credits to enter—in which case, click Save & New).

$ NOTE: If you've agreed that the vendor pays the shipping costs to return items, don't forget to enter that amount in the Expenses tab.

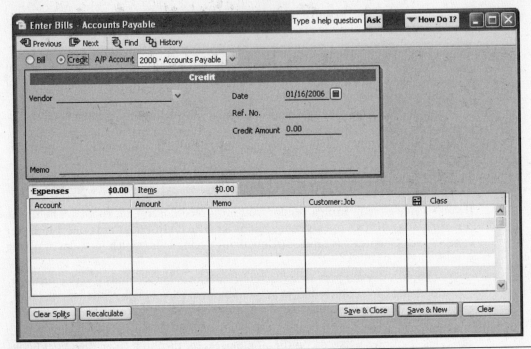

FIGURE 6-11 When you select the Credit option, the Enter Bills transaction window changes—the fields for terms and due date disappear.

Here are the postings to your general ledger when you save a vendor credit:

Account	Debit	Credit
Inventory Asset		Amount of returned items
Applicable expense account(s)		Amounts of expenses in the credit
Accounts Payable	Total credit amount	

 TIP: Don't use an RA (Return Authorization) number you received on the telephone as the basis for your credit. Wait for the credit memo to arrive so your records and the vendor's records match. This makes it much easier to settle disputed amounts.

Entering Recurring Bills

You probably have quite a few bills that you must pay every month. Commonly, the list includes your rent or mortgage payment, payments for assets you purchased with a loan (such as vehicles or equipment), or a retainer fee (for an attorney, accountant, or subcontractor).

You can make it easy to pay those bills every month without entering a bill each time. QuickBooks provides a feature called *memorized transactions,* and you can put it to work to make sure your recurring bills are covered.

Creating a Memorized Bill

To create a memorized transaction for a recurring bill, first open the Enter Bills window and fill out the information, as shown in Figure 6-12.

TIP: If the recurring bill isn't always exactly the same—perhaps the amount is different each month (your utility bills, for instance)—it's okay to leave the Amount Due field blank. You can fill in the amount each time you use the memorized bill.

Before you save the transaction, memorize it. To accomplish this, press CTRL-M (or choose Edit | Memorize Bill from the menu bar). The Memorize Transaction window opens.

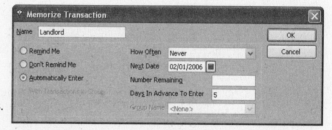

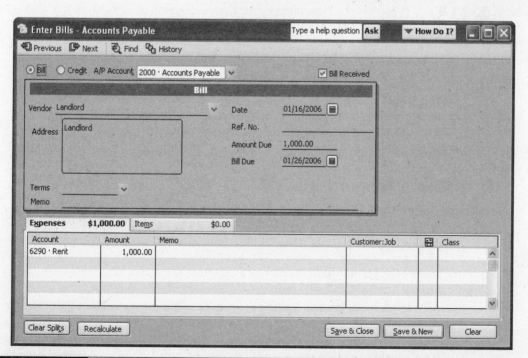

FIGURE 6-12   Enter the bill in the normal fashion, then memorize it to use it again and again.

Use these guidelines to complete the Memorize Transaction window:

- Use the Name field to enter a name for the transaction. QuickBooks automatically enters the vendor name, but you can change it. Use a name that describes the transaction so you don't have to rely on your memory.
- Select Remind Me (the default) to tell QuickBooks to issue a reminder that this bill must be put into the system to be paid.
- Select Don't Remind Me if you want to forego getting a reminder and enter the bill yourself.
- Select Automatically Enter to have QuickBooks enter this bill as a payable automatically, without reminders. Specify the number of Days In Advance To Enter this bill into the system. At the appropriate time, the bill appears in the Select Bills To Pay List you use to pay your bills (covered in Chapter 7).
- Select the interval for this bill from the drop-down list in the How Often field.
- Enter the Next Date this bill is due.
- If this payment is finite, such as a loan that has a specific number of payments, use the Number Remaining field to specify how many times this bill must be paid.

Click OK in the Memorize Transaction window to save it, and then click Save & Close in the Enter Bills window to save the bill.

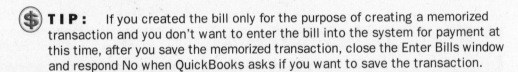 **TIP:**   If you created the bill only for the purpose of creating a memorized transaction and you don't want to enter the bill into the system for payment at this time, after you save the memorized transaction, close the Enter Bills window and respond No when QuickBooks asks if you want to save the transaction.

CAUTION: When you select the reminder options for the memorized bill, the reminders only appear if you're using reminders in QuickBooks. Choose Edit | Preferences and click the Reminders category icon to view or change reminders options.

Using a Memorized Bill

If you've opted to enter the memorized bill yourself (either by asking QuickBooks to remind you to do this, or by trusting your memory), you must bring it up to make it a current payable.

To use a memorized bill, press CTRL-T (or click the MemTx icon on the Icon Bar, or choose Lists | Memorized Transaction List from the menu bar). This opens the Memorized Transaction List window.

Double-click the appropriate listing to open the bill in the usual Enter Bills window with the next due date showing.

If the amount is blank, fill it in. Click Save & Close to save this bill so it becomes a current payable and is listed as a bill that must be paid when you write checks to pay your bills. (See Chapter 7 for information about paying bills.)

Creating Memorized Bill Groups

If you have a whole bunch of memorized transactions to cover all the bills that are due the first of the month (rent, mortgage, utilities, car payments, whatever), you don't have to select them for payment one at a time. You can create a group and then invoke actions on the group (automatically invoking the action on every bill in the group).

The steps to accomplish this are easy:

❶ Press CTRL-T to display the Memorized Transaction List.

❷ Right-click any blank spot in the Memorized Transaction window and choose New Group from the shortcut menu. In the New Memorized Transaction Group window, give this group a name.

❸ Fill out the fields to specify the way you want the bills in this group to be handled.

❹ Click OK to save this group.

Now that you've created the group, you can add memorized transactions to it as follows:

❶ In the Memorized Transaction List window, select the first memorized transaction you want to add to the group.

❷ Right-click and choose Edit Memorized Transaction from the shortcut menu.

❸ When the Schedule Memorized Transaction window opens with this transaction displayed, select the option named With Transactions In Group. Then select the group from the list that appears when you click the arrow next to the Group Name field.

❹ Click OK and repeat this process for each bill in the list.

As you create future memorized bills, just select the same With Transactions In Group option.

If you have other recurring bills with different criteria (perhaps they're due on a different day of the month, or they're due annually), create groups for them and add the individual transactions to the group.

Now that all of your vendor bills are in the system, you have to pay them. Chapter 7 covers everything you need to know about accomplishing that task.

Tracking Mileage Expense

QuickBooks provides a way to track the mileage of your vehicles. You can use the mileage information to track the expenses connected to vehicle use, to use mileage as part of your job-costing efforts, or to bill customers for mileage expenses.

($) TIP: Your accountant may be able to use the vehicle mileage data on your income tax return. You can either deduct the actual mileage expense or your other vehicle expenses; you can't deduct both. Your accountant, working with the figures you provide as a result of mileage tracking, will make the decision.

To track a vehicle, you must add that vehicle to your Vehicle List (covered in Chapter 2). Once the vehicle is in your QuickBooks system, you can begin tracking its mileage. Of course, you also need to make sure that everyone who uses a vehicle for business is tracking the odometer. Create and print a form for this purpose, with the following categories to fill in:

- Trip Start Date
- Trip End Date
- Starting Odometer
- Ending Odometer
- Customer:Job

Entering Mileage Rates

To track the cost of mileage, you must make sure you have accurate mileage rates in your system. These change frequently, so you'll have to keep up with the latest IRS figures. QuickBooks calculates the cost of mileage based on the information you enter. To get the current rate, check with the IRS (www.irs.gov) or ask your accountant.

Now use the following steps to enter the rate:

1. Choose Company | Enter Vehicle Mileage to open the Enter Vehicle Mileage window.
2. Click the Mileage Rates button on the toolbar to open the Mileage Rates window.
3. Select a date from the calendar as the Effective Date.
4. Enter the IRS rate for that date.
5. Click Close.

Notice that you can continue to add dates and rates and QuickBooks will use the appropriate rate, based on the date of your mileage entry, to calculate costs.

Creating a Mileage Item

If you plan to use mileage expenses for job costing, or to bill customers for mileage, you must create an item (call it mileage, travel, or something similar). The item is a Service type. This is the item you select when you're filling in a mileage window.

Attach an income account to the item (for example, Mileage Invoiced). You could create another reimbursement income account to attach to this item because you're collecting reimbursements for travel expenses. However, don't create an expense account for mileage and link the reimbursement account to it because you don't enter accounts payable expenses for mileage—this mileage item is just one part of your existing vehicle expenses (such as vehicle fuel, travel, and so on).

It's important to understand that the mileage rate you entered in the Mileage Rates window (described in the previous section) is not automatically transferred to the item you create for mileage. Therefore, you must independently fill in the rate for the item and update it when the IRS rate changes. You can use the same rate you used in the Mileage Rates window or enter a different rate to create a markup (or a markdown, if you wish to take that approach).

Entering Mileage

Use the following steps to enter mileage:

1 Choose Company | Enter Vehicle Mileage to open the Enter Vehicle Mileage window.

2 Select the vehicle from the drop-down list in the Vehicle field.

3 Enter the dates of the trip.

4 Enter the odometer readings—QuickBooks calculates the total miles.

5 If you want to bill the customer for mileage, place a check mark in the Billable check box and select the Customer:Job, the item you created for mileage, and the Class (if you're tracking classes).

6 If you don't want to bill a customer but you want to track job costs, select the Customer:Job, the item you created for mileage, and the Class (if you're tracking classes). Do *not* place a check mark in the Billable check box.

7 Optionally, enter a note.

8 Click Save & New to enter another trip, or click Save & Close if you're finished entering mileage.

To add the billable mileage to a customer's invoice, follow the instructions for recovering reimbursable expenses earlier in this chapter.

Creating Mileage Reports

QuickBooks includes four vehicle mileage reports, which you can access by choosing Reports | Jobs, Time & Mileage and selecting the appropriate mileage report from the submenu. If you're working in the Enter Vehicle Mileage dialog box, the reports are available in the drop-down list you see if you click the arrow next to the Mileage Reports button.

Mileage By Vehicle Summary

Use the Mileage By Vehicle Summary report to see the total miles and the mileage expense for each vehicle you're tracking. You can run this report for any date range that you want to check, which is a way to determine whether vehicles need servicing. For example, you may need to change the oil and filter every 6,000 miles, or schedule a 50,000-mile checkup. If you deduct mileage expenses on your income tax form, use the entire year as the date range.

Mileage By Vehicle Detail

Use the Mileage By Vehicle Detail report to view details about each mileage slip you created. For each vehicle, the report displays the following information:

- Trip End Date
- Total Miles

- Mileage Rate
- Mileage Expense

No customer information appears in the report, but you can double-click any listing to open the original mileage slip, which shows you whether the trip is linked to a job and whether it's marked billable.

Mileage By Job Summary

Use the Mileage By Job Summary report to view the total number of miles linked to customers or jobs. The report displays total miles for all customers or jobs for which you entered an item and displays billable amounts for any mileage entries you marked billable.

Mileage By Job Detail

Use the Mileage By Job Detail report to see the following information about each trip for each customer or job:

- Trip End Date
- Billing Status
- Item
- Total miles
- Sales Price
- Amount

To gain more knowledge, you can modify the report by clicking the Modify Report button on the report window to open the Modify Report dialog. In the Display tab, select additional columns to reflect what you want to see in this report. For example, you may want to add the Mileage Rate or Mileage Expense (or both). You may even want to add the start date for the trip. If you do, memorize the report so you don't have to repeat the modifications next time.

Reimbursing Employees and Subcontractors for Mileage

You can use the vehicle mileage-tracking feature to reimburse employees, subcontractors, and yourself. Enter each person's car in the Vehicle List (use the person's name for the vehicle), and have everyone keep mileage logs.

If you're doing your own payroll, QuickBooks cannot transfer this money directly to paychecks the way the system can transfer time, but you can run reports to reimburse everyone.

Use the following steps:

1. Open the Mileage By Vehicle Detail report.
2. Enter the date range for which you're reimbursing individuals.
3. Click the Modify Report button to open the Modify Report dialog box.

④ In the Filters tab, select the first person's car from the drop-down list in the Vehicle field.

⑤ Click OK to return to the report window, which now displays information about that person's mileage only.

⑥ Memorize the report, naming it *person* mileage (substitute the real name for *person*).

⑦ Repeat the process for each remaining person.

⑧ Print each person's report and attach it to the reimbursement check.

Additional Features for Premier and Enterprise Editions

If you're running QuickBooks Premier Edition or QuickBooks Enterprise Solutions, you may have some additional features available, above and beyond the features covered in this chapter. (Not all features are in all Premier or Enterprise versions.)

Generate Purchase Orders from Sales Orders Automatically

If you entered a sales order (instead of an invoice) because you were out of product, you have to order the product. Instead of opening a blank purchase order transaction window, and filling in the data, you can tell QuickBooks Premier/Enterprise editions to generate the purchase order from the sales order. This saves a lot of time and effort, and, perhaps more importantly, avoids the possibility of typing errors. To create the purchase order, open the sales order transaction and click the arrow to the right of the Create Invoice icon on the toolbar. Then select Purchase Order from the drop-down menu.

Paying Bills

n this chapter:

- Choose bills to pay
- Apply discounts and credits
- Write checks
- Make direct disbursements
- Set up sales tax payments

The expression "writing checks" doesn't have to be taken literally. You can let QuickBooks do the "writing" part by buying computer checks and printing them. Except for signing the check, QuickBooks can do all the work.

Choosing What to Pay

You don't have to pay every bill that's entered, nor do you have to pay the entire amount due for each bill. Your current bank balance and your relationships with your vendors have a large influence on the decisions you make.

There are all sorts of rules that business consultants recite about how to decide what to pay when money is short, and the term "essential vendors" is prominent. I've never figured out how to define "essential," since having electricity can be just as important as buying inventory items. Having worked with hundreds of clients, however, I can give you two rules to follow that are based on those clients' experiences:

- The government (taxes) comes first. Never, never, never use payroll withholding money to pay bills.
- It's better to send lots of vendors small checks than to send gobs of money to a couple of vendors who have been applying pressure. Vendors hate being ignored much more than they dislike small payments on account.

Viewing Your Unpaid Bills

Start by examining the bills that are due. The best way to see that list is in detailed form instead of a summary total for each vendor. To accomplish this, choose Reports | Vendors & Payables | Unpaid Bills Detail. In the report window, set the Dates field to All to make sure all of your outstanding vendor bills are displayed (see Figure 7-1).

Double-click any entry if you want to see the original bill you entered, including all line items, and notes you made in the Memo column.

You can filter the report to display only certain bills. To accomplish this, click Modify Report and go to the Filters tab in the Modify Report dialog. Use the filters to change the display in any of the following ways:

- Filter for bills that are due today (or previously), eliminating bills due after today.
- Filter for bills that are more or less than a certain amount.
- Filter for bills that are more than a certain number of days overdue.

Print the report, and if you're short on cash, work on a formula that will maintain good relationships with your vendors.

Selecting the Bills to Pay

When you're ready to tell QuickBooks which bills you want to pay, choose Vendors | Pay Bills. The Pay Bills window appears (see Figure 7-2), and you can begin to make your selections using the following guidelines.

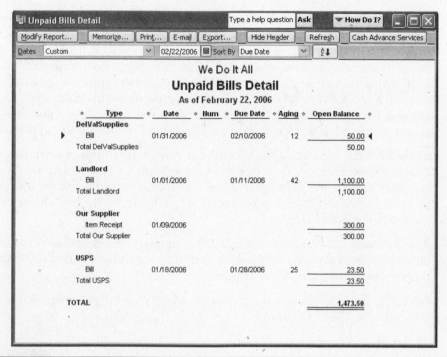

FIGURE 7-1   Check the current unpaid bills.

FIGURE 7-1   Check the current unpaid bills.

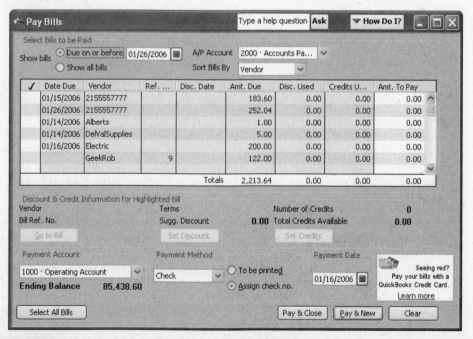

FIGURE 7-2   Paying bills starts in the Pay Bills window.

Due On Or Before   Displays all the bills due within ten days by default, but you can change the date to display more or fewer bills. If you have discounts for timely payments with any vendors, this selection is more important than it seems. The due date isn't the same as the discount date. Therefore, if you have terms of 2%10Net30, a bill that arrived on April 2 is due on May 2 and won't appear on the list if the due date filter you select is April 30. Unfortunately, the discount date is April 12, but you won't know because the bill won't appear. If you want to use a due date filter, go out at least 60 days. (See the section "Applying Discounts" later in this chapter.)

Show All Bills   Shows all the bills in your system, regardless of when they're due. This is the safest option, because you won't accidentally miss a discount date. On the other hand, if you don't get discounts for timely payment (usually offered only by vendors who sell inventory products), it's probably not the best choice because the list can be rather long.

A/P Account   If you have multiple A/P accounts, select the account to which the bills you want to pay were originally posted. If you don't have multiple A/P accounts, this field doesn't appear in the window.

Sort Bills By   Determines the manner in which your bills are displayed in the Pay Bills window. The choices are

- Due Date (the default)
- Discount Date
- Vendor
- Amount Due

Payment Account   The checking or credit card account you want to use for these payments.

Payment Method   The drop-down list displays the available methods of payment: Check and Credit Card are listed by default, but if you've signed up for QuickBooks online bill payment services, that payment method also appears in the list.

If you are paying by check and QuickBooks prints your checks, be sure the To Be Printed option is selected. If you're using manual checks, select Assign Check No., and when you finish configuring bill payments, QuickBooks opens the Assign Check Numbers dialog so you can specify the starting check number for this bill paying session in the Check No. column.

Payment Date   This is the date that appears on your checks. By default, the current date appears in the field, but if you want to predate or postdate your checks, you can change that date. If you merely select the bills today and wait until tomorrow (or later) to print the checks, the payment date set here still appears on the checks.

 TIP: You can tell QuickBooks to date checks using the day of printing by changing the Checking Preferences.

If you made changes to the selection fields (perhaps you changed the due date filter), your list of bills to be paid may change. If all the bills displayed are to be paid either in full or in part, you're ready to move to the next step. If there are still some bills on the list that you're not going to pay, you can just select the ones you do want to pay. Selecting a bill is simple—just click the leftmost column to place a check mark in it.

Selecting the Payment Amounts

If you want to pay in full all the bills that are listed in the Pay Bills window and there aren't any credits or discounts to worry about, the easiest thing to do is to click the Select All Bills button at the bottom of the window. This selects all the bills for payment (and the Select All Bills button changes its name to Clear Selections, so you have a way to reverse your action). Here's what happens in your general ledger when you pay all bills in full:

Account	Debit	Credit
Accounts Payable	Total bill payments	
Bank		Total bill payments

I've had clients ask why they don't see the expense accounts when they look at the postings for bill paying. The answer is that the expenses were posted when they entered the bills. That's a major difference between entering bills and then paying them or writing checks without entering the bills into your QuickBooks system (called *direct disbursement*). If you just write checks, you enter the accounts to which you're assigning those checks. For that system (the cash-based system) of paying bills, the postings debit the expense and credit the bank account. See the section "Using Direct Disbursements" later in this chapter for more information.

Making a Partial Payment

If you don't want to pay a bill in full, you can easily adjust the amount.

Follow these steps:

1. Click the check mark column on the bill's listing to select the bill for payment.
2. Click in the Amt. To Pay column and replace the amount that's displayed with the amount you want to pay. The total will change to match your payment when you save the window.

When the transaction is posted to the general ledger, the amount of the payment is posted as a debit to the Accounts Payable account (the unpaid balance remains in the Accounts Payable account) and as a credit to your bank account.

Applying Discounts

Bills that have terms for discounts for timely payment display the Discount Date (in the Disc. Date column). Bills that have no data in that column do not have discount terms.

Select the bill by clicking the check mark column, and the discount is automatically applied. You can see the amount in the Disc. Used column, and the Amt. To Pay column adjusts accordingly.

If the discount isn't applied automatically, check the date in the Due On Or Before field, which must be equal to or earlier than the discount date. (If it's too late, don't worry, take the discount anyway—see the next section "Taking Discounts After the Discount Date.")

If you're making a partial payment and want to adjust the discount, click the Set Discount button to open the Discount And Credits window, and enter the amount of the discount you want to take. Click Done, and when you return to the Pay Bills window, the discount is applied and the Amt. To Pay column has the correct amount.

Taking Discounts After the Discount Date

Many businesses fill in the discount amount even if the discount period has expired. The resulting payment, with the discount applied, is frequently accepted by the vendor. Businesses that practice this protocol learn which vendors will accept a discounted payment and which won't (most will). Seeing that the discount you took has been added back in the next statement you receive is a pretty good hint that you're not going to get away with it.

To take a discount after the discount date, use the same steps explained in the preceding section for applying a discount. When you click the Set Discount button to open the Discount And Credits window, the amount showing for the discount is zero. Enter the discount you would have been entitled to if you'd paid the bill in a timely fashion, and click Done.

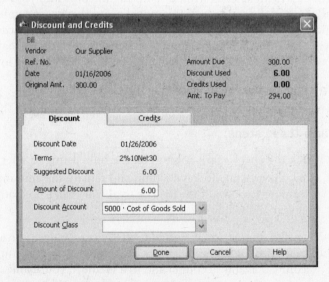

Understanding the Discount Account

Notice that the Discount tab of the Discount And Credits window has a field for the Discount Account. This account accepts the posting for the amount of the discount. If you don't have an account for discounts taken (not to be confused with the account for discounts given to your customers), you can create one now by clicking the arrow to the right of the field and choosing <Add New>.

The account for the discounts you take (sometimes called *earned discounts*) can be either an income or expense account. There's no right and wrong here, although I've seen accountants get into heated debates defending a point of view on this subject. If you think of the discount as income (money you've brought into your system by paying your bills promptly), make the account an income account. If you think of the discount as a reverse expense (money you've saved by paying your bills promptly), make the account an expense account (it posts as a minus amount, which means it reduces total expenses).

If the only vendors who offer discounts are those from whom you buy inventory items, you should put the discount account in the section of your chart of accounts that holds the Cost Of Goods Sold accounts. In fact, the most efficient way to do this is to have a parent account called Cost Of Goods Sold and then create two subaccounts:

- Cost Of Goods
- Discounts Taken

You'll be able to see the individual amounts on your financial reports, and the parent account will report the net COGS.

 TIP: QuickBooks may have created a Cost Of Goods Sold account automatically during your company setup. If not, create one and then create the subaccounts.

Here's what posts to your general ledger when you take a discount. For example, suppose the original amount of the bill was $484.00 and the discount was $9.68; therefore, the check amount was $474.32. (Remember that the original postings when you entered the bill were for the total amount without the discount.)

Account	Debit	Credit
Accounts Payable	$484.00	
Bank		$474.32
Discounts Taken		$9.68

Applying Credits

If the list of bills includes vendors for whom you have credits, you can apply the credits to the bill. Select the bill and, if credits exist for the vendor, the amount of the credit appears in the Credits Used column, and the Amt. To Pay column is adjusted.

If you don't want to take the credit against this bill, click Set Credits to open the Discount And Credits window. Make the appropriate changes and click Done to change the Amt. To Pay column to reflect your adjustments.

If your total credits with the vendor are equal to, or exceed, the bill you select, QuickBooks displays a message telling you no check will be created, because the bill is paid in its entirety with credits.

Saving the Pay Bills Information

There are two ways to save information about paying bills: save as you go or save at the end. You can select a bill, make adjustments (make a partial payment, apply a discount or a credit), and then click Pay & New to save that bill payment. That bill disappears from the list if it's paid in total and reappears with the balance owing if it's partially paid. You can also select each bill that appears in the Pay Bills window, making the appropriate adjustments. Then, when you're finished applying all the credits, discounts, and partial payments, click Pay & Close.

Regardless of the approach, when you're finished selecting the bills to pay, QuickBooks transfers all the information to the general ledger and fills out your checkbook account register (or credit card account register) with the payments. If you're paying bills online, QuickBooks retains the information until you go online.

After you've paid the bills in QuickBooks, the bills aren't really paid; your vendors won't consider them paid until they receive the checks. You can write manual checks or you can print checks.

When you click Pay & Close in the Pay Bills window, all the bills you paid are turned into checks (albeit unwritten checks). You can see those checks in the bank account register, as shown in Figure 7-3 (click the Register icon on the Icon Bar and select the bank account).

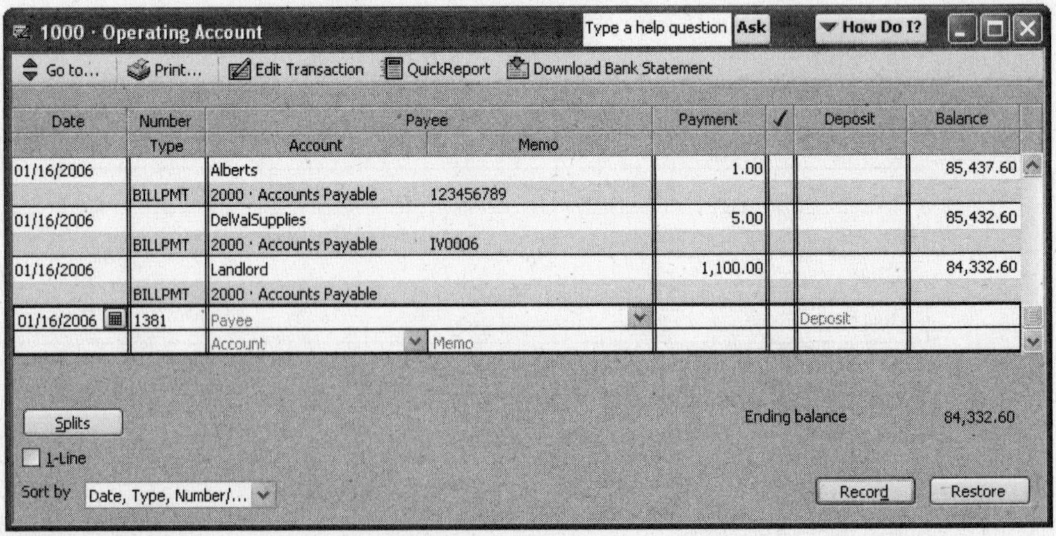

FIGURE 7-3   The checks that pay your bills have been posted to your bank account.

If you indicated in the Pay Bills window that you would be printing checks (by selecting the To Be Printed option), your bank account register displays To Print as the check number. See the upcoming section "Printing Checks."

If you selected the Assign Check No. option because you manually write checks, your bank account register uses the check number you specified in the Assign Check Numbers dialog.

Writing Manual Checks

If you're not printing checks, you must make sure the check numbers in the register are correct. In fact, it's a good idea to print the register and have it with you as you write the checks. To accomplish that, with the register open in the QuickBooks window, click the Print icon at the top of the register window. When the Print Register dialog opens, select the date range that encompasses these checks (usually, they're all dated the same day), and click OK to open the Print Lists dialog, where you can select print options before clicking Print to print. Then, as you write the checks, use the check numbers on the printout.

Printing Checks

Printing your checks is far easier and faster than using manual checks. Before you can print, however, you have some preliminary tasks to take care of. You have to purchase computer checks and set up your printer.

 C A U T I O N :   Lock the room that has the printer with the checks in it when you're not there.

Purchasing Computer Checks

Many vendors sell computer checks, and my own experience has been that there's not a lot of difference in pricing or the range of styles. Computer checks can be purchased for dot matrix printers (the check forms have sprocket holes) or for page printers (laser and inkjet). Investigate the prices and options at the following sources:

- Intuit, the company that makes QuickBooks, sells checks through its Internet marketplace, which you can reach at www.intuitmarket.com.
- Business form companies (there are several well-known national companies, such as Safeguard and NEBS).
- Office supply stores, such as Staples, Office Depot, and others.
- Some banks have a computer-check purchasing arrangement with suppliers; check with your bank.

Dot Matrix Printers for Checks

I use dot matrix printers for checks. I gain a few advantages with this method, and you might like to think about them:

- I never have to change paper when it's time to print checks. I never accidentally print a report on a check. I never accidentally print a check on plain paper.

- They're cheap. Not just cheap—they're frequently free. Gazillions of companies have upgraded to networks and can now share laser printers. As a result, all of those dot matrix printers that were attached to individual computers are sitting in storage bins in the basement. Ask around.

- They're cheap to run (you replace a ribbon every once in a while), and they last forever. I have clients using old printers (such as OKI 92s) that have been running constantly for about 15 years. And I mean constantly—dot matrix printers are great for warehouse pick slips and packing slips, and some of my clients pick and pack 24 hours a day, 7 days a week.

I have two checking accounts and still never have to change paper, because I have one of those dot matrix printers (an OKI 520) that holds two rolls of paper at the same time; one feeds from the back and the other from the bottom. I flip a lever to switch between checks.

I have clients who want the additional security of making copies of printed checks. You can buy multipart checks where the second page is marked "COPY" so nobody tries to use it as a check. Law firms, insurance companies, and other businesses that file a copy of a check appreciate multipart checks, which require a dot matrix printer.

Don't use a dot matrix printer that has a pull tractor for checks, because you'll have to throw away a check to get the print head positioned properly. Use a push-tractor printer.

If you purchase checks from any supplier except Intuit, you have to tell them you use QuickBooks. All check makers know about QuickBooks and offer a line of checks that are designed to work perfectly with the software.

Computer checks come in several varieties (and in a wide range of colors and designs). For QuickBooks, you can order any of the following check types:

- Plain checks
- Checks with stubs (QuickBooks prints information on the stub)
- Checks with special stubs for payroll information (current check and year-to-date information about wages and withholding)
- Wallet-sized checks

Setting Up the Printer

Before you print checks, you have to go through a setup routine. Take heart: you only have to do it once. After you select your configuration options, QuickBooks remembers them and prints your checks without asking you to reinvent the wheel each time.

Your printer needs to know about the type of check you're using, and you supply the information in the Printer Setup window. To get there, choose File | Printer Setup from the menu bar. Select Check/PayCheck as the form. Choose the printer name and type that match the printer you're using for checks. Your Printer Setup window should look similar to Figure 7-4.

Choosing a Check Style

You have to select a check style, and it has to match the check style you purchased, of course. Three styles are available for QuickBooks checks, and a sample of each style appears in the window to show you what the style looks like.

- **Standard checks**   These are just checks. They're the width of a regular business envelope (usually called a *#10 envelope*). If you have a laser printer, there are three checks to a page. A dot matrix pin-feed printer just keeps rolling, since the checks are printed on a continuous sheet with perforations separating the checks.

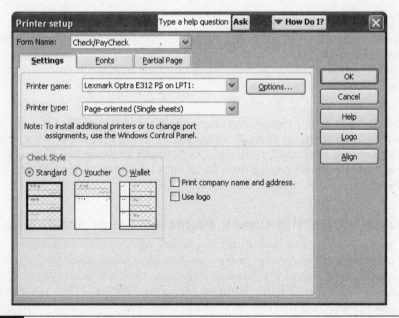

FIGURE 7-4   Set up your printer for check printing.

- **Voucher checks**   These have a detachable section on the check form. QuickBooks prints voucher information if you have voucher checks, including the name of the payee, the date, and the individual amounts of the bills being paid by this check. The voucher is attached to the bottom of the check. The check is the same width as the standard check.
- **Wallet checks**   These are narrower than the other two check styles (so they fit in your wallet). The paper size is the same as the other checks (otherwise, you'd have a problem with your printer), but there's a perforation on the left edge of the check, so you can tear off the check.

Adding a Logo

If your checks have no preprinted logo and you have a file of your company logo, select Use Logo or click the Logo button to open the Logo dialog. Click the File button to locate the graphics file, which must be a bitmapped graphic (the file extension is .bmp).

There's also a selection box for printing your company name and address, but when you buy checks, you should have that information preprinted.

 CAUTION: Dot matrix printers can't handle graphics printing, so don't bother choosing a logo if you're using a dot matrix printer for your checks.

Changing Fonts

Click the Fonts tab in the Printer Setup window to choose different fonts for the check information, such as the spelled-out amounts or the payee's address block. Click the appropriate button and then choose a font, a font style, and a size from the dialog that opens.

 CAUTION: Before you change fonts, make a note of the current settings. No Reset or Default button exists in the Fonts tab. If you make changes and they don't work properly, without knowing the original settings you'll have to mess around with fonts for a long time to get back to where you started.

Handling Partial Check Pages on Laser and Inkjet Printers

If you're printing to a laser or inkjet printer, you don't have the advantage that a pin-feed dot matrix printer provides—printing a check and stopping, leaving the next check waiting in the printer for the next time you print checks. QuickBooks has a nifty solution for this problem, found on the Partial Page tab (see Figure 7-5). Click the selection that matches your printer's capabilities.

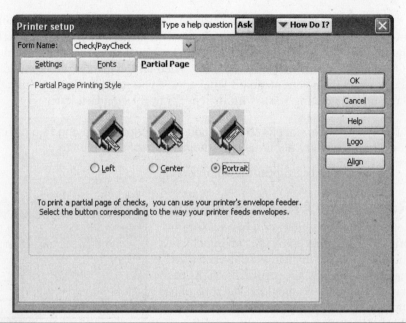

FIGURE 7-5   The Partial Page solution is based on the way your printer handles envelopes.

Printing the Checks

After your printer is configured for your checks, click OK in the Printer Setup window to save the configuration data. Now you can print your checks. Choose File | Print Forms | Checks from the menu bar to bring up the Select Checks To Print window.

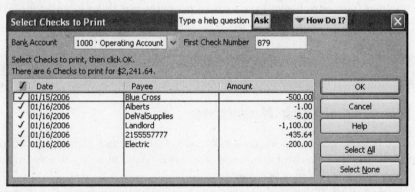

By default, all the unprinted checks are selected for printing. The first time you print checks, the first check number is 1; just replace that number with the first check number in the printer. When everything is correct, click OK to open the Print Checks window.

If you're not using a dot matrix printer, QuickBooks asks how many checks are on the first page (in case you have a page with a check or two remaining). Fill in the number and place the page with leftover blank checks in the manual feed tray (QuickBooks prints those checks first). Then let the printer pull the remaining check pages from your standard letter tray. If you indicate there are three checks on the page, printing starts with the checks in the standard letter tray.

 TIP: Voucher checks for laser and inkjet printers are one to a page, so you don't have to worry about using remaining checks on a page.

Click Print to begin printing your checks.

Reprinting After a Problem

Sometimes things go awry when you're printing. The paper jams, you run out of toner, the ribbon has no ink left, the dog chews the paper as it emerges, the paper falls off the back tray and lands in the shredder—all sorts of bad things can occur. QuickBooks knows this and checks the print run before it finalizes the printing process.

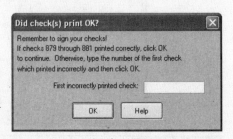

If everything is fine, click OK. If anything untoward happened, enter the number of the first check that is messed up. Put more checks into the printer (unless you're using a dot matrix printer, in which case you don't have to do anything). Then click OK and choose File | Print Forms | Checks. Your unprinted checks are listed in the Select Checks To Print dialog, and the first check number is the next available check number.

After your checks have printed properly, put them in envelopes, stamp them, and mail them. *Now* you can say your bills are paid.

➡ FYI

Missing Check Numbers

If you have to restart the print run with the next available check number, QuickBooks does not track the number(s) of the checks that were misprinted. Those numbers are missing from your bank register, and that's sloppy bookkeeping.

Unfortunately, QuickBooks (unlike all other accounting software I've worked with) has no automatic, easy method for voiding checks. In other accounting software, if you enter a check number with a zero amount, without filling out any other data, the software figures out what you're doing and displays a message asking if this is a void check. Clicking Yes records the check in the account register with a zero amount, and the text VOID is in the memo field (or some other field, depending on the accounting software).

▶▶ FYI

This is useful for tracking check numbers for checks that aren't used, which means not only checks that failed to print, but checks you send as samples either when you buy checks or when you're setting up electronic fund transfers, checks that accidentally fell into the shredder, or checks your dog ate. (When you send sample checks, be sure to write the word VOID across the check.)

In QuickBooks, you must enter the check number, a payee, and the amount (0.00), and post the transaction to some account. Then right-click the transaction line, choose Void, and then choose Record.

This means you have to reconstruct the print run to enter the right payee or account, which is a pain. Of course, since the check is void, you could select any payee and any account to speed up the process of entering the check. However, the void check carries the payee and account information permanently, and it appears on reports for the payee and the account. Consider inventing a vendor and an account for voiding checks.

Using Direct Disbursements

A *direct disbursement* is a disbursement of funds (usually by check) that is performed without matching the check to an existing bill. This is check writing without entering bills.

If you're not entering vendor bills, this is how you'll always pay your vendors. However, even if you are entering vendor bills, you sometimes need to write a quick check without going through the process of entering the vendor bill, selecting it, paying it, and printing the check—for example, when the UPS delivery person is standing in front of you waiting for a C.O.D. check and doesn't have time for you to go through all those steps.

Writing Direct Disbursement Manual Checks

If you use manual checks, you can write your checks and then tell QuickBooks about it later, or you can bring your checkbook to your computer and enter the checks in QuickBooks as you write them. You have two ways to enter your checks in QuickBooks: in the bank register or in the Write Checks window.

Using the Register

To use the bank register, open the bank account register with either of the following actions:

- Click the Check Register button on the Home page, and select your bank account.
- Select Banking | Use Register from the menu bar, and choose your bank account from the Select Account drop-down list.

When the account register opens, you can enter the check on a transaction line, as follows:

1 Enter the date.

2 Press the TAB key to move to the Number field. QuickBooks automatically fills in the next available check number.

3 Press TAB to move through the rest of the fields, filling in the name of the payee, the amount of the payment, and the expense account you're assigning to the transaction.

4 Click the Record button to save the transaction.

5 Repeat the steps for the next check and continue until all the manual checks you've written are entered into the register.

Using the Write Checks Window

If you prefer a graphical approach, you can use the Write Checks window to tell QuickBooks about a check you manually prepared. To get there, click the Write Checks icon on the Home page, or press CTRL-W. When the Write Checks window opens (see Figure 7-6), select the bank account you're using to write the checks.

The next available check number is already filled in unless the To Be Printed option box is checked (if it is, click it to toggle the check mark off and put the check number in the window). QuickBooks warns you if you enter a check number that's

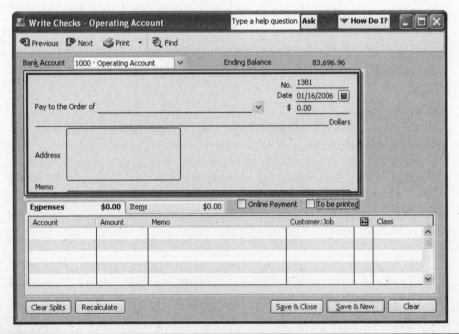

FIGURE 7-6   Fill out the onscreen check the same way you'd fill out a paper check—they look the same.

already been used (unfortunately, the warning doesn't appear until you've filled in all the data and attempt to save the check).

Fill out the check, posting amounts to the appropriate accounts. If the check is for inventory items, use the Items tab to make sure the items are placed into inventory. When you finish, click Save & New to open a new blank check. When you're through writing checks, click Save & Close to close the Write Checks window. All the checks you wrote are recorded in the bank account register.

Printing Direct Disbursement Checks

You can print checks immediately, whether you normally enter bills and print the checks by selecting bills to pay or you normally print checks as direct disbursements.

Printing a Single Check Quickly

If you normally enter vendor bills and then print checks to pay those bills, you can print a check for an expense that isn't entered in your accounts payable system. This is handy for writing a quick check.

Follow these steps to print a single check:

1. Click the Write Checks icon on the Home page, or press CTRL-W to open the Write Checks window. Make sure the To Be Printed option is selected.
2. Fill in the fields in the check and when everything is ready, click Print.
3. A small Print Check window opens to display the next available check number. Make sure that number agrees with the number of the check you're loading in the printer, and then click OK.
4. When the Print Checks window opens, follow the instructions for printing described earlier in this chapter.
5. When you return to the Write Checks window, click Save & New to write another quick check, or click Save & Close if you're finished printing checks.

Printing Direct Disbursement Checks in Batches

If you don't enter vendor bills but instead pay your bills as direct disbursements, you can print checks in a batch instead of one at a time. To do so, open the Write Checks window and make sure the To Be Printed option is selected.

Now follow these steps:

1. Fill out all the fields for the first check and click Save & New to move to the next blank Write Checks window.
2. Repeat step 1 for every check you need to print.
3. Print the checks using one of the following methods:
   - Click Save & Close when you are finished filling out all the checks, and then choose File | Print Forms | Checks from the menu bar.
   - In the last Write Checks window, click the arrow to the right of the Print button at the top of the Write Checks window, and choose Print Batch.

Postings for Direct Disbursements

The postings for direct disbursements are quite simple:

Account	Debit	Credit
Bank account		Total of all checks written
An expense account	Total of all checks assigned to this account	
Another expense account	Total of all checks assigned to this account	
Another expense account	Total of all checks assigned to this account	

Sending Sales Tax Checks and Reports

If you collect sales tax from your customers, you have an inherent accounts payable bill because you have to turn that money over to the state taxing authorities. The same thing is true for payroll withholdings.

In order to print reports on sales tax (so you can fill out those complicated government sales tax forms), you have to configure your sales tax collections in QuickBooks. If you collect multiple sales taxes, that configuration effort can be more complicated than the government forms.

While I will sometimes use the term "state" in the following sections, your tracking and reporting needs may not be limited to state-based activities. In recent years many states have created multiple sales tax authorities within the state (usually a specific location such as a county or a group of ZIP codes, each having its own tax rate). Businesses in those states may have to remit the sales tax they collect to both the state and the local sales tax authority (or to multiple local sales tax authorities). As a result, tracking sales tax properly (which means in a manner that makes it possible to fill out all the forms for all the authorities) has become a very complicated process.

I've received hundreds of messages asking for help from readers on this subject, mostly from readers in states that have made sales taxes more complicated. In the following sections I'll present a rather comprehensive discussion in an effort to cover these complicated scenarios. If your sales tax issues aren't at all complicated, you probably don't have to read the rest of this chapter.

Configuring Sales Tax Settings

If you collect and remit sales tax, you need to configure the sales tax features in QuickBooks. You must set up tax codes to link to your customers, so you know whether a customer is liable for sales tax. You must also set up tax items, so you can set a rate (a percentage rate) and link the item to a taxing authority.

Start your sales tax setup by choosing Edit | Preferences from the menu bar. Click the Sales Tax icon in the left pane and select the Company Preferences tab to see the window shown in Figure 7-7.

If you didn't enable the sales tax feature during the EasyStep Interview, do it now by selecting the Yes option in the section labeled Do You Charge Sales Tax? In the following sections I'll go over the other options in this dialog.

Sales Tax Payment Basis

There are two ways to remit sales tax to the taxing authorities, and they're listed in the Owe Sales Tax section of the Sales Tax Preferences dialog:

- **As Of Invoice Date**, which is accrual-based tax reporting.
- **Upon Receipt Of Payment**, which is cash-based tax reporting.

Check with your accountant (and the taxing authority law) to determine the method you need to select. You don't have a choice, and the options are unrelated to your own tax reporting status (accrual or cash). Each state has its own reporting rule.

Sales Tax Payment Dates

You must indicate the frequency of your remittance to the taxing authority in the Pay Sales Tax section of the Preferences dialog. You don't get to choose—your sales tax license indicates the schedule you must use. Many states base the frequency on

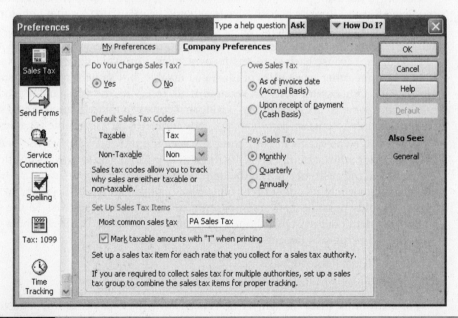

FIGURE 7-7   Be sure your sales tax specifications are correct, because QuickBooks goes on autopilot using these options.

the amount of tax you collect, usually looking at your returns for a specific period of time—perhaps one specific quarter—which is usually referred to as the *lookback* period. If your sales tax liability changes dramatically during the lookback period, you may receive notice from the state that your remittance interval has changed. (They'll probably send you new forms.) If that occurs, don't forget to return to the Preferences window to change the interval.

Default Sales Tax Codes

QuickBooks has two discrete entities for configuring sales tax: Tax Codes and Tax Items. Lots of people get them confused, so I'll attempt to clarify their definitions and use. Let's start with definitions:

- A *tax code* indicates tax liability, which means the entity to which it's linked (a customer or an item) is deemed to be taxable or nontaxable, depending on the code. In addition, if you take the trouble to do so, you can have tax codes that explain *why* an entity is taxable or nontaxable. Tax codes contain no information about the tax rate or the taxing authority (the payee for the check you write when you remit the sales tax you collected).

- *Tax items* contain information about the tax rate and the taxing authority to which you remit taxes and reports. Like all other items, they appear on sales forms, and the tax is calculated when you add the tax item to the taxable line items (products and services) on an invoice or sales receipt.

Linking a sales tax *code* to customers and items lets you (and the QuickBooks invoicing feature) know whether sales tax should be calculated for that item for this customer. If a customer is liable for sales tax, it doesn't mean that every item you sell the customer is taxable, because some items aren't taxable. I can't give you a list of categories, because each state sets its own rules. For example, in Pennsylvania, food and some other necessities of life aren't taxable, but some types of consulting services are. Other states don't tax services at all, reserving the sales tax for products. Some states seem to tax everything—California comes to mind. If an item is taxable, it's taxable only to customers whose tax code indicates they are liable for sales tax.

When you create items in your company file, you indicate whether the item is taxable under your state tax laws. If the item is taxable, the rate that's applied is connected to the customer, not to the item. Technically, a customer's sales tax liability is like a light switch; it's either on or off (techies call this scenario "Boolean," which means the only possible answers or definitions are On/Off or Yes/No). In the spirit of Boolean mathematics, QuickBooks prepopulates the Sales Tax Preferences dialog with the following two tax codes:

- **Tax**   Means liable for sales tax
- **Non**   Means not liable for sales tax

For many of us, that's enough; we don't need any additional tax codes for customers or for items. We can move on to creating tax items so their rates are calculated on sales forms. However, for some companies, those two tax codes aren't enough. State rules governing sales tax reports, and state reporting forms require more information.

For nontaxable customers, some states want to know why a nontaxable customer isn't charged sales tax. Is a customer nontaxable because it's out of state and the rules say you don't have to collect taxes for out-of-state sales? Is a customer nontaxable because it's a nonprofit organization? Is a customer nontaxable because it's a government agency? Is a customer nontaxable because it's a wholesale business and collects sales tax from its own customers? (The last definition may describe your business, and your suppliers have you configured as nontaxable.) If your state requires this information, you must create tax codes to match the reporting needs (covered in the next section "Creating Sales Tax Codes").

For taxable customers, you may want to use tax codes to specify customers as taxable in another state (if you collect taxes from out-of-state customers and remit those taxes to that state's taxing authority).

States that have instituted multiple tax rates depending on a customer's location want to know which location within the state the customer occupies, because that location determines the tax rate. Your reports on sales taxes have to subtotal your collections by location. In fact, in some states, you have to send individual sales tax reports to individual local tax authorities. If your state operates in this manner, you should solve this with tax items, not tax codes, because part of your configuration task is the tax rate (which isn't part of a tax code, it's only part of a tax item).

Creating Sales Tax Codes

If you want to create codes to track customer sales tax status in a manner more detailed than "taxable" and "nontaxable," follow these steps to add a new sales tax code:

1 Choose Lists | Sales Tax Code List.

2 Press CTRL-N to open the New Sales Tax Code window.

3 Enter the name of the new code, using up to three characters.

4 Enter a description to make it easier to interpret the code.

5 Select Taxable if you're entering a code to track taxable sales.

6 Select Non-taxable if you're entering a code to trace nontaxable sales.

7 Click Next to set up another tax code.

8 Click OK when you've finished adding tax codes.

This procedure works nicely for specifying different types of nontaxable customers. For example, you could create the following tax codes for nontaxable categories:

- NPO for nonprofit organizations
- GOV for government agencies
- WSL for wholesale businesses
- OOS for out-of-state customers (if you aren't required to collect taxes from out-of-state customers)

For taxable customers, the permutations and combinations are much broader, of course. If you're required to collect and remit sales tax for some additional states, just create codes for customers in those states, using the postal abbreviations for each state.

The problem is that QuickBooks' tax code setup doesn't work well for categorizing taxable customers if you do business in a state with complicated multiple tax rates. Those states issue codes that match the rules and rates (frequently location-based), and the codes are almost always more than three characters—but three characters is all QuickBooks permits for a sales tax code. The workaround for this is in the ability to assign a sales tax item to a customer, as long as the customer's configuration indicates "taxable" (using the built-in tax code or any taxable code you created). Sales tax items are discussed in the next section.

A larger problem is that sales tax codes don't contain any real information (such as tax rate or taxing authority), so they aren't used in reports that generate your sales tax liabilities. However, you can generate reports about tax codes and use that information in addition to the sales tax reports, if you have to send incredibly detailed reports to your taxing authorities. You can eschew the notion of creating additional tax codes for taxable and nontaxable categories and apply sales tax items to customers (see the following sections to understand that recommendation).

Sales Tax Items

A sales tax item is a collection of data about a sales tax, including the rate and the agency to which the sales tax is remitted. QuickBooks uses sales tax items to calculate the Tax field at the bottom of sales forms, and to prepare reports for tax authorities. The Sales Tax Preferences dialog has a section named Set Up Sales Tax Items, and you can create sales tax items here or in the Item List (see the section "Creating Sales Tax Items").

Most Common Sales Tax

The Sales Tax Preferences dialog has a field named Most Common Sales Tax, and you must enter a sales tax item in that field. Of course, to do that, you must first create at least one sales tax item. This item becomes the default sales tax item for any customers you create hereafter, but you can change any customer's default sales tax item.

Creating Sales Tax Items

You can create a sales tax item in either of the following ways:

- In the Sales Tax Preferences dialog, click the arrow next to the Most Common Sales Tax field and choose <Add New> from the drop-down list.
- Click the Item icon on the toolbar or choose Lists | Item List from the menu bar to open the Item List. Then Press CTRL-N.

Either action opens the New Item dialog.

Follow these steps to create the new sales tax item:

1. Select Sales Tax Item as the item type.
2. Enter a name for the item.
3. Enter a description to describe this sales tax on your transaction forms.
4. Enter the tax rate. QuickBooks knows the rate is a percentage, so it automatically adds the percent sign to the numbers you type (for instance, enter 6.5 if the rate is 6.5 percent).
5. Select the tax agency (which is a vendor) to whom you pay the tax from the drop-down list, or add a new vendor by choosing <Add New>.
6. Click OK.

Use the Name field to enter those complicated, pesky tax rate codes if you're in a state that has codes you couldn't use because of the three-character limitation of the tax code. In fact, if you'd created specific tax codes for multiple state rates, you'd still have to create these tax items in order to calculate rates and track the tax authorities.

Does this make you wonder why QuickBooks doesn't just use tax items and get rid of the tax codes altogether? It certainly makes me wonder, and it seems to me that it would be easy to do this, by adding a "Taxable?" field to the item, to put everything in one place. Then you'd only have to assign a tax item to each customer, instead of both a tax code and a tax item. On the other hand, QuickBooks could do it the other way around, making tax codes the container of rate and payee information, but they'd have to make the number of characters allowed greater than the current limit of three.

Assigning Codes and Items to Customers

By default, QuickBooks assigns the Tax (taxable) tax code to all customers, as well as the tax item you specify as the default in the Sales Tax Preferences dialog. These fields are on the Additional Info tab of the customer's record, and you can edit each customer's record to make changes to either field. Most of the time, it's the default tax item (not the tax code) for a customer that requires changing, especially if you're in a state that bases tax rates (and perhaps taxing authorities) on the delivery location for customers.

If you already created a great many customers, opening each record to make changes can be onerous, and you might want to wait until you use a customer in a sales transaction. Then, in the transaction window, select a new tax code or tax item (or both) from the drop-down list in the appropriate field. When you save the transaction, QuickBooks cooperates with this approach by asking you if you want to change the customer's tax information permanently. The customer record changes, and hereafter the new tax information appears in any transaction window for this customer.

Creating Tax Groups

In some states, the tax imposed is really two taxes, and the taxing authority collects a single check from you but insists on a breakdown in the reports you send. For example, in Pennsylvania, the state sales tax is 6 percent, but businesses in Philadelphia and Pittsburgh must charge an extra 1 percent. The customer pays 7 percent, a check for 7 percent of taxable sales is remitted to the state's revenue department, but the report that accompanies the check must break down the remittance into the individual taxes—the total of the 6 percent tax, and the total of the 1 percent tax. In other states, the customer pays a single tax, but the portion of that tax that represents the basic state sales tax is remitted to the state, and the locally added tax is remitted to the local taxing authority.

The challenge is to display and calculate a single tax for the customer and report multiple taxes to the taxing authorities. Tax groups meet this challenge. A tax group is a single entity that appears on a sales transaction, but it is really multiple entities that have been totaled. QuickBooks creates the tax amount by calculating each of the multiple entries and displaying its total (the customer is being charged the "combo" rate). For example, in Pennsylvania, a Philadelphia business would use a tax group (totaling 7 percent) that includes the 6 percent state sales tax and the 1 percent Philadelphia sales tax.

To create a tax group, you must first create the individual tax items, and then use the following steps to create the group item:

1. Open the Item List by clicking the Item icon on the toolbar, or by choosing Lists | Item List.
2. Press CTRL-N to open the New Item dialog.
3. Select Sales Tax Group as the Type.
4. Enter a name for the group.
5. Enter a description (which appears on your sales forms).
6. In the Tax Item column, choose the individual tax code items you need to create this group. As you move to the next item, QuickBooks fills in the rate, tax agency, and description of each tax you already selected. The calculated total (the group rate) appears at the bottom of the dialog (see Figure 7-8).
7. When you've added all the required tax code items, click OK.

Select this item for the appropriate customers when you're creating sales transactions. QuickBooks will offer to replace the current tax item for the customer (if a different tax item exists) with the new tax group.

Running Sales Tax Reports

At some interval determined by your taxing authority, you need to report your total sales, your nontaxable sales, and your taxable sales, along with any other required breakdowns. Oh, yes, you also have to write a check to remit the taxes.

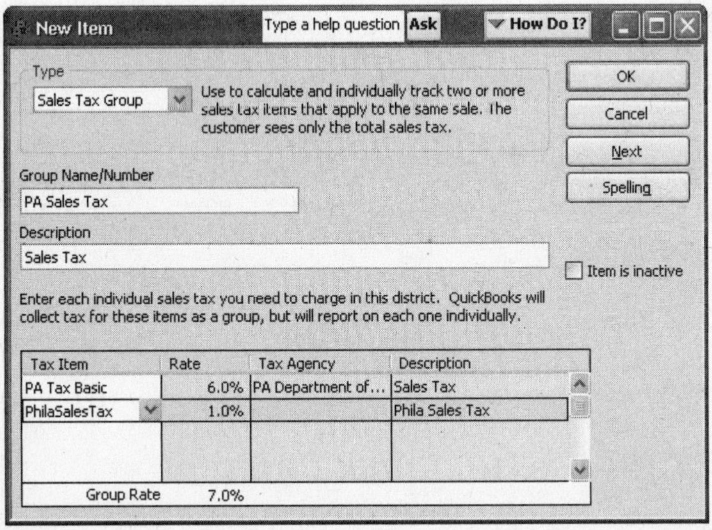

FIGURE 7-8   Create a Sales Tax Group to apply two taxes to transactions.

Sales Tax Liability Report

QuickBooks has reports to help you fill out your sales tax forms. Choose Reports | Vendors & Payables | Sales Tax Liability. Use the Dates drop-down list to select an interval that matches the way you report to the taxing authorities. By default, QuickBooks chooses the interval you configured in the Preferences dialog, but that interval may only apply to your primary sales tax. If you collect multiple taxes, due at different intervals, you must create a separate report with the appropriate interval to display those figures. Figure 7-9 shows a Sales Tax Liability report for a monthly filer.

Tax Code Reports

If you have to report specific types of taxable or nontaxable sales, you can obtain that information by creating a report on the tax code you created to track that information. Choose Lists | Sales Tax Code List and select (highlight) the tax code for which you need a report. Press CTRL-Q to see a report on the sales activity with this tax code (see Figure 7-10). Change the date range to match your reporting interval with the sales tax authority (this isn't a sales tax report, so QuickBooks doesn't automatically match the settings in the Sales Tax Preferences dialog).

You don't have to create these reports one code at a time; you can modify the report window so it reports all of your tax codes, or just those you need for a specific tax authority's report. In fact, you can modify the report so it reports totals instead of every sales transaction.

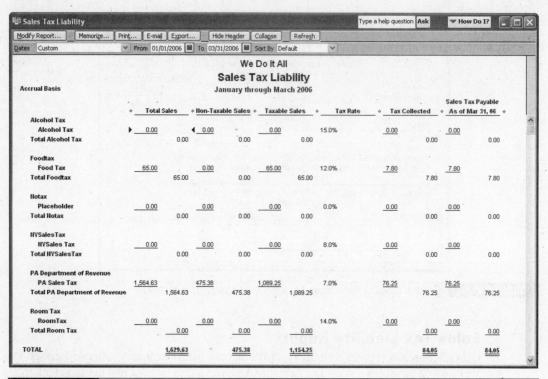

FIGURE 7-9   The Sales Tax Liability report displays taxable and nontaxable sales for each tax code.

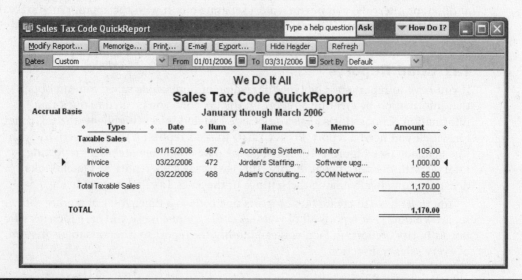

FIGURE 7-10   It's easy to get an activity report on any tax code.

Use the following steps to modify this report:

❶ Click the Modify Report button on the report window.

❷ In the Display tab, use the Columns list to deselect any items you don't require for the report (for example, the Type, Date, and Number of an invoice/sales receipt, and the contents of the Memo field).

❸ In the Filters tab, choose Sales Tax Code from the filter list.

❹ Click the arrow to the right of the Sales Tax Code field and select the appropriate option from the drop-down list, using the following guidelines:

- All Sales Tax Codes, which displays total activity for the period for every code.
- Multiple Sales Tax Codes, which opens the Select Sales Tax Code window, listing all codes, so you can select the specific codes you want to report on.
- All Taxable Codes, which displays total activity for the period for each taxable code.
- All Nontaxable Codes, which displays total activity for the period for each nontaxable code.

❺ Click OK to return to the report window, where your selections are reflected.

❻ Unless you want to take all these steps again when you need this report, click the Memorize button to memorize the report.

Remitting the Sales Tax

After you check the figures (or calculate them, if you have multiple reports with different standards of calculation), it's time to pay the tax.

Follow these steps:

❶ Choose Vendors | Sales Tax | Pay Sales Tax, to open the Pay Sales Tax window.

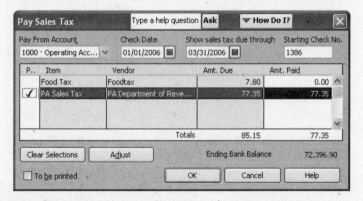

❷ Select the bank account to use if you have more than one.

❸ Check the date that's displayed in the field named Show Sales Tax Due Through. It must match the end date of your current reporting period (for instance, monthly or quarterly).

④ Click in the Pay column to insert a check mark next to those you're paying now. If you're lucky enough to have the same reporting interval for all taxing authorities—it never seems to work that way, though—just click the Pay All Tax button (the name of which then changes to Clear Selections).

⑤ If you're going to print the check, be sure to select the To Be Printed check box at the bottom of the dialog. If you write the check manually, or if you remit sales tax online using an electronic transfer from your bank, deselect the To Be Printed check box. (For electronic payment, open the bank account register and change the check number QuickBooks inserted automatically to ACH or another code indicating an electronic transfer.)

⑥ Click OK when you've completed filling out the information. The next time you print or write checks, the sales tax check is in the group waiting to be completed.

NOTE: QuickBooks doesn't ask for a start date because it uses the period duration defined in your Sales Tax Preferences.

Adjusting Sales Tax Amounts

If you need to adjust the amount of sales tax due (most states offer a discount for timely payment), select the appropriate sales tax item and click the Adjust button to open the Sales Tax Adjustment dialog.

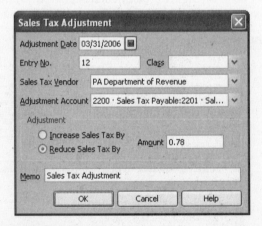

Specify the amount by which to reduce (or increase, if you're late and paying a penalty) the tax amount. Specify an Adjustment Account (you can create a specific account for this adjustment), and click OK to return to the Pay Sales Tax window, where the amount has been changed to reflect your adjustment.

➡ FYI

Sales Tax vs. Use Tax

If you have customers in a state other than the state in which you do business, you might be able to use another approach to sales tax. Technically, some states call this tax a Sales and Use tax, where the "use" part of the name means that the customer is responsible for remitting the tax.

If the state permits it, you can skip the sales tax charge (and therefore skip the need to fill out forms and remit payments) and leave it up to the out-of-state customer. The customer has to tell his or her state taxing authority that he or she purchased taxable goods from an out-of-state vendor (that's you) and remit the appropriate amount.

Businesses that take advantage of this approach usually print a message on the invoice that says, "Sales taxes for this purchase are not collected by us and are your responsibility," or something to that effect. The truth is, you have no legal obligation to warn the customer if the out-of-state taxing authority is willing to let you skip sales tax collections, but it's a nice thing to do.

Running Payroll

In this chapter:

- Choose a payroll service

- Set up payroll

- Check tax status, deductions, and other employee information

- Enter historical data

- Write payroll checks

If you plan to do your own payroll rather than employ a payroll service, the information you need to set up and run payroll is covered in this chapter.

QuickBooks Do-it-yourself Payroll Services

QuickBooks offers a variety of do-it-yourself payroll services, and if you want to do your payroll in-house, here's a brief overview of the offerings:

- Standard payroll, which provides tax tables, automatic calculations of paycheck deductions and employer expenses, and automatic creation of federal forms (941, W-2, and so on).
- Enhanced payroll, which adds state-based functions (such as workers compensation).
- Assisted payroll, which lets you run payroll in the standard or enhanced mode, and then turns the job of depositing withholdings, paying employer contributions, and printing government forms over to QuickBooks.

Additional plans are available based on the standard and enhanced payroll offerings, such as an Enhanced Accountants' service, which lets you prepare payroll for up to 50 companies.

Unless you've signed up for QuickBooks payroll services, no calculations occur against the gross amount of the paycheck. No withholding appears, no amounts are posted to employee and employer liability accounts, and there is no net amount. You can, if you wish, use your own printed tax table (Employer's Circular E from the IRS), calculate the deductions manually, and then issue a paycheck for the net amount to each employee. If you don't want to face that, you must sign up for payroll services.

With any of the payroll services, you can purchase direct deposit services for your employees. Employees must sign a form giving permission for direct deposit, and you can print those forms directly from your QuickBooks software (QuickBooks provides a link to display and print the forms during the sign-up process). Employees can opt to deposit their entire paychecks into one bank account or split the amount between two bank accounts.

 N O T E :   QuickBooks also provides an outsourced payroll solution (similar to those offered by ADP, Paychex, and other well-known payroll services).

To learn about the QuickBooks payroll offerings, or to sign up, choose Employees | Add Payroll Service. From the submenu, choose either Learn About Payroll Options, or Order Payroll Service (both menu choices produce the same result). QuickBooks opens its internal browser and takes you to the Payroll Services web site (see Figure 8-1).

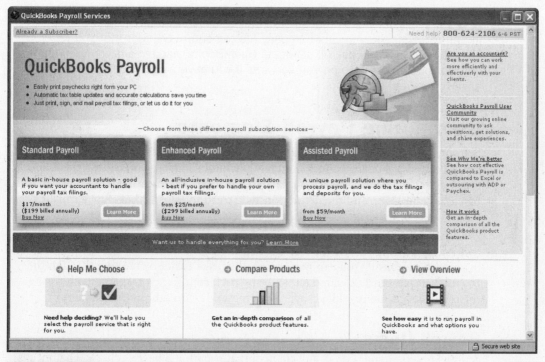

Signing Up for Payroll Services

After you've used the links on the Payroll Services web site to learn about all the payroll offerings, click the Buy Now link for the Payroll Service you want.

A wizard walks you through the enrollment process. You must enter information about your company and provide a credit card number. If you want to sign up for direct deposit, you also need your bank's routing number and your bank account number. Follow the prompts in the ensuing windows, filling in information as required.

When the sign-up process is completed, QuickBooks downloads the files you need to run payroll. The new files are automatically added to your QuickBooks system; you don't have to do anything to install them. In addition to the payroll software, the current tax table is added to your system. After payroll is installed, your Employees menu has all the commands you need to run payroll.

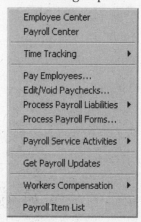

NOTE: During the process of installing the payroll files, QuickBooks installs a service key in your company file to confirm the fact that you've enrolled in one of the payroll services. QuickBooks also e-mails your service key, so you can activate payroll services if you have a computer disaster and have to reinstall QuickBooks.

Configuring Payroll Elements

Before you run the first payroll, all your setup tasks must be completed. You can't produce accurate payroll checks unless QuickBooks knows everything there is to know about the payroll taxes you have to withhold, the payroll taxes you have to pay as an employer, and the deductions you need to take for benefits, garnishes, union dues, or any other reason. And, of course, you need to configure each employee for dependents and deductions.

In the following sections, I'll go over all the elements and components involved in setting up payroll. You can perform all the tasks either by moving through the Payroll Setup wizard (covered later), or by performing each task manually, using the QuickBooks menus. I'll go over both methods throughout this chapter.

Payroll Items

A QuickBooks *payroll item* is any element that is part of a payroll check. That means the elements that go into determining the gross amount of the payroll check (salary, wages, bonuses, and commissions), as well as the elements that determine the net amount of the payroll check (withheld taxes, deductions for benefits, and any other deductions). Additionally, if you have expenses that are attached to payroll, such as company-paid benefits that don't deduct amounts from employee paychecks, those have to be set up as payroll items, too.

QuickBooks creates some payroll items during your EasyStep Interview, if you indicate you'll be using payroll, but you'll probably have to create additional items. Each item you create has to be linked to an account in your chart of accounts. And because all the money you withhold or pay out as a company expense is turned over to somebody else (the government, an insurance company, or a pension administrator), you must have vendors associated with each deduction.

Chapter 2 has directions for setting up payroll items, if you want to perform this task manually. On the other hand, you can use the QuickBooks Payroll Setup wizard.

Employee Information

The information about your employees must be perfectly, pristinely accurate, or you may hear about it in a very unfriendly manner. Your employees won't be happy if the deductions are incorrect; the IRS won't be happy if your payroll records don't accurately reflect employee tax status categories.

Chapter 2 covers the procedure for adding employees to your company records manually, or you can use the QuickBooks Payroll Setup wizard.

Vendors

The money you withhold from paychecks, and the money your business owes for employer expenses, must be sent to the appropriate vendors. You should make sure those vendors are in your system before setting up payroll items.

For withholding of federal taxes, medicare, FICA, and the matching employer medicare and FICA payments, your vendor depends on the way you transmit the funds. If you use electronic transfer of funds, the vendor is the United States Treasury Department. If you use coupons, the vendor is your bank.

For local and state income tax, unemployment, disability, and workers comp, enter a vendor for each agency to which checks are remitted. Read Chapter 2 to learn how to add vendors to your company file.

Chart of Accounts

Your chart of accounts must contain the accounts required for payroll. At the very least you need the following accounts:

- A bank account for writing payroll checks or transferring direct deposit funds (many businesses maintain a separate payroll account)
- A payroll liabilities account to track the money you withhold from paychecks
- A payroll expense account to track employer expenses

QuickBooks automatically adds the payroll liabilities and employer payroll expense accounts when you enable payroll in your company file (either during the EasyStep Interview or in the Preferences dialog).

You can use one liability account and one expense account to hold all the postings, or create separate accounts for each type of liability/expense. I prefer the latter approach, and have created separate liability and expense accounts for each payroll item. I can tell at a glance whether I'm up-to-date on remitting payments by seeing if any of the accounts have a balance (some payments are due monthly and some quarterly).

Name		Type	Balance Total
◇2100 · Payroll Liabilities		Other Current Liability	0.00
◇2110 · FWT		Other Current Liability	0.00
◇2120 · FICA Withheld		Other Current Liability	0.00
◇2130 · Medicare Withheld		Other Current Liability	0.00
◇2140 · PA Income Tax Withheld		Other Current Liability	0.00
◇2150 · Phila Wage Tax		Other Current Liability	0.00
◇2190 · Blue Cross		Other Current Liability	0.00
◇2200 · Sales Tax Payable		Other Current Liability	139.68
◇2600 · Credits owed for Discounts		Other Current Liability	-20.25

Entering Historical Data

If you're not starting your use of QuickBooks at the very beginning of the year, you must enter all the historical information about paychecks. This is the only way to perform all those tasks required at the end of the year. You cannot give your employees two W-2 forms, one from your manual system and another from QuickBooks, nor can you file your annual tax reports on any piecemeal basis.

No matter what your fiscal year is, your payroll year is the calendar year. Even though you can start using payroll for the current period before you enter the historical data, remember that the absence of historical data may affect some tax calculations. If there are withholding amounts that cease after a certain maximum (perhaps your state only requires SUI for the first $8,000.00 in gross payroll), you'll have to adjust the deductions on the current paychecks manually. If the historical data is entered, QuickBooks can calculate the maximum deduction properly and stop deducting these amounts.

 TIP: To avoid a lot of data entry, go live with payroll at the beginning of a calendar quarter.

Understanding Historical Data

The historical data is the payroll you issued before the date on which you let QuickBooks take over your payroll chores (which is called the *go live date*). Starting with the go live date, you'll be entering payroll checks in QuickBooks; those checks are not part of the historical data. It's important to understand how the go live date affects the task of entering historical data, so here are some guidelines:

- Payroll records are summarized quarterly, because your 941 reports are due quarterly.
- You can't enter summarized data for the quarter that's current (the quarter that the go live date falls in). Instead, for the current quarter, you must enter data for each individual pay period (weekly, biweekly, semimonthly, or monthly). For previous quarters, you can enter quarterly totals.
- If your go live date is any date in the first quarter, you have to enter historical data for each pay period, because you don't have a full quarter to summarize.
- If your go live date is in the second quarter, enter a quarterly total for the first quarter and then enter the individual pay period numbers for the second quarter, up to the go live date.
- If your go live date is in the third quarter, enter quarterly totals for the first two quarters and then enter each pay period up to the go live date.
- If your go live date is in the fourth quarter, you can follow the same pattern, but it might be just as easy to wait until next year to begin using QuickBooks payroll.

Entering the History Manually

The truth is, payroll is so easy to do if everything is set up properly that I usually advise clients to enter each historical payroll run individually. It's great training. For the first couple of pay periods, stop to look at the details (the postings to general ledger accounts) after you enter historical totals, and compare them to your manual records. This gives you an opportunity to understand what QuickBooks is doing, in addition to checking accuracy.

However, this is a lot of work, so you can enter the history in batches, using the QuickBooks Payroll Data Wizard (covered next), which walks you through the process using easy-to-understand wizard windows.

Using the QuickBooks Payroll Setup Wizard

QuickBooks provides assistance for setting up payroll in the form of a wizard. You can use the wizard to set up all the components required for payroll, or set up your payroll items and employees manually, and then use the wizard to enter your historical data.

Regardless of whether you use the Payroll Setup Wizard to set up all your components or to enter historical data only, set up all the vendors you need to remit payroll withholding and employer payroll expenses before using the wizard.

To use the wizard, choose Employees | Payroll Service Activities | Payroll Setup from the QuickBooks menu bar. The wizard window opens with all the tasks listed in the left pane (see Figure 8-2).

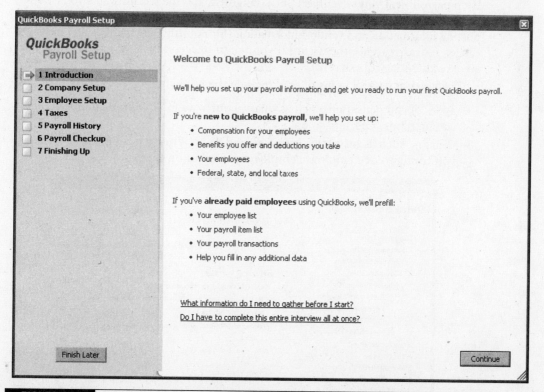

QuickBooks Payroll Setup

QuickBooks
Payroll Setup

1 Introduction
2 Company Setup
3 Employee Setup
4 Taxes
5 Payroll History
6 Payroll Checkup
7 Finishing Up

Welcome to QuickBooks Payroll Setup

We'll help you set up your payroll information and get you ready to run your first QuickBooks payroll.

If you're **new to QuickBooks payroll**, we'll help you set up:

- Compensation for your employees
- Benefits you offer and deductions you take
- Your employees
- Federal, state, and local taxes

If you've **already paid employees** using QuickBooks, we'll prefill:

- Your employee list
- Your payroll item list
- Your payroll transactions
- Help you fill in any additional data

What information do I need to gather before I start?

Do I have to complete this entire interview all at once?

Finish Later   Continue

FIGURE 8-2   The Payroll Setup Wizard is divided into logical sets of tasks.

If you're using the wizard to set up your payroll from scratch (you didn't preconfigure any of the components), the setup process can take as much time as it takes to perform those tasks manually. Luckily, the wizard has a Finish Later button, which you can click if you have to do other work, get tired, or get bored. When you open the wizard again, you pick up where you left off.

 N O T E :   The Payroll Setup Wizard for QuickBooks 2006 is new, replacing the wizard that was available in previous versions of QuickBooks. The new wizard is easier to use, explains each step clearly, and is an effective, uncomplicated way to set up payroll. In fact, it's actually a pleasure to use.

The first few screens are informational, explaining the information you need to complete the wizard (the same information about employees, payroll items, deductions, etc., discussed earlier in this chapter). The real work starts with Section 2, where the wizard asks about your payroll start date. If you select the current calendar year, you're asked whether you've already begun issuing paychecks in this calendar year. If you have, you'll enter the historical information when you get to Section 5.

Setting Up Payroll Items in the Wizard

In the Company Setup section, the wizard also covers all the possible payroll items. Each payroll item you select has to be configured, and the wizard walks you through the configuration process with easy-to-follow instructions. The configuration includes posting information and vendor information (for remitting payments). As I indicated earlier, it's easier to use the wizard if your chart of accounts and vendor information are already set up for payroll.

The types of payroll items offered include the following:

- Types of compensation, such as salary, hourly wages, overtime, bonuses, commissions, tips, and so on.
- Benefits, such as insurance, pension, and so on. For each benefit you select, you configure the employee/employer contribution rates.

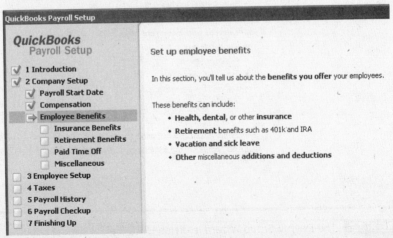

- Paid time off, such as sick leave and vacations. You can configure your formulas for calculating vacation time and sick time, if you let employees accrue time according to time worked.
- Other additions and deductions, such as workers comp, auto expense reimbursement, garnishments, union dues, charitable contributions, and so on.

Setting Up Employees in the Wizard

In Section 3, the wizard moves on to the task of setting up employees.

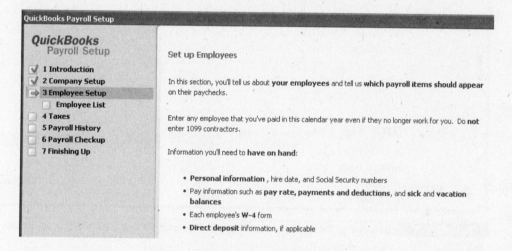

If you didn't set up your employees manually (using the instructions in Chapter 2), you can add each employee in the wizard, moving through a series of windows in which you enter information about the employee's personal information, pay structure, and tax status. For each employee, you designate the taxes and benefits that affect the employee.

When you finish entering your employee information, the wizard displays the list of employees. If any employee is missing information, the wizard indicates the problem, as seen in Figure 8-3. If you entered your employees manually, the wizard automatically finds the employee records and displays the same list.

Some missing information isn't critical to issuing paychecks (for example, the hire date, which is required information in the employee record). If any employee in the list has the notation Fix This Error Now, it means critical information is missing, and the system either won't be able to issue a paycheck or won't be able to issue a W-2 form at the end of the year. Regardless of whether the missing information is critical or not, select the employee and click Edit to fix the problem.

You can also select an employee and click Summary to see all the information in the employee's record.

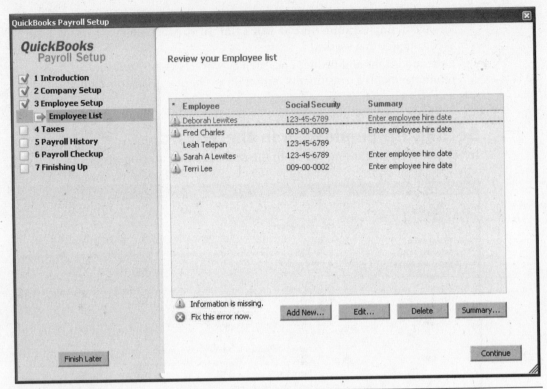

FIGURE 8-3   Supply any information you neglected to enter when you configured employees.

Setting Up Payroll Taxes in the Wizard

In Section 4, you tell the wizard about the federal, state, and local taxes you're responsible for. These are payroll items, so if you haven't set up all these items beforehand, you can use the wizard.

If you're setting up your taxes in the wizard, as you finish each section, the wizard displays a list of all the taxes for that section. If you set up your taxes as payroll items manually, the wizard finds those entries and uses them to populate the list.

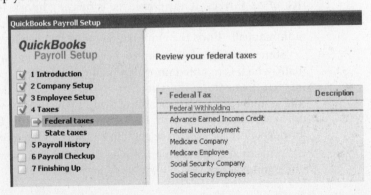

If the wizard finds anything amiss in your setup, the problem is displayed in the Description column. The same type of list, along with the enumeration of any problems, is displayed for your state and local taxes.

Entering Payroll History in the Wizard

In Section 5, you enter your historical payroll data. The wizard presents a set of windows for each employee. The first window asks about the last paycheck you issued (outside of QuickBooks, of course). Using your go live date, the wizard arranges the dates appropriately. For example, if your go live date is the first week of August, the wizard will ask you for data about the first and second quarter totals, and then the pay periods for July. The data entry starts with earnings information.

The wizard then walks through all the withholdings for all the payroll items assigned to each employee.

In the ensuing windows, you'll enter the batch totals for employer contributions and other employer payments (which depend on the benefits you offer, and the state or local municipality in which your business operates).

When you finish entering the batch totals for completed quarters, the wizard asks for the financial information about the paychecks in the current quarter, up to the go live date. If you are performing this task in the second month of the current quarter, the wizard asks for batch information for the first month of the quarter, and then individual paycheck information for the current month.

After the paycheck data is entered, the wizard walks you through the process of entering employer payments (withholding remittances, employer taxes, payments to pension and benefit plans, and so on).

Payroll Checkup

Step 6 is the QuickBooks Payroll Checkup, which you can run whenever you make changes to your payroll components (employees, taxes, etc.) by choosing Employees | Payroll Service Activities | Payroll Checkup. At this point, the wizard automatically launches that program.

Each section of the wizard's task list is checked for errors. The errors the checkup may find include missing information, invalid information (the format of an EIN number or state reporting number may be incorrect), or any other data that doesn't match the standards built into the QuickBooks payroll feature.

The program displays a report on the integrity of the data for prior quarters (unless you're working in the first quarter, of course), and then, separately, the integrity of the data for the current quarter.

Then, the program asks you about the federal and state forms you've filed to remit withholdings and pay employer taxes. After you've filled in the information, the program reconciles the totals against the payroll totals you entered previously. If there are errors, the specifics are displayed, and you can correct the problem and re-run the checkup.

Finishing Steps

After all the data in your payroll system is deemed accurate, the wizard takes care of the details required to use QuickBooks for your payroll from your go live date forward. The wizard asks about the frequency with which you must remit withholding and employer taxes for federal and state taxing authorities (and for local taxes if you configured them).

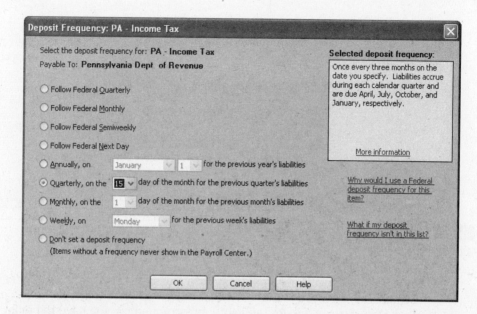

Having completed all the tasks, the wizard opens the Employee Center so you can begin issuing paychecks. If it's not payday, close the Employee Center and perform your other QuickBooks tasks.

Running Payroll

It's payday. All the historical data is entered. It's time to run the payroll. If you're using direct deposit services, you need a two-day lead before the actual payday. If only some of your employees use direct deposit, you have two choices:

- Do all your payroll data entry two days before payday and hold the printed checks until payday (date the checks appropriately).
- Run the payroll procedure twice using the appropriate employees for each run.

Selecting Employees to Pay

To begin, click the Pay Employees icon on the Home page, or choose Employees | Pay Employees from the menu bar. Either action opens the Select Employees To Pay dialog shown in Figure 8-4.

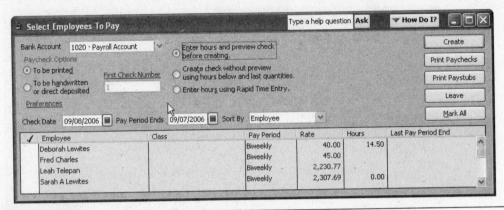

FIGURE 8-4   Select the employees who get a paycheck in this payroll run.

NOTE: QuickBooks may display a message telling you it's been quite some time since you last checked for payroll updates and offering to perform that task. Always accept the invitation so you know you have the most current tax information.

The first time you run payroll, there's no information about the last payroll check for each employee. After you've completed this payroll run, that information will be available:

- For salaried employees, the information usually remains the same so you can create the checks without previewing information about hours.
- For hourly wage employees, if the number of hours is the same as the last check, you can repeat checks as if the employee were on salary.

For this first payroll, however, you must check the details before printing payroll checks, using the following guidelines:

- Make sure the correct bank account is selected.
- Select the option Enter Hours And Preview Check Before Creating.
- Select the employees to be paid by clicking next to their names in the check-mark column. If all employees are included in this payroll run (they're all direct deposit or all printed checks), click the Mark All button.
- Specify the check date and the payroll period end date.

TIP: If you have a separate payroll account, be sure to go to Edit | Preferences and click the Checking icon. On the Company Preferences tab, select the default bank account for creating paychecks and the default bank account for paying payroll liabilities. This way, you won't accidentally use the wrong bank account when you're working in payroll.

Click Create to begin entering paycheck information.

Filling Out the Paycheck Information

The first employee's Preview Paycheck window opens (see Figure 8-5). If the employee is on an hourly wage, everything is blank until you fill in the Hours column. If the employee is salaried, the amounts are displayed.

Make any necessary corrections, such as adding a bonus or entering a one-time deduction. When everything is correct, click Create. The next employee's record appears so you can repeat the process. Continue to move through each employee, and when the last check is created you're returned to the original Select Employees To Pay window. Click Print Paychecks if you're ready to do that; otherwise, click Leave and print the paychecks later (printing is covered next).

Printing the Paychecks

When all the checks have been created, you must print the paychecks. Load the right checks in your printer (don't use your standard bank account checks if you have a separate payroll account).

To print checks, follow these steps:

1 Either click the Print Paychecks button in the Select Employees To Pay window, or choose File | Print Forms | Paychecks to open the Select Paychecks To Print window.

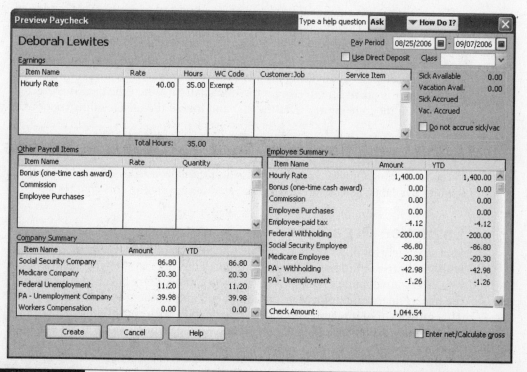

FIGURE 8-5 Enter any missing data for this paycheck.

2 Select the bank account for this paycheck print run.

3 Make sure the First Check Number field contains the correct number for the first check loaded in the printer.

4 Deselect any paycheck you don't want to print at this time by clicking in the check-mark column to remove the existing check mark.

5 If you have both paychecks and direct deposit stubs to print, select the appropriate option at the bottom of the dialog to display (and print) only those items. Then select the other option to print the remaining items.

6 Click OK when everything is configured properly.

The Print Checks window opens. Click Print to print the paychecks. QuickBooks displays a window in which you must confirm that everything printed properly or reprint any checks that had a problem. If everything is fine, click OK. If there's a problem, enter the number of the first check that had a problem and QuickBooks will reprint as necessary, starting with the next available check number.

Sending Direct Deposit Information

If you use direct deposit services, you still go through the payroll process for the employees who opted for this service. You just don't print the checks. Instead, you notify QuickBooks to deposit the checks.

To make the direct deposit, be sure you're connected to the Internet, and then choose Employees | Send Payroll Data from the QuickBooks menu bar (the menu item doesn't exist if you haven't signed up for direct-deposit services).

A window opens to display the data you're about to upload, and you must confirm its accuracy. If anything is amiss, cancel the procedure and return to the Pay Employees procedure to correct the information. When the data is correct, click Go Online to begin the data transfer and follow the onscreen instructions.

Additional Features for Enterprise Solutions

If you're running QuickBooks Enterprise Solutions, you have some additional features available, above and beyond the features covered in this chapter.

Employee Organizer

Sold separately for other versions of QuickBooks, the Employee Organizer comes with Enterprise Solutions, and takes the worry out of even the most complex human resources and compliance tasks. Use Employee Organizer to streamline the management of employee information, and employment laws and regulations. This software tool integrates employee information with payroll information in QuickBooks, making it easy to access, update, and generate reports about employee information.

Stay on Top of Employment Regulations

Employee Organizer includes an Employment Regulations Update Service, which gives you access to current federal and state employment laws and regulations.

Employment-related Processes Are Easier

Employee Organizer provides guidance as you wend your way through employment-related processes. Make sure your processes are always consistent by using the Employee Organizer's step-by-step guidelines for the following processes:

- Recruiting
- Interviewing
- Hiring
- Raises
- Promotions
- Termination
- Leaves of absence

Forms and Templates with a Click of a Mouse

Employee Organizer includes federal and state government forms, as well as a selection of templates for letters, other employment-related documents, and employee management forms, including the following:

- INS Form I-9
- COBRA notification
- Federal Form W-4
- Independent Contractor Agreement
- Job Descriptions Form
- Reference Check Form
- Driving Record Check Form

Expert Help and Advice

Send specific employment questions by e-mail. You'll receive answers including the text of relevant government policies, laws, and regulations on average within two business days. Answers are provided by CCH Incorporated, a leading provider of tax and business law information since 1913.

Government Payroll Reporting

In *this chapter:*

- Make tax deposits

- Prepare quarterly and annual returns

- Print W-2 forms

Doing payroll in-house means having a lot of reports to print, forms to fill out, and checks to write. There's a logical order to these tasks, although the logic differs depending on the state and city (or town) you're in. In this chapter, I'll go over the procedures in the order in which most businesses have to perform the tasks.

If you've signed up for QuickBooks Assisted Payroll services, you don't have to worry about the sections in this chapter that are concerned with remitting federal and state withholdings (except entering them as a journal entry). You do, however, have to remit your local payroll tax withholding yourself.

Making Federal Payroll Tax Deposits

The federal government requires you to deposit the withholding amounts, along with the matching employer contributions, at a specified time. That time period is dependent upon the size of the total withholding amount you've accumulated. You may be required to deposit monthly, semimonthly, weekly, or within three days of the payroll. Check the current limits with the IRS or your accountant.

There's a formula for determining the size of the deposit check—it is the sum of the following amounts for the period:

- Federal withholding
- FICA withholding
- Medicare withholding
- FICA matching contribution from employer
- Medicare matching contribution from employer

You don't have to do the math—QuickBooks does it for you. But it's a good idea to know what the formula is so you can check the numbers yourself.

Select the Liabilities for the Federal Deposit Check

To create the liabilities payment for your federal deposit, follow these steps:

1. Click the Pay Liabilities icon in the Employees section of the Home page, or choose Employees | Process Payroll Liabilities | Pay Payroll Liabilities from the QuickBooks menu bar.
2. Select the Date Range for which you're remitting liabilities.
3. Select or deselect the To Be Printed option (depending on whether you print checks).
4. Select the bank account, if you have more than one bank account.
5. Enter the check date.
6. Specify whether you want to create the check without reviewing it, or review the check before finalizing it (you don't usually need to review the check, unless you're adding penalties or changing the amount for some other reason).
7. Click the federal payments in the check-mark column to select them. Notice that when you choose Medicare or Social Security, selecting the employee

liability automatically selects the company liability (or vice versa). This is, of course, because you must pay the total of withholding and employer contributions at the same time.

8 Click Create when you've selected the liability payments you want to pay. If you opted to review the check, it's displayed, and if you need to make changes, do so.

9 Click Save & Close.

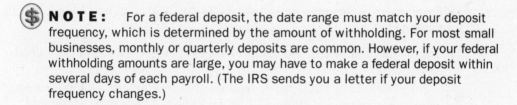

N O T E : For a federal deposit, the date range must match your deposit frequency, which is determined by the amount of withholding. For most small businesses, monthly or quarterly deposits are common. However, if your federal withholding amounts are large, you may have to make a federal deposit within several days of each payroll. (The IRS sends you a letter if your deposit frequency changes.)

Print the Check

If you selected the option to create the check without reviewing it, the check is created and needs only to be printed (if you print checks).

To print the check, use the following steps:

1 Choose File | Print Forms | Checks from the menu bar.

2 When the Select Checks To Print window opens, select the bank account you use for payroll.

3 Be sure all the payroll liability checks you created are selected.

4 Click OK to bring up the Print Checks window so you can print the checks.

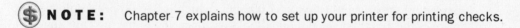

N O T E : Chapter 7 explains how to set up your printer for printing checks.

If you selected the option to review the check before finalizing it, the Write Checks window opens with your check displayed. Make any needed changes, and click the Print button at the top of the window to print the check, or, if you don't print checks, click Save & Close to save the check.

The federal government sent you a book of coupons (Form 8109) you must use when you deposit the funds you owe. Fill out a coupon and take it, along with your check, to the bank in which you have your payroll account. Make the check payable to the bank, unless you've been given different instructions by the bank or your accountant.

N O T E : Don't forget to fill in the little bullets on the coupon: one to indicate this is a 941 deposit, the other to indicate the quarter for which this payment is remitted.

TIP: You can sign up with the IRS for online payment of your liabilities at www.eftpssouth.com/Eftps.

Paying Federal Unemployment Taxes

The Federal Unemployment Tax Act (FUTA) provides unemployment compensation to workers who have lost their jobs, usually after the workers' state benefits have been exhausted. The FUTA tax is paid by employers; no deductions are taken from employee wages. Companies must make FUTA payments if either of the following scenarios exists:

- During this year or last year you paid wages of at least $1,500 in any calendar quarter.
- During this year or last year you had one or more employees for at least part of a day for a period of 20 weeks (the weeks do not have to be contiguous).

Use Form 8109 (the same coupon you use to deposit federal withholding and employer matching contributions) and mark the coupon for 940 Tax, and the quarter in which you are making your deposit. You don't have to make the deposit until you owe the entire amount, but you can make deposits until you reach that amount if you wish.

 CAUTION: Always use a separate coupon and check for FUTA; don't mix the payment with your other federal liabilities payment.

Technically, FUTA tax is 6.2 percent of gross wages up to $7,000.00 per employee, but the federal government gives employers a 5.4-percent credit for paying their state unemployment taxes. Therefore, unless you deliberately ignore your state unemployment payments, you can calculate FUTA at the rate of .8 percent of gross wages (.008 × $7,000.00), which is $56.00 per employee who reaches the $7,000.00 goal. QuickBooks assumes you're paying your state unemployment taxes and calculates your FUTA liability accordingly.

Remitting State and Local Liabilities

Your state and local payroll liabilities vary depending upon where your business is located and where your employees live (and pay taxes). Besides income taxes, you are probably liable for unemployment insurance, as well. And many states have withholding for disability.

State and Local Income Taxes

Most states have some form of an income tax, which might be calculated in any one of a variety of ways:

- A flat percentage of gross income
- A sliding percentage of gross income
- A percentage based on the federal tax for the employee

Local taxes are also widely varied in their approach:

- Some cities have different rates for employees of companies that operate in the city. There may be one rate for employees who live in the same city and a different rate for nonresidents.
- Your business might operate in a city or town that has a *payroll head tax* (a once-a-year payment that is a flat amount per employee).
- You may have a head tax for the town in which your business operates and still be required to withhold local taxes for employees who live in another city.

State and local taxing authorities usually provide coupons or forms to use for remitting income tax withholding. The frequency with which you must remit might depend on the size of your payroll, or it might be quarterly, semiannual, or annual, regardless of the amount.

To remit the withheld income tax for your state and local taxing authorities, choose Employees | Process Payroll Liabilities | Pay Payroll Liabilities from the QuickBooks menu bar. Select the date range this payment covers and click OK to open the Pay Liabilities window. Locate the state and local income tax liabilities. Mark them by clicking in the check-mark column, and then click Create. Follow the steps to print the checks as described earlier. Mail them, along with your coupon or form, to the appropriate addresses.

Other State Liabilities

If your state has SUI or SDI or both, you have to pay those liabilities when they're due. Commonly, these are quarterly payments.

 TIP: It's a good idea to create different vendor names for SUI, SDI, and income tax withholding to make sure you don't accidentally send checks for the wrong component, and to prevent QuickBooks from issuing a single check for the grand total. The vendor record for each vendor name may have the same payee (Department of Revenue), but the records are kept separately.

Not all states have SUI or SDI, and some have one but not the other. Some states collect SUI from the employee and the company; some collect only from the company. Check the rules for your state.

Use the same process described earlier for selecting the amounts due from the Pay Liabilities window when it's time to pay your state liabilities.

Remitting Other Payroll Liabilities

The rules for remitting the paycheck deductions and employer contributions for other reasons—such as health benefits, pension, and workers compensation—are specific to your arrangements with those vendors.

There are a great many ways to handle the way these payments are posted, and you have to decide what makes sense to you (or to your accountant). For example, if you pay a monthly amount to a medical insurer, you may want to post the employee deductions back to the same expense account you use to pay the bill. That way, only the net amount is reported as an expense on your taxes. Or you can track the deductions in a separate account and calculate the net amount at tax time.

You have to perform these tasks in a way that guarantees the vendors get the right amount. For example, before you write the check to the medical insurance company, you must enter a regular vendor bill for the difference between the deducted amounts and the actual bill. That difference is your company contribution, of course. Then, when you write the check, both bills will be in the hopper, and the check will be in the correct amount.

Workers Comp

QuickBooks Enhanced Payroll can manage workers comp, and the setup options are available in the Payroll & Employees category of the Preferences dialog. Click Set Preferences to open the Workers Comp dialog. Select Track Workers Comp to enable the feature.

When workers comp is enabled, you can also opt to see reminder messages to assign workers comp codes when you create paychecks or timesheets. In addition, you can select the option to exclude an overtime premium from your workers comp calculations (check your workers comp insurance policy to see if you can calculate overtime amounts as regular pay).

To set up the workers comp calculations, choose Employees | Workers Compensation | Set Up Workers Comp. Follow the prompts to set up your workers comp insurance premiums.

Preparing Your 941 Form

Every quarter you must file a 941 form that reports the total amount you owe the federal government for withheld taxes and employer expenses. If you have been paying the deposits regularly, no check is remitted with the 941. Instead, it's a report of amounts due and amounts paid, and they should match. The 941 is concerned with the following data:

- Gross wages paid
- Federal income tax withholding
- FICA (social security) withholding and matching employer contributions
- Medicare withholding and matching employer contributions

Many people fill out the 941 form they receive in the mail. You can gather the information you need from a QuickBooks report to do that, or you can have QuickBooks print the 941 form for you.

QuickBooks will prepare your 941 report using the information in your QuickBooks registers.

To prepare the report, follow these steps:

1 Choose Employees | Process Payroll Forms from the QuickBooks menu bar.
2 Select Federal Form.
3 Select Quarterly Form 941.
4 Select the appropriate filing period.
5 Click OK and follow the onscreen instructions to complete the form and print it.

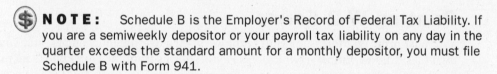 **N O T E :** Schedule B is the Employer's Record of Federal Tax Liability. If you are a semiweekly depositor or your payroll tax liability on any day in the quarter exceeds the standard amount for a monthly depositor, you must file Schedule B with Form 941.

The printed form can be sent to the IRS if you use these printing criteria:

- The form must be printed with black ink on white or cream paper.
- The paper must be 8"×11" or 8.5"×11".
- The paper must be 18lb. weight or heavier.

The printed report doesn't look exactly like the blank form you received, but it's close. More importantly, it's perfectly acceptable to the government.

You could also use the information in the printed report to fill in the blank 941 form you receive or to transmit the information via telephone, and save your QuickBooks printout as your copy.

Preparing Annual Returns

All the taxing authorities want annual returns. The feds, state, and local folks need reports and forms. Some of them need checks. You can get all the information you need from QuickBooks. In fact, all the usual QuickBooks reports work just fine, as long as you remember to set the Dates field to the entire year.

Preparing State and Local Annual Returns

The state and local taxing authorities usually send you a form that asks for a reconciliation for the year. You may have to present quarterly totals as you fill out the form, which you can accomplish by changing the date range in the QuickBooks payroll reports.

Finish your State Unemployment annual report as soon as possible, because the payments you make to the state are relevant to the Federal Unemployment report (Form 940). Incidentally, for many states, the year-end State Unemployment report doesn't require a check because there's a limit to the wages that are eligible for applying the unemployment contribution rate.

Preparing the 940 Report

For small businesses with only a couple of employees, the 940 report (FUTA) is frequently filed annually. To create your Form 940, choose Employees | Process Payroll Forms from the QuickBooks menu bar. Select Federal Form and then select the 940 form. Follow the instructions that appear on the screen. Many small businesses qualify for Form 940EZ, which is shorter and easier.

Printing W-2 Forms

You must print W-2 forms for your employees, the government agencies, and your own files. Choose Employees | Process Payroll Forms from the QuickBooks menu bar, select Federal Form, be sure the filing period year is correct, and then select Form W-2.

In the Process W-2s window, click Mark All to select all the employees, and then choose Review W-2. Each employee's W-2 form is presented on the screen. If there is nonfinancial data missing (such as an address or ZIP code), you must fill it in.

Click Next to move through each employee's form. When everything is correct, load your W-2 forms in the printer and choose Print W-2s. The Print W-2s window opens so you can choose a printer and print the forms. Click OK and click Print.

You must also print the W-3 form, which is a summary of your W-2 forms. It must be in the package you send to the IRS when you transmit the W-2 forms. Unfortunately, you can't preview the W-3 form.

All these payroll reports are a bit time-consuming, but you have no choice: these tasks are legally necessary. At least it's easier because QuickBooks keeps the records and does the math.

Configuring and Tracking Inventory

n this chapter:

- Create inventory items

- Deal with physical inventory counts

- Adjust the count

- Create pre-builds

- Manage backorders

Chapter 10

For many businesses, the warehouse is a source of frustration, bewilderment, rage, and erroneous information. I'm using the term "warehouse" generically to indicate the place where you store inventory (which may be your basement instead of a real warehouse).

Creating Inventory Items

Inventory items are part of the Item List in your QuickBooks system. That list contains all the elements that might ever appear on a customer invoice, or a purchase order, including services you sell, non-inventory products you sell, discounts, sales tax, and so on.

Creating New Items

Instructions for adding items to the Item List are in Chapter 2, but it's worth taking a moment here to go over the steps for creating inventory items.

Click the Items & Services icon on the Home page, or choose Lists | Item List from the menu bar, to open the Item List window. All your items are listed, and the inventory items can be distinguished easily because they have their own type, *Inventory Part*.

To add a new item to your inventory items list, press CTRL-N while the Item List window is open. When the New Item window opens, select Inventory Part as the item type, and then fill in the information (Figure 10-1 is an example of an inventory item).

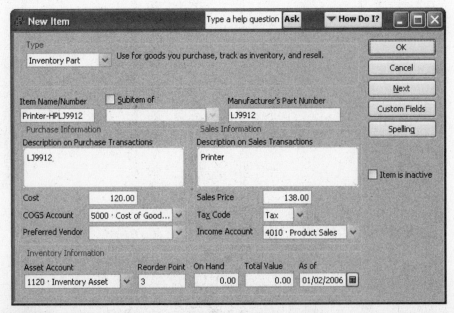

FIGURE 10-1   An inventory item record contains all the information you need to use it in transactions.

Use the following guidelines when you create a new inventory item:

- The Item Name/Number is your code for the item. This field must be unique in your Items List.
- The Manufacturer's Part Number (new in QuickBooks 2006) lets you include the part number on your purchase orders. If you purchase from a distributor instead of a manufacturer, enter the distributor's part number. This makes creating an accurate purchase order much easier.
- The Description fields are optional. The text you enter in the Description On Purchase Transactions field automatically appears when you create a purchase order. The text you enter in the Description On Sales Transactions field automatically appears in sales transaction forms, such as invoices, estimates, sales receipts, and so on.
- The financial information (cost and price) that you enter can be changed on an individual transaction.
- Select the appropriate posting accounts for Cost of Goods and Income.
- Enter a number in the Reorder Point field that reflects the minimum quantity you want to have in stock. When this quantity is reached, QuickBooks will issue a reminder about reordering (if you've enabled the Reminders feature).
- Don't enter anything in the On Hand or Total Value field, because the data won't provide the accurate financial trail your accountant needs. Instead, use the inventory adjustment tool, discussed in the section "Making Inventory Adjustments" later in this chapter.

If you disabled automatic spell checks in the Preferences dialog box, click Spelling to make sure you have no spelling errors. This also lets the QuickBooks spelling checker add the words connected to this item to its dictionary (for example, the item code, the name of the vendor, and any technical jargon in the description). This obviates the need to check the spelling when you create an invoice or purchase order for the item. If you didn't disable automatic spell checks, the spelling tool will start when you click OK to save the item.

If you created any custom fields for items (discussed in Chapter 2), click Custom Fields and enter data in any custom field that's appropriate for this item. (If you want to add additional custom fields, click Define Fields.)

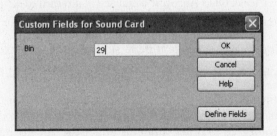

Using the Manufacturer's Part Number in Purchase Orders

You cannot use the Manufacturer's Part Number in a purchase order unless you customize a purchase order template to display this field. To accomplish this, when you're creating your next purchase order, select the built-in Purchase Order template (named Custom Purchase Order), and click the Customize button above the Template drop-down list field.

In the Customize Purchase Order dialog, select Edit, and go to the Columns tab. The Manufacturer's Part Number is listed just below the Description field (but it's not selected). Put a check mark in the Screen check box and also in the Print check box to have the data appear on the PO transaction window and the printed purchase order you send to your supplier. Click OK to save the changes and return to the Create Purchase Orders window.

Creating Subitems

Subitems are useful when there are choices for items and you want all the choices to be part of a larger hierarchy so you can track them efficiently. For instance, if you sell widgets in a variety of colors, you may want to create a subitem for each color: red widget, green widget, and so on. Or perhaps you sell widgets from different widget manufacturers: Jones widgets, Smith widgets, and so on.

In order to have a subitem, you must have a parent item. Figure 10-2 shows a new item that has been specifically created as a parent item (using the Inventory Part type in the Type drop-down list).

Here are some guidelines for creating an inventory item that's designed to be a parent:

- Use a generic name for the item; the details are in the subitem names.
- Don't enter a description, save that for the subitems.
- Don't enter the cost.
- Don't enter the price.
- Don't enter a reorder point.
- Don't enter the quantity on hand.
- Enter the COGS Account because it's a required field for all inventory items.
- Enter the Income Account because it's a required field for all inventory items.

Having created the parent item, subitems are easy to create.

Open a blank New Item window (press CTRL-N) and follow these steps:

1 In the Item Name/Number field, enter the code for this item. It can be an item, a color, a size, a manufacturer name, or any other code that specifies this subitem as compared to other subitems under the same parent item (see Figure 10-3).

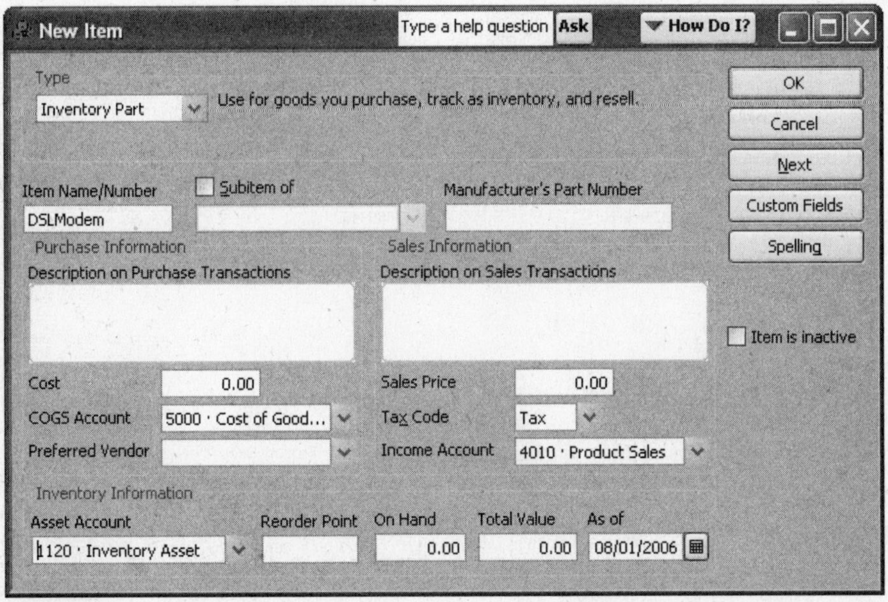

FIGURE 10-2 This item isn't sold to customers—it exists only as a parent item.

2. Check the box named Subitem Of, and then select the parent item from the drop-down list that appears when you click the arrow to the right of the field.
3. Enter the descriptions you want to appear on purchase orders and invoices.
4. Enter the cost and price.
5. Enter the general ledger account information (Cost of Goods and Income accounts).
6. Enter the reorder point if you're using that feature.
7. Continue to add subitems to each parent item in your system.

Making Items Inactive

Sometimes you have inventory items that you aren't buying or selling at the moment. Perhaps they're seasonal, or the cost is too high and you want to delay purchasing and reselling the item until you can get a better price.

As long as you're not using the item, you can make it inactive. It doesn't appear on the Item List when you're entering transactions. To declare an item inactive, open the Item List window and right-click the item. Then choose Make Item Inactive from the shortcut menu.

When an item is inactive, it's not just invisible on the list of items for sale that appears during invoice data entry; it doesn't even appear on the Item List window. However, you can change the appearance of the Item List window to display inactive items.

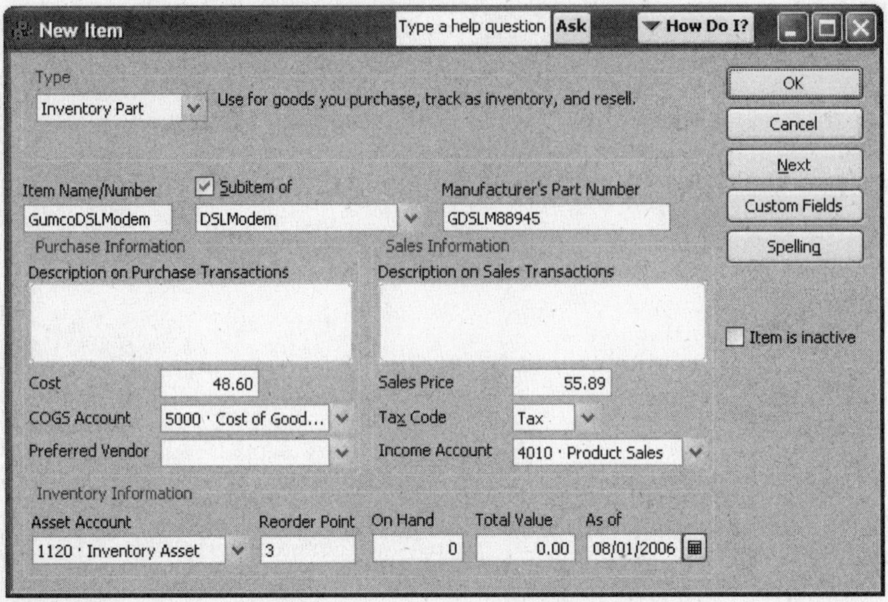

FIGURE 10-3   This subitem has all the data needed for transactions.

When you make any item inactive, the Include Active check box becomes activated in the Item List window. If no items are marked inactive, the Include Active option is grayed out and inaccessible. Click the Include Active check box to display the inactive items along with the active items. Any inactive item is displayed with an X to the left of the item listing. To make an inactive item active again, choose the Include Active option so you can see the inactive items, and then click X to deselect the inactive status.

CAUTION: You can make any subitem inactive, but if you make a parent item inactive, all of its subitems are also made inactive.

Activate All Items Before Running Reports

If you make an item inactive, QuickBooks pretends it doesn't exist. An inactive item doesn't show up in any of the inventory reports available on the Reports | Inventory menu. Worse, all calculations about the worth of your inventory, including reports that aren't directly connected to inventory (such as your balance sheet reports), fail to include any amounts connected to inactive items.

Activate all inventory items except those that have never been received into stock before running any reports on inventory. You should also activate all inventory items before running financial statements.

Running Inventory Reports

You'll probably find that you run reports on your inventory status quite often. For most businesses, tracking the state of the inventory is the second most important set of reports (right behind reports about the current accounts receivable balances).

QuickBooks provides several useful, significant inventory reports, which you can access by choosing Reports | Inventory. The available reports are discussed in this section.

 N O T E : Very few customization options are available for inventory reports—you can change the date range and the headers/footers, and some reports let you filter some of the items. You can't add or remove columns.

Inventory Valuation Summary Report

This report gives you a quick assessment of the value of your inventory. By default, the date range is the current month to date. Each item is listed with the following information displayed in columns:

Item Description The description of the item, if you entered a description for purchase transactions.

On Hand The current quantity on hand, which is the net number of received items and sold items. Because QuickBooks permits you to sell items you don't have in stock (let's hope you really do have them but you haven't used a QuickBooks transaction to bring them into stock), it's possible to have a negative number in this column.

Avg Cost Each transaction for receipt of inventory is used to calculate this figure.

Asset Value The value posted to your Inventory account in the general ledger. The value is calculated by multiplying the number on hand by the average cost.

% of Tot Asset The percentage of your total inventory assets that this item represents.

Sales Price The price you've set for this item. This figure is obtained by looking at the item's configuration window. If you entered a price when you set up the item, that price is displayed. If you didn't enter a price (because you chose to determine the price at the time of sale), $0.00 displays. QuickBooks does not check the sales records for this item to determine this number, so if you routinely change the price when you're filling out a customer invoice, those changes aren't reflected in this report.

Retail Value The current retail value of the item, which is calculated by multiplying the number on hand by the retail price.

% of Tot Retail The percentage of the total retail value of your inventory that this item represents.

Inventory Valuation Detail Report

This report lists each transaction that involved each inventory item. The report shows no financial information about the price charged to customers, because your inventory value is based on cost. You can double-click any sales transaction line to see the details (and the amount you charged for the item).

Inventory Stock Status

There are two Stock Status reports: Inventory Stock Status By Item, and Inventory Stock Status By Vendor. The information is the same in both reports, but the order in which information is arranged and subtotaled is different. You can use these Stock Status reports to get quick numbers about inventory items, including the following information:

- The preferred vendor
- The reorder point
- The number currently on hand
- A reminder (a check mark) for ordering items that are below the reorder point
- The number currently on order (purchase order exists but stock has not yet been received)
- The next delivery date (according to the data in the purchase orders)
- The average number of units sold per week

Physical Inventory Worksheet

This is the report you print when it's time to take an inventory count. See the section "Counting Inventory," later in this chapter, for more information.

Pending Builds

This report details the current state of items you assemble from existing inventory items (called *builds*, or *pre-builds*). Only QuickBooks Premier editions offer built-in features for creating builds (although in the Premier editions they're called *assemblies*).

QuickBooks personnel tell me that this report is listed in case you've opened a company file in your copy of QuickBooks Pro that was created (or worked on) in a QuickBooks Premier edition. Apparently, this report exists so you can view the details on pre-builds that were created in a Premier edition, even though you can't access the QuickBooks pre-build features in QuickBooks Pro.

To learn about a workaround for pre-builds so you can create them in QuickBooks Pro, see the section "Creating Pre-Builds," later in this chapter. To learn how to create real pre-builds in QuickBooks Premier Edition, read *Running QuickBooks 2006 Premier Editions* from CPA911 Publishing (www.cpa911publishing.com). You can purchase the book at your favorite bookstore.

Getting Quick Inventory Reports

QuickBooks provides a reporting feature called QuickReports that provides valuable information about an individual inventory item or all inventory items. QuickReports are available from the Item List window.

In the Item List window, select an item and press CTRL-Q (or click the Reports button and choose QuickReport) to open a QuickReport similar to the one seen in Figure 10-4. You can change the date range for the report, and you can double-click any transaction line to drill down to the transaction details.

Counting Inventory

I can hear the groans. I know—there's nothing worse than doing a physical inventory. However, no matter how careful you are with QuickBooks transactions, no matter how pristine your protocols are for making sure everything that comes and goes is accounted for, you probably aren't going to match your physical inventory to your QuickBooks figures. Sorry about that.

Printing the Physical Inventory Worksheet

The first thing you must do is print a Physical Inventory Worksheet (see Figure 10-5), which is one of the choices on the Inventory Reports submenu. This report lists your

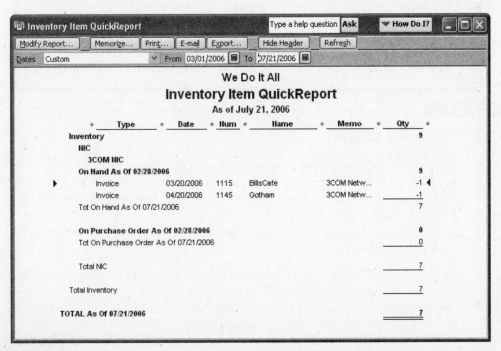

FIGURE 10-4   A QuickReport is an activity report for a specific item.

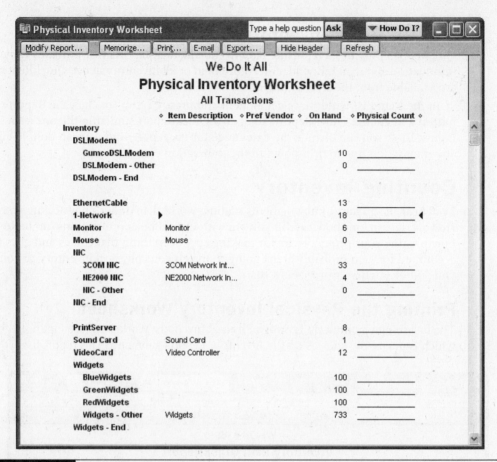

FIGURE 10-5   The most important column is the one with blank lines, which is where you enter the physical count.

inventory items in alphabetical order, along with the current quantity on hand, which is calculated from your QuickBooks transactions. In addition, there's a column that's set up to record the actual count as you walk around your warehouse with this printout (and a pen) in hand.

If you have a large number of inventory items, you may have some problems with this worksheet:

- You cannot change the way the worksheet is sorted, so you cannot arrange the items to match the way you've laid out your warehouse.

- If you use bins, rows, or some other physical entity in your warehouse, QuickBooks has no feature to support it, so you cannot enter the location on this worksheet (nor can you sort by location, which would be an extremely useful method).

I have no idea why the Pref Vendor column exists, because I've never experienced a physical inventory in which that information was used. If you stock by manufacturer, the manufacturer's name is usually referred to in the code or description. You can't get rid of this column.

Click the Print button in the worksheet window to bring up the Print Reports window. In the Number Of Copies box, enter as many copies as you need (one for each person helping with the count).

 T I P : Don't hand every person a full report—cut the report to give each person the pages he or she needs, and keep one full copy to use as a master.

Planning the Physical Count

QuickBooks lacks a "freeze" feature like the one found in most inventory-enabled accounting software. Freezing the inventory means that after you've printed the worksheet and begun counting, any transactions involving inventory are saved to a holding file in order to avoid changing the totals. When you've finished your physical count, you unfreeze the inventory count and print a report on the holding file. You make your adjustments to the count using the information in that file, and then make the final adjustments to the count.

You can perform these actions manually, however. After you print the worksheet (which you don't do until you're ready to start counting), be sure that all sales invoices will be handled differently until after the inventory count is adjusted. There are a number of ways to do this:

- Print an extra copy of each invoice and save the copies in a folder. Don't pick and pack the inventory for the invoices until after the count.
- Prepare a form for sales people to fill out the name and quantity of inventory items sold during the freeze, and delay picking and packing the inventory until after the count.
- Delay entering invoices until after the count is over. (This is not a good idea if counting takes a couple of days.)
- Don't receive inventory in QuickBooks (don't fill out a Receive Items or Enter Bill For Received Items form) until after the count.
- If inventory arrives in the warehouse during the count, don't unpack the boxes until after the count.

When you start counting the inventory, be sure there's a good system in place. The most important element of the system is *having somebody in charge*. One person, with a master inventory worksheet in hand, must know who is counting what. When each counter is finished, his or her sheet should be handed to the person in charge and the numbers should be duplicated onto the master inventory worksheet. (This is why you print multiple copies of the worksheet.) Note the date and time the count was reported.

After the count, bring in any inventory that's arrived during the count. Then start picking and packing your orders so you can generate income again.

Making Inventory Adjustments

After you've finished counting the inventory, you may find that the numbers on the worksheet don't match the physical count. In fact, it's almost a sure bet that the numbers won't match.

Most of the time the physical count is lower than the QuickBooks figures. This is called *shrinkage*. Shrinkage is jargon for "stuff went missing for an unexplained reason," but most of the time the reason is employee theft. Sorry, but that's a well-documented fact. Another reason for shrinkage is breakage, but most of the time that's reported by employees, and you can adjust your inventory because you know about it. When you don't know about it, suspect the worst, because statistics prove that suspicion to be the most accurate.

Adjusting the Count

You have to tell QuickBooks about the results of the physical count, and you accomplish that by choosing Vendors | Inventory Activities | Adjust Quantity/Value On Hand. The Adjust Quantity/Value On Hand window opens, which is shown in Figure 10-6.

 N O T E :   Inactive items appear on the Adjust Quantity/Value On Hand window.

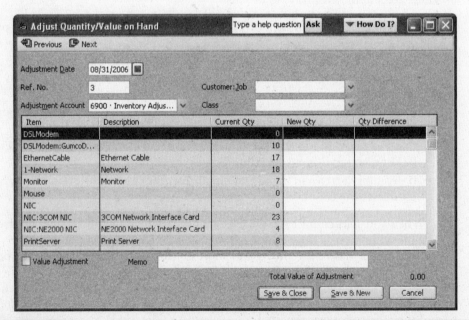

FIGURE 10-6   Correct the quantity and value of inventory to match the physical count.

Here are the guidelines for filling out this window:

- Enter the date (usually inventory adjustments are made at the end of the month, quarter, or year, but there's no rule about that).
- Use an optional reference number to track the adjustment. The next time you enter an adjustment, QuickBooks will increment the reference number by one.
- Enter the inventory adjustment account in your chart of accounts. Click the arrow to see a display of all your accounts. If you don't have an inventory adjustment account, choose <Add New> and create one (it's an expense account).
- The Customer:Job field is there in case you're sending stuff to a customer (or for a job) but you didn't include the items on any invoices for that customer or job (you just transferred the inventory). The inventory count is changed and the cost is posted to the job.
- If you've enabled the Classes feature, a Class field appears.
- This transaction window doesn't differentiate between parent items and subitems. The parent items have a current quantity of zero, but some subitems might also have a zero count. Be careful about the item you're adjusting.
- Use either the New Qty column or the Qty Difference column to enter the count (depending on how you filled out the worksheet and calculated it). Whichever column you use, QuickBooks fills in the other column automatically.
- Anything you enter in the Memo field appears on your Profit & Loss Detail report, which eliminates the question "What's this figure?" from your accountant.

Adjusting the Value

When you complete the entries, the total value of the adjustment you made is displayed in the window. That value is calculated by using the average cost of your inventory. For example, if you received ten widgets into inventory at a cost of $10.00 each and later received ten more at a cost of $12.00 each, your average cost for widgets is $11.00 each. If your adjustment is for minus one widget, your inventory asset value is decreased by $11.00.

You can be more precise about your inventory valuation.

Eliminate the average valuation and enter a true value when you fill out this transaction window:

1. Click the Value Adjustment check box at the bottom of the window. A column named New Value opens in the window (see Figure 10-7).
2. The value of the total adjusted count is displayed for each item, and you can change the value to eliminate the effects of averaging costs.

Of course, in order to enter the correct total value, you must have the information you need and then make the appropriate calculations. To obtain the information, choose Reports | Purchases | Purchases By Vendor Detail. This report presents a history of your purchases so you can make the necessary calculations.

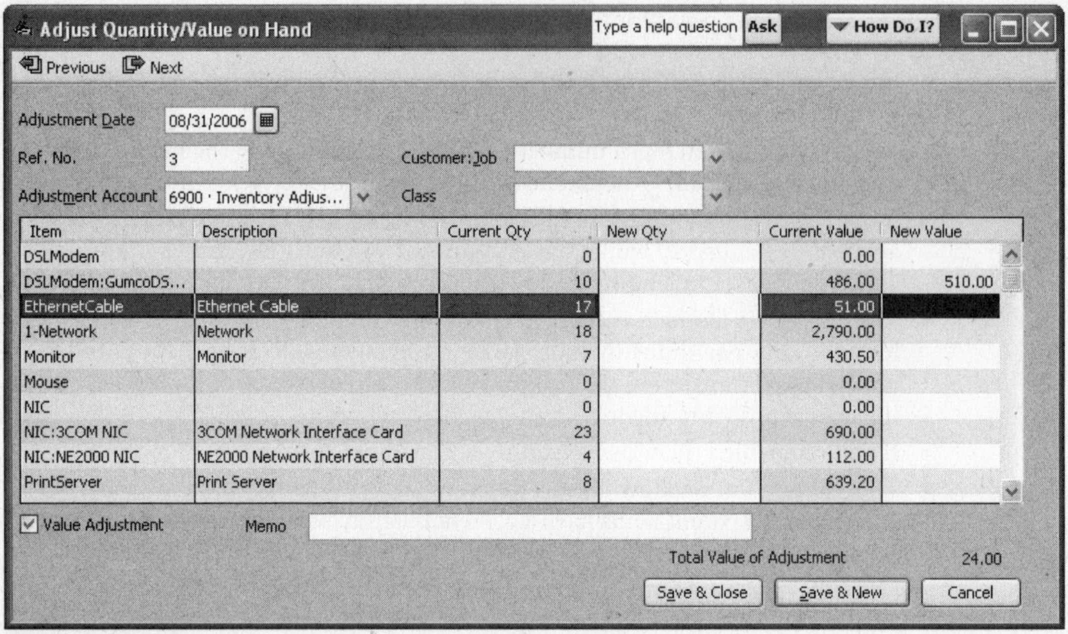

FIGURE 10-7   You can change the current value of any item.

> **$ TIP:**   In case your accountant asks, QuickBooks does not support FIFO or LIFO costing for inventory. Essentially, you create your own FIFO/LIFO calculations by using the information in the vendor reports.

Return to the Adjust Quantity window and enter the data. When you've finished making your changes, click Save & Close to save your new inventory numbers.

Understanding the Postings

When you adjust the inventory count, you're also changing the value of your inventory asset. After you save the adjustment, the inventory asset account register reflects the differences for each item.

But this is double-entry bookkeeping, which means there has to be an equal and opposite entry somewhere else. For example, when you sell items via customer invoices, the balancing entry to the decrement of your inventory account is made to cost of sales. When you're adjusting inventory, however, there is no sale involved (nor is there a purchase involved). In this case, the balancing entry is made to the inventory adjustment account, which must exist in order to adjust your inventory.

If your inventory adjustment lowers the value of your inventory, the inventory asset account is credited and the adjustment account receives a debit in the same amount. If your adjustment raises the value of your inventory, the postings are opposite.

Making Other Adjustments to Inventory

You can use the Adjust Quantity/Value On Hand window to make adjustments to inventory at any time and for a variety of reasons:

- Breakage or other damage
- Customer demo units
- Gifts or bonuses for customers or employees
- Removal of inventory parts in order to create pre-built or pre-assembled inventory items (see the upcoming section on pre-builds).

The important thing to remember is that tracking inventory isn't just to make sure that you have sufficient items on hand to sell to customers (although that's certainly an important point). Equally important is the fact that inventory is a significant asset, just like your cash, equipment, and other assets. It affects your company's worth in a substantial way.

Creating Pre-builds

Pre-builds are products that are assembled or partially assembled using existing inventory parts. Some manufacturers call them *kits*. Only QuickBooks Premier and Enterprise editions offer the software features for assembling pre-builds (and those editions call the items *Assembly Items*). However, even though QuickBooks Pro doesn't have any capacity for building or tracking pre-builds automatically, you can still create a system that works.

I'll start by examining the elements that go into a pre-build. Accounting software that supports pre-builds automates all the processes, using the following rules:

- Ask which existing inventory parts (and how many of each) are used to build the product.
- Receive the pre-built item into inventory (after you notify the software that you've built it) and automatically remove the individual parts that were used from inventory.
- Automatically create a cost for the new pre-built item based on the cost of the individual parts.

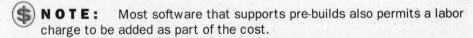 **N O T E :**   Most software that supports pre-builds also permits a labor charge to be added as part of the cost.

Each of these steps can be performed manually in QuickBooks and, although it's more time-consuming, it means you can create pre-builds if you need them.

T I P :   If pre-builds are a large part of your business, you should move up to QuickBooks Premier or QuickBooks Enterprise Solutions. You can learn how to use this feature in *Running QuickBooks 2006 Premier Editions* from CPA911 Publishing (www.cpa911publishing.com). The book is available at your favorite bookstore or online bookseller.

Creating the Pre-built Item

Start a pre-build by putting the item into your items list, as shown in Figure 10-8. The protocols used for entering the item are specially designed for pre-builds, and you may find the guidelines helpful as you make your own entries:

- The Item Name/Number is unique in its starting character to make it clear that this is a special line of products. If you normally use numbers for items, use a letter for the first character of your pre-builds (X or Z usually works well).
- The cost is the aggregate current average cost of the original inventory parts (which means you have to look them up and add them up, before you create the item).
- No startup quantity is entered (it's brought into inventory when built).
- If the item is built-to-order for customers, no reorder point is entered.

Putting Pre-builds into Inventory

When you bring your pre-built items into inventory, you don't receive them the way you receive the inventory items you purchase (there's no vendor and you don't write a check to purchase the parts).

Instead, you must take the items you used to build the new product out of inventory and put the new pre-built product into inventory.

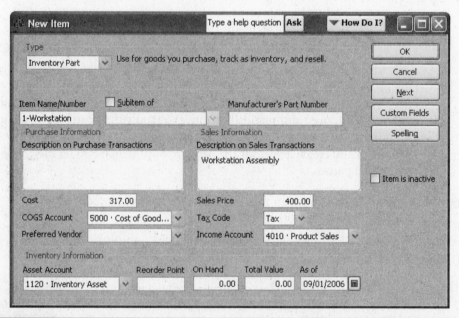

FIGURE 10-8 Create a pre-build the same way you create a regular, purchased item.

Choose Vendors | Inventory Activities | Adjust Quantity/Value On Hand. In the Adjust Quantity/Value On Hand window, use the Qty Difference column to add the number of pre-builds and remove the number of original items that were used to create these pre-builds.

The total value of the inventory adjustment is zero, because you're replacing components that total a certain amount with a pre-build that costs the same amount.

 TIP: If you use other paraphernalia for pre-builds (nails, screws, labels, whatever), add those items to your items list so you can include them in the pre-build, which makes the cost more exact.

Workaround for Backorders

Backorders are nerve-wracking on both ends, whether you're waiting for items that your supplier didn't have (your supplier's backorder problem), or you need to ship items to customers and you're out of them (your backorder problem). Although QuickBooks Pro doesn't offer a backorder feature, you can use existing features to create your own backorder protocols.

 NOTE: QuickBooks Premier and Enterprise Solutions editions have backorder features built in. If backorders are common in your business, consider upgrading. You can learn how to create and track backorders in *Running QuickBooks 2006 Premier Editions* from CPA911 Publishing (www.cpa911publishing.com). The book is available at your favorite bookstore or online retailer.

Determining Customer Backorder Preferences

Part of the trick of keeping your customers' business is keeping your customers' preferences straight. The issue of backorders is important, because not all customers have the same attitude. Generally, there are three different approaches your customers take:

- "Okay, ship me whatever you have and send the backorders when you get them."
- "Just ship me what you have and take the other items off the order, and I'll order the other stuff when you get it." (This may really mean, "I'm going to look elsewhere, but if everyone else is out of it, I'll call you back.")
- "Hold the order until the backordered items are in, and then ship everything at once."

Nobody expects you to remember each customer's preference, but QuickBooks has some features that help you handle backorders to each customer's satisfaction.

Using the Notepad for Backorder Instructions

QuickBooks has this nifty item called "customer notes," which you can use for keeping backorder instructions:

1. Open the Customers & Jobs List, select the customer's listing, and click the Edit Notes button in the right pane of the Customer Center.
2. In the Notepad window, enter a notation about the customer's attitude regarding backorders.
3. Click OK twice to save the note and close the customer record.

When you're filling out an invoice for this customer, you can view the customer notepad. With the customer's invoice on the screen, choose Edit | Notepad from the QuickBooks menu bar, and the notepad for that customer appears.

Using a Backorder Handling Field

You can formalize your backorder handling by creating a Backorders field on the customer cards. Then you can put the field on the invoice form so it's right in front of you when you're filling out an order. To do this, you have to perform the following three tasks (all of which are covered in this section):

- Create the custom field for backorder preferences.
- Add data to the field for each customer.
- Add the field to your invoice form.

Create the Field in the Customer Form

You can add a custom field to all the customer cards in your system by creating the new field in any existing customer record.

To accomplish this:

1. Open the Customers & Jobs List.
2. Double-click the listing for any existing customer.
3. Click the Additional Info tab, and then click Define Fields.
4. When the Define Fields window opens (see Figure 10-9), enter a label for the backorder field.
5. Select Customers:Jobs to use this field on your customer cards, and then click OK. QuickBooks displays a message telling you that you can use this custom field in templates (which is exactly what you're going to do). Click OK to make the message go away. Notice that you can tell it never to come back.
6. When you return to the customer window, click OK.

Enter Data in the Customer Records

The customer list is still on your QuickBooks screen, which is handy because now you must enter information in the new field for each customer that orders inventory items from you.

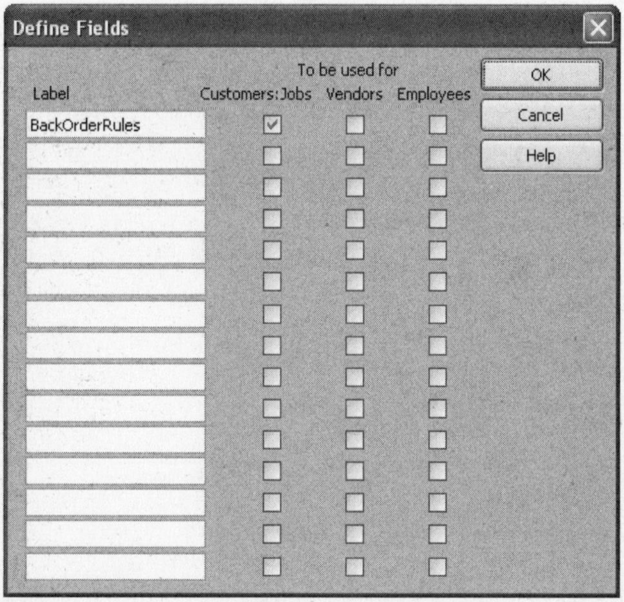

FIGURE 10-9   Create a label for a custom field for all customer records.

Follow these steps:

1. Double-click a customer listing to open an Edit Customer window.
2. Move to the Additional Info tab.
3. Enter this customer's backorder preference in the BackOrderRules field you created (see Figure 10-10).
4. Click OK to save the information.
5. Repeat the process for each customer.

Unlike most of the fields that are built into the customer record, custom fields don't have their own list files; therefore, you don't have a drop-down list available when you want to enter data—data entry is manual. You should create some rules about the way you use this field so everyone in the office uses the same phrases. Don't let people create abbreviations or "cute" entries; make sure the data makes the customer's backorder status absolutely clear. For example, for a backorder preference, consider creating easy-to-understand data entries such as: Ship Separately, Hold Order, and No BOs.

Put the Field on Your Invoice Forms

The information about a customer's backorder preferences is important when you're filling an order and you're out of something the customer wants. So you might as well have the information in front of you, which means putting it right on the

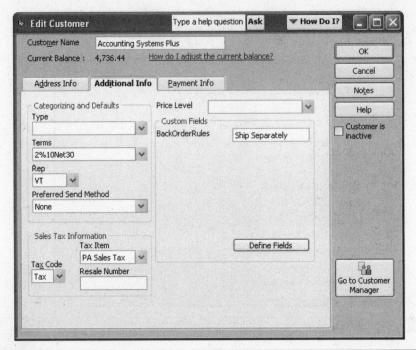

FIGURE 10-10   Enter data specific to each customer's preferences.

invoice form. Complete instructions for customizing invoices appear in Chapter 3, but I'll go over the way you add a new field.

To put a field on your invoice forms:

❶ Click the Invoices icon on the Home page (or press CTRL-I) to open the Create Invoices window.

❷ Click the Customize button above the Template box.

❸ In the Customize Template window, select the Intuit Product Invoice from the Template list and click New to open the Customize Invoice window.

❹ Enter a name for this new invoice template.

❺ Move to the Fields tab, where you'll find that the field you added to the customer form is listed.

❻ Enter the text you want to use for this field on the invoice (see Figure 10-11).

❼ Select Screen to make sure this field and its data are on the screen when you're filling out an invoice. If you want to print the field and its data when you print the invoice (so the customer is reminded of the preference), also select Print.

❽ Click OK to save the new template.

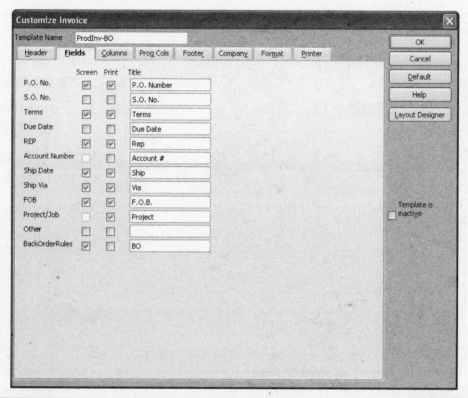

FIGURE 10-11 Put the custom field on the invoice template.

You may get a message from QuickBooks about the position of fields (adding a field may cause fields on the template to overlap), and usually it's best to opt to lay out the fields again. Check Chapter 3 for more information about field positions on templates, including moving your new field to a different position on the invoice.

Now when you need to enter a product invoice, use this new template. As soon as you enter the customer name in the Create Invoices window, the backorder preference for that customer is displayed (see Figure 10-12).

Recording a Backorder Invoice

Now you're all set and can fill backorders the way your customers want them filled.

To create a pending invoice in QuickBooks:

1 Fill out the invoice form, putting backordered items on the line items (see Chapter 3 for information about creating invoices). QuickBooks will flash a message telling you there's insufficient quantity to fill the order (which is not a problem now, so click OK).

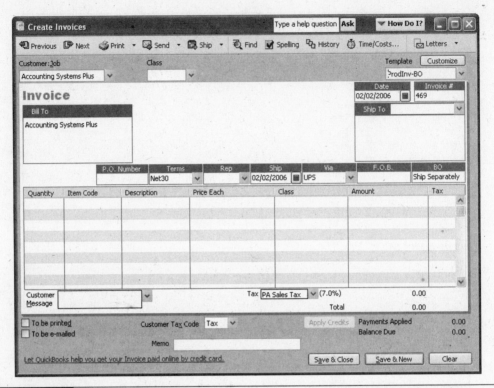

FIGURE 10-12 With the data in your new custom field, you know what each customer's backorder preference is.

❷ When the invoice form is completely filled out, right-click in the header or footer area of the form and choose Mark Invoice As Pending from the shortcut menu. The word "Pending" appears on the invoice form (see Figure 10-13).

❸ Save the invoice by clicking Save & Close (or click Save & New if you have more invoices to complete).

NOTE: A pending invoice does not post any amounts to the general ledger.

Later, when the backordered products arrive and have been entered into inventory, you can release the pending status.

Follow these steps:

❶ Choose Reports | Sales | Pending Sales.

❷ When the list of pending sales appears, double-click the listing for the sale you want to finalize. The original invoice (still marked "Pending") is displayed on your screen.

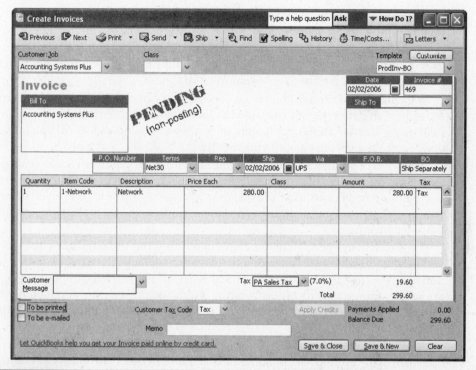

FIGURE 10-13   This order can't be filled until you receive the product, so it's not really a sale yet.

③ Choose Edit | Mark Invoice As Final from the QuickBooks menu bar.

④ Click Save & Close to save the invoice.

⑤ Pick it, pack it, and ship it.

The point of going through this work is to reinforce the notion that the better you satisfy your customers, the more money you'll make.

Another important lesson in this chapter is that even though your edition of QuickBooks doesn't inherently support a feature you want to use, once you understand the software, you can frequently manipulate it to do what you need.

Additional Features for Premier and Enterprise Editions

If you're running QuickBooks Premier Edition or QuickBooks Enterprise Solutions, you may have some additional features available, above and beyond the features covered in this chapter. (Not all features are in all Premier or Enterprise versions.)

Inventory Assemblies

Inventory assemblies are products that are assembled, or partially assembled, using existing inventory parts. QuickBooks Premier and Enterprise editions offer the software functions required for inventory assemblies.

In QuickBooks Premier/Enterprise editions you can create an item of the type Assembly (an item type not available in QuickBooks Basic/Pro editions). The New Item dialog box for an Assembly item includes a components list. All you have to do is enter the existing components required to build this assembly.

When you've built an assembly, you must receive it into inventory so you can sell it. QuickBooks Premier/Enterprise editions provide functions to automate this process. The Build Assemblies window provides an easy way to add your assembled items to your inventory, and automatically decrement your inventory of the components in the assembled items.

If you don't have enough of the components to build the number of assemblies you need, QuickBooks Premier/Enterprise editions accept the data, and mark the build as Pending (and finalizing the build when all the needed components become available). You can track current pending builds so you're sure you remember to order the components. Choose Reports | Inventory | Pending Builds to see a list of pending builds.

When the components needed for pending bills are received into inventory, you can finalize the appropriate pending bills. Choose Reports | Inventory | Pending Builds, and double-click the listing for the build you're ready to finalize. When the build's window opens, the new Quantity on Hand for the components is displayed automatically. If you have sufficient components to build the assemblies, click the Remove Pending Status button at the bottom of the window. QuickBooks automatically brings the assembly into inventory and decrements the components from inventory.

If you overbuild assemblies, or a customer cancels a built-to-order assembly, you can disassemble an assembly by deleting the build, and QuickBooks will automatically return the components to inventory.

Backorders

QuickBooks Premier and Enterprise Solutions editions provide the ability to track customer orders that can't be filled immediately and that need to wait for backordered products. You must start the sales transaction with a Sales Order to take advantage of backorder tracking.

Managing Bank and Credit Card Accounts

In this chapter:

- Make deposits

- Transfer funds between accounts

- Deal with bounced checks

- Void disbursements

- Manage cash

- Balance credit card statements

Before you started using accounting software, did your checkbook register have entries crossed out? Pencil notes next to inked-in entries? Inked notes next to penciled entries? Transactions that were made in April entered in the middle of a string of June transactions ("The statement came—I forgot about that transaction")? Lots of corrections for math errors? If so, relax; QuickBooks can take care of all of those problems.

Making a Deposit

Even though QuickBooks takes care of depositing money into your bank account when you receive money from customers (covered in Chapter 4), there are times when you receive money that's unconnected to a customer payment.

Entering a deposit (one that's not a customer payment) into your QuickBooks check register isn't much different from entering a deposit into a manual checkbook register. Actually, it's easier because you don't have to make any calculations— QuickBooks takes care of that.

Double-click the account in the Account Balances window on the Home page, or press CTRL-A to open the chart of accounts and double-click the bank account you want to work with. Fill in the date, delete the check number if one automatically appears, and then click in the deposit column to enter the amount. Assign the deposit to an account. You should use the Memo field for an explanation because your accountant will probably ask you about the deposit later (and, if necessary, create a journal entry to re-assign the amount to a different account). Click the Record button. That's it!

You can, if it's necessary, enter a payee name in the Payee column, but QuickBooks doesn't require that. Most of the time, you use this method of direct entry to record deposits that are unconnected to sales revenue you want to track. For example, you may receive a rebate on a purchase you made.

If you want to enter a payee that doesn't exist in any of your name lists, QuickBooks displays a Name Not Found message offering you the following selections:

- Quick Add, which lets you enter a name without any additional information
- Set Up, which lets you create a new name using the regular New Name window
- Cancel, which returns you to the account register so you can either choose another name or delete the nonexistent Payee entry

If you select Quick Add or Set Up, you're asked which type of Name you're adding: Vendor, Customer, Employee, or Other. Unless this payee will become a Vendor or Customer (I think we can eliminate Employee from this procedure), choose Other.

If you're depositing your own money into the business, that's capital; you should post the deposit to a capital account (it's an equity account). If you're depositing the proceeds of a loan (from yourself or from a bank), post the deposit to the liability account for the loan (you may have to create the liability account). If you're making a deposit that's a refund from a vendor, you can post the amount to the expense account that was used for the original expense.

When in doubt, post the amount to the most logical place and call your accountant. You can always edit the transaction later or make a journal entry to post the amount to the right account.

TIP: It's a good idea to set up accounts for transactions that you're unsure how to post. I have two such accounts. For income about which I want to ask my accountant, I use account #9998, titled MysteryIncome (it's an Other Income type). Account #9999 is titled MysteryExpense (it's an Other Expense type). If either account has a balance, it means I should call my accountant and find out where to post the income or expense I temporarily "parked" in that account. I can use a journal entry or edit the transaction to put the money into the right account.

Transferring Funds Between Accounts

Moving money between bank accounts is a common procedure in business. If you have a bank account for payroll, you have to move money out of your operating account into your payroll account every payday. Some people deposit all the customer payments into a money market account (which pays interest) and then transfer the necessary funds to an operating account when it's time to pay bills. Others do it the other way around, moving money not immediately needed from the business operating account to a money market account. Lawyers, agents, real estate brokers, and other professionals have to maintain escrow accounts and move money between them and the operating account.

The difference between a regular deposit and a transfer isn't clear if you think about the end result as being nothing more than "money was disbursed from one account and deposited into another account." However, that's not the way to think about it. When you work with accounting issues, every action has an effect on your general ledger, which means there's an effect on your financial reporting (and your taxes). A transfer isn't a disbursement (which is an expense that's assigned to a specific account), and it isn't a regular deposit (income received). A transfer has no effect on your profit and loss. If you don't use the transfer protocol, you run the risk of posting a deductible expense or taxable income to your profit and loss reports.

To make a transfer, follow these steps:

1. Choose Banking | Transfer Funds from the menu bar to open the Transfer Funds Between Accounts dialog (see Figure 11-1).
2. Fill out the fields.
3. Click Save & Close (or Save & New if you have another transfer to make).

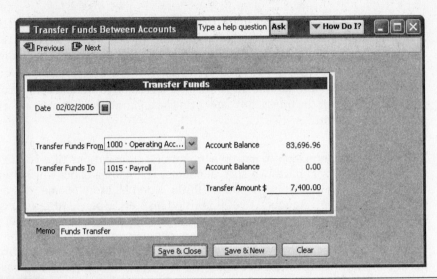

FIGURE 11-1   It's incredibly easy to transfer money between bank accounts.

QuickBooks posts the transaction (you'll see it marked as TRANSFR in both bank accounts if you open their registers) without affecting any totals in your financial reports. All the work is done on the balance sheet, but the bottom line of your balance sheet doesn't change as the following postings are made to the general ledger:

Account	Debit	Credit
Sending Bank Account		Amount of Transfer
Receiving Bank Account	Amount of Transfer	

Handling Bounced Checks

Customer checks sometimes bounce. When that happens, you face the following tasks:

- Deduct the amount of the bounced check from your checking account.
- Record any bank charges you incurred as a result of the bounced check.
- Remove the payment applied to the customer invoice (if it wasn't a cash sale).
- Recover the money from the customer.

In addition, you might want to collect a service charge from the customer (at least for the amount of any charges your own bank assessed).

Adjusting the Account Balances

You must remove the amount of the bounced check from your bank account and also adjust the Accounts Receivable account if the bounced check was an invoice payment. If the check was a payment for a cash sale, nothing was posted to Accounts Receivable, so you must adjust the income account to which you posted the cash sale.

Using the Bank Account Register

If you deposited the check directly into the bank instead of using the Undeposited Funds account, you can make your adjustments right in the account register.

If the deposit was an invoice payment, its listing in the bank register has a type of PMT. You must delete the payment by pressing CTRL-D or by choosing Edit | Delete Payment from the QuickBooks menu bar. (There's no Void option for customer payments of invoices.)

QuickBooks displays a message telling you that the payment was used to pay an invoice and that deleting it will result in unpaid balances (which is exactly what should happen). Click OK, and the invoice that was paid returns to its balance due before the payment. The Accounts Receivable account is also adjusted (the amount now owed to you is increased).

The invoice will show up as unpaid the next time you send a statement to the customer, and you should also invoice the customer for any bounced check charges you incurred and for any service charge you want to charge the customer for the aggravation. (See "Invoicing Customers After Checks Bounce" later in this section.)

If you deposited the money directly into the bank and the transaction was a cash sale (instead of an invoice payment), the deposit type is RCPT. You can right-click the listing and void the transaction.

Using a Journal Entry

If you used the Undeposited Funds account, it's easiest to create a journal entry to remove the amount paid from the customer's balance. Then you must re-invoice the customer (see "Invoicing Customers After Checks Bounce" later in this section).

To create a journal entry to adjust the amounts, choose Company | Make General Journal Entries to open the General Journal Entry window.

Now take the following steps:

1. Click the Account column and then click the arrow to display the account list. Select the bank into which you deposited the payment.
2. Move to the Credit column and enter the amount of the bounced check.
3. Move to the Memo column to write yourself a note (e.g., Smith Ck #2345 bounced).
4. Click in the Account column and choose the Accounts Receivable account from the drop-down list. QuickBooks automatically fills in the amount in the Debit column.
5. Click in the Name column and select the customer whose check bounced.
6. Click Save & Close.

Recording Bank Charges for Bounced Checks

If your bank charged you for a returned check, you have to enter the bank charge. To do so, open the chart of accounts and double-click the bank account listing.

Now fill out the fields as follows:

1. Click the Date field in the blank line at the bottom of the register and enter the date that the bank charge was assessed.
2. In the Number field, QuickBooks automatically fills in the next available check number. Delete that number and press TAB.
3. Leave the Payee field blank.
4. In the Payment field, enter the amount of the service charge for the returned check.
5. In the Account field, assign this transaction to the expense account you use for bank charges.
6. Optionally, enter text in the Memo field (such as the name of the customer whose check bounced).
7. Click the Record button in the register window to save the transaction.

Your bank account balance is reduced by the amount of the service charge. You should charge the customer for this, and in the following sections I'll cover the steps needed to accomplish that.

Invoicing Customers After Checks Bounce

In order to re-invoice your customers after a check bounces, you must create items for bounced checks and for any service charges connected to returned checks. Then you can use those items in the invoice.

Creating an Item for a Bounced Check

You have to re-invoice the customer for the bounced check. To do that, you need an item for bounced checks. You cannot invoice the customer for the original product or service you sold, because you already did that, and the records of the product or service were updated at that time. You just need to replace the money you expected to receive for the product or service you sold.

Use the following steps to create an item for bounced checks:

1. Choose Lists | Item List from the menu bar to open the Item List window.
2. Press CTRL-N to enter a new item.
3. Select Other Charge as the item type.
4. Name the item appropriately (for instance, "Returned Check").
5. Enter an optional description.
6. Leave the amount blank (you fill it in when you create the invoice).
7. Select Non as the tax code.
8. Link the item to your sales income account.

The reason you link the item to the sales income account is to replace the income that was removed when you voided the deposited check. If you have multiple sales income accounts, you can take either of the following approaches:

- Create separate items for returned checks for each account (be sure to name the items in a way that reminds you of the linked sales account).
- Link this item to one sales account, and then edit the invoice after you create it to change the posting account to the appropriate sales account.

Creating an Item for Customer Service Charges

To create an item for invoicing customers for service charges, follow these steps:

1. Open the Item List window.
2. Press CTRL-N to enter a new item.
3. Select Other Charge as the item type.
4. Name the item appropriately (for instance, "RetChkChg").
5. Enter a description (for example, "Service charge for returned check").
6. Leave the amount blank (you fill it in when you create the invoice).
7. Select Non as the tax code.
8. Link the item to an income account, such as to Other Income or to an account you create for situations like this (perhaps "Customer Service Charges").
9. Click OK.

Creating the Invoice

Now that your system has the required items, you can send an invoice to the customer for the bounced check.

Use the following steps to create the invoice:

1. Click the Invoices icon on the Home page, or press CTRL-I.
2. When the Create Invoices window opens, enter the name of the customer who gave you the bad check.
3. Enter the date on which the check bounced.
4. Click in the Item column and select the item you created for returned checks.
5. Enter the amount of the returned check.
6. Optionally, add another line item for the service charge you incurred for the bounced check using the item you created for service charges.

($) TIP: You might want to use the Intuit Service Invoice template for this charge; it's easier and "cleaner" for this type of invoice.

Voiding Disbursements

Sometimes you have to void a check that you've written. Perhaps you decided not to send it for some reason, or perhaps it was lost in the mail. Whatever the reason, if a check isn't going to clear your bank, you should void it.

The process of voiding a check is quite easy, and the only trouble you can cause yourself is *deleting* the check instead of *voiding* it. Deleting a check removes all history of the transaction, and the check number disappears into la-la land. This is not a good way to keep financial records. Voiding a check keeps the check number but sets the amount to zero.

To void a check, open the bank account register and click anywhere on the check's transaction line to select the transaction. Right-click to open the shortcut menu and choose Void Check. The corresponding entry in the expense account (or multiple expense accounts) to which the check was written is automatically adjusted. Click Record to save the transaction.

Tracking Cash

Aren't those ATM gadgets wonderful? They're everywhere, even at the supermarket checkout! It's so easy to take cash out of your bank account. And it's so easy to forget to enter the transaction in your account register!

Another wonderful device is the petty cash box, which many businesses maintain to dispense cash to employees (or owners) who need cash to recover money they've spent for the company or as an advance against future expenditures.

When you use cash, whether it's cash from the petty cash box or a withdrawal via an ATM machine, you have to account for it. That means you have to account for the portion of it you spend and the portion that's still in your pocket. The cash belongs to the business. In this section, I'll cover the accounting procedures involved with petty cash transactions.

Creating a system that ensures your ATM and petty cash withdrawals are accounted for is *your* problem—QuickBooks cannot help you remember to enter transactions. (Well, you could set up a QuickBooks reminder that appears frequently with the message "Did you ATM today????")

Creating a Petty Cash Account

If you spend cash for business expenses, your chart of accounts should have a petty cash account. This account functions like a cash register till: you put money in it, then you account for the money that's spent, leaving the rest in the till until it too is spent. Then you put more money into the till. The petty cash account doesn't represent a real bank account; it just represents that portion of the money in the real bank account that moved into the till.

If you don't have a petty cash account in your chart of accounts, create one as follows:

1. Click the Chart Of Accounts icon on the Home page, or press CTRL-A.
2. When the Chart Of Accounts window appears, press CTRL-N to open a blank New Account window.

❸ Fill in the account information using the following guidelines:
- The Account Type is Bank.
- If you number your accounts, use a number that places your new petty cash account near the other (real) bank accounts in your chart of accounts.
- Leave the opening balance at zero.

Putting Money into Petty Cash

You have to put money into your petty cash till, both literally (get cash) and figuratively (record a withdrawal from your bank account to your petty cash account). Most of the time you'll write a check for petty cash using the following guidelines:

- Create a name in the Other Names list for the payee (usually the name is "cash").
- Post the check to the petty cash account.

You can use the Write Checks window to accomplish the task, or enter the transaction directly in the bank account register.

 TIP: Don't post a petty cash check to an expense, nor to a class. Those postings are recorded when you account for the spent funds, not for the moment at which you withdraw the cash (see "Recording Petty Cash Disbursements").

Recording ATM Withdrawals

When you withdraw money from your bank account with your ATM card, it's not an expense, it's just cash. You've put cash into a till (literally, the till is your pocket, but to QuickBooks it's a petty cash container). It becomes an expense when you spend it (remember to get a receipt so you can enter the expense into your system).

Bring the ATM receipt (and receipts for any stuff you purchased with the ATM cash) back to the office. Now you're ready to perform the procedures necessary to track the cash you took and the part of it you spent.

The first thing you have to do is take the cash out of your QuickBooks bank account because you stood in front of an ATM dispenser and took cash out of your actual bank account. However, this is double-entry bookkeeping, and there has to be an equal and opposite posting to another account. That's what the petty cash account is for. You have a choice of methods for performing this task: transfer the funds between accounts, or enter a transaction in your bank account.

To transfer funds between the bank account and the petty cash account, use the following steps:

❶ Choose Banking | Transfer Funds.
❷ In the Transfer Funds Between Accounts window, fill out the information needed: the two accounts and the amount you withdrew.
❸ Click Save & Close.

To enter the withdrawal as a transaction, open the bank account register and follow these steps:

1. Enter the transaction date.
2. Delete the check number QuickBooks automatically enters in the Number field.
3. Skip the Payee field.
4. Enter the amount of the transaction in the Payment column.
5. In the Account field, post the transaction to the petty cash account. QuickBooks automatically assigns the type TRANSFR to the transaction.

Some bookkeepers are uneasy about skipping the Payee field. If you fall in that category, create a payee named PettyCash in the Other Names list and use that name for petty cash transactions.

Recording Petty Cash Disbursements

As you spend the money you withdraw via an ATM transaction, or by taking cash out of the petty cash box in the office, you must record those expenditures in the petty cash register.

TIP: Don't let anyone take money out of the petty cash till without a receipt. If the money is an advance against a purchase instead of payment for a receipt, use an IOU. Later, replace the IOU with the purchase receipt.

Open the petty cash account register and use the receipts you've collected to assign expense accounts to the transaction. You can enter one transaction, splitting the postings among all the affected expense accounts, or enter individual transactions. Use the following guidelines for entering the transaction:

- You can delete the check number QuickBooks automatically inserts in the Number field, or you can leave the number there (you'll never reconcile the petty cash account, so it doesn't matter).
- You can either skip the Payee field or use a payee named PettyCash, as explained in the previous section.

I constantly encounter bookkeepers who enter a real payee for each petty cash transaction ("Joe's Hardware Store," "Mary's Office Supplies," and so on). As a result, their QuickBooks files grow larger than they need to because the system is carrying the weight of all these vendors. The vendors they enter appear in all their vendor reports, crowding those reports with extraneous names that nobody has any interest in tracking.

Reserve vendors for those payees from whom you receive bills or to whom you disburse checks and for whom you want to track activity. If it's so important to know that you spent a buck eighty for a screwdriver at Joe's Hardware Store, enter that information in the Memo field.

If you spent less than the amount of cash you withdrew from the till, the balance stays in the petty cash account while it's in your pocket. You'll probably spend it later, and at that point you'll repeat this task to account for that spending.

Managing Your Credit Cards

When you use a business credit card, you have a number of choices for tracking and paying the credit card bill. You can either pay the entire bill every month, or pay part of the bill and keep a running credit card balance. For either approach, you can choose between two methods of handling credit card purchases in QuickBooks:

- Treat the credit card bill as an ordinary vendor and enter the bill when it arrives.
- Treat the credit card bill as a liability and enter each transaction as it's made.

Treating Credit Cards as Vendors

You can set up your credit card as an ordinary vendor (instead of a liability account) and enter the bill into QuickBooks when it arrives, or use the Write Checks function to create a direct disbursement. Most of the time, the expenses are posted to multiple accounts, so the credit card bill transaction is a split transaction (see Figure 11-2).

If you don't pay off the card balance, each month you'll have a new bill to enter that has interest charges in addition to your purchases. Post the interest charges to an interest expense account.

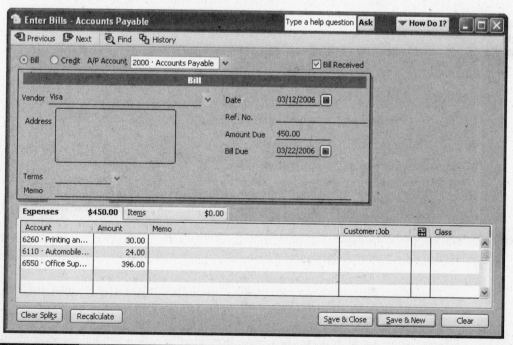

FIGURE 11-2   Credit card bills are usually posted to multiple accounts.

If you enter the bill in the Enter Bills window, and then use the Pay Bills window to write the checks, enter the amount you want to pay against each bill in the system. Always start with the oldest bill, making a partial payment or paying it in full. Then move to the next oldest bill, making a partial payment or paying it in full.

Treating Credit Cards as Liability Accounts

You can also treat credit cards as liability accounts, tracking each transaction against the account as it occurs. Then when the bill arrives, you match the transactions against the bill and decide how much to pay. Your running balance is tracked specifically against the credit card, instead of being part of your Accounts Payable balance.

Creating a Credit Card Account

To use credit cards in this manner, you must have an account for each credit card in your chart of accounts. If you don't have such an account as a result of the EasyStep Interview, you can create one now, using an account type of Credit Card. Check out Chapter 2 for information about adding items to your chart of accounts.

 C A U T I O N :   QuickBooks arranges the chart of accounts by account types. If you're using numbers for your accounts, the numbering is ignored in favor of account types. To make sure your credit card accounts are displayed in the right order, use account numbers that fit into the right section of the chart of accounts—credit card accounts come right after accounts payable accounts.

Entering Credit Card Charges

If you want to track your credit card charges as they're assumed, instead of waiting for the bill, you have to treat your credit card transactions like ATM transactions—enter them as you go. QuickBooks offers two methods to accomplish this:

- Set up your credit card account for online banking and download the transactions (covered in Chapter 16).
- Enter transactions manually.

If your credit card account is enabled for online banking, these are not mutually exclusive methods. You can enter the transactions manually and download data from your credit card server to match those transactions. Or, you can download the transactions and then add each transaction to the credit card register (instructions are in Chapter 16).

To enter credit card charges manually, choose Banking | Enter Credit Card Charges, to open the Enter Credit Card Charges window seen in Figure 11-3.

Select the appropriate credit card account and then use the store receipt as a reference document to fill in the transaction. Here are some guidelines for making this transaction easy and quick to complete:

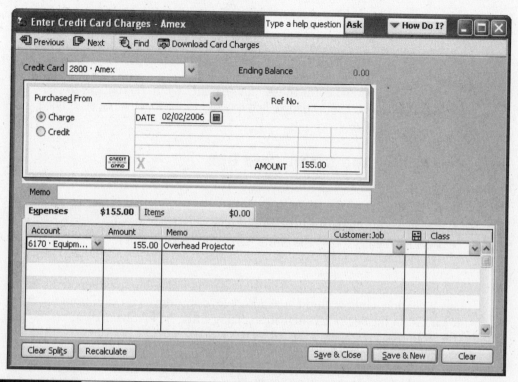

FIGURE 11-3   To track credit card charges as liabilities, enter each transaction.

- You can skip the Purchased From field (or, if you're compulsive about avoiding blank fields, enter a generic vendor—create a vendor named Credit Card Purchase or something similar). Then use the Memo field for each transaction to note the name of the real vendor, if that information is important to you. If you type a vendor name in the Purchased From field, QuickBooks will force you to add the vendor to your vendor list. You'll end up with a gazillion vendors with whom you don't have a real vendor relationship (they don't send you bills), and you won't be able to delete them from your QuickBooks file because they have transactions.

- If the transaction is a return, be sure to select the Credit option at the top of the window.

- Enter the receipt number in the Ref No. field.

- Enter the date of the purchase.

- Use the Expenses tab for general expenses; use the Items tab if you used the credit card to buy inventory items for resale.

- If you use the credit card for an expense or an item for a customer, enter the customer information so you can bill the customer for reimbursement (see Chapter 6 for details about entering reimbursable expenses).

Click Save & New to save the record and move to another blank credit card entry window to enter another credit card transaction, or click Save & Close if you're finished entering credit card charges.

 TIP: You can also enter these charges directly in the register of your credit card account. (Some people find it faster to work in the register than in a transaction window.)

Reconciling the Credit Card Bill

Eventually, the credit card bill arrives, and you have to perform the following chores:

- Reconcile the bill against the entries you recorded.
- Decide whether to pay the entire bill or just a portion of it.
- Write a check.

Choose Banking | Reconcile from the QuickBooks menu bar to open the Begin Reconciliation window. In the Account field, select the credit card from the drop-down list. In the Begin Reconciliation dialog enter the following data:

- The ending balance from the credit card bill
- Any finance charges on the bill in the Finance Charge box, along with the date on which the charges were assessed
- The account you use to post finance charges (create one if you don't have one—it's an expense)

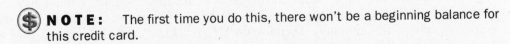 **NOTE:**   The first time you do this, there won't be a beginning balance for this credit card.

Click Continue to open the Reconcile Credit Card window, which displays the purchases you entered into QuickBooks and the payments you made. Click the check mark column for each transaction on your window that has a matching transaction on the credit card bill (make sure the amounts match, too). That includes payments, credits, and charges.

 TIP: If the list of transactions is very long, select the option Show Only Transactions On Or Before The Statement Ending Date. This removes transaction listings past that date, none of which could have cleared.

Add any transactions you forgot to enter by opening the credit card register and entering the transactions. (To find the receipts, search your pockets, desk, pocketbook, the floor of your car, and the kitchen junk drawer.) When you return to the Reconcile Credit Card window, the new transactions are automatically added and you can check them off. (You can also click the Go To button to open the Enter Credit Card Charges window, if you prefer to work in that window.)

($) TIP: Finance charges for businesses are tax deductible; the finance charges you incur for your personal credit cards, or for personal expenses, aren't.

Now look at the box at the bottom of the window where the totals are displayed. If the difference is $0.00, congratulations! Everything's fine. Click Reconcile Now.

If the difference is not $0.00, you have to figure out the problem and make corrections. Read Chapter 12, which is dedicated to the subject of reconciling bank accounts, to learn how to troubleshoot reconciliations.

Paying the Credit Card Bill

When you finish working in the reconciliation window, QuickBooks moves on to pay the bill by asking you whether you want to write a check now, or create a vendor bill that you'll pay the next time you pay your bills.

Select the appropriate response and click OK. QuickBooks offers congratulations and also offers to print a reconciliation report (see Chapter 12 to learn about printing reconciliation reports). Select the report type you want, or click Cancel to skip the report.

If you opted to pay the bill, a transaction window that matches your response to paying the bill opens, so you can either enter a vendor bill or write a check. Fill in all the fields and save the transaction.

($) TIP: All the detailed information you need to create vendor bills is covered in Chapter 6, and information about paying bills and printing checks is in Chapter 7.

Reconciling Bank Accounts

In this chapter:

Chapter 12

Reconciling bank accounts is fancy terminology for "I have to balance my checkbook," which is one of the most annoying tasks connected with financial record keeping. In this chapter I'll go over all the steps required to reconcile your bank accounts.

 N O T E :   If you also have to reconcile credit card statements, read Chapter 11 to learn how.

Getting Ready to Reconcile

After your bank statement arrives, you must find some uninterrupted moments to compare it to the information in the QuickBooks account register.

If your bank sends your canceled checks in the envelope along with the statement (many banks don't include the physical checks), you can arrange the checks in numerical order before you start this task.

However, instead of sorting and collating the physical checks, it's much easier to use the list of check numbers, which appear in numerical order, on your statement. An asterisk or some other mark usually appears to indicate a missing number (usually a check that hasn't cleared yet, a check that cleared previously, or perhaps a voided check).

Open the register for the bank account you're about to reconcile by clicking the Check Register icon on the Home page and selecting the account, or by opening the chart of accounts (CTRL-A) and double-clicking the account's listing.

If the bank statement shows deposits or checks (or both) that are absent from your bank register, add them to the register. If you miss any, don't worry; you can add transactions to the register while you're working in the Reconcile window, but it's usually quicker to get this task out of the way before you start the reconciliation process.

Interest payments and bank charges don't count as missing transactions because the bank reconciliation process treats those transactions separately. You'll have a chance to enter those amounts during bank reconciliation.

Adding Missing Disbursements to the Register

The way you add missing checks to the register depends on whether the checks were payments of vendor bills you entered into your QuickBooks file or direct disbursements.

- To enter a payment, use the Pay Bills command on the Vendors menu.
- To enter a direct disbursement, use the Write Checks window (press CTRL-W) or enter the check directly into the register.

Adding Missing Deposits to the Register

Check the Undeposited Funds account to see if you entered the deposits when they arrived but neglected to run the Make Deposits procedure. If so, click the Record

Deposits icon on the Home page, or choose Banking | Make Deposits from the menu bar. Select the deposits that appear on your statement. If you have multiple deposits listed, you can either deposit the funds in amounts (batches of transactions) to match the transaction list on the statement, or deposit everything and select that deposit amount in the Reconcile window.

For example, your bank statement may show a deposit of $145.78 on one date and another deposit for $3,233.99 on another date. Both deposits appear in the Make Deposits window. Select one of the deposits, process it, and then repeat the procedure for the other deposit. When you reconcile the account, your transactions reflect the transactions in your bank statement.

On the other hand, you could select both deposits and process them in one transaction. When you reconcile the account, the joint deposit adds up correctly, so the reconciliation succeeds.

If a missing deposit isn't in the Undeposited Funds account, you have to create the deposit, which may have been a customer payment of an invoice, a cash sale, a transfer of funds between banks, a payment of a loan, or a deposit of capital.

For customer invoice payments or cash sales, fill out the appropriate transaction window. If you deposit the proceeds to the Undeposited Funds account, don't forget to take the additional step to deposit the funds in the bank so the transaction appears in the reconciliation window. If you deposit the proceeds directly to the bank, the transaction appears in the reconciliation window automatically.

If you made deposits unconnected to customers and earned income, such as putting additional capital into your business or depositing the proceeds of a loan, the fastest way to enter the transaction is to work directly in the bank account's register. Enter the deposit amount and post the transaction to the appropriate account.

Using the Begin Reconciliation Window

Reconciling your bank account starts with the Begin Reconciliation window, which you open by choosing Banking | Reconcile. If you have more than one bank account, or you have credit card accounts you reconcile in addition to bank accounts, select the bank account you want to reconcile from the drop-down list in the Account field.

Check the Beginning Balance field in the window against the beginning balance on the bank statement. (Your bank may call it the *starting balance*.)

If your beginning balances match, enter the ending balance from your statement in the Ending Balance field and enter the statement date. Skip the next sections in this chapter on solving the problem of nonmatching beginning balances. Head for the section "Enter Interest Income and Service Charges" and keep reading from there.

If the beginning balances don't match and this is the first time you've reconciled this account in QuickBooks, that's normal. If the beginning balances don't match and you've previously reconciled this account, that's *not* normal.

You cannot edit the beginning balance in the Begin Reconciliation window, but you can change it by making adjustments in your bank account register, and I'll go over those tasks in this section.

Adjusting the Beginning Balance for the First Reconciliation

The beginning balance in the Begin Reconciliation window probably doesn't match the opening balance on your bank statement the first time you reconcile the account. Your QuickBooks beginning balance is the initial entry you made for this bank account during setup. The number may have been posted to the bank account from the account balance you entered in the EasyStep Interview or from the account balance you entered when you set up the account from the Chart Of Accounts window. If you followed my advice in the chapters covering the EasyStep Interview and creating accounts, you didn't enter an opening balance for any accounts, so the beginning balance in the Begin Reconciliation window is zero.

The bank, of course, is using the last ending balance as the current beginning balance. The last ending balance represents a running total that began way back when, starting when you first opened that bank account. The only QuickBooks users who have it easy are those who opened their bank accounts the same day they started to use QuickBooks. (A minuscule number of people, if any, fit that description.)

You can change the beginning balance in your account register to match the bank's beginning balance, and the changed balance will appear as the Beginning Balance in the Begin Reconciliation window.

Use the following steps to match beginning balances:

1. Click Cancel on the Begin Reconciliation window to close it.
2. Open the bank account register and find that opening balance entry. It's probably the earliest entry in the register, and the Account field shows Opening Bal Equity as the posting account.
3. Change the amount to match the beginning balance on your bank statement.

④ Make sure there's a check mark in the Cleared column (the column heading is a check mark).

⑤ Click Record to save the transaction.

⑥ QuickBooks issues a warning message about changing this transaction and asks if you really want to record your changes. Click Yes.

⑦ Choose Banking | Reconcile to open the Begin Reconciliation window, which displays the same opening balance as the bank statement.

Now you can move on in this chapter to the section "Enter Interest Income and Service Charges" and keep reading from there. Also, write yourself a note so you can give your accountant a coherent explanation, because your Opening Bal Equity account changed and may have to be adjusted at the end of the year.

⑤ TIP: If you don't want to change the beginning balance, QuickBooks can make an automatic adjusting entry to account for the difference when you finish reconciling the account. In fact, QuickBooks posts the adjusting entry to the Opening Bal Equity account, so the bottom line is the same (and will generate the same question from your accountant). See the section "Permitting an Adjusting Entry" later in this chapter for more information.

Resolving Unexpected Differences in the Beginning Balance

If this isn't the first time you've reconciled the bank, the beginning balance that's displayed on the Begin Reconciliation window should match the beginning balance on the bank statement. That beginning balance is the ending balance from the last reconciliation, and nothing should change its amount.

If the beginning balance doesn't match the statement, you have to find out why. Search your memory, because you probably performed one of the following actions (and you need to undo the damage):

- You changed the amount on a transaction that had previously cleared.
- You voided a transaction that had previously cleared.
- You deleted a transaction that had previously cleared.
- You removed the cleared check mark from a transaction that had previously cleared.

You have to figure out which one of those actions you took after you last reconciled the account, and luckily, QuickBooks has a tool to help you. Click the Locate Discrepancies button on the Begin Reconciliation window to open the Locate Discrepancies dialog seen in Figure 12-1.

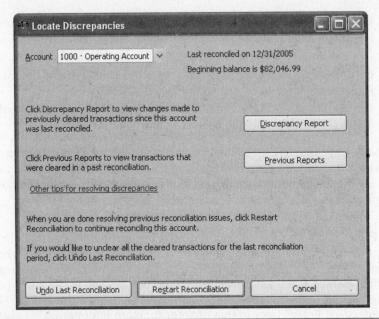

FIGURE 12-1   You have to track down the reason for an incorrect starting balance.

Viewing the Discrepancy Report

Click Discrepancy Report to see any transactions that were cleared during a past reconciliation and then were changed or deleted.

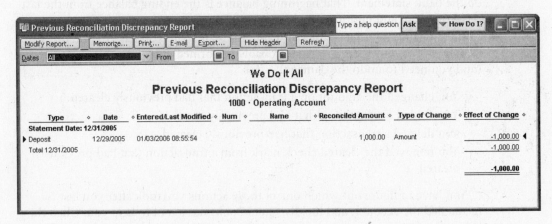

This report shows you the details of the transaction that cleared during a previous reconciliation and the change made to that transaction since that reconciliation. If the Reconciled Amount column shows a positive number, the original cleared transaction was a deposit; a negative number indicates a disbursement.

The Type Of Change column provides a clue about the action you must take to correct the unmatched beginning balances.

- **Uncleared**   Means you removed the check mark in the Cleared column of the register (and you persisted in this action even though QuickBooks issued a stern warning about the dangers).
- **Deleted**   Means you deleted the transaction.
- **Amount**   Is the original amount, which means you changed the amount of the transaction.

The difference between the amount in the Reconciled Amount column and the amount in the Effect Of Change column is the amount of the change.

Unfortunately, QuickBooks doesn't offer a Type Of Change named "Void," so a voided transaction is merely marked as changed, and the Type Of Change is Amount. A transaction with a changed amount equal to and opposite of the original amount was almost certainly a transaction you voided after it cleared.

($) **T I P :**   Even though the Discrepancy Report doesn't specify Void as the reason for a change in the beginning balance, the audit trail is quite clear about what happened. See Chapter 21 to learn about the QuickBooks audit trail.

Open the register and restore the affected transactions to their original state. This is safe because you're undoing your own mistake. You can't justify changing a cleared transaction—*a transaction that cleared cannot be changed, voided, deleted, or uncleared.*

($) **T I P :**   You don't have to be in the Begin Reconciliation window to see a Discrepancy Report. You can view the contents at any time by choosing Reports | Banking | Reconciliation Discrepancy.

Viewing the Last Reconciliation Report

Even if you don't display or print a reconciliation report after you reconcile an account, QuickBooks saves the report. If you're trying to track down a discrepancy in the beginning balance, viewing the last reconciliation report may be helpful. QuickBooks Pro can save only the last reconciliation report, and each time you reconcile an account the report is overwritten.

($) **T I P :**   QuickBooks Premier editions save multiple reconciliation reports. Instructions for viewing and using older reconciliation reports are available in *Running QuickBooks 2006 Premier Editions*, from CPA911 Publishing (www.cpa911publishing.com). You can buy the book at your favorite bookstore.

Click Previous Reports to open the Select Previous Reconciliation Report dialog, and select the options for the type and format of the report you want to see.

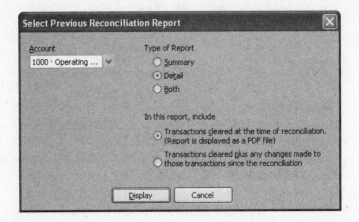

 TIP: You can view the Previous Reconciliation Report at any time by choosing Reports | Banking | Previous Reconciliation.

Choose the Reconciliation Report Type

Select Summary to see the totals for transactions that were cleared and uncleared at the time of the last reconciliation. The report also lists the totals for new transactions (transactions entered after the reconciliation). Totals are by type, so there is one total for inflow (deposits and credits) and another total for outflow (checks and payments).

Select Detail to see each transaction that was cleared or not cleared in a previous reconciliation and also see each new transaction. Select Both to open both reports (not one report with both sets of listings).

Choose the File Type for the Reconciliation Report

QuickBooks offers this report in two file types: PDF and the regular QuickBooks report window.

PDF, which you choose by selecting the option Transactions Cleared At The Time Of Reconciliation (Report Is Displayed As A PDF File), is a Portable Document Format file. In order to view a PDF file, you must have Adobe Reader (or another PDF reader program) installed on your computer. If you don't, when you select this report QuickBooks opens a dialog with a link to the Adobe web site, where you can download Acrobat Reader (it's free!).

PDF files are graphical and let you view and print information. You cannot drill down to see details because this report is not directly linked to your QuickBooks data. However, the report gives you an accurate account of the last reconciliation.

(If you printed a reconciliation report the last time you reconciled the account, the PDF file matches your printout.)

The standard QuickBooks report window, which you choose by selecting the option Transactions Cleared Plus Any Changes Made To Those Transactions Since The Reconciliation, is neither useful nor accurate. It is not, as its name implies, a reconciliation report. It's merely a report on the current state of the account register, sorted in a way to display the account's transactions according to cleared/uncleared/new categories. If you, or someone else, changed a cleared transaction, the new information appears in this report, not the information that was extant at the time you reconciled the account. If you're viewing the previous reconciliation to try to determine whether any changes were made to cleared transactions, this report fools you—it's dangerous to rely on its contents.

Here's the bottom line: If you need to see an accurate, trustworthy, previous reconciliation report in order to track down discrepancies, either use the PDF file or make sure you print and file a detailed reconciliation report every time you reconcile a bank account.

Finding and Resolving Differences

If you view the Discrepancy Report, changed transactions are displayed. If you haven't found the problem that's causing the discrepancy in the beginning balances and want to search for it manually, you can compare the reconciliation report and the account register. Any transaction that is listed in the reconciliation report should also be in the register.

- If a transaction is there but marked VOID, re-enter it, using the data in the reconciliation report. That transaction wasn't void when you performed the last reconciliation; it had cleared. Therefore, it doesn't meet any of the reasons to void a transaction.
- If a transaction appears in the reconciliation report but is not in the register, it was deleted. Re-enter it, using the data in the reconciliation report.

Check the amounts on the printed check reconciliation report against the data in the register to see if any amount was changed after the account was reconciled. If so, restore the original amount.

Undoing the Last Reconciliation

QuickBooks lets you undo the last reconciliation, which means that all transactions cleared during the reconciliation are uncleared. This is a good way to start over if you're mired in difficulties and confusion during the current reconciliation, and the problems seem to stem from the previous reconciliation (especially if you'd forced reconciliation by having QuickBooks make an adjusting entry).

Just in case this process doesn't work, back up your company file so you can restore the data in its reconciled state.

Now follow these steps to undo the last reconciliation:

1. Click the Locate Discrepancies button in the Begin Reconciliation dialog.
2. In the Locate Discrepancies dialog, select the appropriate account.
3. Click Undo Last Reconciliation.
4. Click Continue.

QuickBooks performs the following actions:

- Removes the cleared status of all transactions you cleared during the last reconciliation
- Leaves the amounts you entered for interest and bank charges

When the process completes, QuickBooks displays a message to describe those actions and tell you they were performed. Click OK to clear the message and return to the Locate Discrepancies dialog.

If you'd let QuickBooks make an adjustment entry during the last reconciliation (which almost certainly is the case; otherwise, you wouldn't have to undo and redo the reconciliation), click Cancel to close the dialog. Open the account's register and delete the adjustment entry—it's the entry posted to the Opening Bal Equity account. Hopefully, this time the reconciliation will work and you won't need another adjusting entry.

Start the reconciliation process again. When the Begin Reconciliation window opens, the data that appears is the same data that appeared when you started the last reconciliation—the last reconciliation date, the statement date, and the beginning balance are back.

Enter the ending balance from the bank statement. Do *not* enter the interest and bank charges again; they weren't removed when QuickBooks undid the last reconciliation.

Good luck!

Giving Up the Search for a Reason

You may not be able to find a reason for the difference in the beginning balances. If a changed transaction cleared in a previous reconciliation, you can't compare the reconciliation report against the register if you didn't print and save those reports (unless you're running QuickBooks Premier Edition, which stores them).

There's a point at which it isn't worth your time to keep looking, so just give up and perform the reconciliation, even though it won't balance. QuickBooks will make an adjusting transaction at the end of the reconciliation process, and if you ever learn the reason, you can remove that transaction.

Enter Interest Income and Service Charges

Your statement shows any interest and bank service charges if either or both are applicable to your account. Enter those numbers in the Begin Reconciliation window and choose the appropriate account for posting.

If you have online banking and the interest payments and bank charges have already been entered into your register as a result of downloading transactions, don't enter them again in the Begin Reconciliation window.

By "bank charges," I mean the standard charges banks assess, such as monthly charges that may be assessed for failure to maintain a minimum balance. Bank charges do not include special charges for bounced checks (yours or your customers'), nor any purchases you made that are charged to your account (such as the purchase of checks or deposit slips). Those should be entered as discrete transactions (using the Memo field to explain the transaction), which makes them easier to find in case you have to talk to the bank about your account.

Reconcile the Transactions

After you've filled out the information in the Begin Reconciliation dialog, click Continue to open the Reconcile window, shown in Figure 12-2.

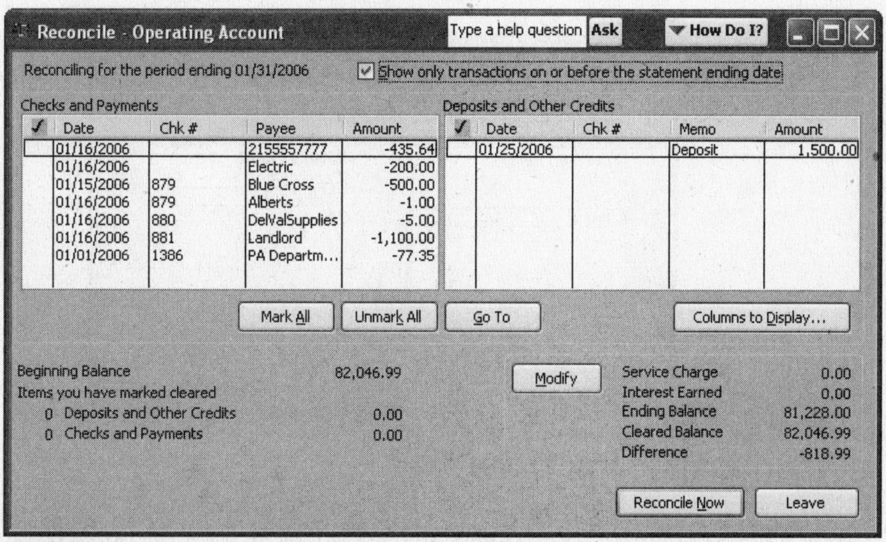

FIGURE 12-2 Uncleared transactions appear in the Reconcile window.

Configuring the Reconcile Window

You can configure the way transactions are displayed to make it easier to work in the window.

Eliminate Future Transactions

If the list is long, you can shorten it by selecting the option Show Only Transactions On Or Before The Statement Ending Date. Theoretically, transactions that weren't created before the ending date couldn't have cleared the bank. Removing them from the window leaves only those transactions likely to have cleared. If you select this option and your reconciliation doesn't balance, deselect the option so you can clear the transactions in case one of the following scenarios applies:

- You issued a postdated check and the recipient cashed it early. Since it's rare for a bank to enforce the date, this is a real possibility.
- You made a mistake when you entered the date of the original transaction. You may have entered a wrong month or even a wrong year, which resulted in moving the transaction date into the future.

Customize the Column Display

You can change the columns that display on each pane of the Reconcile window by clicking Columns To Display. Add or remove columns, depending on their usefulness to you as you clear transactions.

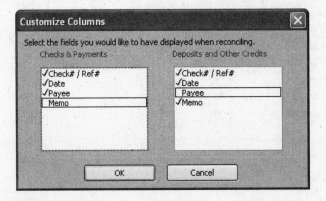

Clearing Transactions

Now you must tell QuickBooks which transactions have cleared. All the transactions that are on your bank statement are cleared transactions. If the transactions are not listed on the statement, they have not cleared.

Click each transaction that cleared. A check mark appears in the leftmost column to indicate that the transaction has cleared the bank. If you clear a transaction in error, click again to remove the check mark—it's a toggle.

Use the following shortcuts to speed your work:

- If all, or almost all, of the transactions have cleared, click Mark All. Then deselect the transactions that didn't clear.
- Mark multiple, contiguous transactions by dragging down the Cleared column.
- If the account you're reconciling is enabled for online access, click Matched to automatically clear all transactions that were matched in the QuickStatements you've downloaded over the month. QuickBooks asks for the ending date on the statement and clears each matched transaction up to that date.

As you check each cleared transaction, the Difference amount in the lower-right corner of the Reconcile window changes. The goal is to get that figure to 0.00.

Viewing Transactions During Reconciliation

If you need to look at the original transaction window for any transaction in the reconcile window, double-click its listing (or select the listing and click the button labeled Go To).

Adding Transactions During Reconciliation

While you're working in the Reconcile window, if you find a transaction on the statement that you haven't entered into your QuickBooks software (probably one of those ATM transactions you forgot to enter), you don't have to shut down the reconciliation process to remedy the situation. You can just enter the transaction into your register.

To open the bank account register, right-click anywhere in the Reconcile window and choose Use Register from the shortcut menu. When the account register opens, record the transaction. Return to the Reconcile window, where that transaction is now listed. Pretty nifty! Check it off as cleared, of course, because it was on the statement.

You can switch between the Reconcile window and the register for the account you're reconciling all through this process. Use the Window menu item to move between them.

 TIP: I automatically open the register of the account I'm reconciling as soon as I start the reconciliation process, to make it easier to switch over if I have to enter a transaction in the account register.

Deleting Transactions During Reconciliation

Sometimes you find that a transaction that was transferred from your account register to this Reconcile window shouldn't be there. This commonly occurs if you entered an ATM withdrawal twice. Or perhaps you forgot that you'd entered a deposit, and a couple of days later you entered it again. Whatever the reason, occasionally there are transactions that should be deleted.

To delete a transaction, move to the account register and select that transaction. Press CTRL-D to delete it (QuickBooks asks you to confirm the deletion). When you return to the Reconcile window, the transaction is gone.

Editing Transactions During Reconciliation

Sometimes you'll want to change some of the information in a transaction. For example, when you see the real check, you realize the amount you entered in QuickBooks is wrong. You might even have the wrong date on a check. (These things only happen, of course, if you write checks manually; they don't happen to QuickBooks users who let QuickBooks take care of printing checks.)

Whatever the problem, you can correct it by editing the transaction. Double-click the transaction's listing in the Reconcile window to open the original transaction window. Enter the necessary changes and close the window. Answer Yes when QuickBooks asks if you want to record the changes, and you're returned to the Reconcile window where the changes are displayed.

Resolving Missing Check Numbers

Most bank statements list your checks in order and indicate a missing number with an asterisk. For instance, you may see check number 1234 followed by check number *1236 or 1236*. When a check number is missing, it means one of three things:

- The check cleared in a previous reconciliation.
- The check is still outstanding.
- The check number is unused and is probably literally missing.

If a missing check number on your bank statement is puzzling, you can check its status. To see if the check cleared in the last reconciliation, open the Previous Reconciliation report (discussed earlier in this chapter) by choosing Reports | Banking | Previous Reconciliation.

To investigate further, right-click anywhere in the Reconcile window and choose Missing Checks Report from the shortcut menu. When the QuickBooks Missing Checks Report opens, select the appropriate account. You'll see asterisks indicating missing check numbers, as seen in Figure 12-3.

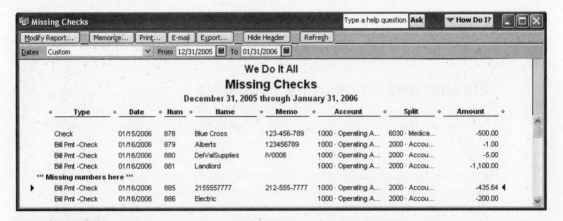

FIGURE 12-3 Three checks are missing, all of which are in somebody's wallet.

If the check number is listed in your Missing Checks Report, it's truly missing; it doesn't exist in the register. Investigate the following possible causes:

- You deleted the check.
- The check is physically missing (usually because somebody grabbed one or more checks to carry with her).
- Checks jammed while printing, and you restarted the print run with the number of the first available check (QuickBooks doesn't mark checks as void in that case, it just omits the numbers in the register).

Finishing the Reconciliation

If this isn't the first reconciliation you're performing, there's a good chance that the Difference figure at the bottom of the Reconcile window displays 0.00. If this is the first reconciliation and you changed the opening balance in the account register (as explained earlier in this chapter), you probably also see 0.00 as the difference.

If that's true, you've finished this part of the reconciliation. Click Reconcile Now and read the section "Printing the Reconciliation Report" later in this chapter. If the Difference amount is an amount other than 0.00, read the following sections.

Pausing the Reconciliation Process

If the account doesn't reconcile (the Difference figure isn't 0.00), and you don't have the time, energy, or emotional fortitude to track down the problem at the moment, you can stop the reconciliation process without losing all the transactions you cleared.

Click the Leave button in the Reconcile window and do something else for a while. Have dinner, play with the cat, help the kids with homework, whatever. When you restart the reconciliation process, all the entries you made are still there.

Finding and Correcting Problems

When you're ready to investigate the cause of a difference between the ending balance and the cleared balance, follow the guidelines I present here to find the problem.

Count the number of transactions on the bank statement. Then look in the lower-left corner of the Reconcile window, where the number of items you have marked cleared is displayed. Mentally add another item to that number for each of the following:

- A service charge you entered in the Begin Reconciliation box
- An interest amount you entered in the Begin Reconciliation box

If the numbers now differ, the problem is in your QuickBooks records; there's a transaction you should have cleared but didn't, or a transaction you cleared that you shouldn't have.

If you're sure you didn't make any mistakes clearing transactions, do the following:

- Check the amount of each transaction against the amount in the bank statement.
- Check your transactions and make sure a deposit wasn't inadvertently entered as a payment (or vice versa). A clue for this is a transaction that's half the difference. If the difference is $220.00, find a transaction that has an amount of $110.00 and make sure it's a deduction if it's supposed to be a deduction (or the other way around).
- Check for transposed figures. Perhaps you entered a figure incorrectly in the register, such as $549.00 when the bank clears the transaction as $594.00. A clue that a transposed number is the problem is that the reconciliation difference can be divided by nine.

If you find the problem, correct it. When the Difference figure is 0.00, click Reconcile Now.

 TIP: You might want to let somebody else check over the statement and the register, because sometimes you can't see your own mistakes.

Permitting an Adjusting Entry

If you cannot find the problem, you can tell QuickBooks to make an adjusting entry to force the reconciliation to balance. The adjusting entry is placed in the bank account register and is offset in the Beginning Bal Equity account. If you ever figure out what the problem is, you can make the proper adjustment transaction and delete the adjusting entry.

To force a reconciliation, click Reconcile Now, even though there's a difference. A message appears to offer the opportunity to make an adjusting entry. Click Enter Adjustment.

Printing the Reconciliation Report

When you have a balanced reconciliation (even if it results from an adjusting entry), QuickBooks offers congratulations and also offers to print a reconciliation report. (The dialog has a Cancel button to skip the report, but it's not a good idea to do so.)

QuickBooks saves the report whether you print it, view it, or cancel it, and you can view it in the future by choosing Reports | Banking | Previous Reconciliation. Of course, next month, this report disappears in favor of the new report—QuickBooks only stores the last report (unlike QuickBooks Premier editions).

Deciding on the Type of Report

QuickBooks offers two reconciliation report types: Detail and Summary. Here are the differences between them:

- The Detail Report shows all the transactions that are cleared and all the transactions that haven't cleared (called *in transit* transactions by your bank) as of the statement closing date. Any transactions dated after the statement closing date are listed as *new transactions*.
- The Summary Report breaks down your transactions in the same way, but it doesn't list the individual transactions; it shows only the totals for each category: Cleared, Uncleared (in transit), and New.

Selecting the Detail Report makes it easier to resolve problems in the future. You have a list of every check and deposit and when it cleared.

Print vs. Display

You also have to decide whether to print or to display the report. Make your decision according to how you think you might use the report.

Printing a Reconciliation Report

If you opt to print both reports, the Print Reports dialog opens so you can select the printer. If you select either the Summary or Detail Report, the Print Reports dialog offers options, as follows:

- Print the report to the selected Printer. You can file the printout in case you ever need to refer to it.
- Print the report to a file. The file option offers several formats in a drop-down list, so you can load the resulting file into the software of your choice. This gives you the opportunity to store multiple reports in one application (or even one file) and sort the data as you wish. The following file options are available:

  - **ASCII text**   Is straight, unformatted text.
  - **Comma delimited**   Automatically puts a comma between each field (column). Select this option if you want to use the file in a spreadsheet or database program capable of importing comma-delimited files. Most spreadsheet software can handle comma-delimited files.
  - **Tab delimited**   Is the same as comma delimited, but the field delimiter is a tab marker instead of a comma. All spreadsheet and database software can handle tab-delimited files.

When you print a report to a disk file, QuickBooks opens a Create Disk File window with the folder that holds your QuickBooks software as the target folder. The file extension matches the file type you selected.

You can change the container to any other folder in the system—you might want to create a subfolder in your My Documents folder to hold these files. Hereafter, that folder becomes the default container for your reconciliation reports. Be sure to save each month's reconciliation report file with a unique name—the date and the account name (if you reconcile more than one bank account) are good selections for filenames.

Displaying a Reconciliation Report

If you choose to display the report, you see the usual QuickBooks report format. You can modify the report to change the font, the columns, and so on. In addition, you can click the Export icon at the top of the report window and send the report to Excel.

Additional Features for Premier and Enterprise Editions

If you're running QuickBooks Premier Edition or QuickBooks Enterprise Solutions, you may have some additional features available, above and beyond the features covered in this chapter. (Not all features are in all Premier or Enterprise versions.)

Previous Bank Reconciliation Reports

Unlike QuickBooks Pro, which only saves the last bank reconciliation report, QuickBooks Premier/Enterprise Solutions editions save all bank reconciliation reports in your company file. This means you don't have to print a report each month, and file it away in case you have to refer to it later (usually because you have a problem reconciling the current month's statement). The previous reconciliation reports are available in two places:

- Choose Reports | Banking | Previous Reconciliation.
- In the Begin Reconciliation dialog box, click Locate Discrepancies, then click Previous Reports.

Even if you never remember (or bother) to print a reconciliation report, you can get your hands on any month's report because QuickBooks saves them for you.

Using Budgets and Planning Tools

In this chapter:

- Configure a budget

- Report on budgets versus actual figures

- Export budgets

- Project cash flow

- Use QuickBooks Decision Tools

A *budget* is a tool for tracking your progress against your plans. A well-prepared budget can also help you draw money out of your business wisely, because knowing what you plan to spend on staff, overhead, or other expenses in the future prevents you from carelessly withdrawing profits and living high on the hog whenever you have a good month.

How QuickBooks Handles Budgets

Before you begin creating a budget, you need to know how QuickBooks manages budgets and the processes connected to budgets. In this section, I'll present an overview of the QuickBooks budget features, so you can understand them and bear them in mind when you create your budgets.

Types of Budgets

QuickBooks offers several types of budgets:

- Budgets based on your Balance Sheet accounts
- P&L budgets based on your income and expense accounts
- P&L budgets based on income and expense accounts and a customer or job
- P&L budgets based on income and expense accounts and a class (if you've enabled class tracking)

P&L budgets can be created from scratch or by using the actual figures from the previous year. The latter option, of course, only works if you've upgraded to QuickBooks 2006 from an earlier version.

Budgets Aren't Really Documents

In QuickBooks, a budget is the data you enter in a budget window. Once you begin creating a budget, the data you record is more or less permanently ensconced in the budget window and reappears whenever you open that budget window. You create a budget by choosing Company | Planning & Budgeting | Set Up Budgets.

You can only create one of each type of budget. For example, if you create a P&L budget, enter and record some figures, and then decide to start all over by launching the Create New Budget wizard, you can't create a new P&L budget. Instead of creating a new budget, the wizard displays the data you already configured. You have no way of telling QuickBooks, "Okay, save that one, I'm going to do another one with different figures." You can change the figures, but the changes replace the original figures. You're editing a budget; you're not creating a new budget document.

Creating Multiple Budgets

Once you've created your first budget, regardless of type, the next time you select Company | Planning & Budgeting | Set Up Budgets, the budget window opens with the last budget you created.

If the budget is a P&L or Balance Sheet budget, you cannot create a second budget of the same type. However, you can create a budget of a different type (P&L Customer:Job or P&L Class). To do so, click the Create New Budget button in the budget window and go through the wizard to select different criteria (Customer:Job or Class).

After you've created a Customer:Job budget or a Class budget, you can create another budget using a different customer or job (or different accounts for the same customer or job). See the sections "Customer:Job Budgets" and "Class Budgets" for instructions on creating multiple budgets of those types.

Deleting a Budget

QuickBooks lets you delete a budget. This means if you want to create multiple budgets of the same type (perhaps you feel better if you have a "Plan B"), you have a workaround to the "no two budgets of the same type" rule. Export the original budget to a spreadsheet application, and then delete the original budget and start the process again. See the section "Exporting Budgets," later in this chapter.

To delete a budget, choose Edit | Delete Budget from the QuickBooks menu bar while the budget window is open.

Understanding the Budget Window

Before you start entering figures, you need to learn how to manage your work using the buttons on the budget window.

- **Clear** Deletes all figures in the budget window—you cannot use this button to clear a row or column.
- **Save** Records the current figures and leaves the window open so you can continue to work.
- **OK** Records the current figures and closes the window.
- **Cancel** Closes the window without any offer to record the figures.
- **Create New Budget** Starts the budget process anew, opening the Create New Budget wizard. If you've entered any data, QuickBooks asks if you want to record your budget before closing the window. If you record your data (or have previously recorded your data with the Save button), when you start anew, the budget window opens with the same recorded data.
- **Show Next 6 Months** Exists only if the display resolution of your computer is set lower than 1024×768; otherwise, you can see all twelve months in the budget window. With lower resolution, only six months of the budget can be seen in the window. In that case, QuickBooks adds buttons to the window to move the display to the next six-month display, and the button changes its name to Show Prev 6 Months.

The other buttons in the budget window are used when you're entering data, and I go over them later in this chapter. See the section "Enter Budget Amounts."

Tasks to Perform Before You Start Your Budget

Before you create a budget, you need to check the following details:

- The accounts you need must be available; you cannot add accounts while you're working in a budget.
- The first month of the budget must be the same as the first month of your fiscal year.

Activate All Necessary Accounts

Make sure all the accounts you want to include on the budget are included in the accounts list in the budget window. Any account you marked "inactive" is not available.

If you want to create a budget that includes an account that's currently inactive, follow these steps before you begin your budget:

1. Click the Chart Of Accounts icon on the Home page or press CTRL-A to open the Chart Of Accounts window.
2. Make sure a check mark appears in the Include Inactive check box at the bottom of the window. Your inactive accounts have an X in the leftmost column.
3. Right-click any inactive account you want to use in the budget and choose Make Account Active from the shortcut menu.
4. Close the Chart Of Accounts window.

Check the Starting Month

The first month that's displayed in the budget window must be the first month of your fiscal year, or your budget won't work properly. If you don't run your company on a calendar year (or if you want to create a budget that's not based on your fiscal year), you must make sure your company configuration has the correct starting month.

Follow these steps:

1. Choose Company | Company Information from the menu bar.
2. Enter the correct starting month for your fiscal year and click OK. (The tax year doesn't matter for budgeting, but if it's wrong, you should correct it while you have the dialog open.)

A Word About Balance Sheet Budgets

It's highly unusual to have a need to create a Balance Sheet budget because you can't predict the amounts for most Balance Sheet accounts. Even if you want to keep an eye on the few accounts over which you have control (fixed assets and loans), there's little reason to use a budget to do so. The transactions for fixed assets and loans are usually planned and therefore don't need budget-to-reality comparisons to allow you to keep an eye on them.

As a result, I'm not going to spend time discussing Balance Sheet budgets. If you feel you need to create one, choose Company | Planning & Budgeting | Set Up Budgets. If this is your first budget, the Create New Budget wizard opens. Otherwise, when an existing budget appears, click the Create New Budget button. When the Create New Budget wizard opens, select the year for which you want to create the budget and select the Balance Sheet option. Then click Next, and because the next window has no options, there's nothing for you to do except click Finish. The budget window opens, listing all your Balance Sheet accounts, and you can enter the budget figures. See the following sections on creating P&L budgets to learn the procedures for entering budget figures.

P&L Budgets

The most common (and useful) budget is based on your income and expenses. After you've set up a good chart of accounts, creating a budget is quite easy.

Create the Budget and Its Criteria

To create a P&L budget, choose Company | Planning & Budgeting | Set Up Budgets. If this is the first budget you're creating, the Create New Budget wizard opens to walk you through the process. (If you've already created a budget, the Set Up Budgets window appears with your existing budget loaded—click Create New Budget to open the Create New Budget wizard.) Enter the year for which you're creating the budget and select the P&L budget option.

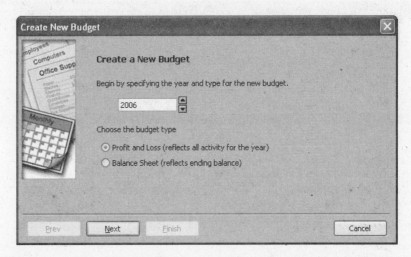

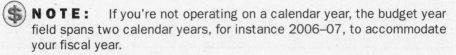
N O T E :   If you're not operating on a calendar year, the budget year field spans two calendar years, for instance 2006–07, to accommodate your fiscal year.

Click Next to select any additional criteria for this budget. You can include customers (and jobs) or classes in your budget.

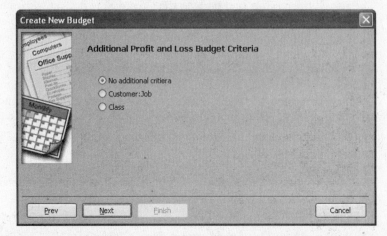

For this discussion, I'll go over regular P&L budgets (unconnected to customers or classes), and I'll explain later in this chapter how to budget for customers and jobs, and for classes. Click Next to choose between creating a budget from scratch or from the figures from last year's activities. I'll start by creating a budget from scratch. Click Finish to open the budget window, where all your income and expense accounts are displayed (see Figure 13-1).

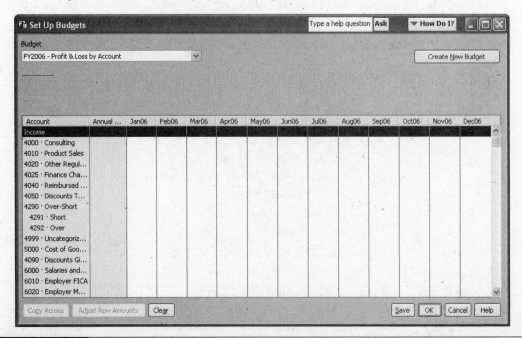

FIGURE 13-1   All active income and expense accounts are available for your budget.

Enter Budget Amounts

To create budget figures for an account, select the account and then click in the column of the first month you want to budget. Enter the budget figure, press TAB to move to the next month, and enter the appropriate amount. Repeat until all the months for this account have your budget figures. As you enter each monthly amount and press TAB, QuickBooks automatically calculates and displays the annual total for the account (see Figure 13-2).

If you see the Show Next 6 Months button, when you enter the amount for the sixth month, you must click it to continue through the rest of the months. Pressing TAB in the sixth month column moves your cursor to the first month of the next account, not to the seventh month column of the current account (isn't that annoying?). When you finish entering the figures in the twelfth month, click Show Prev 6 Months to return to the first half of the year and the next row.

Using Budget Entry Shortcuts

To save yourself from contracting a case of terminal ennui, QuickBooks provides some shortcuts for entering budget figures.

Copy Numbers Across the Months

To copy a monthly figure from the current month (the month where your cursor is) to all the following months, enter the figure and click Copy Across. The numbers are copied to all the rest of the months of the year.

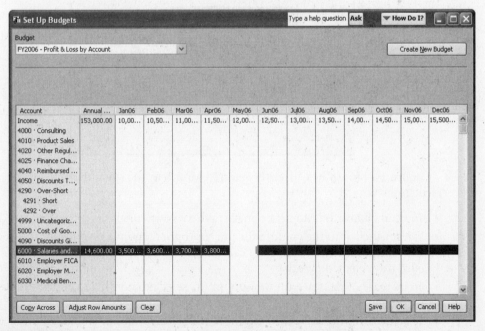

FIGURE 13-2 QuickBooks takes care of tracking the running totals.

You can perform this shortcut as soon as you enter an amount (but before you press TAB), or you can return to the month you want to designate the first month by clicking its column (useful if you've entered figures for several months and then remember this shortcut).

This is handier than it seems at first glance. It's obvious that if you enter your rent in the first month and choose Copy Across, you've saved a lot of manual data entry. However, suppose your landlord sends you a notice that your rent is increasing beginning in July? To adjust the July–December budget figures, just move your cursor to July, enter the new rate, and click Copy Across.

The Copy Across button is also the only way to clear a row. Delete the figure in the first month (or enter a zero) and click Copy Across. The entire row is now blank (or filled with zeros).

Automatically Increase or Decrease Monthly Figures

After you've entered figures into all the months on an account's row (manually, by using the Copy Across button, or by bringing in last year's figures), you can raise or lower monthly figures automatically. For example, you may want to raise an income account by an amount or a percentage starting in a certain month because you expect to sign a new customer or a new contract.

Select the first month that needs the adjustment and click Adjust Row Amounts to open the Adjust Row Amounts dialog.

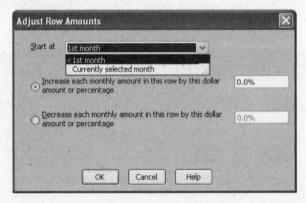

Choose 1st Month or Currently Selected Month as the starting point for the calculations.

- You can choose 1st Month no matter where your cursor is on the account's row.
- You must click in the column for the appropriate month if you want to choose Currently Selected Month (you can click the first month to make that the currently selected month).
- To increase or decrease the amount in the selected month and all the months following by a specific amount, enter the amount.
- To increase or decrease the amount in the selected month and all columns to the right by a percentage, enter the percentage rate and the percentage sign.

Compound the Changes

If you select Currently Selected Month, the Adjust Row Amounts dialog adds an additional option named Enable Compounding.

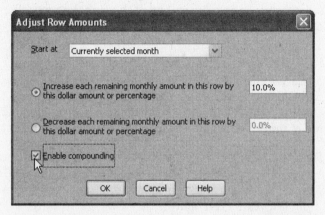

$ TIP: Although the Enable Compounding option appears only when you select Currently Selected Month, if your cursor is in the first month and you select the Currently Selected Month option, you can use compounding for the entire year.

When you enable compounding, the calculations for each month are increased or decreased based on a formula starting with the currently selected month and taking into consideration the resulting change in the previous month.

For example, if you entered $1,000.00 in the current month and indicated a $100.00 increase, the results differ from amounts that are not being compounded.

Compounding Enabled?	Current Month Original Figure	Current Month New Figure	Next Month	Next Month	Next Month	Next Month
Yes	1,000.00	1,000.00	1,100.00	1,200.00	1,300.00	1,400.00
No	1,000.00	1,100.00	1,100.00	1,100.00	1,100.00	1,100.00

Create a Budget from Last Year's Data

If you used QuickBooks last year, you can create a budget based on last year's figures. To use last year's real data as the basis of your budget, open the Create New Budget wizard by choosing Company | Planning & Budgeting | Set Up Budgets. When the Create New Budget wizard opens, enter the year for which you're creating the budget, and select the P&L budget option. In the next window, select any additional criteria, such as a customer, job, or class. (I'm skipping additional criteria for this example.) In the next window, select the option to create the budget from the previous year's actual figures, and click Finish.

The budget window opens with last year's actual data displayed (see Figure 13-3). For each account that had activity, the ending monthly balances are entered in the appropriate month.

You can change any figures you wish using the procedures and shortcuts described earlier in this chapter.

Customer:Job Budgets

If you have a customer or a job that warrants it, you can create a P&L budget to track the financials for that customer or job against a budget. Usually, you only do this for a project that involves a substantial amount of money and/or covers a long period of time.

Creating the First Customer:Job Budget

To create your first budget for a customer or a job, choose Company | Planning & Budgeting | Set Up Budgets. I'm assuming you're creating the budget from scratch, not from last year's P&L figures.

- If you already created another budget of a different type (P&L or Class), the budget window opens with the last budget you created. Click the Create New Budget button in the budget window to launch the Create New Budget wizard.
- If this is your first-ever budget, the Create New Budget wizard appears automatically.

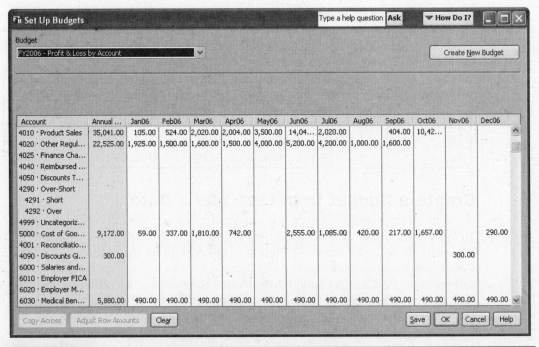

FIGURE 13-3 Start your budget by looking at last year's figures.

Select the year for your budget and choose P&L as the type. In the next wizard window, select the option Customer:Job. When the budget window opens, an additional field labeled Current Customer: Job appears so you can select the Customer:Job for this budget from the drop-down list.

Select the account, or multiple accounts, for which you want to budget this job—these will probably be only expense accounts (the anticipated income is usually already known). The expenses you track depend on the scope of the job. For example, you may only want to budget the cost of outside contractors or supplies, so if prices rise you can have a conversation with the customer about overruns.

You can enter a monthly budget figure for each account or for each month the project exists, or enter a total budget figure in the first month. The latter option lets you compare accumulated data for expenses against the total budgeted figure by creating modified reports (where you change the report date to reflect the elapsed time for the project and filter the report for this job only).

If the project is lengthy, you may budget some accounts for some months and other accounts for other months. For example, if you have a project that involves purchases of goods, followed by installation of those goods, or training for the customer's employees, you might choose to budget the purchases for the first few months and then the cost of the installation or training (either by tracking payroll or outside contractors) for the months in which those activities occur.

If you want to track payroll costs against a job, use the QuickBooks Time and Billing features that are discussed in Chapter 18. If you do your own payroll, also read Chapter 19 to learn how to move the Time and Billing features to your payroll computations. It's nerve-wracking to attempt payroll job-costing manually.

 CAUTION: Customer:Job budgets don't work unless you're faithful about assigning transactions to the customer or job. If you've only been filling in the Customer:Job fields when the customer is billable, you won't have accurate budget-to-reality reports.

Creating Additional Customer:Job Budgets

After you've created one budget based on a customer or job, creating a budget for a different customer or job requires different steps.

To create a budget for another customer immediately while the Customer:Job budget you just created is still in the budget window, select another customer from the drop-down list. Begin entering data and click Yes when QuickBooks asks if you want to record the budget you just finished.

To create a budget for another customer later, choose Company | Planning & Budgeting | Set Up Budgets. The budget window opens immediately with the last budget you worked on.

- If the budget that appears is a Customer:Job budget, select a different customer or job from the Current Customer:Job drop-down list and begin entering data.

- If the budget that appears is a different type of budget, click the arrow to the right of the Budget field and select Profit And Loss By Account And Customer:Job as the budget type. Then select a customer from the Current Customer:Job drop-down list and begin entering data.

Class Budgets

You can link your budget to any class you've created (if you're using class tracking). I've learned that this works well for certain types of classes and not for others. If you're using classes to track branch offices, company divisions, or company departments, you can create useful budgets. If, on the other hand, you're using classes to divide your transactions in some esoteric way, budgeting may not work well.

Look at your class-based reports, and if you find yourself asking, "Aren't those expenses higher than they should be?" or "Why is one class less profitable than the other classes?", you might want to budget each month to get a handle on where and when expenses got out of hand. Also, if you ask, "Is this department contributing the income I expected?", include income accounts in your budget. You can use income accounts in class budgets to provide incentives to your employees—perhaps a bonus to a manager if the reality is better than the budget.

To create a class-based budget, use the steps described earlier to create a budget and choose Class in the Additional Profit And Loss Budget Criteria wizard window. When the budget window opens, a Current Class field appears. Select the class for which you're creating a budget from the drop-down list. Then begin entering data.

To create additional class budgets (for other classes, of course), use the same approach discussed in the previous section on creating additional customer or job budgets.

Budget Reports

QuickBooks provides a number of budget reports you can use to see how you're doing. I'll discuss each of them in this section. To get to the reports, choose Reports | Budgets from the menu bar and then select one of the following reports:

- Budget Overview
- Budget vs. Actual
- Profit & Loss Budget Performance
- Budget vs. Actual Graph

Budget Overview

This report shows the accounts you budgeted and the amounts you budgeted for each month. Accounts that you didn't include in the budget aren't displayed.

Profit & Loss Budget Overview

If you created a P&L budget, select Profit & Loss By Account in the first Budget Report window and click Next. In the next window, you're asked to select a report layout, but the only option available in the drop-down list is Account By Month. Click Next, and then click Finish. The report opens and looks like the P&L budget report in Figure 13-4. Essentially, the Overview report type produces the display you'd see if the window you use to create a budget had a button labeled Print The Budget.

If you use subaccounts in your budget, you can click the Collapse button at the top of the report window to see only the parent account totals. The button name changes to Expand, and clicking it puts the subaccount lines back into the display.

To condense the numbers, use the Columns drop-down list to select a different interval. The default is Month, but you can choose another interval and QuickBooks will calculate the figures to fit. For example, you might want to select Quarter to see four columns of three-month subtotals.

If you want to tweak the budget, or play "what if" games by experimenting with different numbers, click the Export button to send the report to Microsoft Excel. See Appendix B for more information about integrating QuickBooks reports with Excel.

Profit & Loss Budget Overview							
Dates Custom	From 01/01/2006 To 12/31/2006 Colums Month			Sort By Default			

We Do It All
Profit & Loss Budget Overview
January through December 2006

Accrual Basis

	Jan 06	Feb 06	Mar 06	Apr 06	May 06	Jun 06	Jul 06
Ordinary Income/Expense							
Income							
Income	3,525.00	10,000.00	2,085.00	750.00	885.00	6,060.00	3,67
4010 · Product Sales	105.00	524.00	2,020.00	2,004.00	3,500.00	14,040.00	2,02
4020 · Other Regular Income	1,925.00	1,500.00	1,600.00	1,500.00	4,000.00	5,200.00	4,20
Total Income	5,555.00	12,024.00	5,705.00	4,254.00	8,385.00	25,300.00	9,89
Cost of Goods Sold							
5000 · Cost of Goods Sold	59.00	337.00	1,810.00	742.00		2,555.00	1,08
Total COGS	59.00	337.00	1,810.00	742.00		2,555.00	1,08
Gross Profit	5,496.00	11,687.00	3,895.00	3,512.00	8,385.00	22,745.00	8,81
Expense							
4090 · Discounts Given							
6030 · Medical Benefits	490.00	490.00	490.00	490.00	490.00	490.00	49
6250 · Postage and Delivery		39.00	37.00		37.00		3
6260 · Printing and Reproduction			239.25			185.99	
6290 · Rent	1,000.00	1,000.00	1,000.00	1,000.00	1,000.00	1,000.00	1,00
6300 · Repairs							
6750 · Janitorial Exp	45.00	45.00	45.00	45.00	45.00	45.00	45.00
Total 6300 · Repairs	45.00	45.00	45.00	45.00	45.00	45.00	4
6340 · Telephone	145.25	152.39	124.85	119.58	188.25	155.78	14
6390 · Utilities							
6400 · Gas and Electric	180.00	177.00	168.00	182.00	174.00	177.00	163.00

FIGURE 13-4 The P&L Budget Overview is an easy-to-read display of your budget.

Balance Sheet Budget Overview

If you created a Balance Sheet budget, select Balance Sheet By Account in the first window and then click Next. QuickBooks displays a graphical representation of the report's layout (it's a monthly layout similar to the layout for the P&L budget). Click Finish to see the report.

Customer:Job Budget Overview

If you created one or more budgets for a customer or a job, select Profit & Loss By Account And Customer:Job in the first window and click Next. Select a report layout from the drop-down list (as you select each option from the list, QuickBooks displays a diagram of the layout). The following choices are available:

- **Account By Month**   Lists each account you used in the budget and displays the total budget amounts (for all customer budgets you created) for each month that has data. No budget information for individual customers appears.
- **Account By Customer:Job**   Lists each account you used in the budget and displays the yearly total for that account for each customer (each customer has its own column).
- **Customer:Job By Month**   Displays a row for each customer that has a budget and a column for each month. The budget totals (for all accounts—individual accounts are not displayed) appear under each month. Under each customer's row is a row for each job that has a budget.

 TIP: The name of each layout choice is a hint about the way it displays in the report. The first word represents the rows, and the word after the word "by" represents the columns.

Class Budget Overview

If you created a Class budget, select Profit & Loss By Account And Class in the first window and click Next. Select a report layout from the drop-down list. You have the following choices:

- **Account By Month**   Lists each account you used in the budget and displays the total budget amounts (for all Class budgets you created) for each month that has data. No budget information for individual classes appears.
- **Account By Class**   Lists each account you used in the budget and displays the yearly total for that account for each class (each class has its own column).
- **Class By Month**   Displays a row for each class that has a budget and a column for each month. The total budget (not broken down by account) appears for each month.

Budget vs. Actual

This report's name says it all—you can see how your real numbers compare to your budget figures. For a straight P&L budget, the report displays the following data for each month of your budget, for each account:

- Amount posted
- Amount budgeted
- Difference in dollars
- Difference in percentage

The choices for the budget type are the same as the Budget Overview, so you can see account totals, customer totals, or class totals to match the budgets you've created.

The first thing you'll notice in the report is that all the accounts in your general ledger are listed, regardless of whether or not you included them in your budget. However, only the accounts you used in your budget show budget figures. You can change that by customizing the report to include only your budgeted accounts.

Click the Modify Report button at the top of the budget report window. In the Modify Report window, click the Advanced button to open the Advanced Options window. Click the option labeled Show Only Rows And Columns With Budgets.

Click OK to return to the Modify Report window, and then click OK again to return to the Budget Vs. Actual Report window. The data that's displayed is only that data connected to your budgeted accounts.

You can also use the options in the Modify Report window to make other changes:

- Change the report dates.
- Change the calculations from Accrual to Cash (which means that unpaid invoices and bills are removed from the calculations, and only actual income and expenses are reported).

You should memorize the report so you don't have to make these modifications the next time you want to view a comparison report. Click the Memorize button at the top of the report window and then give the report a meaningful name. Only the formatting changes you make are memorized, not the data. Every time you open the report, it displays current data. To view the report after you memorize it, choose Reports | Memorized Reports from the QuickBooks menu bar.

Profit & Loss Budget Performance

This report is similar to the Budget vs. Actual report, but it's based on the current month and the year to date. For that time period, the report displays your actual income and expenses compared to what you budgeted.

By default, the date range is the current month, but you can change that to see last month's figures or the figures for any previous month. This report is also available for all types, as described in "Budget Overview," earlier in this section, and can also be modified to customize the display.

Budget vs. Actual Graph

This report just opens; you have no choices to select first. All the choices are in the graph that displays, in the form of buttons across the top of the report window. Merely click the type of report you want to see.

Exporting Budgets

If you need to manipulate your budgets, export them to other software applications. However, you can't select specific budgets to export—it's all or nothing.

You can export the budgets to any software program that supports documents that contain delimited fields (this usually means spreadsheet or database programs).

Use the following steps:

1. Choose File | Utilities | Export | Lists to IIF Files, from the QuickBooks menu bar.
2. When the Export dialog opens, it displays all the QuickBooks lists. Select the item named Budgets and click OK.
3. Another Export dialog opens (this one looks like the Save dialog you're used to seeing in Windows software). Select a folder in which to save this exported file, or leave it in your QuickBooks folder (the default location). I usually change the folder to the location where I keep files for the program I'm going to use for the exported file.
4. Give the exported list a filename (for example, 2006Budgets). QuickBooks will automatically add the extension .iif to the filename.
5. Click Save. QuickBooks displays a message telling you that your data has been exported successfully. Click OK.

Using Exported Budgets in Other Software

You can view and manipulate your exported budgets in the software application that received the exported budgets. One common task is to change the budget dates to the following year, so you can import your budgets back into QuickBooks and use them as the basis of next year's budgets.

Here's how to import the .iif file into the target software application:

1. Click the Open icon (or use the Open command) in the software you're using. When the Open dialog appears, move to the folder where you stored your .iif file.

❷ In the Files Of Type field of the Open dialog, change the specification to All Files (otherwise, you won't see your .iif file in the listings).

❸ Double-click your exported .iif file to open it.

Your software application should recognize that this file doesn't match its own file type and therefore begin the procedures for importing a file. In case your software doesn't figure it out, your .iif file is a *tab-delimited file*.

When the import procedures are completed, your budget is displayed in the window of your software program.

You can use the features in this software to manipulate the budget by changing the way the items are sorted or by applying formulas to budget data. If you want to change the budget dates so you can use the budgets next year in QuickBooks, move to the column labeled STARTDATE and update the dates so they apply to the following year.

If you're planning to import the budgets back into QuickBooks (covered next), be sure to save the file as a tab-delimited document and give the file the extension .iif.

Importing Budgets Back into QuickBooks

The only circumstances under which you'd import budgets back into QuickBooks is to copy a budget to another year. If you wanted to edit figures, you'd work in the QuickBooks budget window. To play "what if" games or to sort the budget differently, you'd work in the appropriate software (such as Excel) because QuickBooks doesn't provide those features.

If you changed the dates to next year, import the file so you can use the data in budget reports, or edit data right in the QuickBooks budget window.

Import the budgets back into QuickBooks, using the following steps:

❶ Choose File | Utilities | Import | IIF Files, from the menu bar.

❷ When the Import dialog opens, locate and double-click the file you saved.

❸ QuickBooks displays a message to tell you the import was successful. Click OK.

You can view the imported budgets in any budget report or in the budget window. QuickBooks checks the dates and changes the budget's name to reflect the dates. Budget names start with FY*xxxx*, where *xxxx* is the fiscal year.

When you select a budget report or choose a budget to edit in the budget window, the available budgets include both the budgets you created in QuickBooks (FY2006) and the budgets you imported after changing the date (FY2007). Next year, you can delete the FY2006 budgets.

Projecting Cash Flow

The Cash Flow Projector is a tool you can use to build a report that projects your cash flows using your own criteria. Like the cash flow reports available in the QuickBooks Reports menu (covered in Chapter 15), this tool uses data in your company file. However, the Projector lets you remove and add accounts and even adjust figures. These features make it easier to achieve the projection parameters and results you need.

The Cash Flow Projector is rather powerful if you understand the accounting terminology and principles of determining cash flows. You can design very specific cash flow scenarios, which might be useful in planning for expansion or other major business events.

It's beyond the scope of this book to provide a detailed explanation of the best ways to use this tool, but in this section I'll give you an overview.

 NOTE   Unless you have quite a bit of expertise in accounting, it's best to work with your accountant when you use the Cash Flow Projector.

To ensure accuracy, make sure you've entered all transactions, including memorized transactions, into your QuickBooks company file. Then launch the Cash Flow Projector by choosing Company | Planning & Budgeting | Cash Flow Projector. The program operates like a wizard, and the opening window (see Figure 13-5) welcomes you and offers links to information you should read before you begin.

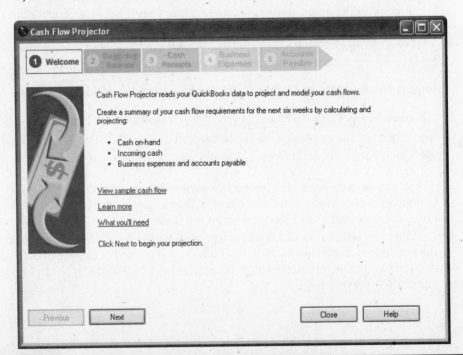

FIGURE 13-5   Use the links to familiarize yourself with the information the wizard needs.

TIP   Each ensuing wizard window has a button labeled Preview Projection. Click it to see your results so far.

Click Next to display the Beginning Balance window (see Figure 13-6), and select the cash accounts you want to include in your projection.

The software calculates a beginning balance by adding together the balances of all the accounts you select. You can make an adjustment to that calculated balance to change the beginning balance of the cash flows projection. This is useful if you know the current balance of any account contains an amount that you don't want included in the projection, such as an income item that is earmarked for spending tomorrow.

Click Next to move to the Cash Receipts window (see Figure 13-7). You must select a projection method from the drop-down list. If you don't understand the terminology in the list, discuss it with your accountant. One of the choices is manual entry, which is useful if your accountant has some particular paradigm in mind, or if you don't have A/R totals to guide you because you run a retail business.

The next two wizard windows look similar to Figure 13-7, but they deal with expenses, starting with expenses that are not accounts-payable expenses (such as unique expenses that qualify as "one-time-only") and moving on to accounts-payable expenses (including recurring bills you've entered into your system). In both windows you can enter specific expenses or enter adjusted total expenses.

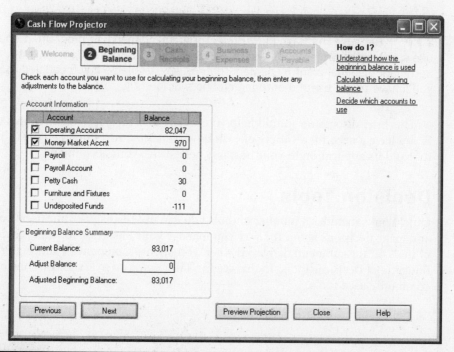

FIGURE 13-6   Select the accounts to use.

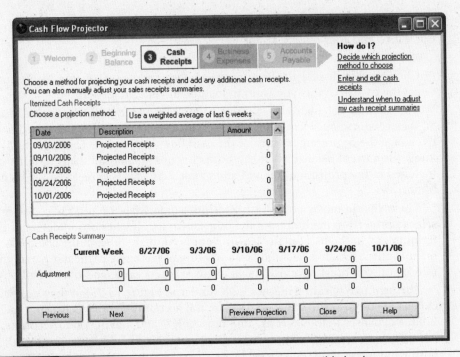

FIGURE 13-7   Summarize your projected cash receipts on a weekly basis.

$ TIP   Because the Cash Flow Projector is an independent program, it doesn't use some of the preferences you established in QuickBooks. Consequently, the automatic decimal point placement feature isn't available if you enabled it, so you'll have to get used to entering numbers differently.

This brief discussion should help you understand the possibilities in this tool. If you have a need for a variety of cash flow scenarios, you should go over this tool and its application to your business needs with your accountant.

Decision Tools

QuickBooks includes a number of tools you can use to analyze your fiscal condition and make decisions about the way you manage your business. You can see the list of tools on the submenu displayed when you choose Company | Planning & Budgeting | Decision Tools. In this section I'll provide an overview of some of the commonly used tools.

Measure Profitability

The Measure Profitability tool looks at your profit margin and offers advice based on that data. When the tool opens, the Basics tab is selected (see Figure 13-8) and displays a graph of your net profit margin by quarter for the last 12 months, along with the income/expense dollar amounts for the current quarter and your profit margin percentage. Use the Next button to move through the tabs.

The Interpret Results tab offers guidelines on interpreting your numbers. The advice is rather generic (and bland), and you should also consider industry-specific common trends. For example, different types of industries operate at different "acceptable" profit margins. Retailers commonly have lower profit margins (but higher volume) than service industries.

The Improve Results tab has some guidelines (including a number of questions to ask yourself) for improving your profit margin if the displayed figures are disappointing.

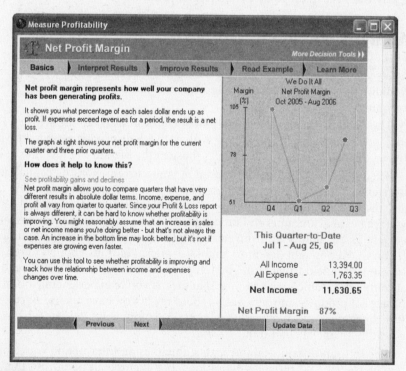

FIGURE 13-8   Check your profit margin and learn how to improve it.

The Read Example tab presents data and explanations for a sample (imaginary) company. The narrative explains the fluctuations in the sample company's quarterly net profit margin and offers solutions for overcoming the problems.

The Learn More tab explains how the Measure Profitability tool gets the numbers it presents. Because there is no single "correct" way to calculate profit margin, it's important to know the algorithms the tool uses. Then you or your accountant (who probably has more experience with this stuff) can analyze the results within the proper perspective.

To compute your net profit margin, the Measure Profitability tool performs an analysis of your company's Profit & Loss report using the following steps:

1 Totals the income account totals (the Total Income and Total Other Income accounts)

2 Totals the expense accounts (Total COGS, Total Expense, and Total Other Expense)

3 Reduces the income total by the expense total to get the net income

4 Divides the net income by the total income

Analyze Financial Strength

This tool concerns itself with your liquidity, which means the amount of cash and assets your business has available. A business that is financially strong has enough liquidity to manage emergencies and can continue to operate in spite of slow accounts receivable collections.

The Analyze Financial Strength tool operates similarly to the Measure Profitability tool, presenting a multitab window, with each tab displaying a different type of data. In fact, the tab names are the same as those in the Measure Profitability tool.

The Basics tab displays the amount of your current working capital, which is the difference between your current assets and your current liabilities. The difference is also displayed as a ratio. While a ratio of 2 or higher is considered healthy, sometimes working capital amounts and ratio figures can be deceiving. That's because your current assets include your inventory and accounts receivable, in addition to cash. If you've over-bought inventory and sales aren't vigorous enough to recoup the investment quickly, that's not good. If your current assets are enhanced by a large accounts receivable, don't assume that means you're experiencing a healthy number of sales of products and services. It could mean you have a lot of uncollected sales. Run an aging report (covered in Chapter 5) before you celebrate what seems to be a healthy financial condition.

The Interpret Results tab presents guidelines on interpreting your numbers. The text on the tab also provides definitions. For example, it points out that a ratio of 1.0 (which is quite low) means that your finances are operating at a one-to-one ratio. For every dollar you owe, you have one dollar available payment. This leaves nothing for emergencies (even minor ones), which is quite risky.

The Improve Results tab offers suggestions for improving your ratio, if it's too low. Some of the advice may fall under the category "obvious," but that doesn't mean it's not good advice. For example, the suggestions to convert inventory and receivables to cash more quickly may produce a reaction of "duh, who doesn't know that?", but those suggestions are eternal truths.

The Read Example tab presents the same sample company, with accompanying data, that you see in the Measure Profitability tool, but the subject matter is financial strength (liquidity).

The Learn More tab explains the numbers and calculations the tool uses to produce the analysis (see Figure 13-9).

Compare Debt and Ownership

This tool examines your data and calculates what's commonly called the debt-to-equity ratio, which is simply an analysis of the amount of assets in your business that's controlled by debt. The tool displays a graph that shows how much of your total assets came from ownership (equity) and how much came from creditors (see Figure 13-10). The more equity-owned assets, the easier it is to use your company's assets as collateral. Inventory and accounts receivable are often used as collateral.

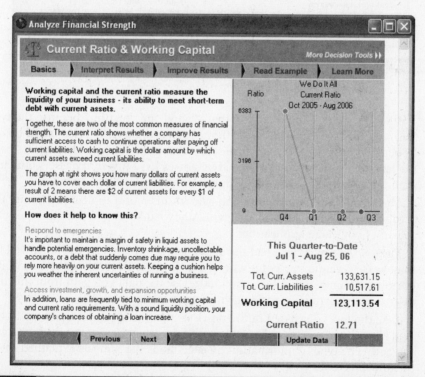

FIGURE 13-9 The source information is enumerated and explained in the Learn More tab.

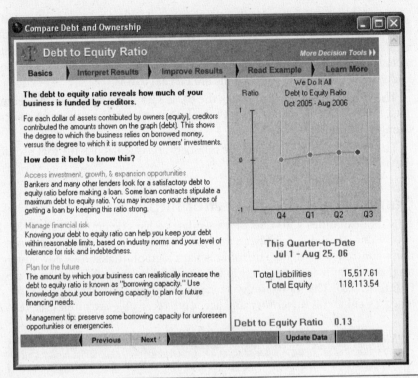

FIGURE 13-10   Check the ratio of debt to equity for your company.

It's difficult to pinpoint a ratio that's "good" or "healthy," because the type of business has a great deal to do with that determination. Service-based businesses frequently don't have as high an asset total as product-based businesses because of the lack of inventory assets. Retail businesses have inventory assets but lack the accounts receivable assets that wholesale businesses experience.

You can use the information you gain in this report to decide whether to seek credit in order to expand (or survive). Many banks want a debt-to-equity figure as part of your loan application.

Debt isn't necessarily a bad thing in business. If you can use borrowed funds to increase revenue to a point where your profit is larger than the cost of debt, borrowing money might be a good idea. Use the data you gain from this tool to discuss your borrowing options with your accountant.

Like the tools discussed in the previous two sections, the Compare Debt And Ownership tool presents information in categories, with tabs for each category. The type of information on each tab is the same as explained for the previous tools.

Depreciate Your Assets

This tool has the same look as the three tools discussed in the previous paragraphs, but that's the only similarity. Each of the first four tabs contains overview information about depreciation, lacking any information about the data in your company file. The last tab, named Depreciate Your Assets Now (see Figure 13-11), is a semi-tool.

Unlike the other tools, the Depreciate Your Assets tool can't read data from your QuickBooks company file. If you've already entered your depreciable fixed assets in the QuickBooks Fixed Asset Item list, you have to enter all the same information in this dialog. The tab labeled View All Assets is unconnected to your QuickBooks company file and presents only the list of assets you've entered in this dialog.

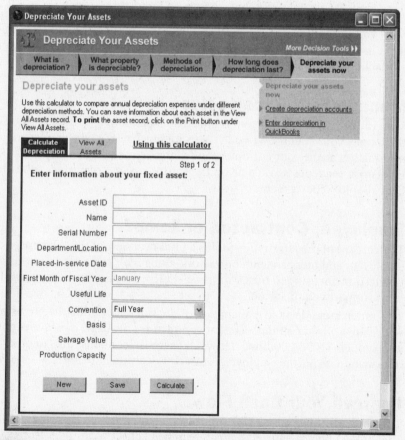

FIGURE 13-11   The Depreciate Your Assets tool has limited functions.

Two other links on the right side of the window seem to offer tools, but they don't:

- **Create Depreciation Accounts**   Clicking this link opens a page with an explanation of the reason for creating depreciation accounts. It does not present any way to create the accounts in your company file from the dialog and, in fact, does not present specific instructions for creating an account in QuickBooks. (Instructions for creating an account are in Chapter 2.)

- **Enter Depreciation In QuickBooks**   Clicking this link opens a page with an explanation of the difference between spending money for office supplies and spending part of the useful life of a fixed asset (depreciation). It does not contain a way to create a depreciation transaction directly in your company file and does not contain instructions for creating a depreciation entry in QuickBooks. (Instructions for creating journal entries for depreciation are in Chapter 14.)

If you want to use this tool to calculate depreciation for any assets you've entered here, you must know the IRS rules (which are complicated) and must calculate them manually; no list of IRS Depreciation Basis rules or calculation algorithms is available.

Manage Your Receivables

Most of the content of this tool is aimed at explaining why it's important to collect the money your clients owe you. There are links on the tabs that let you display information about your customers and your accounts receivable balances. The links open the reports available on the Customers & Receivables submenu of your QuickBooks Reports menu.

Employee, Contractor, or Temp?

The content of the tabs in this tool is a brief overview of the differences between employees and independent contractors, along with some explanations of the risks involved in choosing to treat workers as independent contractors when IRS rules don't support your decision.

A much more detailed explanation of the rules governing the provisions required to declare a worker an independent contractor is available at www.irs.gov/govt/fslg/article/0,,id=110344,00.html. This web page also contains links to other important information about the employee/contractor decision guidelines.

Improve Your Cash Flow

This tool offers suggestions for improving your cash flow and provides information about QuickBooks features that can help you collect receivables (for example, using the Write Letters feature to send letters to customers that are overdue by a specific number of days).

Periodic Tasks

This tool provides general advice (actually, reminders) about QuickBooks tasks that should be performed on a periodic basis. A tab exists for each period (see Figure 13-12).

Additional Features for Premier and Enterprise Editions

If you're running QuickBooks Premier Edition or QuickBooks Enterprise Solutions, you may have some additional features available, above and beyond the features covered in this chapter. (Not all features are in all Premier or Enterprise versions.)

Create a Business Plan

QuickBooks Premier/Enterprise editions include a robust software tool named Business Planner. You can use the software to create a detailed business plan, which is a way to predict, plan for, and control your company's future growth. You can create a business plan for your own business or, if you're an accounting professional, for a client's business.

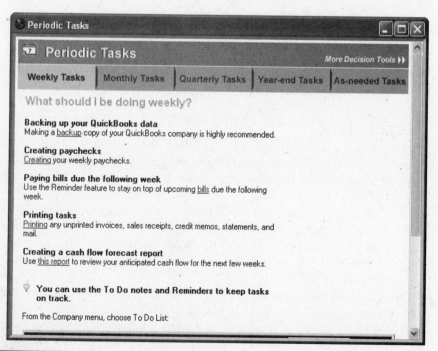

FIGURE 13-12   Get hints about scheduling tasks.

The tool operates like the EasyStep Interview you used when you set up your QuickBooks company file, which is, of course, a wizard (anyone who uses Windows knows about wizards). You click Next to move through a series of windows, divided into sections (topics), answering questions and providing information in each window.

The software is extremely powerful, so the business plan it creates is extremely detailed. Don't plan on getting the entire plan written in one session; it takes a lot of time to do this right. Luckily, the Business Planner saves the information you enter, so whenever you go back to the software you can pick up where you left off.

The Business Planner uses existing data from your QuickBooks company file, and then asks a slew of questions about your expectations for the business. You don't need an MBA to answer the questions; they're simple and to the point. You know your own businesses well enough to answer these questions.

The Business Planner produces a pro forma balance sheet, a profit and loss statement, and a statement of cash flow for the next three years, based on the projections it makes from the data you enter. You can publish your plan in PDF format, which makes the document extremely portable—you can send it to anybody, regardless of the word processing software they use. Additionally, you can export the plan's financial projections to Microsoft Excel for those "what if" exercises that are always so valuable.

TIP   A good business plan is more than a blueprint you can use for growing your business, it's a useful tool for gaining investment funds or a line of credit. The format of the QuickBooks business plan matches the recommendations of the United States Small Business Administration for a loan application or a line of credit.

Forecasting

You can create a forecast for revenue and cash flow with the QuickBooks Set Up Forecast feature, available only in Premier and Enterprise editions. The process, the user interface, and the linked reports for the forecast feature all closely resemble the QuickBooks budget feature.

You can start your forecast with existing company data, and then use "what if" scenarios to manipulate that data so it more closely matches your expectations (or hopes) for the coming year. As with the budget feature, you can base your forecast on your P&L accounts, or narrow the scope of a forecast to one customer (or customer:job), or one class.

You can also create your forecast from scratch, ignoring the data in your company file. This is a good approach if you've changed your business substantially, or are planning to. Perhaps you're adding services or products, or hiring employees who bring a new, specialized expertise that will provide new sales opportunities and a new customer base. On the other hand, perhaps your current financials reflect losses and you've decided to remove the service or products that caused those losses.

After you create your forecast, you can generate reports on the forecast, including a Forecast To Real Figures report.

Expert Analysis

Expert Analysis is a product of Sageworks, Inc., which you can read about at www.sageworksinc.com. The company's Expert Analysis product is offered without any fee (for one year) to Premier edition users.

Expert Analysis benchmarks your company's financial performance against past performance (if your company file has previous year data), and also against other companies in the same industry. The reports are incredibly comprehensive, which makes them a powerful resource for analyzing your company and planning for future growth.

Accountants can use Expert Analysis to examine and report on the performance of client companies, providing an opportunity for accountants to offer their clients a valuable professional service.

To create an Expert Analysis report on your company's financial condition, choose Company | Planning & Budgeting | Use Expert Analysis Tool. Using a wizard interface, Expert Analysis walks you through a series of windows in which you're asked to answer questions and enter information.

 C A U T I O N :   If you're using the QuickBooks logins and permissions features, only a user with permission to access sensitive reports can use Expert Analysis.

Expert Analysis calculates period comparisons, and you can select monthly, quarterly, or yearly analysis periods. You can further refine the way the periods are analyzed. For example, if you select quarterly analysis, you can compare this quarter to the previous quarter, or this quarter to the same quarter last year.

In a wonderful concession to reality, the software lets you make adjustments for scenarios that are specific to your business environment. For example, you can tell Expert Analysis to put back a proprietor's salary (instead of making it an expense), since those amounts are really part of the profit for a proprietorship. You can also tell Expert Analysis to consider expenses you don't currently have but plan to incur in the future. For example, you may be planning to move your home-based business (no rent expense) to an office building, or you may be ready to hire somebody to replace the free labor you're getting from family members.

The reports you get from Expert Analysis are slick and professional. Every imaginable category is covered in detail.

Depreciating Assets

The tools for asset tracking built into QuickBooks Pro don't interact; that is, you can't use the Depreciate Your Assets tool using the data you entered into the Fixed Assets List. However, QuickBooks Premier Accountant Edition and all of the Enterprise Solutions editions can bring the information in the Fixed Assets List into the Fixed Asset Manager. This powerful tool is discussed in Appendix A.

Using Journal Entries

In *this chapter:*

- The QuickBooks journal entry window

- Enter the opening trial balance

- Make adjustments to the general ledger

- Depreciate fixed assets

- Journalize outside payroll services

As you work in QuickBooks, the amounts involved in the financial transactions you complete are transferred to your general ledger. In addition to transaction data, numbers can be placed into the general ledger directly. This action is called a *journal entry*.

Journal entries shouldn't be used without a specific purpose, and usually that purpose is to enter figures that cannot be added to an account via a standard transaction.

 NOTE: The standard jargon for this transaction type is *journal entry*, usually abbreviated JE. However, QuickBooks refers to the transaction as *general journal entry* and uses GJE as the abbreviation.

The QuickBooks Journal Entry Window

For journal entries, QuickBooks provides the Make General Journal Entries window, seen in Figure 14-1. The format of the transaction window matches the standard approach to viewing the general ledger: columns for account numbers, debit amounts, and credit amounts (called a *T-Account* format). In addition, QuickBooks provides columns you can use to link the GJE data to customers and classes, and also enter a memo.

To create a journal entry, follow these steps:

1 Choose Company | Make General Journal Entries. QuickBooks displays a message telling you that automatic numbers are now assigned to journal entries (a feature introduced several years ago). Select the option Do Not Display This Message In The Future, and then click OK (you can enable and disable the feature in the Accounting category of the Preferences dialog).

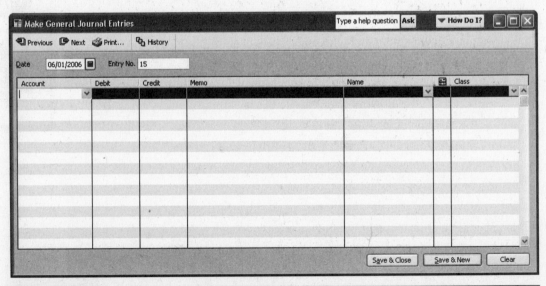

FIGURE 14-1   The QuickBooks GJE window has more columns than the standard T-Account format so you can track additional information.

2️⃣ Click in the Account column, and then click the arrow to see a drop-down list of your chart of accounts. Choose the account you need.

3️⃣ Move to the Debit or Credit column (depending on the data you're entering) and enter the amount for that account.

4️⃣ Repeat for all the accounts in the journal entry.

As you enter each amount, QuickBooks presents the offsetting total in the next line. For example, if the line items you've entered so far have a higher total for the credit side than the debit side, the next entry presents the balancing offset (see Figure 14-2).

Here are the guidelines for using the columns QuickBooks adds to a traditional journal entry window:

- Use the Memo column to write a comment about the reason for the journal entry. The memo text appears in the entry of the account's register and on reports, so you should enter the text on every line of the entry in order to see the explanation no matter which account register you're viewing.

💲 **N O T E :**   If you're using QuickBooks Premier, you can select the AutoFill Memo option to have the memo you enter on the first line appear automatically on all lines. This is a very handy feature. To learn how to use this and other Premier Edition features, buy *Running QuickBooks 2006 Premier Editions* (CPA911 Publishing—www.cpa911publishing.com) at your favorite bookstore or online book seller.

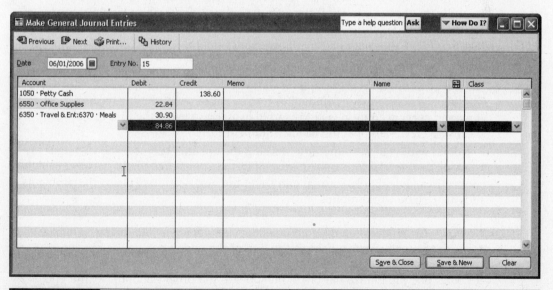

FIGURE 14-2   QuickBooks keeps the running offset figure available so you don't have to enter an amount for the last entry.

- Use the Name column to assign a customer, vendor, employee, or other name to the amount on this line of the entry, if you're linking the entry to a name. If the account you're posting to is an A/R or A/P account, an entry in the Name column is required.
- The column with the icon is a "billable" flag, which means that the amount is billable to the name in the Name column. Click the column to insert the "billable" icon if you are using an expense account and you enter a customer name in the Name column.
- If you are using the Classes feature, a Class column is present, and you can link the entry to a class. (See Chapter 21 for information about classes.)

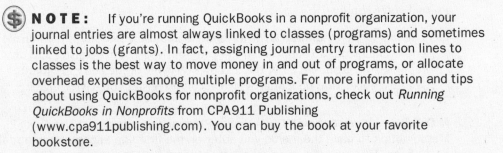 **NOTE:**   If you're running QuickBooks in a nonprofit organization, your journal entries are almost always linked to classes (programs) and sometimes linked to jobs (grants). In fact, assigning journal entry transaction lines to classes is the best way to move money in and out of programs, or allocate overhead expenses among multiple programs. For more information and tips about using QuickBooks for nonprofit organizations, check out *Running QuickBooks in Nonprofits* from CPA911 Publishing (www.cpa911publishing.com). You can buy the book at your favorite bookstore.

Opening Trial Balance

If you opted to skip entering opening balances during your EasyStep Interview, or when you created new accounts, you need to enter the opening balances for your accounts. All that's necessary is the opening balances for the balance sheet accounts. Then you can add all the transactions that took place since the beginning of the year to create a thorough history of transactions.

Entering the Opening Balances

QuickBooks does not have an item or feature called the "opening balance," per se. However, every account register is sorted by date, so using the first day of your fiscal year creates an opening balance automatically.

Confer with your accountant to develop the opening balance, and then enter it as a journal entry. Unfortunately, some of the accounts in the balance sheet can't be entered in a QuickBooks journal entry, and the next section explains the problems and offers some workarounds.

 TIP: Create a separate equity account for your previous equity; it makes it easier to maneuver numbers at the end of the year when you're closing books. QuickBooks will post profit (or loss) to the retained earnings equity account, but you'll have historical numbers in the other account. At the end of each year, you can make a journal entry to move the current year's equity change into the previous equity account.

Workarounds for QuickBooks Limitations

There are a couple of QuickBooks idiosyncrasies you may run into when working with journal entries.

In QuickBooks, a journal entry can contain only the A/P account or the A/R account; you cannot use both of those accounts in the same journal entry (and the odds are good that both accounts appear in your opening balance). You'll get an error message that says, "You cannot use more than one A/R or A/P account in the same transaction" (which is not a clear explanation). Unfortunately, QuickBooks doesn't issue the error message until after you enter all the data and try to save the journal entry (and an opening balance JE can contain a great many rows).

This restriction does not have its roots in accounting standards. It's an arbitrary rule built into the QuickBooks software.

Another problem is that QuickBooks insists you attach a single customer or vendor name to the entry if you're making a journal entry that involves either the A/R or the A/P account. You can't just enter an A/R or A/P balance against your previous equity (or against income or expenses, for that matter). If you're keeping customer info outside of QuickBooks (perhaps you have a retail business and keep customer charges elsewhere), you're out of luck.

If you decide that's okay, and you're willing to enter customer opening balances in your JE, you have another problem: you can't enter A/R for more than one customer in the JE. QuickBooks won't permit more than one A/R line in the journal entry, and that A/R line has to have one customer (the same restrictions apply to A/P).

QuickBooks' approach is to enter the opening balance when you create a customer or vendor. Both the New Customer and New Vendor windows have a field for this purpose. Those totals are posted to A/R and A/P as of the date you enter, which should be the first day of the fiscal year if you're trying to create an opening trial balance.

As a special "trick" to drive accountants into a frenzy, when you enter an opening balance for a customer or vendor as you create the entity, QuickBooks uses the Opening Bal Equity account as the offset account. That's not a standard equity account; it's another QuickBooks invention (probably invented by the QuickBooks programmers to have an offset account after they decided it would be a good idea to enter opening balances when you create customers, vendors, and accounts). Most accountants don't want to see any balance in the Opening Bal Equity account, ever.

($) TIP: If you're an accountant faced with clients who have balances in the Opening Bal Equity account, *Running QuickBooks 2006 Premier Editions* from CPA911 Publishing (www.cpa911publishing.com) has information, tricks, and tips to manage the account so it doesn't have a balance. You can buy the book at your favorite bookstore.

Neither of these data entry methods—A/R lines or opening balances during customer setup—is a good idea. The entry is only a total, and you don't have discrete invoices or bills, saddling you with several annoying drawbacks, such as:

- You can't easily deal with disputes over specific invoices or bills (you'll have to try to find the original paperwork).
- Customer payments have to be applied as partial payments against the total you entered. This makes it more difficult to have conversations with customers about their accounts.
- You don't have the opportunity to enter memos on invoices or bills.
- It makes it difficult to track those amounts that are for reimbursed expenses.

The solution is to enter your opening trial balance without the A/R and A/P entries (and always avoid entering an opening balance when you set up customers and vendors.) Adjust the equity account (Retained Earnings or Prior Retained Earnings) if your accountant preconfigured the opening trial balance for you with A/R and A/P included.

Then, enter the open invoices for customers and the open bills from vendors, using your opening balance date for the transactions, and let QuickBooks post the totals to the general ledger.

You can create one comprehensive invoice for the entire open balance per customer/vendor and pay it off if you don't want to bother with the individual invoices that created the opening balance. The equity account will automatically adjust itself back to your accountant's original totals as you enter the transactions.

Making Adjusting Entries

There are some circumstances, such as changing accounts and tracking depreciation, that require adjusting entries to your general ledger. Read on to find out how to handle these situations.

Making Journal Entries for Changed Accounts

I've had many clients who decided, after they'd been using QuickBooks for a while, that they wanted to track income differently. Instead of one income account, they opted for separate income accounts that are more specific. For example, having an income account for fees, and another income account for products sold, makes business analysis easier.

This transaction is quite simple. Create the new account and then take the appropriate amount of funds out of the original account and put it into the new account. Revenue is a credit-side item, so that means

- Debit the original account for the amount that belongs in the new account.
- Credit the new account for that same amount.

Then, of course, you'll have to go to the items list and change the necessary items to reflect the new income account so you don't have to keep making journal entries. (If QuickBooks didn't force you to link items to accounts, this wouldn't be necessary— sigh!)

The same decision is frequently made about expenses, as business owners decide to split heretofore comprehensive accounts. Perhaps you feel your insurance accounts should be separated for car insurance, equipment insurance, building insurance, malpractice insurance, and so on.

For expense accounts, the journal entry goes to the opposite side of the ledger because expenses are a debit-side item, so do the following:

- Credit the original expense account for the amount you're taking out of it and putting into the new account(s).
- Debit the new account(s) for the appropriate amount(s).

This logic also applies to a fixed-asset account named Vehicles that you want to divide into more specific accounts (to track the truck separately from the car, for instance, especially if they were purchased in different years). This means you can also separate out any accumulated depreciation so it's assigned to the correct asset. (You can get that information from your tax returns, or ask your accountant.)

Making Depreciation Entries

Depreciation is a way to track the current value of a fixed asset that loses value as it ages. The basis of an asset's depreciation from an accounting point of view is determined by a complicated set of rules. The IRS makes these rules, and the rules change frequently.

Depreciation is a journal entry activity. Most small businesses enter the depreciation of their assets at the end of the year, but some companies perform depreciation tasks monthly or quarterly.

Depreciation is a special journal entry because the accounts involved are very restricted—this is not a free choice where you can use whichever account strikes your fancy. The account that is being depreciated must be a fixed asset. The offset entry is to an account named Depreciation Expense (or Depreciation), and it is in the expense section of your chart of accounts.

Creating Accounts for Tracking Depreciation

I'm assuming that you've created your fixed-asset account and that the assets you've purchased have been posted there. You might have multiple fixed-asset accounts if you want to track different types of fixed assets separately. (For instance, my chart of accounts has three fixed-asset account sections: Equipment, Furn & Fixtures, and Vehicle.)

When it comes to accounting procedures that have a direct bearing on my taxes and for which I might need information at a glance (especially if I'm called on to explain it), I like to be very explicit in the way I work. Therefore, for every fixed-asset account in my chart of accounts, I have families of accounts for depreciation. I create a parent (account) and children (subaccounts) for each type of fixed asset. For example, the fixed-asset section of a chart of accounts I create would look like this:

Parent Accounts	Subaccounts
Equipment Assets	
	Equipment Purchases
	AccumDepr-Equipment
Furn & Fixtures Assets	
	Furn & Fixtures Purchases
	AccumDepr-Furn & Fixtures
Vehicle Assets	
	Vehicle Purchases
	AccumDepr-Vehicles

If you use numbers for your chart of accounts, create a numbering system that makes sense for this setup. For example, if Equipment is 1600, the subaccounts start with 1601; Furn & Fixtures starts with 1620, and the subaccounts start with 1621; Vehicle starts with 1640, and so on.

I post asset purchases to a subaccount I create for the specific purchase, and I make my journal entry for depreciation in the AccumDepr subaccount. I never use the parent account. There are several reasons for this:

- Both the asset subaccount and the depreciation asset subaccount are "pure." I can look at either one to see a running total instead of a calculated net total.
- Tracing the year-to-year depreciation is easy. I just open the depreciation asset subaccount register—each line represents a year.
- It's easier and quicker to open the depreciation asset subaccount if I'm asked about the depreciation total (handy if you sell the asset and have to add back the depreciation).
- The net value of my fixed assets is correct. A Balance Sheet report shows me the details (see Figure 14-3).

You can further refine this paradigm by creating subaccounts for specific fixed assets. For instance, you may want to create a subaccount for each vehicle asset (or one for all cars and one for all trucks) and its accompanying accumulated depreciation. If your equipment falls under a variety of depreciation rules (for example, manufacturing equipment vs. computer equipment), you may want to have a set of subaccounts for each type.

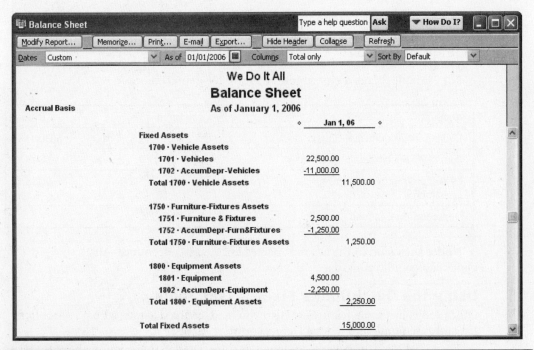

FIGURE 14-3   Subaccounts provide a detailed view of depreciation activity.

If you're really obsessive, you can create a different subaccount for each year of depreciation; for instance, under your AccumDepr-Vehicle subaccount, you could have Vehicle-Depr 2000, Vehicle-Depr 2001, Vehicle-Depr 2002, and so on. Then your balance sheet shows a complete year-by-year depreciation schedule instead of accumulated depreciation—and the math still works properly. Of course, after a number of years, you'll have destroyed an entire forest with all the paper it takes to print your balance sheet.

Creating a Depreciation Entry

To depreciate fixed assets, you must have a depreciation offset account in the Expense section of your chart of accounts.

Once that account exists, here's how to make your depreciation entry:

1. Choose Company | Make General Journal Entries from the menu bar.
2. Choose the first asset depreciation subaccount.
3. Enter the depreciation amount in the Credit column.
4. Choose the next asset depreciation subaccount and enter its depreciation amount in the Credit column. (QuickBooks automatically puts the offsetting amount in the Debit column, but just keep moving to the Credit column as you work.)
5. Continue until all your depreciation figures are entered in the Credit column.

6 Choose the Depreciation Expense account. The total amount of the credits is automatically placed in the Debit column.

7 Click Save & Close.

For example, here's a typical journal entry for depreciation:

Account	Debit	Credit
Equipment:AccumDepr-Equip		5,000.00
Furn & Fix:AccumDepr-Furn & Fix		700.00
LeaseholdImprov:AccumDepr-LeasImprov		1,000.00
Depreciation Expense	6,700.00	

Notice the colon in the account names for the asset accounts—that's the QuickBooks indication of a subaccount.

Using the QuickBooks Fixed Asset Tools

QuickBooks has some features to help you manage fixed assets: a Fixed Asset Item list and a planning tool named Depreciate Your Assets.

The Fixed Asset Item list is designed to store detailed information about fixed assets. Information about the list and the kind of data you can store in each asset's record is in Chapter 2.

The Depreciate Your Assets tool can be used to determine depreciation rates, but it doesn't pay any attention to the Fixed Asset Item list—instead, you have to enter your asset information to use the tool (the same information you entered in the Fixed Asset Item list). This is a planning tool, and it doesn't perform depreciation journal entries. You can learn more about this tool in Chapter 13.

QuickBooks Premier: Accountant Edition has a tool (Fixed Asset Manager) for managing assets on your Fixed Asset Item list. If your accountant has installed this product, depreciation calculations and entries can be written to your file when you send an Accountant's Copy. Chapter 15 explains how to create an Accountant's Copy of your file. If you're an accountant, you can learn how to use the Fixed Asset Manager in *QuickBooks 2006 Premier Editions* from CPA911 Publishing (www.cpa911publishing). The book is available at your favorite bookstore.

Reversing Entries

Your accountant may enter, or tell you to enter, *reversing entries*. These are general journal entries that are applied on one date and then reversed on another (later) date. For example, on 12/31/06, you may have a journal entry that adjusts your A/R and A/P accounts in order to prepare for tax filing on a cash basis (some accountants prefer this method to creating cash-basis reports). On 1/1/07, the entry has to be reversed. You enter both journal entries, and the totals you see are dictated by the dates selected in report windows.

N O T E : QuickBooks Premier editions have an automated reversing journal entry. Merely click the Reversing icon on the GJE window, and enter the reversal date.

Journalizing Outside Payroll Services

If you have an outside payroll service, you have to tell QuickBooks about the payroll transactions that took place. You get a report from the service, so all the numbers are available. It's just a matter of entering them.

It's common for businesses to perform this task via a journal entry. Like all other journal entries, this one is just a matter of entering debits and credits. There are three parts to recording payroll:

- Transferring money to the payroll account
- Entering the payroll figures
- Entering the employer expense figures

Transferring Money to the Payroll Account

You should have a separate bank account for payroll if you have an outside payroll service—in fact, a separate payroll account is a good idea even if you do your own payroll. Outside payroll services reach into your checking account; in fact, they have checks, and you certainly don't want to give away checks for your regular operating account.

Another reason for a separate payroll account, even if you do your own payroll, is the discipline involved in holding on to your employee withholdings until you pass them along to insurance companies, other vendors, and the government—*especially* the government. The money you withhold and leave in your bank account until you're ready to transmit it to the government is not your money. You cannot spend it. It doesn't matter if you need the money to save your business from total bankruptcy—you cannot spend the money. People have done that and gotten into serious trouble, including going to jail. Keeping all the money associated with payroll in a separate bank account makes it more difficult to "inadvertently" use that money to run your business.

To transfer the money you need for this payroll, choose Banking | Transfer Funds. Then, transfer the money from your regular operating account to your payroll account. Be sure to transfer enough money for the gross payroll plus the employer payroll expenses, which include the following:

- Employer-matching contributions to FICA and Medicare
- Employer-matching contributions to pension plans
- Employer-matching contributions to benefits
- Employer state unemployment assessments
- Employer FUTA
- Any other government or benefit payments paid by the employer

Even though some of these aren't transmitted every payday, you should transfer the amounts at that time anyway. Then, when it's time to pay them, the correct amount of money will have been amassed in the payroll account.

Recording the Payroll

The *payroll run* (jargon for "printing the paychecks") produces a fairly complicated set of debits and credits. Many businesses record a journal entry for the run, then a separate journal entry for the employer expenses when they're transmitted.

If your payroll service takes care of remitting employer expenses, you can journalize the payments. If you do the employer reports yourself and send the checks directly, your check-writing activity will record the payments, so you don't need a journal entry.

It's possible that you don't have all the expenses shown in this list (for instance, not all states have employee unemployment assessments). And you may have additional withholding categories such as union dues, garnishments against wages, and so on. Be sure you've created a liability account in your chart of accounts for each withholding category you need and a vendor for each transmittal check. Table 14-1 shows a typical template for recording the payroll run as a journal entry.

Account	Debit	Credit
Salaries and Wages (Expense)	Gross Payroll	
FWT (liability)		Total Federal Withheld
FICA (liability)		Total FICA Withheld
Medicare (liability)		Total Medicare Withheld
State Income Tax (liability)		Total State Tax Withheld
Local Income Tax (liability)		Total Local Tax Withheld
State SDI (liability)		Total State SDI Withheld
State SUI (liability)		Total State SUI Withheld
Benefits Contrib. (liability)		Total Benefits Withheld
401(k) Contrib. (liability)		Total 401(k) Withheld
Other Deductions (liability)		Total Other Deductions Withheld

TABLE 14-1   Typical journal entry to record payroll by an outside service

Recording Employer Payments

You need to journalize the employer remittances if your payroll service is taking care of them for you (if you do it yourself, just write the checks from the payroll account and each item will post to the general ledger correctly). Table 14-2 is a sample journal entry for recording payroll remittances.

The entry involving the transmittal of withholdings is posted to the same account you used when you withheld the amounts. In effect, you "wash" the liability accounts; you're not really spending money, you're remitting money you've withheld from employees.

You can have as many individual employer expense accounts as you think you need, or you can post all the employer expenses to one account named "payroll expenses."

 CAUTION: Don't have your payroll service take their fee from the payroll account. Instead, write them a check from your operating account. The fee for the service is not a payroll expense; it's an operating expense.

Create Your Own Boilerplate

You can save a lot of time and effort by creating a template for the payroll journal entries. Open a Make General Journal Entries window and fill out the Account column only. Enter the first account, then press the Down arrow and enter the next account, and keep going until all accounts are listed. QuickBooks automatically inserts 0.00 as you skip the Debit and Credit columns (see Figure 14-4).

Account	Debit	Credit
Federal Payroll Expenses (expense)	Employer FICA and Medicare	
Federal Withholdings (liability)	All federal withholding	
State and Local Withholdings (liability)	All local withholding	
SUTA (expense)	Employer SUTA	
FUTA (expense)	Employer FUTA	
Employer Contributions (expense)	All employer benefit, pension, etc.	
Payroll Bank Account (asset)		Total of checks written

TABLE 14-2   Typical journal entry for employer-side transactions

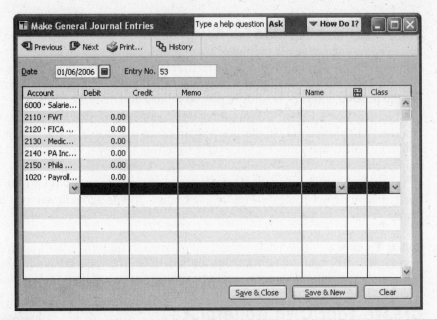

FIGURE 14-4   Create a boilerplate for payroll journal entries.

When all the accounts are listed, press CTRL-M to open the Memorize Transaction dialog. Name the memorized transaction Payroll (or something similar) and select the option Don't Remind Me (the reports from the payroll company are your reminder).

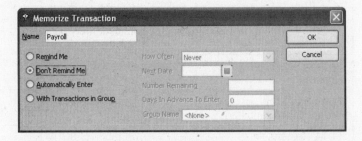

Close the Make General Journal Entries window. QuickBooks displays a message asking if you want to save the transaction you just created. Click No (you don't have to save a GJE to memorize it, isn't that handy?). Do the same thing for the journal entry you create to record employer remittances.

When you're ready to record payroll, open the memorized transaction, fill in the correct data and figures, and save it.

Reconciling the Payroll Account

The problem with journal entries for payroll is that when the bank statement comes for the payroll account, reconciling it is a bit different. You don't have a record of the check numbers and payees. When you open the payroll account in the Reconcile window, you see the journal entry totals instead of the individual checks.

Reconciling Outside QuickBooks

You have the report from the payroll service, and it lists each check number. You can therefore reconcile the account outside of the Reconcile window (using a manual system or using your spreadsheet software).

TIP: See if your payroll service can send you a file containing check#/ payee/amount information that can be opened in spreadsheet or database software.
A tab-delimited file is the best file type.

Entering Fake Payroll Checks in QuickBooks

If you want to perform the reconciliation in QuickBooks, you can enter the checks and post them back to the payroll account. (The journal entry took care of all the real postings.) You have a little bit of setup to do, and then you can perform this task every payday.

Create a name in the Other Names list, and name the new entity Payroll. You can use this name for every check (and put the employee's name in the memo field).

Alternatively, you can create a name for each employee in the Other Names list, using initials, last name only, or some other name that isn't the same as the original employee name. The reason you have to create these fake names is that QuickBooks will not let you write a check directly to an employee. Employee checks can be written only via the real Payroll feature.

Now you have a payee name for the payroll checks. Grab the report from the payroll service and enter the individual checks:

① Press CTRL-A to open the chart of accounts and double-click the Payroll account to open the register.

② On the next available transaction line, enter the payroll check date.

③ Tab to the Number field and enter the first check number on the payroll service report.

④ Enter the payee Payroll (unless you've entered all your employee names as Other Names, in which case enter the appropriate name).

⑤ Enter the amount of the net paycheck.

⑥ In the Account field, choose the Payroll account (the account you're currently working in). QuickBooks will flash a message warning you that you're posting the payment to the source account.

❼ Click OK (because you want to post the payment to the source account) and click the check box that tells QuickBooks to omit this warning in the future.

❽ Click the Record button to save this check, and then enter the next check.

You can also enter the checks the payroll service wrote to transmit your withholdings or pay your taxes. As long as each entry you make was entered into the journal entry, you can post everything back to the payroll account. You're "washing" every transaction, not changing the balance of the account. Then, when you want to reconcile the payroll account, the individual checks are in the Reconcile window. The fact is, this procedure is quite easy and fast, and you have to do it only on payday (or once a month if you want to wait until the bank statement comes in).

Additional Features for Premier and Enterprise Editions

If you're running QuickBooks Premier Edition or QuickBooks Enterprise Solutions, you may have some additional features available, above and beyond the features covered in this chapter. (Not all features are in all Premier or Enterprise versions.)

Advanced Options for General Journal Entries

QuickBooks Premier and Enterprise editions offer some unique functions you can apply when you're entering general journal entries. The additional power available in these functions makes it easier to create and track journal entries.

AutoFill Memos in General Journal Entries

When you're creating a GJE, any text you enter in the Memo field on the first line of the transaction can be automatically entered on all lines of the transaction. When you view the registers of any accounts involved in the journal entry, the memo text is available to help you remember or understand the reason for the transaction. To take advantage of AutoFill Memos in GJEs, you must enable the feature in Preferences. The option is on the My Preferences tab of the Accounting Preferences dialog box.

Without this feature, you have to enter (or copy and paste) the text in the memo field manually, on each line of the general journal entry. If you enter text in the memo field only on the first line of the transaction, then only the register for that account reveals the reason for the GJE. When you're examining account registers for other accounts involved in the transaction, you won't see any explanation for the transaction unless you open the original transaction. Think of the frustration and extra steps this feature saves!

AutoReverse General Journal Entries

Reversing general journal entries are a common transaction type. Frequently, your accountant makes the entry (or sends you instructions for creating the transaction yourself) at the end of the year. Many times, these entries adjust figures for the purpose of creating an accurate business tax return, and then reverse themselves so your reports provide the same view of your financial situation that you saw before the entry.

In QuickBooks Premier/Enterprise, you can automate the reversal process by clicking the Reverse icon at the top of the GJE window after you save the GJE. By default, when QuickBooks Premier/Enterprise creates the new, reversed GJE, it's dated the first day of the following month (the normal and usual method for reversing journal entries). However, if circumstances warrant it, you can change the date.

GJE Adjusting Entries

This feature is only available in the Premier Accountant and Enterprise Solutions Accountant editions.

Frequently, a GJE is an adjustment, made to correct a problem, or "clean up" an account. However, when you examine account registers and see a GJE, you have to rely on your memory for the reason behind the entry. Sometimes, even the text you put into the Memo field doesn't jog your memory sufficiently—it made sense when you wrote, but not any more. If you can't remember, you have to use all those extra keystrokes to open the original transaction window, and even then, you may not find enough information to determine the reason for the transaction.

Some GJEs are easy to figure out later; an entry in a fixed asset is almost certainly a depreciation or amortization entry. You don't even have to bother opening the original transaction window, because you know you'll find a depreciation expense account among the listings.

But what if the entry affects an income or expense account? Was this an adjustment, or did it represent some major change in the way books are kept? Most accountants want to know (and an auditor definitely wants to know).

In the Premier Accountant edition, you can specifically mark a GJE as an adjusting entry, via a check box available at the top of the GJE window. In fact, the Adjusting Entry check box has a check mark in it by default (because the majority of GJEs are created to make an adjustment).

To make this feature even more efficient, the Premier Accountant edition has a report named Adjusting Journal Entries in the Accountant & Tax Reports submenu. As you'd expect, it's a display of the adjusting GJEs you created.

GJE Reports in the Transaction Window

This feature is only available in the Premier Accountant and Enterprise Solutions Accountant editions.

When you open a GJE transaction window, the bottom of the window displays existing GJEs. By default, the window displays the previous month's transactions, but you can change the selection to match your needs (last year, this quarter, and so on). This provides access to earlier GJEs without the need to click the Previous button multiple times.

If you don't want to see the previous transactions, click Hide List of Entries (the button's name changes to Show List of Entries so you can reverse your decision).

 TIP: Hiding the previous transactions enlarges the transaction window you're working on, which makes it easier to see all your entry lines when you're creating a large GJE.

Running Financial Reports

n this chapter:

- Trial balance
- Balance Sheet
- Profit & Loss statement
- Accountant's review copy
- Cash flow

If QuickBooks is your first accounting software program and you've been using manual bookkeeping procedures, you've already discovered how much easier it is to accomplish bookkeeping tasks. However, even with the ease and power you've gained with QuickBooks, bookkeeping probably isn't fun. I can' give you any QuickBooks tips to make it fun (it isn't—it's precise, repetitive work), but I can tell you how to feel better about all the work you do in QuickBooks.

It's the reports you get out of the software that make the work worthwhile. These are reports you'd have to spend hours on using a manual bookkeeping system. And you can change, customize, and manipulate these reports to get all sorts of information about your business. Much of the data you obtain from QuickBooks reports couldn't be gained from a manual system.

Reporting the Trial Balance

A *trial balance* is a list of all your general ledger accounts and their current balances. It's a quick way to see what's what on an account-by-account basis. In fact, you can use the individual totals and subtotal them to create a Balance Sheet and a Profit & Loss (P&L) statement. However, you don't have to do that because both of those important reports are also available in QuickBooks. Most accountants ask to see a trial balance when they're preparing your taxes or analyzing the health of your business.

To see a trial balance, choose Reports | Accountant and Taxes | Trial Balance. Your company's trial balance is displayed on your screen and looks similar (in form, not content) to Figure 15-1. You can scroll through it to see all the account balances. The bottom of the report has a total for debits and a total for credits, and they're equal. Click the Print button on the report's button bar to print the report.

Configuring the Trial Balance Report

You can change the way the trial balance report displays information using the configuration options available for this report. Click the Modify Report button on the report's button bar to bring up the Modify Report window shown in Figure 15-2. If you make changes that don't work as you thought they would, click the Revert button that appears on each tab of the Modify Report window to reset all options to their default state.

Accrual vs. Cash Trial Balance

One important control in the Display tab of the Modify Report window is the Report Basis selection. QuickBooks can show you your balances on an accrual basis or on a cash basis.

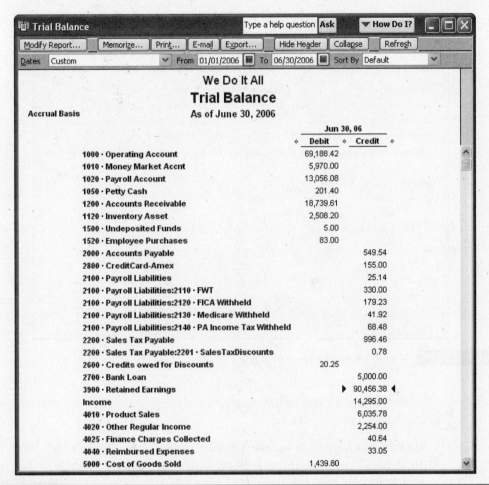

	Jun 30, 06	
	Debit	Credit
1000 · Operating Account	69,188.42	
1010 · Money Market Accnt	5,970.00	
1020 · Payroll Account	13,056.08	
1050 · Petty Cash	201.40	
1200 · Accounts Receivable	18,739.61	
1120 · Inventory Asset	2,508.20	
1500 · Undeposited Funds	5.00	
1520 · Employee Purchases	83.00	
2000 · Accounts Payable		549.54
2800 · CreditCard-Amex		155.00
2100 · Payroll Liabilities		25.14
2100 · Payroll Liabilities:2110 · FWT		330.00
2100 · Payroll Liabilities:2120 · FICA Withheld		179.23
2100 · Payroll Liabilities:2130 · Medicare Withheld		41.92
2100 · Payroll Liabilities:2140 · PA Income Tax Withheld		68.48
2200 · Sales Tax Payable		996.46
2200 · Sales Tax Payable:2201 · SalesTaxDiscounts		0.78
2600 · Credits owed for Discounts	20.25	
2700 · Bank Loan		5,000.00
3900 · Retained Earnings		90,456.38
Income		14,295.00
4010 · Product Sales		6,035.78
4020 · Other Regular Income		2,254.00
4025 · Finance Charges Collected		40.64
4040 · Reimbursed Expenses		33.05
5000 · Cost of Goods Sold	1,439.80	

FIGURE 15-1 A trial balance reports the current balances for every account.

- Accrual numbers are based on your transaction activity. When you invoice a customer, that amount is considered to be revenue. When you enter a vendor bill, you've entered an expense.
- Cash numbers are based on the flow of cash. Revenue isn't real until the customer pays the bill, and your vendor bills aren't expenses until you write the check.

By default, QuickBooks, like most accounting software, displays accrual reports. Accrual reports are generally more useful for analyzing your business. However, unless you pay taxes on an accrual basis (most small businesses don't), your accountant may want to see a cash basis trial balance.

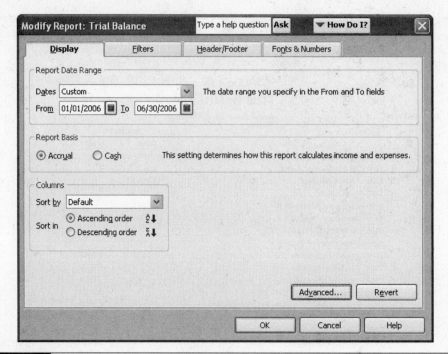

FIGURE 15-2   Modify the report by changing configuration options.

In the Columns section of the Display tab you can select the sort criterion. For the trial balance the choices are

- Default, which sorts the accounts in the usual order (assets, liabilities, and so on)
- Total, which sorts the accounts depending on the current balance (rather useless for this report)

 N O T E :   The report window itself has a field labeled Sort By, which you can use to change the sorting scheme.

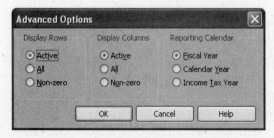

Setting Advanced Options

Click the Advanced button on the Display tab to see the Advanced Options window, where you have two choices for changing the criteria for displaying information and a choice for determining the calendar basis of the report.

The two display choices (Rows and Columns) change the criteria for displaying information.

- Select Active to display only those accounts in which financial activity occurred. This includes accounts that have amounts of $0.00 as a result of financial activity.
- Select All to see all accounts, irrespective of whether they had activity or have a balance of $0.00.
- Select Non-Zero to see only those accounts that had activity and have a balance other than $0.00.

($) **CAUTION:**   The term "Active" has nothing to do with the account's status as active or inactive (hidden). Accounts marked Inactive always appear on the report, because their balances are part of your trial balance.

($) **TIP:**   Most accountants want to see zero-balance accounts, because it's a way to see all the accounts in your system and because sometimes the fact that an account has a zero balance is significant.

The Reporting Calendar option determines the calendar basis of the report. You can change the option if your company preferences are not set for a fiscal and tax year that coincides with the calendar year:

- Fiscal Year sets the reporting calendar to start at the first month of your company's fiscal year.
- Calendar Year sets the reporting calendar to start at January 1.
- Income Tax Year sets the reporting calendar to start on the first day of the first month of your company's tax year.

Click OK to return to the Modify Report window.

Filtering the Data

Click the Filters tab in the Modify Report window to filter the contents of the report (see Figure 15-3). Select a filter from the list in the Choose Filter section and decide how it should be displayed. Different categories have different filtering criteria. For instance, you can filter amounts that are less or greater than a certain amount.

($) **CAUTION:**   Once you start filtering accounts and amounts, you probably will have a trial balance that no longer balances. At that point, you can't call it a trial balance; you're merely creating a list of account balances.

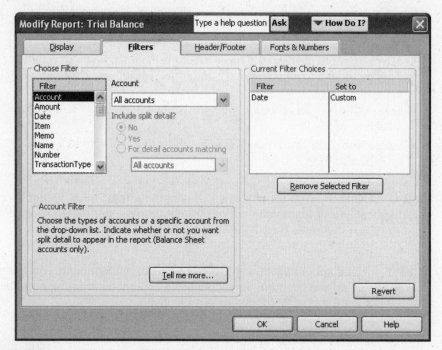

FIGURE 15-3 Change what's reported by filtering the data to meet your criteria.

Changing the Header and Footer

You can customize what appears on the header and footer of your report by changing the options on the Header/Footer tab, shown in Figure 15-4.

The options you configure here have no bearing on the figures in the report; this is just the informational stuff. Most of the fields are self-explanatory, but the Date Prepared field may confuse you. The date you see in this tab has nothing to do with the current date; it's just a sample format. Click the arrow to the right of the field to see other formats for displaying the date.

Changing the Fonts and Number Display

The Fonts & Numbers tab, shown in Figure 15-5, lets you change the font you use for the various elements in the report. Select any part of the report from the list on the left side of the dialog and click Change Font. Then select a font, a style (bold, italic, etc.), a size, and special effects such as underline.

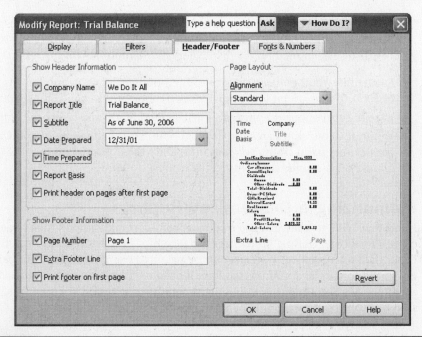

FIGURE 15-4   Configure the top and bottom of the report page in the Header/Footer tab.

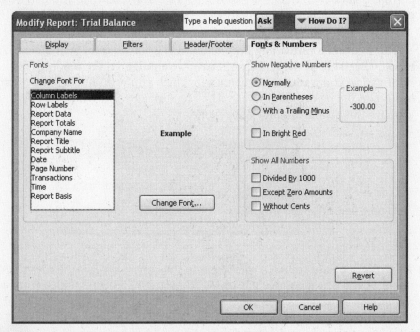

FIGURE 15-5   Change the appearance of the data in the report.

On the right side of the dialog, you can configure the way numbers display and print on your report. Select a method for showing negative numbers. If you wish, you can also select a method for displaying all the numbers on the report:

- Divided By 1000 reduces the size of the numbers by showing them as multiples of 1000. This is useful for companies that report seven- and eight-digit numbers.
- Except Zero Amounts removes all instances of $0.00 and leaves the entry blank.
- Without Cents eliminates the decimal point and the two digits to the right of the decimal point from every amount. Only the dollars show, not the cents. QuickBooks rounds the cents to the nearest dollar.

Memorizing a Customized Report

I find that I like to glance at the trial balance report occasionally, just to see what certain totals are. Calling up the trial balance to view five or six account balances is faster than opening five or six account registers to examine the current balance. I only need to see the accounts that have a balance; I have no interest in zero-balance accounts. My accountant, on the other hand, likes to see all the accounts. He finds significance in some accounts being at zero.

$ TIP: Balance Sheet accounts (assets, liabilities, and equity) display their current balances in the Chart Of Accounts List window, so you don't have to print a report to view those numbers.

The solution to providing both of us with what we want is in memorizing each modified version of the report. After you've configured the report to display the information you want in the manner in which you want it, click the Memorize button on the report's button bar. The Memorize Report window appears so you can give this customized format a name.

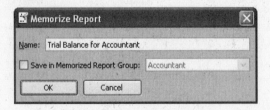

$ TIP: Be sure to use a reference to the report type in the memorized name. If you use a name such as My Report, you'll have no idea what the report displays.

Open a memorized report by choosing Reports | Memorized Reports from the QuickBooks menu bar and selecting the report name from the submenu.

Generating a Balance Sheet

QuickBooks offers several Balance Sheet reports, and each of them is explained in this section. Select the one you want to see by choosing Reports | Company & Financial and then choosing the report.

A Balance Sheet report is specifically designed to show only the totals of the Balance Sheet accounts (assets, liabilities, and equity) from your chart of accounts. It's really a report on your financial health. The reason a Balance Sheet balances is that it's based on a formula:

Assets = Liabilities + Equity

Before you glance at the trial balance you just printed and prepare to write me a note saying, "Excuse me, you don't know what you're talking about; I just added those accounts up, and it doesn't balance," let me redefine one of the terms: equity.

When you generate a Balance Sheet report, the equity number is a calculated number and is arrived at with these steps:

1. All the income accounts are added up.
2. All the expense accounts are added up.
3. The expense total is subtracted from the income total.
4. The result of the calculation in Step 3 is added to the totals in existing equity accounts (which could be Opening Balance Equity, Prior Retained Earnings, Retained Earnings, and so on).
5. The total that's calculated in Step 4 becomes the figure for equity in a Balance Sheet.

If you have more expenses than you have income, you're operating at a loss; consequently, it's a negative number that is combined with the existing equity accounts. This means that the equity number that appears on your Balance Sheet could be lower than the equity number that shows on your trial balance.

Balance Sheet Standard Report

The Balance Sheet Standard reports the balance in every Balance Sheet account (unless the account has a zero balance) and subtotals each account type: asset, liability, and equity. The report is automatically configured for year-to-date figures, using your fiscal year and the current date. (The fiscal year is the same as the calendar year for most small businesses.)

Balance Sheet Detail Report

This report displays every transaction in every Balance Sheet account. By default, the report covers a date range of the current month to date. Even if it's early in the month, this report is lengthy. If you change the date range to encompass a longer period (the quarter or year), the report goes on forever.

If you want to see a Balance Sheet only to get an idea of your company's financial health, this is probably more than you wanted to know.

Balance Sheet Summary Report

This report is a quick way to see totals, and it's also the easiest way to answer the question, "How am I doing?" All the balance sheet accounts are listed and subtotaled by type, as shown in Figure 15-6.

Balance Sheet Previous Year Comparison Report

The comparison Balance Sheet is designed to show you what your financial situation is compared to a year ago. There are four columns in this report:

- The year-to-date balance for each Balance Sheet account
- The year-to-date balance for each Balance Sheet account for last year
- The amount of change between last year and this year
- The percentage of change between last year and this year

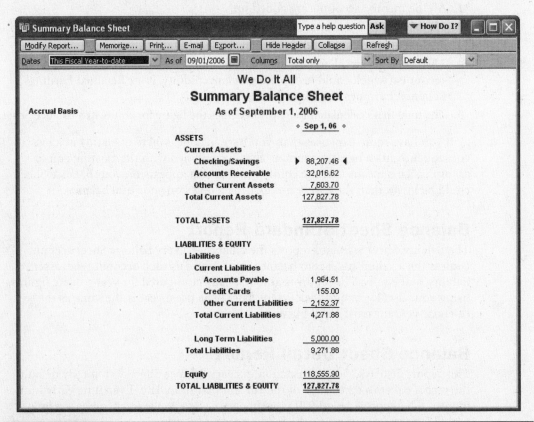

FIGURE 15-6   Check your financial health with the Summary Balance Sheet.

If you've just started using QuickBooks this year, there's little reason to run this report. Next year, however, it'll be interesting to see how you're doing compared to this year.

Customizing and Memorizing a Balance Sheet

When your Balance Sheet is on the screen, you can use all of the customization features covered earlier in this chapter for the trial balance report. Then, when you have the configuration you need, memorize the report by clicking the Memorize button in the report window.

Generating a Profit & Loss Statement

Your P&L report is probably the one you'll run most often. It's natural to want to know if you're making any money. A P&L report is sometimes called an *income report*. It shows all your income accounts (and displays the total), all your expense accounts (displaying the total), and then puts the difference between the two totals on the last line. If you have more income than expenses, the last line is a profit.

All of the P&L reports are available by choosing Reports | Company & Financial, and are explained in this section.

Profit & Loss Standard Report

The standard P&L report is a straightforward document, following the normal format for an income statement:

- The income is listed and totaled.
- The Cost of Goods Sold accounts are listed (if any exist), and the total is deducted from the income total in order to show the gross profit.
- The expenses are listed and totaled.
- The difference between the gross profit and the total expenses is displayed as your Net Ordinary Income (or Loss).

 N O T E :   If you don't sell inventory items, you probably don't have a Cost of Goods Sold section in your P&L.

While the format is that of a normal income statement, the date isn't. The default date range for the QuickBooks standard P&L is the current month to date. This is not a year-to-date figure; it uses only the transactions from the current month, and it's almost certainly not what you want to see. Click the arrow to the right of the Dates field and change the date range to This Fiscal Year-To-Date. The resulting display is what you want to see—a normal income statement for your business so far this year.

Profit & Loss Detail Report

The Profit & Loss Detail report is for terminally curious people. It lists every transaction for every account in the P&L format. It goes on and on.

This report is almost like an audit trail, and it's good to have if you notice some numbers that seem "not quite right" in the standard P&L. I don't recommend it as the report to run when you just need to know if you're making money.

Profit & Loss YTD Comparison Report

The YTD (year-to-date) comparison report compares the current month's income and expense totals with the year-to-date totals. Each income and expense account is listed.

Profit & Loss Prev Year Comparison Report

If you've been using QuickBooks for more than a year, this is a great report! If you recently started with QuickBooks, next year you'll say, "This is a great report!"

This is an income statement for the current year to date, with a column that shows last year's figure for the same period. This gives you an instant appraisal of your business growth (or ebb). So that you don't have to tax your brain doing the math, there are two additional columns: the difference between the years in dollars and in percentage.

Profit & Loss By Job Report

This report presents a year-to-date summary of income and expenses posted to customers and jobs. In effect, it's a customer P&L. Each customer or job gets its own column, and the bottom row of each column is the net income (or loss) for this customer or job.

Profit & Loss By Class Report

If you've enabled class tracking, this report appears on the Reports menu. Each class is subtotaled for its own P&L. If you use classes for branch offices or company divisions, this is the way to get a separate P&L for each.

Profit & Loss Unclassified Report

If you've enabled class tracking, you should run the Profit & Loss Unclassified report, which displays a P&L generated from transactions that had no class assignment. Even if you think you don't care about assigning classes to these transactions, you should examine the report and drill down (double-click the listing) to view the individual transactions. If any transaction should have been assigned a class, you can add the class and click Yes when QuickBooks asks if you want to save the changes you made to the transaction.

 TIP: Because this report uses filtered accounts and transactions, instead of all the transactions in your system, it isn't really a P&L, and you can ignore the bottom line profit/loss figure.

Customizing and Memorizing P&L Reports

Use the QuickBooks Customize features discussed earlier in this chapter to tailor P&L reports so they print exactly the way you want to see the information. You might want to customize several formats: for you, for your accountant, and perhaps for your bank (if you have a loan or line of credit, or are applying for either, your bank also wants to see a Balance Sheet). Then, when a report is perfect, memorize it.

Creating an Accountant's Review

Many accountants support QuickBooks directly, which means they understand the software and know how to use it. In fact, they have a copy of QuickBooks on their own computer systems.

At various times during the year, your accountant might want to look at your books. There might be quarterly reports and adjustments, a physical inventory that resulted in serious changes in your Balance Sheet, expenses that should be posted to different accounts, or any of a hundred other reasons to examine your transactions. Almost definitely this will occur at the end-of-year process you have to go through in order to close your books for the year.

This could result in your accountant showing up and sitting in front of your computer, making the necessary changes (almost always journal entries), moving this, reversing that, and generally making sense out of your daily transaction postings. By "making sense," I mean putting transaction postings into categories that fit your tax reporting needs.

While your accountant is using the software, you can't get much accomplished. You could say, "Excuse me, could you move? I have to enter an invoice." But remember, you're paying for the accountant's time.

If your accountant doesn't want to visit, he or she may request printouts of various reports, then write notes on those printouts: "Move this, split that, credit this number here, debit that number there." Or you might receive a spreadsheet-like printout with a complicated journal entry, which means you have to stop entering your day-to-day transactions to make all those changes.

Some accountants ask for a copy of the company file, a backup of your company file (which they restore), or a portable company file (covered in Chapter 21). While the accountant has the file and is tweaking transactions or making journal entries, you can't do any work. If you continue to work, the transactions you enter won't be in the company file you restore when your accountant returns it to you, because it overwrites the company file you'd continued to use.

QuickBooks has a better solution. Give your accountant a specially-designed review copy of your company file. Let your accountant do the work back at his or her office, while you continue to work in your copy. When the file comes back to you, with the accountant's changes, QuickBooks can merge the changes in the review copy into your copy of the company file, which saves the work you did while the accountant's copy was out.

NOTE: To work with your QuickBooks 2006 files, your accountant must have installed an edition of QuickBooks 2006.

Creating an Accountant's Review Copy

You can create the accountant's review copy on a floppy disk or save it to a file and send it to your accountant via e-mail.

To accomplish this, follow these steps:

❶ Choose File | Accountant's Review | Create Accountant's Copy from the QuickBooks menu bar. You may see a message indicating you must be in single-user mode to do this, and you may see a message telling you that all open QuickBooks windows will be closed (depending on your QuickBooks environment). Then the Save Accountant's Copy To dialog appears so you can save the information for your accountant.

❷ The location to which QuickBooks saves the file is the same location to which you last saved a file (a backup, or an export file). If necessary, change the location to match the media you want to use for this file. For example, use your floppy drive if you plan to send a floppy disk to your accountant, or save it to your hard drive if you're going to transmit the file via e-mail or burn a CD.

❸ The filename has an extension of .qbx, added automatically by QuickBooks. You can change the name of the file if you want to, but generally it's a good idea to keep the filename QuickBooks suggests (which is based on your company name).

❹ Click Save to create the accountant's copy.

QuickBooks notifies you when the process is complete. If the file won't fit on a single floppy disk, you're asked to insert additional floppy disks to complete the process.

 CAUTION: If you've password-protected your QuickBooks data file, you must tell your accountant what the admin password is. Otherwise, your accountant won't be able to open the file.

Working During the Accountant's Review

When you create the accountant's copy, parts of your QuickBooks system are locked, so you can't make changes that won't be compatible with the data that comes back from your accountant. It's important to know what you can and cannot accomplish until you receive data back from your accountant. Your accountant also has restrictions. Table 15-1 describes what you (the client) can and can't do while your files are locked, and Table 15-2 describes what an accountant can and cannot do with the accountant's copy file.

Clients Can...	Clients Cannot...
Create transactions	Delete an entry in a list
Edit transactions created after copy is sent	Rename an item in a list
Delete transactions	Change an account to a subaccount
Add new items to lists	Change a subaccount to an account
Edit items in lists	

TABLE 15-1   What you can and cannot do during an accountant's review

To remind you that an accountant's copy was created, the title bar of your QuickBooks software changes to include that fact.

Accountants Can...	Accountants Cannot...
Create journal entries	Delete list entries
Edit account names	Make list entries inactive
Change account numbers (if you use numbers for your chart of accounts)	Create transactions (except journal entries)
Add accounts and items	
Edit tax information for accounts	
Adjust inventory quantities and values	
Print 1099 forms	
Print 941 forms	
Print 940 forms	
Print W-2 forms	

TABLE 15-2   What an accountant can and cannot do with a review copy

Merging the Accountant's Changes

When your accountant returns your files to you, the changes have to be imported into your QuickBooks files.

Follow these steps to make changes:

❶ Place the floppy disk you received from your accountant into the floppy drive. If you received the file via e-mail, note the folder and filename you used to store it on your hard drive.

❷ Choose File | Accountant's Review | Import Accountant's Changes.

❸ QuickBooks closes all open QuickBooks windows and insists on backing up your current file before importing (a good safety measure). Click OK to proceed with the backup.

❹ When the backup is complete, QuickBooks automatically opens the Import Changes From Accountant's Copy window. Make sure the Look In field at the top of the window matches the location of the accountant's review file.

❺ Choose the import file, which has an extension of .aif, and click Open (or double-click the .aif file).

Your QuickBooks data now contains the changes your accountant made, and you can work with your files normally.

 TIP: Make sure your accountant sends you a note or calls to tell you about the changes. QuickBooks does not indicate what has changed after the import, and you should know what specific alterations were made to your financial records.

Unlocking Your Files Without Receiving a Review

If you make an accountant's review copy in error, or if your accountant tells you there are no changes to be made, you can unlock your files. This puts everything back as if you'd never created an accountant's review copy. To accomplish this, choose File | Accountant's Review | Cancel Accountant's Changes. QuickBooks asks you to confirm your decision.

Voided and Deleted Transactions Reports

QuickBooks offers two reports you can use to track voided and deleted transactions. Both reports are available by choosing Reports | Accountant & Taxes and then selecting either of these reports: Voided/Deleted Transactions or Voided/Deleted Transactions History.

Voided/Deleted Transactions Report

This report displays a summary of all voided and deleted transactions in the selected period (the default period is Last Month). The report shows the current state (void or deleted) and the original state (including the amount) of each affected transaction.

Voided/Deleted Transactions History Report

This report is the "Details" version of the Voided/Deleted Transactions report. It provides more information about both the original transaction and the change. In addition to the information provided by the Voided/Deleted Transactions report, this report displays the credit and debit postings and the posting accounts. If items (including payroll items) were involved in the transaction, they're also displayed.

Cash Flow Reports

QuickBooks offers two cash flow reports in the Company & Financial Reports menu: Statement of Cash Flows and Cash Flow Forecast. Essentially, the difference between them is that the Statement of Cash Flows looks back, and the Cash Flow Forecast looks ahead. Both of these reports can be useful for analyzing the current state (health) of your business.

Cash flow reports are complicated documents and are accurate to the degree that the accounts included in the reports contain transaction figures that should actually be included. Your accountant can look at the activity in any account to determine whether it's appropriate to include or exclude that account's activities in the calculation of cash flow reports.

 NOTE: It's beyond the scope of this book to provide detailed instructions about verifying and modifying cash flow reports, because that's a complicated accounting subject, not a software subject.

Statement of Cash Flows

The Statement of Cash Flows report displays information about your cash position over a period of time (by default, year-to-date). You can see where your cash came from and where it went, categorized as follows:

- **Operating Activities** The transactions involved with maintaining the business
- **Investing Activities** The transactions involved with the acquisition of fixed assets
- **Financing Activities** The transactions involved with long-term liabilities and owners' activities (such as investments and draws)

Accounts Used for the Statement of Cash Flows

QuickBooks predetermines the accounts used in the Statement of Cash Flows report, and you can view the account list by choosing Edit | Preferences and selecting the Reports & Graphs icon in the left pane. On the Company Preferences tab, click Classify Cash to open the Classify Cash dialog seen in Figure 15-7.

You can add and remove accounts and move selected accounts to a different category, but that's dangerous unless your accountant recommends such a step.

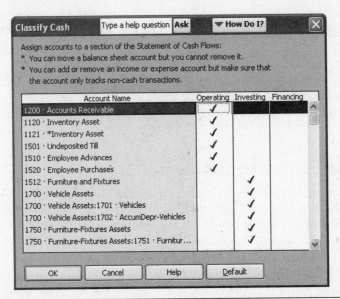

FIGURE 15-7   Don't change the selections without conferring with your accountant.

By and large, the default settings that QuickBooks established work quite well. If your accountant knows you're using an account that's not selected for transactions that should be included in the report, or vice versa, it's okay to make changes.

 CAUTION: Make sure your accountant knows that QuickBooks doesn't permit Balance Sheet accounts to be removed from the list, although they can be moved to a different category.

Creating a Statement of Cash Flows

To create the Statement of Cash Flows report, choose Reports | Company & Financial | Statement Of Cash Flows. The report opens, showing your cash flow from the first day of your fiscal year to the current date, as seen in Figure 15-8.

If you want to see how your cash flow changed during another interval (perhaps this month, this quarter, or during a previous month or quarter), change the date range.

This report is generated on an accrual basis, and unlike most QuickBooks reports, you can't specify accrual or cash-based calculations. Because cash flow is a cash-based figure, QuickBooks adjusts amounts to turn this accrual-based report into a cash-based report. The bottom line is cash-based, but instead of just displaying cash-based figures, QuickBooks takes an accrual-based report and shows you the adjustments that had to be made. Of course, if you have no accrual-based totals (you don't owe money; nobody owes you money), you won't see any adjustments.

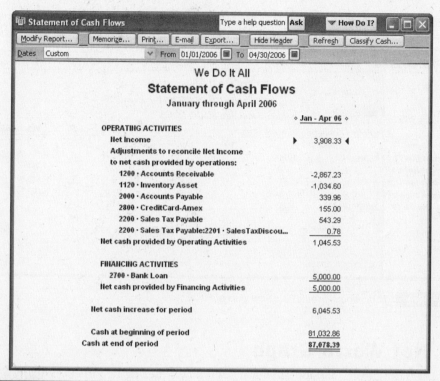

See how your cash position changed during the interval you specified in the Dates fields.

Cash Flow Forecast

The Cash Flow Forecast report does what its name implies—forecasts your cash flow as of a given future date (by default, four weeks hence). The forecast includes cash in, cash out, and the consequent cash (bank) balances.

To create the report, choose Reports | Company & Financial | Cash Flow Forecast. The report window opens with estimated cash flow figures for the next four weeks, as seen in Figure 15-9.

Remember that this forecast is made with the assumption that all A/R will arrive when due, and all A/P will be paid when due. That may or may not be a realistic assumption for your business. To enhance the reality of the report, you can use the Delay Receipts field to tell QuickBooks to assume that your customers will pay late by the amount of days you specify in that field. This is useful if you know that by and large there's a pattern indicating your customers are late by an average of x number of days.

To view a forecast for a different date range, select a different interval from the drop-down list in the Dates field or enter specific From and To dates.

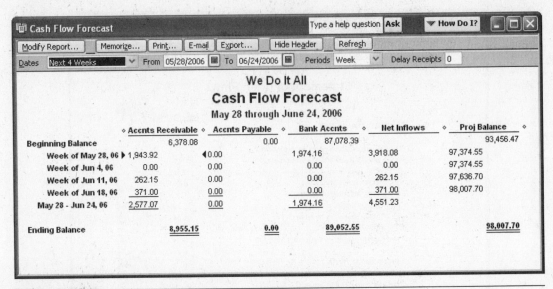

FIGURE 15-9   This report predicts inflow and outflow.

Net Worth Graph

You can display a graph of your net work by choosing Reports | Company & Financial | Net Worth Graph. Like all graphs, this display provides a quick overview of your company's worth (see Figure 15-10). Each graphical element represents a specific month. Because it's reporting net worth, it's based on balance sheet accounts, as follows:

- Your total assets, which are represented by the bars above the line.
- Your total liabilities, which appear below the line.
- Your equity (net worth), which is the calculated difference between assets and liabilities. This figure appears as a small yellow box, and if it's a positive figure, it's above the line.

If you double-click a graphical element (asset bar, liability bar, or equity box), you can see a pie chart graph representing the percentage that each account balance contributed to the total.

Additional Features for Premier and Enterprise Editions

If you're running QuickBooks Premier Edition or QuickBooks Enterprise Solutions, you may have some additional features available, above and beyond the features covered in this chapter. (Not all features are in all Premier or Enterprise versions.)

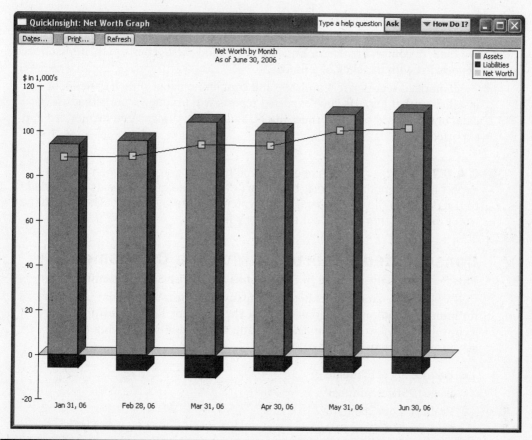

FIGURE 15-10 This graph provides an at-a-glance view of your financial position.

Export Memorized Reports

If you customize a report that has absolutely everything you need, arranged in a beautifully logical order, you can memorize it. Then, it's available every time you need exactly that information, in exactly that format.

To add more power to this already potent feature, QuickBooks Premier/Enterprise editions offer an Export function for memorized reports. If you're an accountant, this means that after you develop memorized reports that provide the information you need, exactly the way you need it, you can export those reports to a file, and e-mail the file to your clients. If you're a bookkeeper, you can travel to client sites with the memorized reports you've created on a floppy disk (the exported report files are quite small).

The real beauty of this feature is that all QuickBooks editions can import the exported memorized reports (only the export feature, not the import feature, is limited to Premier/Enterprise editions). Because the Import Memorize Report feature is a standard QuickBooks function, clients running QuickBooks Basic or Pro (and, of course, Premier or Enterprise) can add these reports to their Memorized Reports list with the click of a mouse.

Memorized reports are templates, and contain no data, so each QuickBooks installation that imports your exported reports will produce reports that use local data, but are based on the format, filters, and sorting designs you memorized and exported.

 CAUTION: There is one thing you must be careful of when you're exporting a memorized report: the report cannot use custom fields you added to the company file you're using when you memorize the report. Those fields won't exist in other QuickBooks company files.

Consolidated Reports for Multiple Companies

This feature is only available in QuickBooks Enterprise Solutions editions.

If you have separate QuickBooks company files for multiple companies, or for multiple locations, divisions, etc., use the Combine Reports feature to get a consolidated view of all the data files. You can create the following reports as consolidated reports:

- Balance Sheet Standard
- Balance Sheet Summary
- Profit & Loss Standard
- Statement of Cash Flows
- Trial Balance

The configuration of the consolidated reports is completed in QuickBooks (selecting the companies, and selecting the report types). However, the data is sent to Microsoft Excel for consolidation, so you must have Excel installed on your computer to use this feature.

Using Online Banking Services

In this chapter:

- Understand online banking

- Set up a connection to QuickBooks on the Web

- Set up online bank accounts

- Perform online transactions

- Receive online payments from your customers

If you have an Internet connection, you can use the wide range of online services offered by QuickBooks. Internet-based banking chores are the subjects covered in this chapter. You'll discover that QuickBooks and most banks have taken advantage of the Internet to make banking a snap. Using QuickBooks, you can sign up for the following online features:

- Online banking, which means you can view the status of your bank accounts, see which transactions have cleared, and generally maintain your accounts via your Internet connection.
- Online payments, which means you send money to vendors via the Internet instead of writing checks. The money is deposited directly into your vendor's bank account, or a check for the vendor is automatically generated and mailed (depending on whether the vendor accepts electronic deposits).
- Online receipts, so your customers can pay your invoices online.

Online banking also includes your credit card accounts, so you can see credit card transactions and enter them in your credit card account register. To take advantage of online credit card tracking, you must set up your credit cards as liability accounts, which is discussed in Chapter 11.

Understanding Online Banking

Online banking is nothing more than using the Internet to access information about your accounts from your bank's computer. The bank's computer is a server, configured for the secure exchange of data that provides information about your accounts. QuickBooks provides two methods for using the online banking services your bank offers:

- **WebConnect**   This is the method you use when your bank doesn't provide a way to connect your QuickBooks data directly to the data on the bank's server. Actually, this means your bank chose not to install the software required to work interactively with QuickBooks. Instead, the bank maintains a web page on its web site that lets you view and download your bank statement and import the downloaded file into QuickBooks.
- **Direct Connection**   Your bank exchanges data interactively with QuickBooks. This allows you to take advantage of all types of online banking services (transaction data downloads, transfers between bank accounts, e-mail messages between you and the bank, and online bill payments). Of course, those features are limited to the online services provided by your bank.

Instructions for using the WebConnect and Direct Connection features appear later in this chapter, in the section "Getting Bank Account Data Online."

Setting Up a Connection

Before you can use the QuickBooks online services, you have to let the software know how you get online. After this simple, initial step, QuickBooks does its online work on autopilot.

The first step is to let QuickBooks know how you reach the Internet. Choose Help | Internet Connection Setup from the menu bar. This launches the Internet Connection Setup wizard (see Figure 16-1).

The choices on the first wizard window cover all the possibilities. One of them fits your situation, and in this section I'll explain how QuickBooks handles the setup for each type of connection.

 NOTE: No matter which selection you choose, when you click Next, the last window wizard appears (it's a small, efficient wizard). Click Done when you've read the information in the second window.

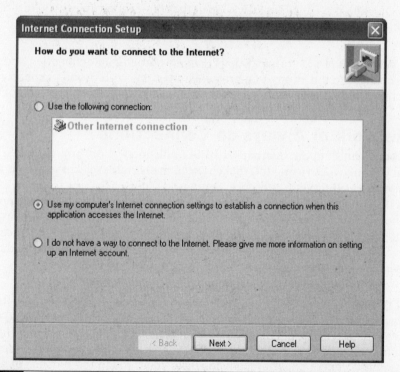

Internet Connection Setup	

How do you want to connect to the Internet?

○ Use the following connection:

  🌐 Other Internet connection

⊙ Use my computer's Internet connection settings to establish a connection when this application accesses the Internet.

○ I do not have a way to connect to the Internet. Please give me more information on setting up an Internet account.

[< Back] [Next >] [Cancel] [Help]

FIGURE 16-1   Tell QuickBooks how to get to the Internet from this computer.

Dial-up Connections

The option Use The Following Connection refers to a dial-up connection, using a modem. This connection could be through an ISP (Internet service provider), which you reach using the dial-up capabilities built into your operating system (Dial-Up Networking). Or you may have a connection through a proprietary software program that connects you to a particular host such as America Online. These proprietary programs first connect you to their host computer, where there are preconfigured sections of information. Then the systems permit you to wander off on your own on the Internet.

Any dial-up connections you've configured appear in the Internet Connection Setup window. If no connection appears and you know you've configured a dial-up connection to your ISP, QuickBooks had a problem finding it or identifying it. Close the window (but don't shut down QuickBooks), open your dial-up connection, and connect to the Internet. Then open this window again, and QuickBooks should find it.

Select (highlight) the connection. Then click Next, and click Done on the next window. You're all set. Anytime you need to travel to the Internet while you're working in QuickBooks, QuickBooks will open the connection (unless you're already connected to the Internet) and take you to the right site.

 CAUTION: If QuickBooks doesn't detect your connection and you had to connect to the Internet before configuring this wizard, you'll probably have to connect manually every time you want to use Internet services in QuickBooks.

Network or Always-on Connections

If you connect to the Internet via a DSL/cable modem or through another computer on your network (using Internet connection sharing), select the option Use My Computer's Internet Connection Settings.... Then click Next to see an explanation of the connection QuickBooks found, which is referred to as a direct connection. The window has an Advanced Connection Settings button, which opens the Internet Properties dialog for Internet Explorer (the same dialog you see if you select Tools | Internet Options from Control Panel). You shouldn't need to check these settings unless you have a problem connecting. Click Done.

 NOTE: If you don't yet have Internet access, select the option I Do Not Have A Way To Connect To The Internet..., and click Next, where you'll see an explanation that you must sign up for Internet service before using the Internet Connection Setup wizard. The window has an option to launch the Windows Internet Connection wizard, which walks you through the process of setting up a new connection. After you sign up with an ISP, return to this window and set up your QuickBooks online connection.

Setting Up Online Banking

To use online banking, your bank must support QuickBooks online access procedures. There are three online banking services available:

- Online account access
- Online bill paying
- Online credit card services

You can sign up for any or all of these services. If your bank only supports online account access and doesn't support online bill paying or online credit card services, you can work directly with QuickBooks online banking sites. See "Using the QuickBooks Online Payment Service" and "Using a QuickBooks Credit Card," later in this chapter.

The process of enabling online banking has three steps (all of which are covered in this section):

1. Apply for online services with your bank.
2. Receive a personal identification number (PIN) from your bank to make sure your online account is secure.
3. Enable a QuickBooks account (or multiple accounts) for online services.

To get started, choose Banking | Online Banking from the menu bar. The submenu has three commands:

- Setup Account For Online Access
- Available Financial Institutions
- Learn About Online Bill Payment

Finding Your Bank Online

If you haven't signed up for (or discussed) online services with your bank, choose Available Financial Institutions to see if your bank participates. QuickBooks displays a dialog telling you it has to open a browser to travel to the Internet. Click OK, and when you're connected to the Internet, you see the Financial Institutions Directory web site (see Figure 16-2).

The four choices at the top of the left pane determine the contents of the Financial Institution Directory list. The window opens with the choice Any Services preselected, and all the banks listed provide some type of online service.

If you're interested in a particular online service (for example, you only care about online access), select that option, and the list of banks changes to those banks that offer the selected service.

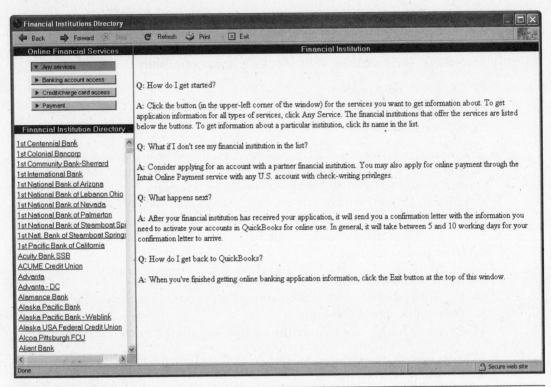

FIGURE 16-2   Select the type of online service you want, and then scroll through the list to see if *your* bank is included.

Scroll through the list to find your bank and click its listing. The right pane of the Financial Institutions Directory window displays information about the bank's online services (see Figure 16-3) and a telephone number you can call for more information or to apply for online services. You may also see an Apply Now button (or one similarly named), if your bank supports online signup.

Click the Apply Now button if you want to start the application process here and now. If no Apply Now button exists, follow the instructions for setting up online services at the bank—usually the bank displays a phone number. If online applications are available, fill out the form and submit the information. Your bank will send you information about using its online service, along with a PIN that's been assigned. All banks provide a method of changing the PIN to one of your own choosing. In fact, many banks insist that you change the PIN the first time you access online services.

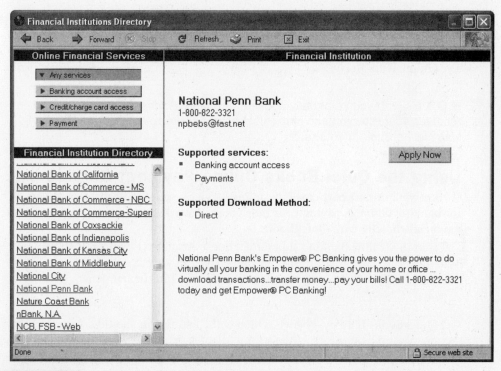

FIGURE 16-3   My bank has the services I want.

CAUTION: You may see a warning that you are about to send information to an Internet zone in which it might be possible for other people to see the data you send. Select Yes to continue (you might want to select the option not to be warned in the future). If this makes you nervous, forget online banking, because there's no guaranteed security on the Internet—even though Intuit and your bank both make every possible effort to keep data secure.

Setting Up Online Access

The Setup Account For Online Access command under the Online Banking menu launches a wizard that walks you through either of the following functions (depending on your selections in the wizard windows):

- It searches for your bank on the Internet so you can apply online (if your bank supports online setup) or get information about applying by telephone or in person. These functions duplicate the functions you perform by choosing the Available Financial Institutions command.

- After you've completed the paperwork at your bank and received a PIN, it walks you through the process of enabling your bank account for online banking in QuickBooks. These functions are discussed in the section "Enabling Your Online Bank Accounts."

 NOTE: If you've already applied for online services at your bank and received your PIN, you can skip this part and move to the section "Enabling Your Online Bank Accounts."

Using the QuickBooks Online Payment Service

If your bank doesn't participate in online services, and if your prime motivation for banking online is paying your bills via the Internet, you can sign up for online payments directly with QuickBooks.

From the Online Banking submenu, choose Available Financial Institutions. When the Financial Institutions list is displayed in your browser window, scroll through the list to find QuickBooks Bill Pay Service in the left pane.

You'll see two listings:

- QuickBooks Bill Pay—New!, which is the listing you should select.
- QuickBooks Bill Pay™, which is the listing for existing customers of this older service (for users of older versions of QuickBooks) and doesn't provide online signup anymore.

When you select QuickBooks Bill Pay—New!, the right pane displays information about this service (see Figure 16-4).

To sign up, click Apply Now. After you answer a couple of questions about your business, click the Continue button. An application form appears on your screen. Follow the prompts and instructions to complete the enrollment process.

Using a QuickBooks Credit Card

If your credit card issuer doesn't support online access and that feature is important to you, you can sign up for a QuickBooks credit card. In the Financial Institutions list, select QuickBooks Platinum Plus and follow the instructions for signing up.

Enabling Your Online Bank Accounts

After you've signed up with your bank and have your secret PIN, you must configure your QuickBooks bank account(s) for online services. The following instructions are for setting up an account with a bank that provides Direct Connection. If your bank doesn't support QuickBooks Direct Connection, you can use your browser to go to the bank's web site, enter your PIN, and download the QBO file.

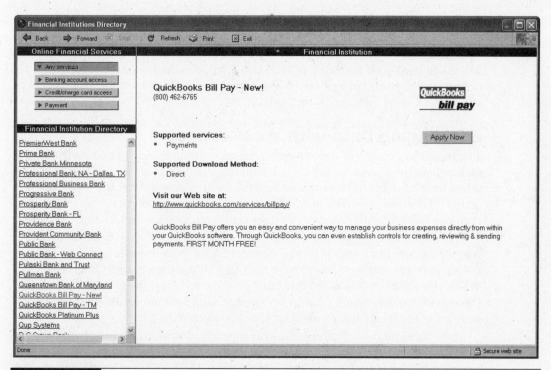

FIGURE 16-4   If your bank doesn't offer online bill paying, sign up with QuickBooks.

 N O T E :   Some banks use passwords instead of PINs.

Choose Banking | Online Banking | Setup Account For Online Access. QuickBooks displays a message telling you that it must close any open windows to complete this task. Click Yes to continue.

The Online Banking Setup Interview wizard appears. Click the Enable Accounts tab, and step through the instructions the wizard presents, answering the questions the wizard poses. As you go through the steps in the wizard, you're configuring a bank account as an online account. You'll be asked to select the online services you'll use with this account. Choose online account access, online payments, or both (depending on the services you've signed up for).

 T I P :   You can create online bank accounts in QuickBooks for as many accounts and different financial institutions as you need (and have signed up for).

Getting Bank Account Data Online

After you've set up your online banking permissions with your financial institutions and established your online bank account(s) in QuickBooks, you're ready to use the online services your bank offers. In this section, I'll go over both the WebConnect and Direct Connection access methods.

Exchanging Data with WebConnect

To connect to your WebConnect-enabled bank, choose Banking | Online Banking | Online Banking Center. In the Online Banking Center dialog, seen in Figure 16-5, select your bank from the Financial Institution drop-down list at the top of the dialog. (The drop-down list only offers multiple entries if you've configured more than one bank for online access or credit card transaction access.) Click Go Online.

When QuickBooks opens the bank's web page, log in and view your bank statements. You can either print the statement from your browser and then enter transactions manually, or download a file that you can import into QuickBooks. When you click the Download File button on the web site, the standard Windows Download dialog appears. Choose Save and select a location for the file (most people use the folder that holds their QuickBooks files).

Make sure you download the right file type; the download button should say QuickBooks. Many banks that provide download files offer selection buttons representing file types for Quicken, QuickBooks, and CSV (or other delimited

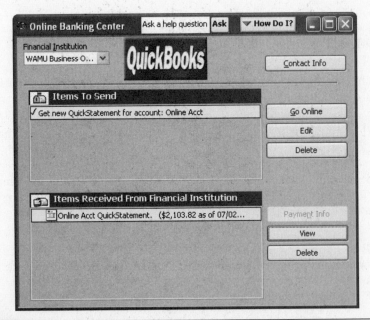

FIGURE 16-5   Online access starts in the Online Banking Center dialog.

formats). While it's possible to modify a CSV file so it will import transactions into QuickBooks, it's far from a cakewalk, and although I almost never recommend "key the data in manually," this is one scenario that elicits that response from me.

After the file is on your hard drive, you can import the data into QuickBooks.

To import a downloaded QuickBooks transaction file, follow these steps:

1 Choose File | Utilities | Import | Web Connect Files from the QuickBooks menu bar.
2 In the Open Online Data File dialog, select the file you downloaded (the file extension is .qbo) and click Open.
3 The Select Bank Account dialog opens, offering you two options: use an existing online account (those you've configured for online access) or create a new one.
4 Click Continue to begin the import process.

When the file is imported, QuickBooks issues a message to inform you of that fact. Click OK.

Exchanging Data with Direct Connection

If your bank supports the Direct Connection method of online banking, you can perform the following tasks online, although you're limited to the specific functions your bank offers:

- Send a message (it's really an e-mail message) to your bank.
- Receive e-mail messages from your bank.
- Send data to the bank regarding the transfer of funds between accounts at that bank.
- Receive a list of transactions that have cleared your account.
- Pay bills.

Some banks won't let you pay bills interactively through QuickBooks, although they may have a bill-paying service available outside of QuickBooks, which you can access on the bank's web site. If that's the case, and you prefer to pay your bills online through QuickBooks, see the section earlier in this chapter on using the QuickBooks Bill Pay Service.

Creating Messages to Send to Your Bank

Banks that support Direct Connection have a two-way message feature: you can both send and receive messages. To send a message to your bank, choose Banking | Create Online Banking Message. Enter the message text in the Online Banking Message dialog, and click OK. You send the message when you connect to your bank (covered next).

Connecting to Your Bank

To connect to your bank, choose Banking | Online Banking | Online Banking Center to open the Online Banking Center dialog.

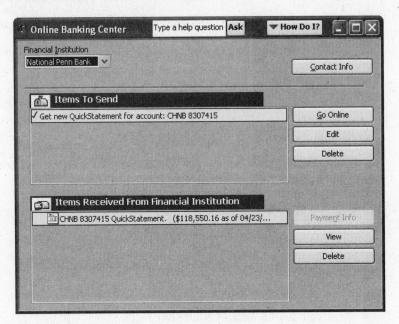

If you have online banking at more than one bank, select the appropriate bank from the drop-down list in the Financial Institution field at the top of the dialog. For example, you may have online bank account access at one bank and online credit card access at another bank. The dialog has two sections:

- Items To Send, which always includes a request for a QuickStatement and may include a message to your bank if you created one.
- Items Received From Financial Institution, which includes the latest QuickStatement from your bank along with any messages from your bank. If the listing for the QuickStatement has a check mark, you haven't yet viewed it.

Details about these functions are covered in the following sections.

Sending Data to Your Bank

The Items To Send section of the Online Banking Center dialog contains the data you send to your bank. A request for a QuickStatement is always on the list, and if you created any messages to send to the bank, they're listed too. (A QuickStatement is a list of transactions that have cleared the account since the last time you received a QuickStatement.)

By default, all items have a check mark, which means they'll be sent to the bank when you click the Go Online button.

- If you don't want to send an item, click its check mark to remove it (it's a toggle). You can click again to put the check mark back when you're ready to send the item.
- You can edit any item except a request for a QuickStatement. Select the item, click the Edit button, make the necessary changes, and click OK.
- You can remove any item except the request for a QuickStatement. Select the item and click the Delete button.

Click the Go Online button to contact your bank over the Internet. A dialog opens to accept your PIN or password (depending on the way your bank manages security).

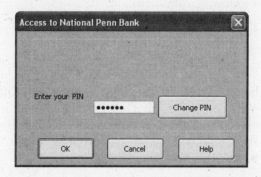

 N O T E :   If you want to change your PIN during this interactive session, click Change PIN and enter your new PIN.

Click OK to begin communications. You'll see progress messages as QuickBooks contacts the bank's server, sends any messages you created, and delivers the request for a QuickStatement.

If your bank account has not cleared any new transactions since the last time you received a QuickStatement, a dialog reports that fact and encourages you to try again tomorrow. If new transactions have cleared, the Online Transmission Summary dialog displays a report. Click Print if you want to print the new transactions (I can't think of any reason to do so), and click Close to return to the Online Banking Center dialog.

Viewing the Received Data

The Online Banking Center dialog displays all the items received from your bank during the online session in the Items Received section. The list includes a QuickStatement for each online account at that bank (the current online balance is displayed next to the bank's listing) and any e-mail messages from the bank. Select an item and click View to see it. Read any e-mail messages and delete those you don't care to save (although it would be unusual to want to save any, since most of the time the messages contain information about upcoming bank holiday closings or announcements about new mortgage or CD rates).

To see the new transactions in your account, select the QuickStatement and click View. QuickBooks opens the Match Transactions dialog, which displays the account register at the top and the list of new transactions at the bottom. (If the account register isn't displayed, select the Show Register option.)

Matching Transactions

QuickBooks automatically tries to match the transactions in the QuickStatement to the transactions in your register and marks each QuickStatement transaction with one of the following conditions:

- **Matched**   Means the downloaded transaction matches a transaction in the register.
- **Unmatched**   Means no match was found for the downloaded transaction.

If all the downloaded transactions are matched, you have nothing else to do. QuickBooks inserts a lightning bolt in the Cleared column of your register (the column with a check mark heading) for every matched transaction, indicating the fact that the transaction has cleared the bank. Whenever you open the register, you know which transactions have cleared:

- A check mark indicates a transaction has cleared and has also been through reconciliation.
- A lightning bolt indicates a transaction has cleared but has not been through a bank reconciliation.

(Chapter 12 covers the topic of bank reconciliations.)

Matching Unmatched Transactions

If any transactions are marked unmatched, you have to correct the register. Any of several conditions will cause a failure when QuickBooks is trying to match transactions in the QuickStatement to the transactions in the register.

Differing Check Numbers and Amounts

If a transaction's check number and amount differs, QuickBooks won't match the transaction. For example, you may have entered check 2034 in the amount of $100.00 in your register, but the only $100 check in the QuickStatement is listed as check 2035. Or, you may have entered check 2034 for $100.00 in your register, but the QuickStatement shows check 2034 with an amount of $1000.00.

Correct the transaction in the register. If the problem is a check number, change the check number in the register because it's unlikely the QuickStatement check number is wrong. Banks read check numbers electronically, using the metallic ink at the bottom of your check.

If the problem is a difference in the amount for a specific check number, it could be either your error or the bank's error. However, for the time being, change the registry to give the victory to the QuickStatement because the QuickStatement always wins (by virtue of the fact that you can't change the items in the QuickStatement). Then contact your bank to find out what happened. If the bank made a mistake in the amount, it will credit or debit your account for the appropriate amount and that transaction will show up in a future QuickStatement, matching the adjusting entry you make in the register when you finish talking to the person at the bank.

Often, the QuickStatement contains transactions that aren't in your register. I'll go over some of the common reasons for this scenario and provide the remedies.

Unmatched Bank Charges

Bank charges appear in the QuickStatement when they're assessed (people who don't have online banking have to wait for the statement to arrive to learn what the monthly bank charge is). Add the bank charges to the register by selecting the transaction in the QuickStatement and clicking the Add One To Register button. In the Unmatched Transaction dialog, select the method you want to use to add the transaction (the choices differ depending on whether you're working with a bank account or a credit card account). Follow the prompts and enter the information. You don't have to enter a payee for a bank charge, you just have to enter the account to which you post bank charges.

If you have a merchant account (you accept credit cards for customer payments), you're assessed a monthly charge that appears as an unmatched transaction just like a bank charge. Use the same remedy described for entering bank charges, posting the merchant card fee/charge to the appropriate account.

Unmatched Checks

A check that has no matching transaction means you wrote and sent a check but didn't enter it in the register. (If this occurs frequently, you should stop writing manual checks and have QuickBooks print your checks.) Click Add One To Register, enter the check in the register, and when you click Record, QuickBooks automatically matches the transaction to the QuickStatement.

Of course, if you print checks, or you know you entered every manual check you wrote in your QuickBooks register, you may have a more serious problem—someone has stolen a check. Call your bank immediately.

Unmatched Withdrawals

If you use an ATM card to withdraw cash from your bank account, any withdrawals you didn't enter in the register are unmatched in the QuickStatement. Click Add One To Register, enter the transactions, and QuickBooks will match it as soon as you click Record.

Unmatched Deposits

If a deposit appears in the QuickStatement for which no matching transaction is found in the register, it's usually rather easy to remedy.

Check to see whether income you recorded in a Sales Receipt or Received Payment transaction is still in the Undeposited Funds account (because you forgot to move the funds to the bank with the Make Deposits window). If so, open the Make Deposits window, select the appropriate transaction(s), and walk through the steps to make the deposit. As soon as you finish, QuickBooks automatically matches the deposit to the QuickStatement.

If a deposit doesn't exist in your QuickBooks file, either because you never entered it or because it was a direct deposit about which you lacked prior knowledge (either lacking information about the date or the amount of the deposit), you need to create the transaction. Use either a Sales Receipt for a direct sale, or a Received Payment for a customer's invoice payment. When you finish recording the transaction, QuickBooks automatically matches it to the QuickStatement.

Matching Merchant Card Deposits

Most of the time, your merchant card deposits are unmatched in the QuickStatement, because you keep the merchant card funds in the Undeposited Funds account until your merchant card provider deposits the money (which could take several days). Merchant card deposits work in one of the two following ways:

- The entire amount of the sale is deposited, and all fees incurred during the month are removed from your account once a month.
- The fee is deducted before the proceeds of the sale are deposited (and your Undeposited Funds account lists the total amount of the sale).

If your merchant card provider deposits the gross sale proceeds, match the transaction by selecting the transaction in the Make Deposits window and following the steps for depositing the funds.

If your merchant card provider deposits the net after deducting the fee (and you didn't deduct the fee when you entered the sales transaction), you need to deduct the fee in order to match the deposit.

Click the Record Deposits icon on the Home page (or choose Banking | Make Deposits from the menu bar), and select the credit card transaction in the Payments To Deposit dialog. Click OK to open the next Make Deposits dialog, where you must create an additional line for this transaction, as follows:

- In the From Account column, enter the account to which you post merchant card fees.
- In the Amount column, enter the fee as a minus figure (you have to calculate the amount—it's the difference between your sale amount and the amount in the QuickStatement).

The net deposit, displayed at the bottom of the dialog, matches the QuickStatement. When you click Save & Close, QuickBooks automatically matches the transaction.

Using Aliases to Match Online Bill Payments

If you use your bank's online bill-paying service (on the bank's web site) and download the transactions for import into QuickBooks, online bill payments have the name of the payee in the downloaded file. (Regular checks have the check number, not the name of the payee, in the downloaded file.)

You may see transactions marked as "unmatched," even though you entered the transaction in your bank register. The problem is that the payee name on the online transaction doesn't match the payee name on your register entry.

In addition, if you didn't enter the transaction in your bank register, your efforts to add the unmatched transaction are thwarted by the fact that QuickBooks can't find a vendor to match the name on the downloaded transaction.

The payee name on the online transaction may be a code your vendor asked you to use for online bill payments. For example, you may have a vendor named BigBank to whom you make online payments, but the bank asked you to use BB4445 (representing your loan payment) when creating online payments. In that case, you have two options for matching (or adding) the transaction in the Online Banking Center dialog:

- Change the name of the vendor to BB4445 in your QuickBooks file.
- Create an alias to match BB4445 to BigBank when a payment appears in a downloaded file.

The same problem occurs when the difference in the payee name is inadvertent. For example, you may have a vendor named Backstroke, with a company name Arthur Backstroke, but when you go online to create the check you may fill in the payee name as Art Backstroke, or Artie Backstroke. If you aren't consistent about the way you fill in payee names online, changing the vendor name isn't efficient (because you'd have to change the name every time you spelled it differently online). Creating an alias for each payee entry you've used resolves your problem.

When you download your online payments, the entries that don't have a matching vendor are marked "unmatched."

Use the following steps to add an alias to online payees that don't match the names of vendors that exist in your company file:

1. Select a transaction and click Add One To Register.
2. Select the way to add the transaction (Add To Register, Write Checks, or Pay Bills). Because the Payee in the downloaded transaction does not match an existing vendor, a Name Not Found dialog appears.
3. Choose Create Alias to open the Create Alias dialog.
4. Select an existing vendor name from the drop-down list.
5. Click OK and confirm the addition of this alias for this vendor.

The next time you download transactions with this payee name, QuickBooks recognizes the alias and matches the transaction if it exists in the register. If the transaction doesn't exist in the register, select the downloaded transaction and click Add One To Register. QuickBooks automatically adds it to the register, replacing the alias with the vendor name.

If you use more than one "wrong name" for an existing vendor, you can add multiple aliases to the same vendor name. For example, perhaps over the months your vendor "Bob Smith" is entered as Bobby Smith, Robert Smith, and Bob Smitz, depending on your memory or how many typos you make when entering payee names for online payments. Don't worry, you can let QuickBooks figure it out accurately by entering a new alias for Bob Smith every time you create an online transaction with the inaccurate name.

Transferring Money Between Accounts Online

If you have multiple accounts at your financial institution, you can transfer money between those accounts. For example, you may have a money market account for your business in addition to your checking account.

To transfer money online, you must have applied at your financial institution for online banking for both accounts. You'll probably have a unique PIN for each account. To make your life less complicated, you should make changes while you're online to ensure both accounts have the same PIN. In addition, you must have enabled both accounts for online access within QuickBooks.

There are two methods you can use to transfer funds between online accounts: the transfer funds function, or direct data entry in the register for either account.

Using the Transfer Funds Function

The simplest way to move money between your online accounts is to use the QuickBooks Transfer Funds Between Accounts window, which you reach by choosing Banking | Transfer Funds from the menu bar.

Specify the sending and receiving accounts (remember, both must be enabled for online access) and enter the amount you want to transfer. Be sure to select the option for Online Funds Transfer. Click Save & Close. Then choose Banking | Online Banking Center, make sure the transaction has a check mark, and click Go Online.

Using the Bank Register to Transfer Funds

You can enter a transfer directly into the account register of the bank account from which you are sending the money. The significant data entry is the one in the Check Number column; instead of a check number, type the word **send**. Don't enter a payee; enter the amount, and enter the receiving account in the Account field. Then choose Banking | Online Banking | Online Banking Center, make sure the transaction has a check mark, and click Go Online.

Paying Bills Online

You can pay your bills in QuickBooks, then go online to send the payments to the payees. You can either use your own bank (if it's capable of working with QuickBooks to pay bills online), or use the QuickBooks bill-paying service. In this section, when

I say "bank," you can mentally substitute the QuickBooks service if that's what you're using.

When you make an online payment, the following information is transmitted to your vendor in addition to money:

- The date and number of the vendor's bill(s)
- Information about any discounts or credits you've applied
- Anything you inserted as a memo or note when you prepared the payment

If the vendor is set up to receive electronic payments, the money is transferred directly from your bank account to the vendor's bank account. Incidentally, being set up to receive electronic payments does not mean your vendor must be using QuickBooks; there are many and varied methods for receiving electronic payments, and many companies have these arrangements with their banks. If the vendor's account is not accessible for online payments, your bank writes a check and mails it, along with all the necessary payment information.

If your vendor can accept electronic funds, making an online payment is a breeze. What happens is that your bank's software transmits the payment electronically, and the vendor's bank uses its software to accept it—no paper, no mail, no delays. If your vendor cannot accept electronic funds, your bank actually prints a check and mails it.

There are three methods for creating the transaction in QuickBooks (each of which requires that you select the option to transmit the transaction online):

- Use the Write Checks window.
- Use the Pay Bills window.
- Use the register for the bank account you use for online payments.

 CAUTION: If you add a memo, your text can only be delivered as a voucher or stub. This means that your payment will not be made electronically even if the vendor is able to accept electronic payments. Instead, a check is sent, which delays the payment.

Go online to transmit the information to the Online Banking Center. Choose Banking | Online Banking | Online Banking Center. In the Online Banking Center window, click Go Online. Your payments are sent to the big bill-paying machine on the Net.

Creating Online Transaction Reports

You can track your online activities using the available QuickBooks reports. The quickest way to see your online transactions is to choose Reports | Accountant & Taxes | Transaction Detail By Account.

In the report window, click the Modify Report button and click the Filters tab. In the Filter list box, select Online Status. Click the arrow to the right of the Online Status box and select the online status option you need (most of the following options are only available for bank accounts that are enabled for Direct Connection online access):

- **All**   Reports all transactions whether they were online transactions or not (don't choose this option if you're trying to get a report on your online transactions).
- **Online To Send**   Reports the online transactions you've created but not yet sent online.
- **Online Sent**   Reports only the online transactions you've sent.
- **Any Online**   Reports on all the online transactions you've created, both sent and waiting.
- **Not Online**   Excludes the online transactions from the report. (Obviously, you don't want to choose this option.)

After you've set the filter options, click OK to return to the report window.

Receiving Customer Payments Online

Besides the online activities that permit you to track your own bank account activity, transfer money, and pay your own bills, QuickBooks offers a way for your customers to pay you online. This service is provided by the QuickBooks online billing service.

The QuickBooks online billing service offers your customers a way to pay their bills on the QuickBooks online payment site. The customer can enter a credit card number to pay the bills or use an online payment service.

You can notify the customer about this online service by e-mailing the invoice with the online service URL in the cover note, or by snail-mailing the invoice and sending an e-mail message with the online service URL. The customer clicks the link to the URL to travel to the QuickBooks web site and arrange for payment.

QuickBooks notifies you that the payment is made, and you can download the payment information into your bank register using the standard online banking procedures.

To learn more about this service or to sign up, click the Add QuickBooks Services link on the Home page. Follow the prompts to get to the QuickBooks Billing Services, and complete the enrollment information.

Year-end Procedures

In this chapter:

- Run reports on your financial condition

- Print 1099 forms

- Make year-end journal entries

- Get ready for tax time

- Close the books

The end of the year is a madhouse for bookkeepers, and that's true for major corporations as well as for small businesses. There is so much to do: so many reports to examine, corrections to make, entries to create, adjustments to apply—whew!

You can relax a bit. You don't have to show up at the office on January 1 (or the first day of your new fiscal year if you're not on a calendar year). Everything doesn't have to be accomplished immediately. QuickBooks is date-sensitive so you can continue to work in the new year. As long as the dates of new transactions are after the last day of your fiscal year, the transactions won't work their way into your year-end calculations.

Running Year-end Financial Reports

The standard financial reports you run at year-end provide a couple of services for you:

- You can see the economic health of your business.
- You can examine the report to make sure everything is posted correctly before you organize information for paying taxes.

To run financial reports, click the Reports menu listing. For year-end reports, you'll need to access several types of reports (see Chapter 15 for information about modifying and customizing the standard financial reports).

Don't forget that reports have date ranges like "current year" and "last fiscal year." If you perform these tasks before the end of your fiscal year, you're still in the current year. However, if you're working after the last date of your fiscal year (which is the norm), the current year isn't the year of interest.

Year-end P&L Report

Start with a Profit & Loss Standard report (also called an *income statement*), by choosing Reports | Company & Financial | Profit & Loss Standard. When the report opens, be sure the date range is the entire fiscal year (by default, the date range is the current month to date).

The report displays the year-end balances for all the income and expense accounts in your general ledger that had any activity this year. Examine the report, and if anything seems out of whack, double-click the line to see the postings for that account. If the data you see doesn't reassure you, double-click any of the posting lines to see the original transaction.

If there's a transaction that seems to be in error, you can take corrective action. You cannot delete or void a bill you paid or a customer invoice for which you received payment, of course. However, you might be able to talk to a customer or vendor for whom you've found a problem and work out a satisfactory arrangement for credits. Or you may find that you posted an expense or income transaction to the wrong general ledger account. If so, make a journal entry to correct it (see Chapter 14 for information on journal entries). Then run the year-end P&L report again and print it.

Year-end Balance Sheet

Your real financial health is demonstrated in your Balance Sheet. To run a year-end balance sheet, choose Reports | Company & Financial | Balance Sheet Standard. The Balance Sheet figures are more than a list of numbers; they're a list of chores. Check with your accountant first, but most of the time you'll find that the following advice is offered:

- Pay any payroll withholding liabilities with a check dated in the current year (the year in which they were accumulated) in order to clear them from the Balance Sheet. Also pay employer contributions.
- If you have an A/P balance, pay some bills ahead of time. For example, pay your rent or mortgage payment that's due the first day of the next fiscal year during the last month of this fiscal year. Enter and pay vendor bills earlier than their due dates (if those dates fall in the next year) in order to pay them this year and gain the expense deduction for this year.

Issuing 1099 Forms

If any vendors are eligible for 1099 forms, you need to print and mail the forms to them. First, make sure your 1099 setup is correct by choosing Edit | Preferences and selecting the Tax: 1099 icon. Click Company Preferences to see your settings (see Figure 17-1).

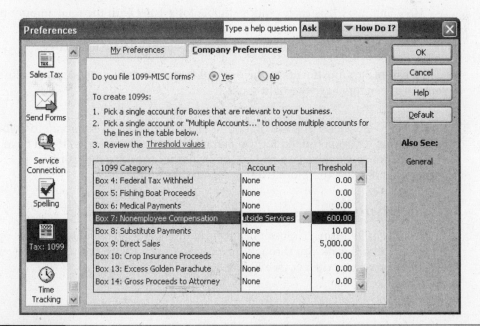

FIGURE 17-1   Make sure your 1099 options are configured correctly.

Check the latest IRS rules and make any changes to the threshold amounts for the categories you need. Also assign an account to each category for which you'll be issuing Form 1099 to vendors. You can assign multiple accounts to a 1099 category, but you cannot assign any accounts to more than one 1099 category.

For example, if you have an expense account "subcontractors" and an expense account "outside consultants," both of the accounts can be linked to the same 1099 category (Nonemployee Compensation). However, once you link those accounts to that category, you cannot use those same accounts in any other 1099 category.

To assign a single account to a category, click the category to select it. Click the text in the account column (it probably says "None") and then click the arrow to select the account for this category.

To assign multiple accounts to a category, instead of selecting an account after you click the arrow, choose the Multiple Accounts option (at the top of the list). In the Select Account dialog, click each account to put a check mark next to its listing. Click OK to assign all the accounts you checked. Then click OK to close the Preferences dialog.

Run a 1099 Report

Before you print the forms, you should print a report on your 1099 vendors. To do this, choose Reports | Vendors & Payables and select one of the following 1099 reports:

- 1099 Summary lists each vendor eligible for a 1099 with the total amount paid to the vendor.
- 1099 Detail lists each transaction for each vendor eligible for a 1099.

You can make adjustments to the original transactions, if necessary, to make sure your 1099 vendors have the right totals.

 N O T E :   Business that are organized as LLCs can opt to be proprietorships, partnerships, or corporations for the purpose of filing tax returns. If you have a vendor that is organized as an LLC, ask whether they are reporting as a corporation and are therefore exempt from 1099 forms.

Print 1099 Forms

To print the 1099 forms, choose File | Print Forms | 1099s/1096. QuickBooks opens a wizard that will walk you through the process to make sure every step is covered and every amount is correct (see Figure 17-2).

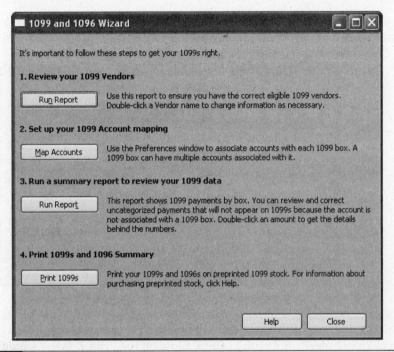

FIGURE 17-2 The 1099 And 1096 Wizard makes it easy to issue end-of-year forms to 1099 vendors.

This isn't a standard wizard, because you don't walk through a series of windows. Instead, as you check each item in the window, QuickBooks opens the appropriate system window so you can check and, if necessary, change the data. When you close the window, you're returned to the wizard window.

When all the data is correct, click Print 1099s in the wizard window. The wizard asks you to confirm the year for which you're printing (I'm assuming you're performing this task in January of next year).

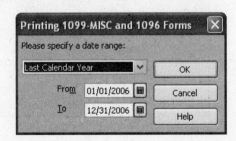

Click OK to move to the Select 1099s To Print dialog. QuickBooks displays the vendors for whom you should be printing 1099s.

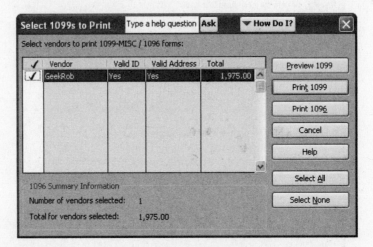

Click Preview 1099 to see what the form will look like when it prints. Zoom in to make sure your company name, address, and EIN number are correct, and also check the vendor's information. Click Close on the Print Preview window to return to the Select 1099s window.

Then load the 1099 forms into your printer and click Print 1099. If you're using a laser or inkjet printer, set the number of copies at three. Dot matrix printers use three-part forms.

When the forms are printed, click Print 1096 in the Select 1099s To Print dialog. Enter the name of the contact person in your company that can answer questions about these forms (the name is printed on the 1096 Form). Print two copies of the 1096, so you have one for your files.

Send each vendor a copy of his or her 1099 by January 31st. Send the government a copy of each 1099, along with a 1096 Transmittal Form.

Repeat these procedures for each type of 1099 form you are required to print (most businesses need to worry only about the 1099-MISC form).

Making Year-end Journal Entries

Your accountant may want you to make some journal entries before you close your books for the year:

- Depreciation entries
- Prior retained earnings moved to a different account or retained earnings moved to owner or partner equity accounts
- Any adjustments needed for cash versus accrual reporting (these are usually reversed on the first day of the next fiscal year)
- Adjustment of prepaid expenses from asset accounts to expense accounts

 N O T E :   See Chapter 14 for detailed information about creating journal entries.

You can send the P&L and Balance Sheet reports to your accountant by exporting the reports to Excel. Ask your accountant for journal entry instructions.

You can also send your accountant an Accountant's Review copy of your company data and let your accountant make the journal entries. You import the changes when the review copy is returned. (See Chapter 15 to learn how to use the Accountant's Review Copy feature.)

Running Tax Reports

Most small businesses turn over the tax preparation chores to their accountants, but some business owners prepare their own taxes manually or by using a tax software program like TurboTax.

No matter which method you choose for tax preparation, you should run the reports that tell you whether your QuickBooks data files are ready for tax preparation. Is all the necessary data entered? Do the bottom-line numbers call for some special tax planning or special tax considerations? Even if your taxes are prepared by your accountant, the more organized your records are, the less time the accountant spends on your return (which makes your bill from the accountant smaller).

Check Tax Line Information

If you're going to do your own taxes, every account in your chart of accounts that is tax related must have the right tax form in the account's tax line assignment. To see if any tax line assignments are missing, choose Reports | Accountant & Taxes | Income Tax Preparation. When the report appears, all your accounts are listed, along with the tax form assigned to each account. If you created your own chart of accounts, instead of accepting a chart of accounts during company setup, the number of accounts that lack a tax form assignment is likely to be quite large.

Before you can prepare your own taxes, you must edit each account to add the tax information. To do so, open the chart of accounts and select an account. Press CTRL-E to edit the account and select a tax form from the Tax Line entry drop-down list.

Your selections vary depending upon the organizational type of your company (proprietorship, partnership, S corp, C corp, and so on).

 NOTE: Be sure the Income Tax Form Used field is filled out properly on your Company Information dialog (on the Company menu). If it's blank, you won't see the tax information fields on any accounts.

If you don't know which form and category to assign to an account, here's an easy trick for getting that information:

1. Choose File | New Company to open the EasyStep Interview wizard.
2. Click Skip Interview.
3. In the Creating New Company dialog, enter a name in the Company Name field (it doesn't matter what name you use; you're not really creating a company file).
4. Be sure to select the correct organizational type from the drop-down list in the Income Tax Form Used field, then click Next.
5. Select the type of company that best describes your business. (If nothing comes close to matching your business, select General Business.)
6. Click Next, and save the new company file.

When the new company file is loaded into the QuickBooks window, open the chart of accounts list and press CTRL-P to print the list. The printed list has the tax form information you need. Open your real company, open the chart of accounts, and use the information on the printed document to enter tax form information.

Calculate Other Important Tax Information

There are some taxable numbers that aren't available through the normal QuickBooks reports. One of the most common is the report on company officer compensation if your business is incorporated.

If your business is a C corporation, you file tax form 1120, while a Subchapter S corporation files tax form 1120S. Both of these forms require you to separate compensation for corporate officers from the other employee compensation. You will have to add those totals from payroll reports (either QuickBooks payroll or an outside payroll service).

You can avoid the need to calculate this by creating a separate Payroll item called Officer Compensation and assigning it to its own account (which you'll also have to create). Then open the Employee card for each officer and change the Earnings item to the new item. Do this for next year; it's probably too late for this year's end-of-year process.

Using TurboTax

If you purchase TurboTax to do your taxes, you don't have to do anything special in QuickBooks to transfer the information. Open TurboTax and tell it to import your QuickBooks company file.

Almost everything you need is transferred to TurboTax. There are some details you'll have to enter directly into TurboTax (for example, home-office expenses for a Schedule C form). You can learn more about TurboTax at www.turbotax.com.

Closing Your Books

After all the year-end reports have been run, any necessary journal entries have been entered, and your taxes have been filed (and paid), it's traditional to go through the exercise of closing the books. Typically, closing the books occurs some time after the end of the fiscal year, usually within the first couple of months of the next fiscal year, as soon as your business tax forms have been filed.

The exercise of closing the books is performed to lock the books, so no user can add, remove, or change any transactions. After taxes have been filed based on the information in the system, nothing should ever be changed. It's too late. This is it. The information is etched in stone.

Understanding Closing in QuickBooks

QuickBooks doesn't use the traditional accounting software closing procedures. In most other business accounting software, closing the year means you cannot post transactions to any date in that year, nor can you manipulate any transactions in the closed year. Closing the books in QuickBooks does not set the information in cement; it can be changed and/or deleted by users with the appropriate permissions.

QuickBooks does not require you to close the books in order to keep working in the software. You can work forever, year after year, without performing a closing process. However, many QuickBooks users prefer to lock the transactions for a year as a way to prevent any changes to the data except by users with the appropriate permissions.

Closing the Year

In QuickBooks, you close the year by entering a closing date. This inherently does nothing more than lock users out of the previous year's transactions. At the same time, you can configure user rights to enable or disable a user's ability to see or manipulate closed transactions.

To accomplish this, follow these steps:

1. Choose Edit | Preferences to open the Preferences dialog.
2. Click the Accounting icon.
3. Select the Company Preferences tab.
4. Enter the closing date, which is the last date of your fiscal year (see Figure 17-3).

TIP: If your fiscal year is different from a calendar year, don't worry about payroll. The payroll files and features (including 1099s) are locked into a calendar year configuration, and closing your books doesn't have any effect on your ability to work with payroll transactions.

Preventing Access to Closed Books

To prevent users from changing transactions in the closed year, and to permit certain users to access those transactions when needed, assign a password for manipulating closed data. Click Set Password and enter the password in the Set Closing Date Password dialog. Press TAB and enter it again in the Confirm Password field.

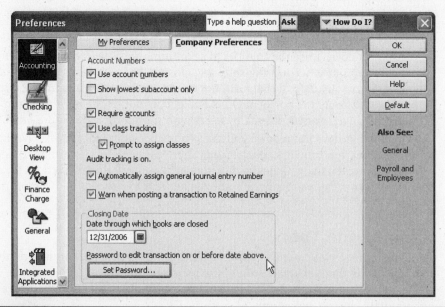

FIGURE 17-3   Entering the closing date is the first step in locking down the previous year's data.

CAUTION: If you've set up users and passwords for access to your QuickBooks data file, only the QuickBooks administrator can set the closing date and password.

Creating a Year-end Backup

After all the numbers are checked, all the journal entries are made, and the books have been closed by entering a closing date as described in the previous section, do a separate backup in addition to your normal daily backup. Don't put this backup on one of the disks you're using for your normal backups—use a fresh disk, label it "Year-End Backup 2006," and put it in a safe place. See Chapter 21 to learn about backing up your QuickBooks files.

Additional Features for Premier and Enterprise Editions

If you're running a QuickBooks Premier edition or QuickBooks Enterprise Solutions, you may have some additional features available, above and beyond the features covered in this chapter. (Not all features are in all Premier or Enterprise versions.)

Closing Date Exception Report

Want to drive an accountant crazy? Create a report that shows opening balances for accounts as of the current year, where those opening balances don't match last year's closing balances for the same accounts. The "rule" is that this year's opening balances should be exactly the same as last year's closing balances. When they're not, accountants go into a frenzy, and sometimes they won't leave your office until they've found the reason the balances don't match. They don't have an easy time in their quest for the answer to the question, "What changed, and why did it change?" The business owner is usually interested in the answer to the question, "Who changed it?"

It's almost impossible to find the cause of these mismatched balances, unless you happen to have a detailed report of every transaction that occurred last year (printed at the moment you recorded the closing balances), so you can compare each transaction to the transactions currently in the registers. This can take days or weeks, and it's going to cost you a lot of money no matter how reasonable your accountant's fees seem to be.

QuickBooks Premier and Enterprise Solutions editions offer a Closing Date Exception Report, which lists all transactions that were added or changed after the closing date. (A transaction that was changed shows the date and amount of the modification, as well as the date and amount of the original transaction.) If your QuickBooks configuration includes user logins, the report displays the login name of the user who created the transaction.

To view the Closing Date Exception Report, choose Reports | Accountant & Taxes | Closing Date Exception Report. Any transactions that occurred after the closing date appear in the report.

Tracking Time and Mileage

Most service businesses sell time; it's the most important commodity they have. Actually, most service businesses are really selling knowledge and expertise, but nobody's ever figured out how to put a value on those talents. The solution, therefore, is to charge for the time it takes to pass along and use all that expertise (that explanation was originally voiced by Abraham Lincoln as he explained why and how attorneys charge for time). Even businesses that are product-based might need to track time for employees or outside consultants.

Tracking mileage is a universal need for any business in which vehicles are used to deliver services or products. Vehicle expense deductions on your tax return need to be able to pass an audit, and many companies insist that every employee keep a travel log. In addition, many service businesses bill clients for mileage when employees work at the client site or travel at the client's behest.

Beyond the need to track time and mileage, you may need to track time and activities by outside contractors or off-site employees.

Part Three of this book covers all the steps you need to take to set your system up for tracking time and mileage with maximum efficiency and accuracy.

Using Time Tracking

In *this chapter:*

- Configure time tracking
- Fill out timesheets
- Edit timesheets
- Bill for time

QuickBooks includes a time-tracking feature that lets you record the amount of time you and your staff spend completing a project, working for a customer, or working for your company (administrative tasks). You can use that information to invoice customers for time.

In addition to tracking billable time, you can also use this information to analyze your business. For example, if you charge retainer fees for your services, time tracking is a terrific way to figure out which customers may need to have the retainer amount raised.

Configuring Time Tracking

When you create a company in QuickBooks, one of the EasyStep Interview windows queries you about your desire to track time. If you respond affirmatively, QuickBooks turns on the time-tracking features. If you opt to skip time tracking, you can turn it on later if you change your mind. In fact, if you turn it on, you can turn it off if you find you're not using it.

If you're not sure whether you turned on time tracking when you installed your company, choose Edit | Preferences from the QuickBooks menu bar. Select the Time Tracking icon and click the Company Preferences tab. Make sure the Yes option is selected.

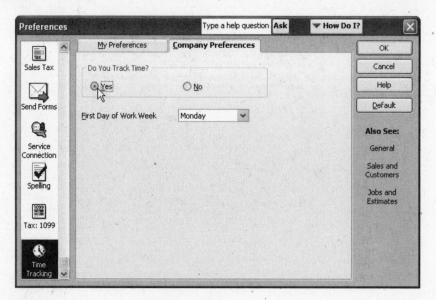

Configuring Your Workweek

By default, QuickBooks assumes your workweek starts on Monday. However, if your business is open every day of the week, you might want to use a Sunday-to-Saturday pattern for tracking time.

If you're tracking time for employees and you plan to use the timesheets for payroll, it's a good idea to match the workweek to the week your pay period covers. Of course, this only works if your pay periods are weekly.

Configuring Workers

If you're tracking time for your employees, outside contractors, or yourself, everybody who must keep track of his or her time must exist in the system. Each person must also fill out timesheets.

Tracking Employee Time

If you're running the QuickBooks payroll feature, you already have employees in your QuickBooks system. You can track the time of any employee who fills out a timesheet (timesheets are covered later in this chapter).

You can also use the timesheet data to pay an employee, using the number of hours reported in the time-tracking system to determine the number of hours for which the employee is paid. For this to work, however, the employee must be linked to his or her timesheet.

As a result, you must modify the employee record as follows:

1. Open the Employee Center (click the Employee icon on the left side of the Home page, or on the toolbar).
2. Click the Employees tab to display the list of employees.
3. Double-click the listing of the employee you want to link to time tracking.
4. In the Change Tabs field at the top of the window, select Payroll And Compensation Info from the drop-down list.
5. Select the Use Time Data To Create Paychecks check box (see Figure 18-1).
6. Click OK.

You don't have to link employees to time tracking in order for them to use the timesheets to record their time—the time-tracking configuration is required only if you want to create the paychecks with the timesheets.

If you *do* link an employee to time tracking, while that employee is filling out timesheets, a QuickBooks message may appear saying that the activity the employee is reporting is not linked to an hourly rate. QuickBooks will report the rate at $0.00/hour, which is fine (especially if your employees are on salary).

Tracking Vendor Time

Any vendor in your system who is paid for his or her time can have that time tracked for the purpose of billing customers. Most of the time, these vendors are outside contractors or subcontractors. You don't have to do anything to the vendor record to effect time tracking; you merely need to record the time used as the vendor sends bills.

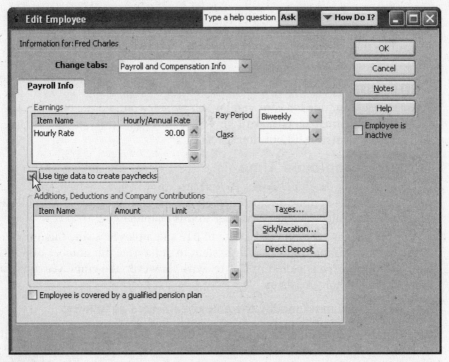

FIGURE 18-1   Link employees to time tracking if you want to use timesheets to prepare paychecks.

Tracking Other Worker Time

You may need to track the time of people who are neither employees nor vendors. The word *employee* means you have enabled do-it-yourself payroll in QuickBooks. If you have employees but you don't use QuickBooks payroll, they're not employees to your QuickBooks software.

QuickBooks provides a system list called Other Names, and you can use this list to collect names that don't fit in the other QuickBooks lists. Following are some situations in which you'll need to use the Other Names list:

- You have employees and use QuickBooks payroll, but you are not an employee because you take a draw instead of a paycheck. In this case, you must add your name to the Other Names list if you want to track your own time.
- You have employees and are not using QuickBooks payroll, so there is no Employees list in your system. You must add each employee name to the Other Names list to track employee time.
- You have no employees and your business is a proprietorship or a partnership. Owner or partner names must be entered into the Other Names list in order to track time.

Configuring the Tasks

Most of the tasks you track already exist in your system as service items. These are the items you use when you invoice customers for services. However, because you can use time tracking to analyze the way people in your organization spend their time, you may want to add service items that are relevant to noncustomer tasks.

For example, if you want to track the time people spend performing administrative tasks for the business, you can add a service item called Administrative to your items list. If you want to be more specific, you can name the particular administrative tasks you want to track (for example, bookkeeping, equipment repair, new sales calls, public relations, and so on).

To enter new items, click the Items & Services icon on the Home page (or choose Lists | Item List from the menu bar). When the Item List window opens, press CTRL-N to open a new item form. Select Service as the item type (only service items are tracked in timesheets) and name the new item. Here are some guidelines for administrative items:

- If you're specifying administrative tasks, create a service named Administration and then make each specific administrative task a subitem of Administration.
- Don't put an amount in the Rate box. You're not charging a customer for this service, and you can calculate the amount you're paying the recipient when you make the payment (via payroll or vendor checks).
- Because QuickBooks insists that you assign an account to a service, choose or create an innocuous revenue account (such as Other Revenue, or Time Tracking Revenue). Don't worry, no money is ever posted to the account because you don't ever sell these services to customers.

The option to configure the item for subcontractors, owners, or partners isn't important if you're creating a service for the purpose of tracking time, because you're entering time on the timesheets; you're not entering amounts.

$ NOTE: When you actually pay a subcontractor, owner, or partner for work, you must create specific accounts for those payments. For subcontractors, you post payments to an expense account that is linked to your 1099 configuration (covered in Chapter 17). For owners and partners, payments must be posted to a draw account (which is an equity account).

Because time tracking is connected to customers, in order to track administrative work, you must also create a customer for the occasions when no real customer is being tracked (those administrative tasks). The easiest way to do that is to create a new customer to represent your company. For example, you may want to create a customer named House, or InHouse.

Configuring User Permissions

If you're using user and password features in QuickBooks, you must make sure each user who uses timesheets has permission to do so. See Chapter 21 for detailed information about performing this task.

Using Timesheets

QuickBooks offers two methods for recording the time you spend on tasks: Single Activity and Weekly Timesheet.

- Single Activity is a form you use to enter what you did when you performed a single task at a specific time on a specific date. For example, a Single Activity form may record the fact that you made a telephone call on behalf of a customer, you repaired some piece of equipment for a customer, or you performed some administrative task for the company.
- Weekly Timesheet is a form in which you indicate how much time and on which date you performed work. Each Weekly Timesheet entry can also include the name of the customer for whom the work was performed.

Your decision about which method to use depends on the type of work you do and on the efficiency of your workers' memories. People tend to put off filling in Weekly Timesheets and then attempt to reconstruct their activities in order to complete the timesheets. This frequently ends up being a less-than-accurate approach. The method works properly only if everyone remembers to open the timesheets and fill them in as soon as they complete each task. Uh huh, sure.

 TIP: When you fill out a Single Activity form, every time you open a Weekly Timesheet form, any single activity within that week is automatically inserted into the Weekly Timesheet.

Tracking a Single Activity

To track one event or task with a Single Activity form (see Figure 18-2), click the Enter Timesheets icon on the Home page, and choose Time/Enter Single Activity (or choose Employees | Time Tracking | Time/Enter Single Activity from the menu bar). Use the guidelines in this section to fill out the form.

The Date field is automatically filled in with the current date. If this activity took place previously, change the date.

Click the arrow to the right of the Name field and select the name of the person who performed the work from the list that appears (usually, the person who is filling out the form). The list contains vendors, employees, and names from the Other Names list. (You can use <Add New> to add a new name.)

If this time was spent working on a task for a customer rather than performing an administrative task, select the customer in the Customer:Job field. Do this

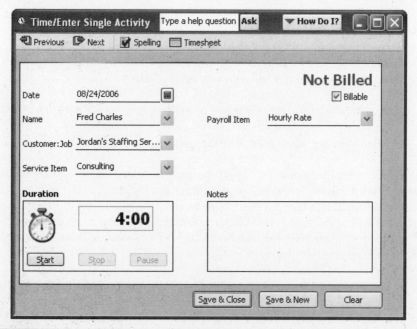

FIGURE 18-2   Fill out the details to indicate how you spent your time.

whether or not the customer is going to be billed for the time. If the task is specific to a job, select the job instead of the customer.

In the Service Item field, select the task, and in the Duration box, enter the amount of time you're reporting, using the format hh:mm.

If this time is billable to the customer, the Billable check box should be marked (it is by default). If the time is not going to be billed to the customer, click the box to remove the check mark.

If the Payroll Item field appears, select the payroll item that applies to this time (for example, salary or hourly wages). This field appears only if the name (in the Name field) is an employee, and the employee record has been linked to the time-tracking system (explained earlier in this chapter).

Use the Notes box to enter any comments or additional information you want to record about this activity.

When you've finished creating the activity, click Save & New to fill out another Single Activity form, or click Save & Close to finish.

NOTE: If an employee is not configured for using time data to create paychecks, QuickBooks asks if you'd like to change that configuration. If the employee is just tracking time for job-costing purposes and is not paid from these timesheets, click No.

Using the Stopwatch

You can let QuickBooks track the time you're spending on a specific task. Click the Start button in the Duration box of the Activity window when you begin the task. QuickBooks tracks hours and minutes as they elapse.

- To pause the counting when you're interrupted, click Pause. Then click Start to pick up where you left off.
- To stop timing, click Stop. The elapsed time is displayed.

You can set the format for reporting time, both on the activity sheet and in the stopwatch window. Some companies prefer the hh:mm format; others prefer a decimal format (such as 1.5 hours). To establish a default based on your preference, choose Edit | Preferences and click the General category. Then select the Company Preferences tab and use the options in the Time Format section of the dialog to select the appropriate format.

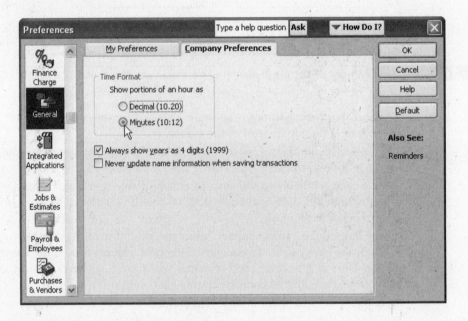

Using Weekly Timesheets

A Weekly Timesheet records the same information as the Single Activity form, except that the information is recorded in week-at-a-time blocks. To use this form, click the Enter Timesheets icon on the Home page, and choose Enter Weekly Timesheet (or choose Employees | Time Tracking | Use Weekly Timesheet from the menu bar). The Weekly Timesheet window opens (see Figure 18-3).

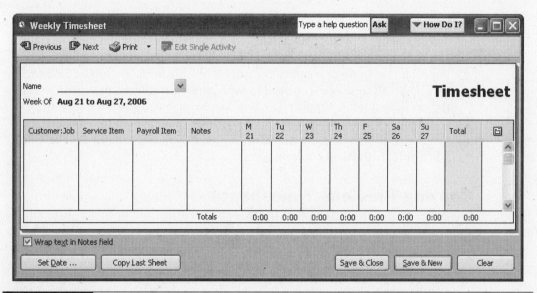

FIGURE 18-3 You may find it easier to enter information on a weekly basis.

Use the following steps to fill out the timesheet:

1. Select your name from the list that appears when you click the arrow to the right of the Name field. (If you're filling out a timesheet for a subcontractor who reported time to you, select the subcontractor's name.)

2. If you want to enter time for a different week, click the Set Date button and enter the first day of any week for which you want to enter activities. (The first day of your company workweek is set in Edit | Preferences | Time Tracking, as explained earlier in this chapter.)

3. Click in the Customer:Job column to display an arrow that you click to see the Customer List. Select the customer connected to the activity (or select the in-house listing if you're performing administrative work unconnected to a customer).

4. Enter the service item that describes your activity.

5. If you're an employee whose paycheck is linked to your timesheets, select the Payroll Item that fits the activity. If your name is attached to the Other Names or Vendor list, or you're an employee who is not paid from the timesheets, you won't see a Payroll Item column.

6. In the Notes column, enter any comments you feel are necessary.

7. Click the column that represents the day for which you are entering this activity and enter the number of hours worked on this task. Repeat for each day that you performed this activity. If you're linking the activity to a customer, all the days you indicate must be for this activity for this customer.

⑧ Move to the beginning of the next row to enter the next timesheet entry (a different activity, or the same activity for a different customer), repeating until you've accounted for your time for the week.

⑨ For each row, indicate whether the time is billable in the rightmost column. By default, all time entries linked to a customer are billable. (The icon in the rightmost column is supposed to look like an invoice.) Click the icon to put an X atop it if the time on this row is not billable.

⑩ Click Save & New to use a timesheet for a different week. Click Save & Close when you are finished entering time.

Copying Previous Timesheets

You can copy the previous week's timesheet by clicking the Copy Last Sheet button after you enter the current date in the timesheet window and select a name. This is useful for employees who have the similar timesheet data every week, a description that frequently applies to your office staff. Because many staff tasks aren't charged against a customer or job, the timesheet may be identical from week to week. For many staff employees, the only entry is the administrative service you created for in-house work, and the only customer is your own company. The only reason to fill in the data is to make sure every hour worked is transferred to the payroll data.

 T I P :　If timesheets are similar, but not identical, from week to week, it's efficient to copy the previous week's timesheet and then make adjustments.

Reporting Timesheet Information

Before you use the information on the timesheets to bill customers or pay workers, check the data on the timesheet reports. You can view and customize reports, edit information, and print the original timesheets.

Running Timesheet Reports

To run reports on timesheets, choose Reports | Jobs, Time & Mileage. You'll see a long list of available reports, but the following reports provide information on time tracking:

- **Time By Job Summary**　Reports the amount of time spent for each service on your customers and their jobs.
- **Time By Job Detail**　Reports the details of the time spent for each customer and job, including dates and whether or not the time was marked as billable (see Figure 18-4). A billing status of Unbilled indicates the time is billable but hasn't yet been transferred to a customer invoice.
- **Time By Name**　Reports the amount of time each user tracked.
- **Time By Item**　Provides a quick analysis of the amount of time spent performing services your company is providing and to whom.

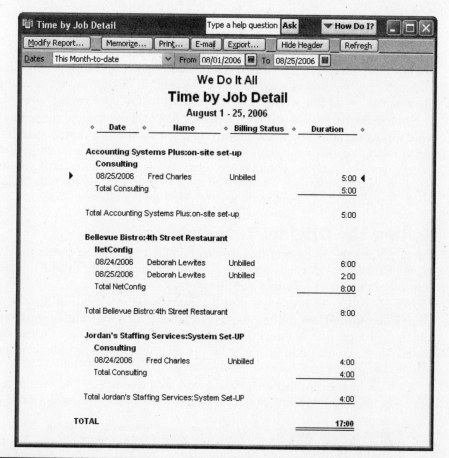

FIGURE 18-4 Generate a report to check everything, before billing customers or entering payroll information.

If you've made it a practice to encourage people to enter comments in the Notes section of the timesheet, you should customize the report format so it includes those comments.

You can do this only in the Time By Job Detail report:

1. Open the Time By Job Detail report and click the Modify Report button on the button bar.
2. In the Modify Report window, select Notes from the Columns list that appears on the Display tab.
3. Click OK.

To make sure you always see the notes, you should memorize this report. Click the Memorize button on the report button bar to open the Memorize Report dialog, and enter a name for the report. Hereafter, it will be available in the Memorized Reports list.

Editing Entries in a Report

While you're browsing the report, you can double-click an activity listing to see the original entry, an example of which is seen in Figure 18-5. You can make changes in the original entry, such as selecting or deselecting the billable option or changing the note field by adding a note or editing the content of the existing note.

If you make changes, when you click Save & Close to return to the report window, QuickBooks displays a message to ask whether you want to refresh the report to accommodate the changes. Click Yes to see the new, accurate information in the report. In fact, it's a good idea to select the option to stop asking you the question, because any time you make changes in transactions that you accessed from a report window, you want to see the effect on the report.

Editing the Original Timesheets

Before you use the timesheets for customer billing or payroll, make sure you examine them and make any needed corrections. In fact, you may want to take this step before you view any of the Jobs & Time reports.

The most common revision is the billable status. If you have outside contractors or employees filling out timesheets, it's not unusual to have some confusion about which customers receive direct time billings. In fact, you may have customers to whom you send direct time bills only for certain activities and provide the remaining activities as part of your basic services.

To check timesheets, just open a new weekly timesheet (choose Employees | Time Tracking | Use Weekly Timesheet from the menu bar). Enter the name of the

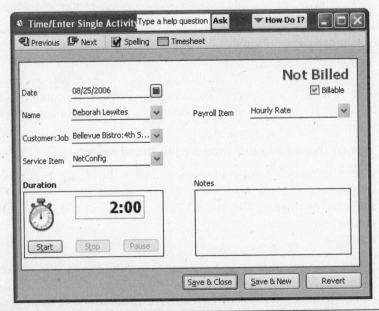

FIGURE 18-5   You can open any entry listed on the report to view the details.

person connected to the timesheet you want to inspect. Use the Previous or Next arrow at the top of the timesheet window, or click the Set Date button at the bottom of the window to move to the timesheet you want to inspect. Then edit the information as necessary:

- You can change the number of hours for any activity item.
- Click the icon in the Billable column (the last column) to reverse the current status (it's a toggle). Line entries that are not billable have an X over the icon.
- To view (and edit if necessary) any notes, first click in any of the weekday columns to activate the Edit Single Activity icon at the top of the timesheet window. Click that icon to see the entry as a single activity, with the entire note available for viewing or editing.

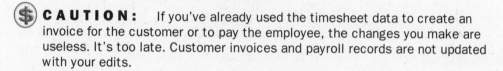 **CAUTION:**   If you've already used the timesheet data to create an invoice for the customer or to pay the employee, the changes you make are useless. It's too late. Customer invoices and payroll records are not updated with your edits.

Printing the Weekly Timesheets

It's a common practice to have employees print their Weekly Timesheets and deliver them to the appropriate management people. Usually that means your payroll person (or the person who phones in the payroll if you use an outside payroll service) or a personnel manager. However, instead of having each user be responsible for handing in the timesheet, it's a good idea to designate someone (such as your payroll manager) to perform this task. That way, all the timesheets are printed and available in a timely manner.

To print timesheets, choose File | Print Forms | Timesheets from the QuickBooks menu bar to open the Select Timesheets To Print window shown in Figure 18-6.

- Change the date range to match the timesheets you want to print.
- By default, all timesheets are selected. To remove a timesheet, select its listing and click the column with the check mark to deselect that listing. You can click Select None to deselect all listings, then select one or more specific users.
- To see any notes in their entirety, select the Print Full Activity Notes option. Otherwise, the default selection to print only the first line of any note is empowered.

The Select Timesheets To Print dialog has a Preview button, and clicking it displays a print preview of the selected timesheets. If you click the Print button in the Preview window, the timesheets are sent to the printer immediately, giving you no opportunity to change the printer or any printing options. Clicking the Close button in the Preview window returns you to the Select Timesheets To Print dialog, where clicking OK brings up the Print Timesheets dialog. Click OK to open the Print Timesheets window, where you can change the printer or printing options.

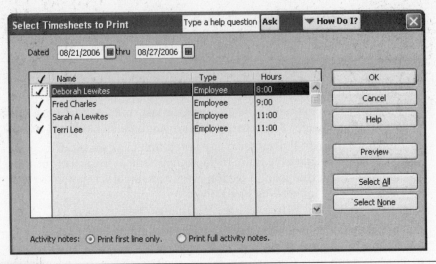

FIGURE 18-6 Print the timesheets for every person who tracks time.

You should change the number of copies to print to match the number of people to whom you're distributing the timesheets.

One thing you should notice about printed (or previewed) timesheets is the last column, which indicates the billing status. The entries are codes, as follows:

- **B** Billable but not yet invoiced to the customer
- **N** Not billable
- **D** Billable and already invoiced to the customer

Creating Invoices with Timesheets Data

After you've configured QuickBooks to track time, you can use the data you amass to help you create customer invoices quickly. For a full and detailed discussion about invoicing customers, please turn to Chapter 3.

Plugging In Time Charges

When you're ready to invoice customers for time, click the Invoice button on Home page and follow these steps:

1. In the Create Invoices window, select the customer or job. If the customer or job as billable time charges, QuickBooks notifies you of that fact.

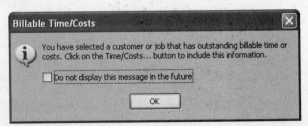

2 Enter the date of this invoice.

3 Click the Time/Costs button on the top of the invoice form to open the Choose Billable Time And Costs window. Click the Time tab to see the entries from timesheets, as shown in Figure 18-7.

4 Select the entries you want to include on this invoice (click Select All to use all the entries, otherwise click in the Use column to put a check mark on the entries you want to include).

5 If you don't want to change any options (see the following section if you want to make changes), click OK to transfer the items to the invoice.

6 Click Save & New to continue to the next invoice or Save & Close if you are finished creating invoices.

Changing Invoicing Options for Time Charges

You can change the way you transfer data from the timesheets to the invoice. You're not changing data or amounts, you're just altering the way in which data is presented on the invoice the client receives.

Printing One Invoice Item

If you just want to invoice the total amount for time charges instead of showing each activity, click the check box next to the selection Print Selected Time And Costs As One Invoice Item. Then click OK to return to the invoice.

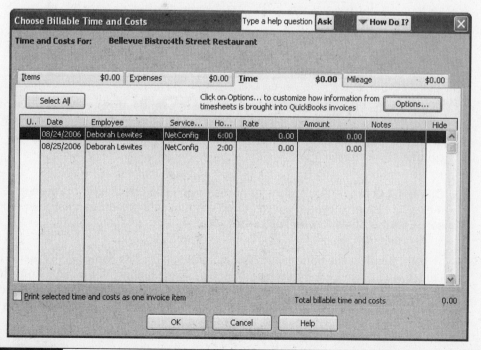

| **FIGURE 18-7** | Select the timesheet entries you want to include on the invoice. |

Now you're going to go crazy unless you realize you have to take the word "print" literally. After you make the selection and return to the invoice form, you see every individual item listed on the invoice, with individual totals for each item.

However, two things have changed on the onscreen invoice: the first line item is now an item named Reimb Group, and it has no amount. A new description appears below the individual time items, and it has an amount that is the total of the individual time charges. This entry is the description attached to the Reimb Group item.

Don't worry, the only thing that prints is that Reimb Group (the last item). It prints as one item called Total Reimbursable Expenses; the onscreen invoice is not the same as the printed invoice. If you're a skeptic, click the arrow to the right of the Print button at the top of the invoice and select Preview to see what the printed invoice will look like (told ya so!).

If you don't want to combine all the time charges into one line, you can still be selective about the way information is transferred to the invoice. Click the Options button at the top of the Choose Billable Time And Costs dialog to see your choices.

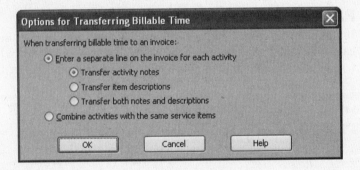

If you select the option to enter a separate line on the invoice for each activity, you can choose to print the notes on each timesheet, the service item description, or both. The text for both the notes and description appear in the Description column of the invoice.

$ CAUTION: Don't transfer notes unless you check every timesheet to make sure an employee hasn't entered a note you'd prefer the customer didn't see. Edit the timesheet to delete the note.

You can select the option Combine Activities With The Same Service Items to enter a single line item for each activity type. For example, if you have Consulting and Training as separate services, and there are several activities for each of those services, the invoice will have a line item for Consulting and another line item for Training. Each line will have the total for that service.

Using Timesheets for Payroll Job Costing

In this chapter:

- Configure payroll from timesheets
- Configure services and reports for job costing

When you turn on time tracking (covered in Chapter 18), you can connect it to your QuickBooks payroll functions. You just move the information about each employee's time into the employee's paycheck. In addition to speeding up the process of creating paychecks, this means you can improve job costing by tracking your payroll expenses against jobs.

Setting Up Payroll Data

If you want to link employee time to payroll or job costing, you must configure your QuickBooks system for those features.

Configuring the Employee Record

To link an employee to time tracking, select the time-tracking option on the Payroll Info tab of the employee record.

To accomplish this, follow these steps:

1. Open the Employee Center by clicking the Employees icon on the left side of the Home page, or by clicking the Employee Center icon on the toolbar.
2. Select the Employees tab to display the employee list.
3. Double-click the listing for an employee you want to link to time tracking (or select the listing and click the Edit Employee Info button in the right pane).
4. In the Change Tabs drop-down list, choose Payroll And Compensation Info.
5. Select the option Use Time Data To Create Paychecks.
6. Click OK to close the employee record and return to the Employee list.

Opting to link paychecks to time-tracking data doesn't mean that the employee's paycheck is absolutely and irrevocably linked to the employee's timesheets. It means only that when you prepare paychecks, QuickBooks checks timesheets before presenting the employee's paycheck form. You have total control over the hours and pay rate for the paycheck.

For hourly workers, if the employee's payroll information includes the hourly rate (and, optionally, the overtime hourly rate), that information is automatically inserted in that employee's timesheet.

If you haven't configured the employee's hourly rate during the data entry process in the timesheet, QuickBooks displays a message that no hourly rate exists, so the system will use a rate of $0.00. You can enter a rate when you're creating paychecks, or you can go through the employee information and set a rate for each hourly worker.

For salaried workers, the QuickBooks message about the lack of an hourly rate isn't "fixable." In fact, while the link to time tracking is advantageous for creating paychecks for hourly workers, the only reason to link salaried employees to time tracking is to track job costing.

Configuring Payroll Preferences for Job Costing

If your time tracking is just as important for job-costing analysis as it is for making payroll easier, you can configure your payroll reporting for that purpose.

Follow these steps:

1. Choose Edit | Preferences from the menu bar.

2. Click the Payroll & Employees icon, and then click the Company Preferences tab.

3. At the bottom of the window (see Figure 19-1), be sure the option Job Costing, Class And Item Tracking For Paycheck Expenses is selected. (QuickBooks preselects the option as the default setting.)

4. If you're using classes, specify the way to assign a class (see the next section, "Using Classes for Payroll Job Costing").

5. Click OK to save your preferences.

Using Classes for Payroll Job Costing

If you've established classes, you may be able to use those classes for the payroll expenses you're tracking as part of your job costing. The class feature won't work for payroll unless your classes match the available options in the Payroll & Employees Preferences dialog. QuickBooks makes the following choices available:

- **Entire Paycheck**   Means you assign a class to all payroll expenses on a check (including company-paid taxes) instead of assigning a class to individual payroll items.

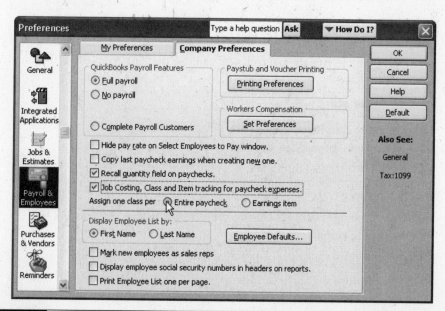

FIGURE 19-1   Configure QuickBooks to include your payroll costs in job costing.

- **Earnings Item**   Means you can assign a class to each payroll item (in the Earnings section of the paycheck) that's used in the paycheck.

If your classes provide a tidy way to fit each employee into a class, the entire paycheck option will work. For example, if you have branch offices, each of which is a class, you can assign the paychecks according to the location of the employee. If your classes divide your company by the products or services you provide, then you'll have to track classes by payroll item to produce useful reports. If your classes don't match the tracking options, you can just ignore the Class column when you're entering data or creating reports.

Using Timesheets Efficiently

If your employees only keep timesheets to indicate the billable work they do, that's not going to do much to automate the payroll process. Few employees fill every hour of their workday with billable activity, and you'll have to fill in the remaining information manually when you create the paycheck.

- Create at least one payroll item to cover nonbillable work. You can call it Administration, In-Office, or any other designation. The customer attached to this work is your own company (create a customer named InHouse or something similar).
- Make sure employees account for every hour of the day and every day of the week.
- Have employees fill in days for sick pay or vacation pay on their timesheets. Those items are probably already part of your payroll items.

Running Payroll with Timesheet Data

When it's time to run the payroll, you can use the data from the timesheets to create the paychecks.

Follow these steps:

1. Open the Employee Center, and select the Payroll tab.
2. In the right pane, click the Pay Employees button.
3. When the Select Employees To Pay window opens, the Hours column displays the number of hours that employees accounted for in their timesheets (see Figure 19-2).
4. Select the option Enter Hours And Preview Check Before Creating.
5. Select the employees to pay.
6. Click Create.

Each employee's paycheck is previewed. For employees who are configured to have their paychecks generated from timesheets, the data from the employee's timesheet is transferred to the Earnings section.

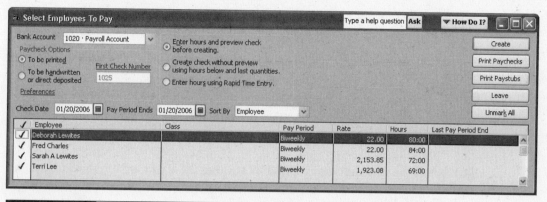

FIGURE 19-2   Some employees don't follow directions about accounting for every hour of the workweek—this biweekly pay period has 80 hours.

Of course, some hourly employees will have billable hours that filled their week, and other employees may have administrative tasks that filled their week. Still others will have entered only the billable hours, and you'll have to fill in the hours devoted to administrative work yourself. If the timesheet data that is transferred to the paycheck doesn't account for all the time the employee is entitled to, you'll have to fill in the hours by adding administrative items.

Use these steps:

1 Click the Item Name column in the Earnings section, and enter a nonbillable (administrative) payroll item.

2 In the Rate column, enter this employee's pay rate.

3 In the Hours column, enter the number of hours needed to complete this employee's work week.

4 Click Create.

Changes you make in the payroll window are not updated on the timesheet. If you want accurate historical timesheets, exit the payroll window, open the timesheets, and fill them in. Then start the payroll run again. Chapter 8 has all the information you need to create checks and direct deposit stubs.

Running Payroll Reports for Cost Information

When you use time tracking, you can see reports on your payroll expenses as they relate to customers and jobs. The one I find most useful is the Payroll Transaction Detail report. To get to it, choose Reports | Employees & Payroll | Payroll Transaction Detail. When the Payroll Transaction Detail report appears, enter the date range you want to examine.

This report probably has more information than you really need, but the customer and job data is there. However, I've found that this report needs a bit of customization to make it useful. Click the Modify Report button to start customizing the report.

Follow these steps:

1 On the Display tab, make the following changes in the Columns section:
- Deselect the Wage Base column, because it's not important.
- Make sure both Name (the customer) and Source Name (the employee) are selected.

2 Change the way the data is sorted by clicking the arrow next to the Sort By text box and selecting a different category. Sorting by Source Name and Name are both useful views.

3 Click the Filters tab, and in the Filter list, select Payroll Item.

4 Click the arrow to the right of the Payroll Item field and choose Multiple Payroll Items.

5 Select the payroll items you want to track for customers and jobs (Salary, Hourly Rate, and Overtime Hourly Rate are the ones I find useful).

6 Click OK twice to return to the report window with its new configuration (see Figure 19-3).

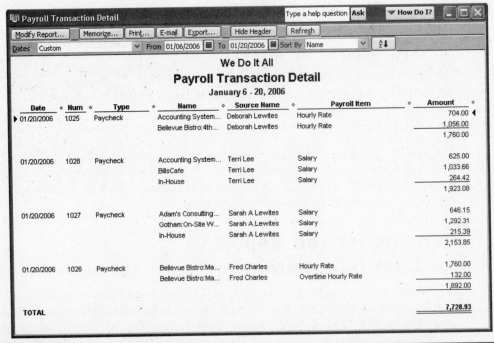

FIGURE 19-3   This customized report is a quick, accurate view of payroll job costs.

7 Click the Memorize button to make this configuration permanent, giving it a name that reminds you of why you need the report (for example, Payroll Job Costing).

You can use the Sort By drop-down list on the report to change the Sort By selection every time you use the memorized report, to see totals by employee (Source Name) or totals by customer (Name).

Managing QuickBooks

All software needs TLC, and accounting software needs regular maintenance to ensure its accuracy and usefulness.

In Part Four of this book, you'll learn how to customize QuickBooks so it works more efficiently. The chapters in Part Four cover the features and tools you can use to make QuickBooks even more powerful. In addition, you'll learn how to maintain the file system, create additional company files, and use QuickBooks in network mode (so more than one person can work in QuickBooks at the same time).

Of course, I'm going to cover backing up your data, which is the most important maintenance task in the world. Once you put your accounting data into QuickBooks, your business life depends on it. Hard drives die, motherboards freak out, power supplies go to la-la land, and all sorts of other calamities are just waiting to happen. Backing up saves your life (at least your business life).

Customizing QuickBooks

In this chapter:

- Configure preferences
- Manage users and passwords
- Create classes
- Customize the QuickBooks window

QuickBooks "out of the box" is set to run efficiently, providing powerful bookkeeping tools that are easy to use. However, you may have specific requirements because of the way you run your company, the way your accountant likes things done, or the way you use your computer. No matter what your special requirements are, it's likely that QuickBooks can accommodate you.

Configuring Preferences

The preferences you establish in QuickBooks have a great impact on the way data is kept and reported. It's not uncommon for QuickBooks users to change or tweak these preferences periodically. In fact, the more you use QuickBooks and understand the way it works, the more comfortable you'll be about changing preferences.

You can reach the Preferences dialog by choosing Edit | Preferences from the QuickBooks menu bar. When the dialog opens the first time, the General category is selected (see Figure 20-1). If you've used the Preferences dialog previously, it opens to the category you were using when you closed the window.

Each category in the Preferences dialog is accessed by clicking the appropriate icon in the left pane. No matter which category you view, you see two tabs: My Preferences and Company Preferences.

- The My Preferences tab is where you configure your preferences as a QuickBooks user. Each user you create in QuickBooks can set his or her own preferences. QuickBooks will apply the correct preferences as each user logs into the software. (Many categories lack options in this tab.)
- The Company Preferences tab is the place to configure the way the QuickBooks accounting features work for the current company, regardless of which user logs in.

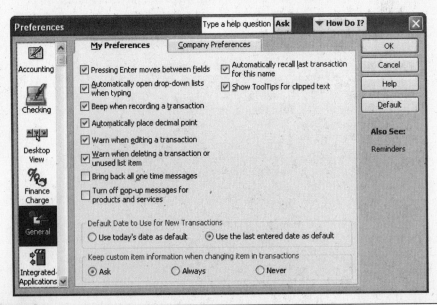

FIGURE 20-1   Configure QuickBooks to behave the way you prefer.

As you select options and move from one category of the Preferences window to another, you'll be asked whether you want to save the changes in the section you just left.

General Preferences

Since the Preferences dialog starts us in the General section, let's begin there.

Setting My Preferences for the General Category

The My Preferences tab of the General category offers a number of options you can select. They're all designed to let you control the way QuickBooks behaves while you're working in transaction windows.

Pressing Enter Moves Between Fields

This option exists for people who constantly forget that the default (normal, usual) key for moving from field to field in Windows software is the TAB key. Of course, when they press ENTER instead of TAB, the record they're working on is saved even though they haven't finished filling out all the fields. Rather than force you to get used to the way Windows works, QuickBooks lets you change the procedure.

Beep When Recording A Transaction

If you don't want to hear sound effects as you work in QuickBooks, you can deselect the option. On the other hand, you can configure the sounds so that some actions produce sound effects and other actions don't. You can even specify which sound you want for the actions that you've configured to play sounds. To learn how to change the sound schemes, see the section "Desktop View Preferences," later in this chapter.

Automatically Place Decimal Point

This is a handy feature once you get used to it (I couldn't live without it—and my desk calculator is configured for the same behavior). When you enter monetary characters in a field, a decimal point is placed automatically to the left of the last two digits when you enable this feature. Therefore, if you type 5421, when you move to the next field the number changes to 54.21. If you want to type in even dollar amounts, type a period after you enter 54, and QuickBooks will automatically add two zeros to the right of the period (or you can enter the zeros, as in 5400, which automatically becomes 54.00).

Warn When Editing A Transaction

This option, which is selected by default, tells QuickBooks to flash a warning message when you change any transaction and try to close the transaction window without explicitly saving the changed transaction. This means you have a chance to abandon the edits. If you deselect the option, the edited transaction is saved as changed, unless it is linked to other transactions (in which case, the warning message explaining that problem appears).

Warn When Deleting A Transaction Or Unused List Item

When selected, this option produces a warning when you delete a transaction or a list entry that has not been used in a transaction—it's a standard message asking you to confirm your action.

If you try to delete an item or a name that has been used in a transaction, QuickBooks won't permit you to complete the deletion.

Bring Back All One Time Messages

One-time messages are those informational dialogs that include a Don't Show This Message Again option. If you've selected the Don't Show option, select this check box to see those messages again (and you can once again select the Don't Show option).

Turn Off Pop-up Messages For Products And Services

Selecting this option stops pop-up messages from QuickBooks that are connected to products and services available from Intuit. For example, when creating checks, Intuit displays a pop-up message explaining that you can buy checks at the Intuit Marketplace.

Automatically Recall Last Transaction For This Name

This option means that QuickBooks will prefill the data for a bill, check, or credit card charge when you select a vendor in the transaction window. This feature is useful for repeating transactions, even if one item (such as the amount) changes for the current transaction.

Show ToolTips For Clipped Text

This option (enabled by default) means that if there is more text in a field than you can see, hovering your mouse over the field causes the entire block of text to display. Very handy!

Default Date To Use For New Transactions

Use this option to tell QuickBooks whether you want the Date field to show the current date or the date of the last transaction you entered, when you open a transaction window. If you frequently enter transactions for the same date over a period of several days (for example, you start preparing invoices on the 27th of the month, but the invoice date is the last day of the month), select the option to use the last entered date so you can just keep going.

Keep Custom Item Information When Changing Item In Transactions

The selection you make for this option determines what QuickBooks does when you change the description text or the price for an item you insert in a sales transaction form, and then change the item. For example, you select an item named Widget, and then in the Description field, you type text to describe this widget, changing the default description that displayed when you selected the item. Or, perhaps the item had no default description, and you entered text to correct that omission. Then, you realize that you didn't really mean to sell the customer a Widget, you meant a Gadget, and the descriptive text you just typed was meant for the item named Gadget (which you thought you'd selected in the Item column). You return to the Item column (on the same line), click the arrow to see your item list, and select Gadget. Now, you think you have to type all that descriptive text again, because Gadget has its own descriptive text, and it will automatically replace your work.

This option prevents that work going to waste. If you select Always, QuickBooks will keep the descriptive text you wrote, even though you changed the Item. This descriptive text is linked to this different item only for this invoice; no changes are made to any item's record.

If you select Never, QuickBooks just fills in the description that goes with the new item you selected.

If you select Ask, as soon as you change the item, QuickBooks asks if you want to change only the item and keep your customized description on the invoice. You can answer Yes (or No) and you can also tell QuickBooks to change this Preferences option permanently to match your answer.

The same thing happens if you entered a different price (instead of, or in addition to, the description), and then changed the item.

Setting Company Preferences for the General Section

The Company Preferences tab in the General section has three choices, explained here.

Time Format

Select a format for entering time, choosing between decimal (for example, 11.5 hours) or minutes (11:30).

Always Show Years As 4 Digits

If you prefer to display the year with four digits (01/01/2006 instead of 01/01/06), select this option.

Never Update Name Information When Saving Transactions

By default, QuickBooks asks if you want to update the original information for a name when you change it during a transaction entry. For example, if you're entering a vendor bill and you change the address, QuickBooks offers to make that change back on the vendor record. If you don't want to be offered this opportunity, and want the record to remain as is, select this option.

Accounting Preferences

Click the Accounting icon on the left pane of the Preferences dialog to move to the Accounting category. There are only Company Preferences available for this section (see Figure 20-2); the My Preferences tab has no options available.

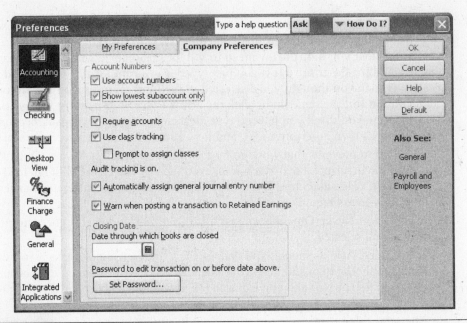

FIGURE 20-2   Select the options you require for efficiency and ease of use.

Use Account Numbers

Choose this option if you want to use numbers for your chart of accounts in addition to names.

Show Lowest Subaccount Only

This option, which is available only if you use account numbers, is useful because it means that when you see an account number in a drop-down list (in a transaction window), you only see the subaccount. If the option is not selected, you see the parent account followed by the subaccount, and since the field display doesn't show the entire text unless you scroll through it, it's hard to determine which account has been selected.

Require Accounts

When enabled, this option means that every item and transaction you create in QuickBooks has to be assigned to an account. If you disable this option, transaction amounts that aren't manually assigned to an account are posted to Uncategorized Income or Uncategorized Expense. I don't know any way to produce a tax return or a report that analyzes your business if you don't post transactions to accounts.

Use Class Tracking

This option turns on the Class feature for your QuickBooks system (which is discussed later in this chapter in the section "Configuring Classes"). The Prompt

To Assign Classes suboption for this setting is to have QuickBooks prompt you to fill in the Class field whenever you close a transaction window without doing so.

Audit Tracking Is On

This is not an option; it's a notice that the audit tracking feature is permanently enabled. (In previous versions of QuickBooks, this was an option.) This feature tracks all the work done in the company file, and can be read by choosing Reports | Accountant & Taxes | Audit Trail.

Automatically Assign General Journal Entry Number

With this option selected, every time you create a general journal entry, QuickBooks automatically assigns the next available number to it.

Warn When Posting A Transaction To Retained Earnings

By default, QuickBooks issues a warning if you use the Retained Earnings account in a general journal entry. It doesn't stop you from performing this action; it just issues a warning. If you're comfortable with journal entries and you move amounts into the Retained Earnings account (usually from the Opening Bal. Equity account), you can disable this option.

Closing Date

Enabling this option lets you set a password-protected closing date for your QuickBooks data file. Once you set the date and create a password, users can't manipulate any transactions that are dated on or before the closing date unless they know the password. See Chapter 17 to learn about closing your file.

Checking Preferences

This category has options in both the My Preferences and Company Preferences tabs. On the My Preferences tab (see Figure 20-3), you can select default bank accounts for different types of transactions. You can skip these options if you only have one bank account.

The Company Preferences tab (see Figure 20-4) offers several options concerned with check printing, which are described in the following paragraphs.

Print Account Names On Voucher

This option is useful only if you print your checks and the check forms you purchase have vouchers (stubs). If so, selecting this option means that the text on the stub will display posting accounts.

Change Check Date When Check Is Printed

Selecting this option means that at the time you print checks, the current date becomes the check date. If you don't select this option, the check date you specified when you filled out the check window is used (even if that date has already passed).

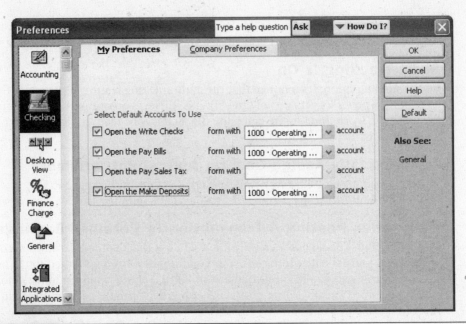

Save time and avoid mistakes by automatically selecting the right bank
account for transactions.

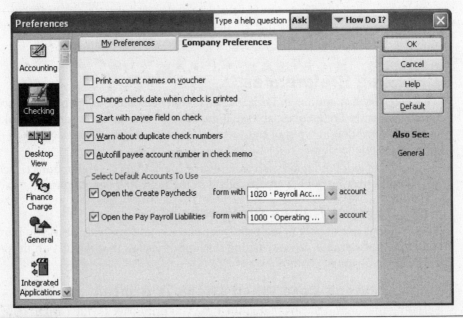

Select the options you need to make check writing more efficient.

Start With Payee Field On Check

Enabling this option forces your cursor to the Payee field when you first bring up the Write Checks window. If the option is not enabled, the bank account field is the first active field. If you always write checks from one specific bank account, enable the option to save yourself the inconvenience of pressing TAB.

Warn About Duplicate Check Numbers

This option means that QuickBooks will warn you if a check number you're filling in already exists.

Autofill Payee Account Number In Check Memo

Most vendors maintain an account number for their customers, and your account number can be automatically printed when you print checks. In order for this to occur, you must fill in your account number in the Vendor card (on the Additional Information tab). The printout appears on the lower-left section of the check.

Select Default Accounts To Use

You can set the default bank accounts for different types of payroll transactions. Then, when you print these checks, you don't have to select the bank account from a drop-down list in the transaction window. This avoids the common error of printing the payroll checks on operating account checks, screaming "Eek!," voiding the checks, and starting again with the right account.

Desktop View Preferences

This section of the preferences configuration lets you design the way the QuickBooks window looks and acts. The My Preferences tab (see Figure 20-5) contains basic configuration options.

In the View section, you can specify whether you always want to see one QuickBooks window at a time or view multiple windows.

- Choose One Window to limit the QuickBooks screen to showing one window at a time, even if you have multiple windows open. The windows are stacked atop each other, and only the top window is visible. To switch between multiple windows, use the Window menu.
- Choose Multiple Windows to make it possible to view multiple windows on your screen. Selecting this option activates the arrangement commands on the Windows menu item, which allow you to stack or arrange windows so that more than one window is visible at a time.

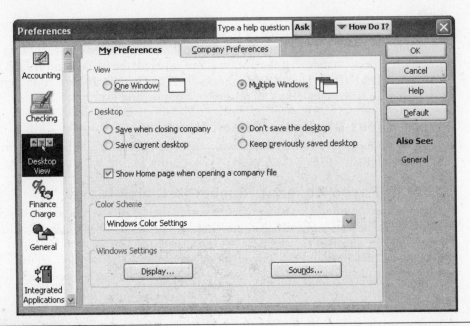

FIGURE 20-5   Configure the look and behavior of QuickBooks.

In the Desktop section, you can specify what QuickBooks should do when you exit the software, choosing among the following options:

- **Save When Closing Company**   Means that the state of the desktop is remembered when you close the company (or exit QuickBooks). Whatever QuickBooks windows were open when you left will reappear when you return. You can pick up where you left off. If you select the option Show Home Page When Opening A Company File, that option overrides this option, so if you close the company file after closing the Home page, the Home page returns when you open the company file.

- **Save Current Desktop**   Displays the desktop as it is at this moment every time you open QuickBooks. Select this option after you've opened or closed the QuickBooks windows you want to see when you start the software. If you select the option Show Home Page When Opening A Company File, that option overrides this option if you close the Home page.

- **Don't Save The Desktop**   Tells QuickBooks to display an empty QuickBooks desktop (unless you enable the Show Home Page When Opening A Company File option) when you open this company file or when you start QuickBooks again after using this company file. The desktop isn't really empty—the menu bar, Icon Bar, and any other navigation bars are on the desktop, but no transaction or list windows are open.

- **Keep Previously Saved Desktop**   Available only when you select Save Current Desktop, this option tells QuickBooks to display the desktop as it was the last time you used the Save Current Desktop option.
- **Show Home Page When Opening A Company File**   Tells QuickBooks to display the Home page when you open the company file. When this option is selected, it overrides the other desktop settings.

In the Color Scheme section, you can select a scheme from the drop-down list. In addition, buttons are available to configure Windows settings for Display and Sounds. Clicking either button opens the associated applet in your Windows Control Panel. The display configuration options you change affect your computer and all your software, not just QuickBooks.

In the Company Preferences tab, you can customize the contents of the Home page.

Finance Charge Preferences

Click the Finance Charge icon (which has only Company Preferences available) to turn on, turn off, and configure finance charges. Finance charges can get complicated, so read the complete discussion about this topic in Chapter 5.

Integrated Applications Preferences

You can let third-party software have access to the data in your QuickBooks files. Click the Integrated Applications icon and move to the Company Preferences tab to specify the way QuickBooks works with other software programs. You can give permission to access all data, no data, or some data.

Jobs & Estimates Preferences

Use the Company Preferences tab to configure the way your estimates and invoices work, as shown in Figure 20-6. The options are self-explanatory. Read Chapter 3 to learn everything about creating estimates and invoices.

Payroll & Employees Preferences

Use the Company Preferences tab of this category to set all the configuration options for payroll. Read Chapter 8 to understand the selections in this window.

Purchases & Vendors Preferences

The Company Preferences tab (see Figure 20-7) has several configuration options for using purchase orders and paying vendor bills:

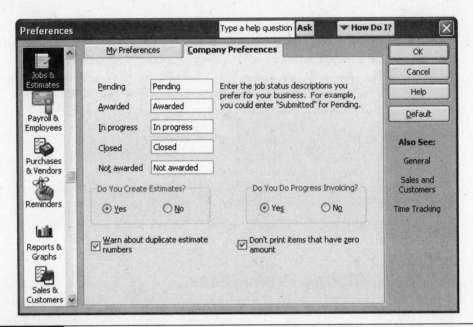

FIGURE 20-6   Set up and configure estimates.

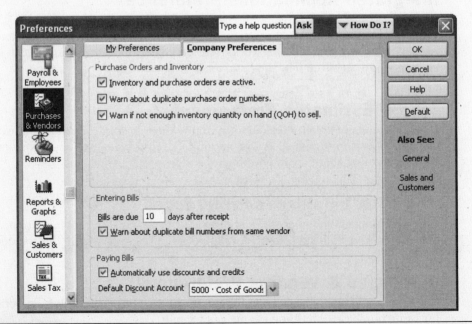

FIGURE 20-7   Manage inventory efficiently by setting the options you need.

Inventory And Purchase Orders Are Active

Select this option to tell QuickBooks that you want to enable the inventory features; the purchase orders are automatically enabled with that action.

Warn About Duplicate Purchase Order Numbers

When this option is enabled, any attempt to issue a purchase order with a PO number that already exists will generate a warning.

Warn If Not Enough Inventory Quantity On Hand (QOH) To Sell

This option turns on the warning feature that is useful during customer invoicing. If you sell ten widgets but your stock of widgets is fewer than ten, QuickBooks displays a message telling you there's insufficient stock to fill the order. You can still complete the invoice; it's just a message, not a functional limitation, but you should order more widgets immediately.

Entering Bills

Use the options in this section to set default payment terms for vendors (you can change the terms for individual vendors) and to issue a warning if you enter a vendor bill that has the number of a bill you already entered from this vendor. The default terms you enter here are assumed for all vendors, until you actually set each individual vendor's terms.

Paying Bills

If you select the automatic discounts option, QuickBooks will apply any credits from the vendor to the open bills automatically and take any discount that the vendor's terms permit. (The vendor terms are specified in the vendor's file.) If you select this option, enter the account to which you want to post discounts taken. See Chapter 7 for detailed information about paying bills.

Reminders Preferences

The Reminders category of the Preferences dialog has options on both tabs. The My Preferences tab has one option, which turns on the Reminders feature. When the Reminders feature is enabled, QuickBooks displays a Reminders list when you open a company file.

The Company Preferences tab enumerates the available reminders, and you can select the ones you want to use (see Figure 20-8). Of course, these selections are meaningless unless you enabled Reminders in the My Preferences tab.

 CAUTION: The Reminders List window is sometimes hidden behind the Home page. Click Window on the menu bar to switch to it, or minimize the Home page to reveal it.

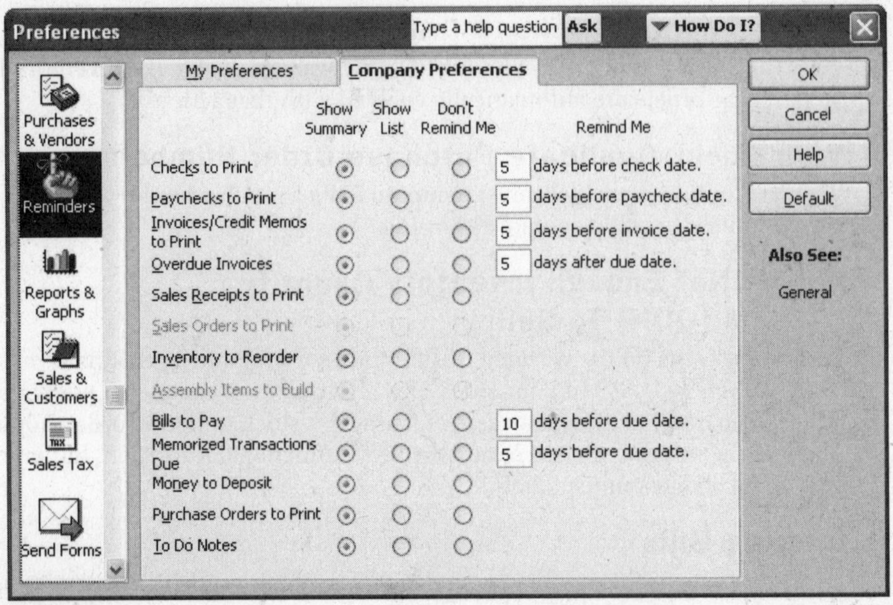

FIGURE 20-8   Decide which tasks you want to be reminded about.

For each item, decide whether you want to see a summary (just a listing and the total amount of money involved), a complete detailed list, or nothing at all. You can also determine the amount of lead time you want for your reminders. (Some of the items are grayed out because they're only available in QuickBooks Premier editions.)

NOTE: If you choose Show Summary, the Reminders List window has an Expand All button you can click to see the details.

Reports & Graphs Preferences

This is another section of the Preferences window that has choices on both tabs, so you can set your own user preferences and then set those options that affect the current company.

The My Preferences tab (see Figure 20-9) configures performance issues for reports and graphs.

Prompt Me To Modify Report Options Before Opening A Report

If you find that almost every time you select a report you have to customize it, you can tell QuickBooks to open the Modify Report window whenever a report is brought to the screen. If you find this feature useful, click the check box next to Prompt Me To Modify Report Options Before Opening A Report.

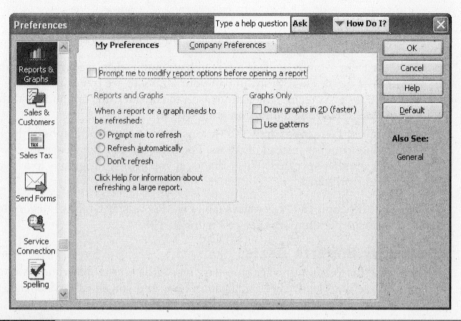

FIGURE 20-9 Set the parameters you want when you're creating reports.

Reports and Graphs Settings

While you're viewing a report or a graph, you can make changes to the format, the filters, or to the data behind it (by opening the appropriate transaction window and changing data). Most of the time, QuickBooks automatically changes the report/graph to match the changes. However, if there is anything else going on (perhaps you're also online, or you're in a network environment and other users are manipulating data that's in your report or graph), QuickBooks may not make changes automatically. The reason for the shutdown of automatic refreshing is to keep your computer running as quickly and efficiently as possible. At that point, QuickBooks has to make a decision about when and how to refresh the report or graph. You must give QuickBooks the parameters for making the decision to refresh.

- Choose Prompt Me To Refresh to see a message asking you whether you want to refresh the report or the graph after you've made changes to the data behind it. When the reminder appears, you can click Yes to refresh the data in the report.

- Choose Refresh Automatically if want up-to-the-second data, and don't want to bother to click the Refresh button. If you work with QuickBooks across a network, this could slow down your work a bit because whenever any user makes a change to data that's used in the report/graph, it will refresh itself.

- Choose Don't Refresh if you want to decide for yourself, without any reminder from QuickBooks, when to click the Refresh button on the report window.

Graphs Only

Give QuickBooks instructions about creating your graphs, as follows:

- Choose Draw Graphs In 2D (Faster) to have graphs displayed in two dimensions instead of three. This doesn't impair your ability to see trends at a glance; it's just not as "high-tech." The main reason to consider this option is that the 2-D graph takes less time to draw on your screen.
- Choose Use Patterns to draw the various elements in your graphs with black-and-white patterns instead of colors. For example, one pie wedge may be striped, another speckled. This is handy if you print your graphs to a black-and-white printer.

Move to the Company Preferences tab of the Reports & Graphs category to set company preferences for reports (see Figure 20-10).

Summary Reports Basis

Specify whether you want to see summary reports as accrual-based or cash-based. You're only setting the default specification here, and you can always change the basis in the Modify Report dialog when you actually display the report.

Aging Reports

Specify whether you want to generate A/R and A/P aging reports using the due date or the transaction date.

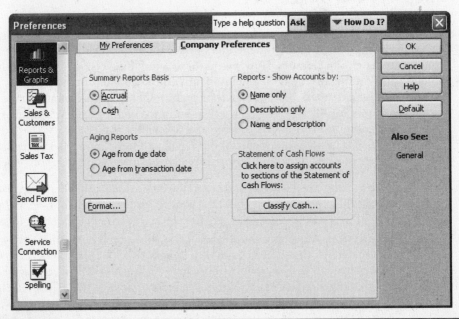

FIGURE 20-10   Set the default options for reports.

Reports—Show Accounts By

Specify whether you want reports to display account names, account descriptions, or both.

Setting Report Format Defaults

You can set the default formatting for reports by clicking the Format button and making changes to the default configuration options for parts of reports that aren't data related but instead control the look of the reports (see Figure 20-11). Use this feature if you find yourself making the same modifications to the formats over and over. See Chapter 15 for detailed information on creating and customizing reports.

Configuring the Cash Flow Report

A cash flow report is really a complicated document, and before the days of accounting software, accountants spent many hours creating such a report (and charged a lot of money for doing so). QuickBooks has configured a cash flow report format that is used to produce the cash flow reports available in the list of Company & Financial reports.

You can view the format by clicking the Classify Cash button, but you shouldn't mess around with the selections in the window that appears until you check with your accountant. You can learn about cash flow reports in Chapter 15.

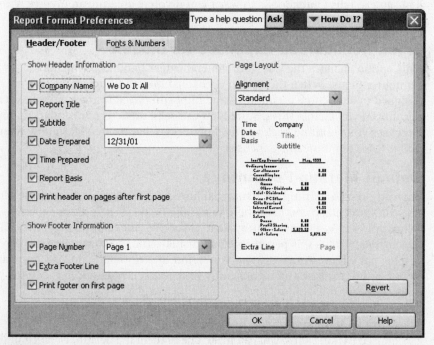

FIGURE 20-11   Set default options for report formats and fonts.

Sales & Customers Preferences

You can set some default options in the Sales & Customers category on the Company Preferences window:

Usual Shipping Method

Use this to set the default shipping method, if you use the same shipping method most of the time. This saves you the trouble of making a selection from the drop-down list unless you're changing the shipper for a particular invoice.

Usual FOB

Set the FOB language for invoices. FOB (Free On Board) is the location from which shipping is determined to be the customer's responsibility. This means more than just paying for freight; it's a statement that says, "At this point you have become the owner of this product." The side effects include assigning responsibility if goods are lost, damaged, or stolen. FOB settings have no impact on your financial records. For instance, if your business is in East Overcoat, Iowa, EastOvercoat might be your FOB entry. Don't let the size of the text box fool you; you're limited to 13 characters. The FOB has absolutely nothing to do with your finances.

Warn About Duplicate Invoice Numbers

This option tells QuickBooks to warn you if you're creating an invoice with an invoice number that's already in use.

Track Reimbursed Expenses As Income

This option changes the way your general ledger handles payments for reimbursements. When the option is enabled, the reimbursement can be assigned to an income account instead of posting back to the original expense account. If you enable this feature, you can set a predetermined markup for expenses you're billing back to customers. See Chapter 6 to learn how to enter and invoice reimbursable expenses.

Default Markup Percentage

You can preset a markup for items that have both a cost and price. QuickBooks uses the percentage you enter here to automate the pricing of inventory items. When you're creating an inventory item, as soon as you enter the cost, QuickBooks automatically adds this percentage and displays the result as the price. If your pricing paradigm isn't consistent, you'll find this automatic process more annoying than helpful, because you'll constantly find yourself re-entering the item's price.

Choose Template For Packing Slip

Select a default packing slip to use when you print packing slips. If you've created customized packing slips, you can make one of them the default. Detailed information on using templates is in Chapter 3.

Use Price Levels

This option turns on the Price Level feature, which is explained in Chapter 2.

Automatically Apply Payments

This option tells QuickBooks to apply payments automatically to open invoices. If the payment amount is an exact match for an open invoice, it is applied to that invoice. If the payment amount is smaller than any open invoice, QuickBooks applies the payment to the oldest invoice. If the payment amount is larger than any open invoice, QuickBooks applies payments, starting with the oldest invoice, until the payment amount is used up.

Without this option, you must manually apply each payment to an invoice. That's not as onerous as it may sound, and in fact, this is the way I prefer to work, because the customer's check almost always indicates the invoice the customer wants to pay (even if the check doesn't cover the entire amount of that invoice). Sometimes customers don't mark the invoice number on the check and instead enclose a copy of the invoice in the envelope. Read Chapter 4 to learn about receiving and applying customer payments.

Automatically Calculate Payments

When this option is enabled, you can begin selecting invoices to pay in the Receive Payment window before entering the amount of the customer's payment check. When you've finished selecting invoices, either paying them entirely or applying a partial payment, the amounts you've applied should equal the amount of the check you received.

This is efficient if a customer has many invoices (some of which may have credits or may have an amount in dispute), and has attached instructions about the way to apply the checks.

Use Undeposited Funds As A Default Deposit To Account

Selecting this option automates the process of depositing all cash received into the Undeposited Funds account. If the option isn't selected, each cash receipts transaction window (customer payments and cash sales) offers the choice of depositing the cash into a bank account or into the Undeposited Funds account.

Sales Tax Preferences

If you collect sales tax, you must set your sales tax options. These options are easy to configure because most of the selections are predefined by state tax laws and state tax report rules. Check with your accountant and read the information that came with your state sales tax license. For more information about managing sales taxes (a very complicated issue in many states), see Chapter 7.

Send Forms Preferences

If you send transactions to customers via e-mail, use this window to design the message that accompanies the invoice. See Chapter 3 for more information.

Service Connection Preferences

If you use QuickBooks services on the Internet, use this category to specify the way you want to connect to the Internet for those services.

The My Preferences tab contains options related to online banking if your bank uses the WebConnect method of online access. (Chapter 16 has detailed information about online banking services.)

- **Give Me The Option Of Saving A File Whenever I Download Web Connect Data**   Select this option if you want QuickBooks to provide a choice to save WebConnect data for later processing instead of automatically processing the transactions. QuickBooks provides the choice by opening a dialog that lets you choose whether to import the data immediately, or save it to a file so you can import it later (you have to supply a filename). The QuickBooks dialog also includes an option to reset this option. This option only works when you select Open on the File Download dialog. If you disable this option, the data is automatically imported into QuickBooks.

- **If QuickBooks Is Run By My Browser, Don't Close It After Web Connect Is Done**   Selecting this option means that when QuickBooks is launched automatically when you download WebConnect data from your Financial Institution (after selecting Open on the Download dialog), QuickBooks remains open after you process the data. If you deselect this option, QuickBooks closes automatically as soon as your data is processed.

The following connection options are available on the Company Preferences tab:

- **Automatically Connect Without Asking For A Password**   Lets all users log into the QuickBooks Business Services network automatically.
- **Always Ask For A Password Before Connecting**   Forces users to enter a login name and password in order to access QuickBooks Business Services.
- **Allow Background Downloading Of Service Messages**   Lets QuickBooks check the Intuit web site for updates and information periodically when you're connected to the Internet.

Spelling Preferences

The Spelling section presents options only on the My Preferences tab. This is where you control the way the QuickBooks spell checker works. You can instruct QuickBooks to check spelling automatically before saving or printing any form. In addition, you can specify those words you want the spelling checker to skip, such as Internet addresses, numbers, and solid capital letters that probably indicate an abbreviation.

Tax:1099 Preferences

Use this window to establish the 1099 form options you need. For each type of 1099 payment, you must assign an account from your chart of accounts. See Chapter 17 for more information about configuring and issuing 1099 forms.

Time-tracking Preferences

Use this section to turn on Time Tracking and to tell QuickBooks the first day of your workweek (which becomes the first day listed on your timesheets). Read all about tracking time in Chapter 18.

Managing Multiple Users

Many businesses have multiple users accessing their QuickBooks company files. You can have multiple users who access QuickBooks on the same computer (taking turns using QuickBooks), or in a multi-user network environment (if you purchased a multi-user version of QuickBooks).

Creating, Removing, and Changing User Information

When you want to create or modify users, choose Company | Set Up Users from the QuickBooks menu bar. If you are setting up multiple users for the first time, QuickBooks displays the Set Up QuickBooks Administrator dialog. You must have an administrator (I'm assuming it's you) to manage all the other user tasks.

The administrator can determine who can use the various features in QuickBooks, adding, deleting, and configuring permissions for users. It's a good idea to leave the administrator's name as Admin. To password-protect the administrator's login, move to the Administrator's Password box and enter a password. Enter the same password in the Confirm Password box to confirm it. You won't see the text you're typing; instead, the system shows asterisks as a security measure (in case someone is watching over your shoulder). You don't have to use a password, but omitting this step could put your QuickBooks files at risk because an intruder could examine or manipulate your files.

 CAUTION: If you forget the administrator's password, you can call QuickBooks support and arrange to have them recover the password—for a fee.

Creating a New User

When you click OK in the Set Up QuickBooks Administrator dialog (or if you set up the configuration option to have multiple users during the EasyStep Interview) you see the User List window.

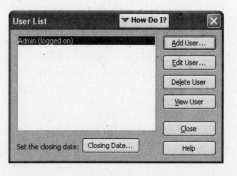

To add a new user to the list, click Add User. This launches a wizard that assists you in setting up the new user.

In the first wizard window, fill in the necessary information, as follows:

1. Enter the username, which is the name this user must type to log into QuickBooks.
2. If you want to establish a password for this user (it's optional), enter and confirm the user's password.
3. Click Next to set up the user's access to QuickBooks features. See the upcoming "Setting User Permissions" section in this chapter.

 TIP: Make a note of all user passwords and keep that list in a secure (hidden) place. Inevitably, a user will come to you because he or she cannot remember a password.

Deleting a User

If you want to remove a user from the User List, select the name and then click the Delete User button. QuickBooks asks you to confirm your decision. You can't delete the administrator.

Editing User Information

You can change the configuration options for any user. Select the username in the User List window and click Edit User. This launches a wizard similar to the Add User wizard, and you can change the username, password, and access permissions.

Setting User Permissions

When you're adding a new user or editing an existing user, the wizard walks you through the steps for configuring the user's permissions. Click Next on each wizard window after you've supplied the necessary information.

The first permissions window asks if you want this user to have access to selected areas of QuickBooks or all areas. If you give the user full permission to do everything, when you click Next. you're asked to confirm your decision, and there's no further work to do in the wizard. Click Finish to return to the User List window.

If you want to limit the user's access to selected areas of QuickBooks, select that option and click Next. The ensuing wizard windows take you through all the QuickBooks features (Accounts Receivable, Check Writing, Payroll, and so on) so you can establish permissions on a feature-by-feature basis for this user. You should configure permissions for every component of QuickBooks. Any component not configured is set as No Access for this user. For each QuickBooks component, you can select one of the following permission options:

No Access   The user is denied permission to open any windows in that section of QuickBooks.

Full Access   The user can open all windows and perform all tasks in that section of QuickBooks.

Selective Access   The user will be permitted to perform tasks as you see fit.

If you choose to give selective access permissions, you're asked to specify the rights this user should have. Those rights vary slightly from component to component, but generally you're asked to choose one of these permission levels:

- Create transactions only
- Create and print transactions
- Create transactions and create reports

T I P :   You can select only one of the three levels, so if you need to give the user rights to more than one of these choices, you must select Full Access instead of configuring Selective Access.

Configuring Special Areas of QuickBooks

There are two wizard windows for setting permissions that are not directly related to any specific area of the software: sensitive accounting activities and sensitive financial reports.

Sensitive accounting activities are those tasks that aren't directly related to QuickBooks transactions, such as

- Making changes to the chart of accounts
- Manipulating the register for any balance sheet account
- Using online banking
- Transferring funds between banks
- Reconciling bank accounts
- Creating journal entries
- Preparing an accountant's review
- Working with budgets

Sensitive financial reports are those reports that reveal important financial information about your company, such as

- Profit & Loss reports
- Balance Sheet reports
- Budget reports
- Cash flow reports
- Income tax reports
- Trial balance reports
- Audit trail reports

Configuring Rights for Existing Transactions

If a user has permissions for certain areas of QuickBooks, you can limit his or her ability to manipulate existing transactions within those areas. This means the user can't change or delete a transaction, even if he or she created it in the first place.

When you have finished configuring user permissions, the last wizard page presents a list of the permissions you've granted and refused. If everything is correct, click Finish. If there's something you want to change, use the Prev button to back up to the appropriate page.

Configuring Classes

QuickBooks provides a feature called Class Tracking that permits you to group items and transactions in a way that matches the kind of reporting you want to perform. Think of this feature as a way to "classify" your business activities. To use classes, you must enable the feature, which is listed in the Accounting section of the Preferences window.

Some of the common reasons to configure classes include

- Reporting by location if you have more than one office
- Reporting by division or department
- Reporting by business type (perhaps you have both retail and wholesale businesses under your company umbrella)

You should use classes for a single purpose; otherwise, the feature won't work properly. For example, you can use classes to separate your business into locations or by type of business, but don't try to do both. If you need to further define a class or narrow its definition, you can use subclasses.

When you enable classes, QuickBooks adds a Class field to transaction forms. For each transaction or each line of any transaction, you can assign one of the classes you created.

Creating a Class

To create a class, choose Lists | Class List from the QuickBooks menu bar to display the Class List window. Remember that you must enable the feature in the Accounting Preferences dialog to have access to the Class List menu item.

Press CTRL-N to add a new class. Fill in the name of the class in the New Class window. Click Next to add another class, or click OK if you are finished.

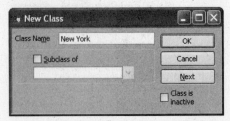

TIP: It's a good idea to create a class called "Other." This gives you a way to sort reports in a logical fashion when a transaction has no link to one of your real classes.

Creating a Subclass

Subclasses let you post transactions to specific subcategories of classes, and they work similarly to subaccounts in your chart of accounts. If you set up a subclass, you must post transactions only to the subclass, never to the parent class. However, unlike the chart of accounts, classes have no option to force the display of only the subclass when you're working in a transaction window. As a result, if you're using subclasses you must keep the name of the parent class short, to lessen the need to scroll through the field to see the entire class name.

You create a subclass using the same steps required to create a class.

Choose Lists | Class List from the QuickBooks menu bar and follow these steps:

1. Press CTRL-N to open the New Class dialog box.
2. Enter a name for the subclass in the Class Name box.
3. Click the check box next to the option Subclass Of to insert a check mark.
4. Click the arrow next to the field at the bottom of the dialog and choose the appropriate parent class from the drop-down list.

Editing, Deleting, and Merging Classes

You can change, remove, and merge classes right from the Class List window, which you open by choosing Lists | Class List.

To edit a class, double-click the class listing you want to modify. You can enter a new name, turn a parent class into a subclass, turn a subclass into a parent class, or mark the class Inactive.

To delete a class, select its listing in the Class List window and press CTRL-D, If the class has been used in transactions or has subclasses, QuickBooks won't let you delete it. (If the problem is subclasses, delete the subclasses and then you can delete the class.)

To merge two classes, start by editing the class you want to get rid of, which you do by double-clicking its listing. Change the name to match the name of the class you want to keep. QuickBooks displays a message telling you that the name is in use and asking if you want to merge the classes. Clicking Yes tells QuickBooks to go through all transactions that contain the now-removed class and replace the Class field with the remaining class.

Using a Class in Transactions

When you're entering transactions, each transaction window provides a field for entering the class. For example, the invoice form adds a Class field at the top (next to the Customer:Job field) so you can assign the entire invoice to a class. However, you can instead link a class to each line item of the invoice (if the line items require links to separate classes).

Reporting by Class

There are two types of reports you can run for classes:

- Individual class reports
- Reports on all classes

Reporting on a Single Class

To report on a single class, open the Class list and select the class you want to report on. Then press CTRL-Q to open a QuickReport on the class. When the Class QuickReport appears, you can change the date range or customize the report as needed.

Reporting on All Classes

If you want to see one report in which all classes are used, open the Class list and click the Reports button at the bottom of the list window. Choose Reports On All Classes and then select either Profit & Loss By Class, Profit & Loss Unclassified, or Graphs. The Graphs menu item offers a choice of an Income & Expenses Graph or a Budget Vs. Actual Graph.

Profit & Loss By Class Report

The Profit & Loss By Class report is the same as a standard Profit & Loss report, except that each class uses a separate column. The Totals column provides the usual P&L information for your company. This report is also available on the submenu under Reports | Company & Financial.

Profit & Loss Unclassified Report

This report displays P & L totals for transactions in which items were not assigned to a class. You can drill down to the transactions and add the appropriate class to each transaction. (This is likely to be a rather lengthy report if you enabled class tracking after you'd already begun using QuickBooks.)

You can find detailed information about running and customizing Profit & Loss reports in Chapter 15.

Graphs That Use Class Data

You can also display graphs for income and expenses sorted by class, or one that compares budget versus actual figures sorted by class.

Customizing Other Reports for Class Reporting

Many of the reports you run regularly can also be customized to report class information (for example, aging reports). Use the Filters tab to configure the report for all, some, or one class.

Customizing the Icon Bar

QuickBooks put icons on the Icon Bar, but the icons QuickBooks chose may not match the features you use most frequently. Putting your own icons on the Icon Bar makes using QuickBooks easier and faster. You can also change the way the Icon Bar and the icons it holds look.

To customize the Icon Bar, choose View | Customize Icon Bar to open the Customize Icon Bar dialog, which displays a list of the icons currently occupying your Icon Bar.

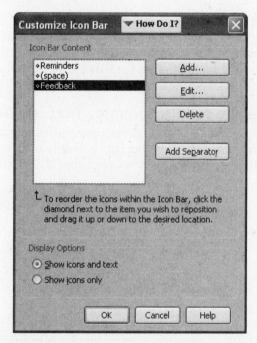

If you updated to QuickBooks 2006 from a previous version, the Icon Bar retains all the icons from the previous version. For new users or new companies, the default Icon Bar has a limited number of icons. The QuickBooks Centers icons (Home, Customer, Vendor, and Employee) don't appear in the Customize Icon Bar dialog, because you cannot change or eliminate them.

 TIP: If you log into QuickBooks, either because a single computer is set up for multiple users, or because you're using QuickBooks on a network, the settings you establish are linked to your login name. You are not changing the Icon Bar for other users.

Changing the Order of Icons

You can change the order in which icons appear on the Icon Bar. The list of icons in the Customize Icon Bar dialog reads top to bottom, representing the left-to-right display on the Icon Bar. Therefore, moving an icon's listing up moves it to the left on the Icon Bar (and vice versa).

To move an icon, click the small diamond to the left of the icon's listing, hold down the left mouse button, and drag the listing to a new position.

Changing the Icon Bar Display

You can change the way the icons display in several ways, which I'll explain in this section.

Display Icons Without Title Text

By default, icons and text display on the Icon Bar. You can select Show Icons Only to remove the title text under the icons. As a result, the icons are much smaller (and you can fit more icons on the Icon Bar). Positioning your mouse pointer over a small icon displays the icon's description as a Tool Tip.

Change the Icon's Graphic, Text, or Description

To change an individual icon's appearance, select the icon's listing and click Edit. Then choose a different graphic (the currently selected graphic is enclosed in a box), change the Label (the title), or change the Description (the Tool Tip text).

Separate Icons

You can insert a separator between two icons, which is an effective way to create groups of icons (after you move icons into logical groups). The separator is a gray vertical line. In the Customize Icon Bar dialog, select the icon that should appear to the left of the separator bar and click Add Separator. QuickBooks inserts the separator on the icon bar and "(space)" in the listing to indicate the location of the separator.

Removing an Icon

If there are any icons you never use or use so infrequently that you'd rather use the space they take up for icons representing features you use a lot, remove them. Select the icon in the Customize Icon Bar dialog and click Delete. QuickBooks does not ask you to confirm the deletion; the icon is just zapped from the Icon Bar.

Adding an Icon

You can add an icon to the Icon Bar in either of two ways:

- Choose Add in the Customize Icon Bar dialog.
- Automatically add an icon for a window (transaction or report) you're currently using.

Using the Customize Icon Bar Dialog to Add an Icon

To add an icon from the Customize Icon Bar dialog, click Add. If you want to position your new icon at a specific place within the existing row of icons (instead of at the right end of the Icon Bar), first select the existing icon that you want to sit to the left of your new icon. Then click Add. The Add Icon Bar Item dialog opens.

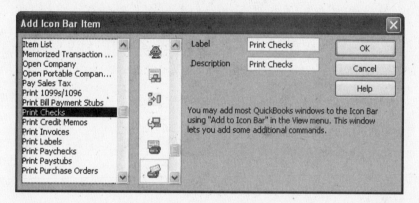

Scroll through the list to select the task you want to add to the Icon Bar. Then choose a graphic to represent the new icon (QuickBooks selects a default graphic, which appears within a box). If you wish, you can change the label (the title that appears below the icon) or the description (the text that appears in the Tool Tip when you hold your mouse pointer over the icon).

Adding an Icon for the Current Window

If you're currently working in a QuickBooks window, and it strikes you that it would be handy to have an icon for fast access to this window, you can accomplish the deed quickly. While the window is active, choose View | Add *Name Of Window* To Icon Bar (substitute the name of the current window for *Name Of Window*). A dialog appears so you can choose a graphic, name, and description for the new icon.

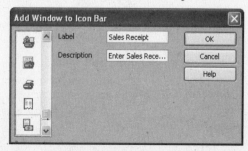

Managing Your QuickBooks Files

Chapter 21

n this chapter:

- Create companies

- Back up and restore company files

- Use a portable company file

- Clean up data

- Use the audit trail

- Update QuickBooks software

In addition to performing bookkeeping chores in QuickBooks, you need to take care of some computer file housekeeping tasks. It's important to keep your software up-to-date and to make sure your data is accurate and available. QuickBooks provides some features to help you accomplish these responsibilities.

Creating Companies in QuickBooks

You can create as many companies in QuickBooks as you wish. You can have your business in one company and your personal finances in another company. If you have enough time and energy, you can also volunteer to run the local community association, open a second business, keep your mother-in-law's books, or create companies for any of a zillion reasons.

 TIP: If you volunteer to use your QuickBooks software for a nonprofit organization, check out *Running QuickBooks in Nonprofits*, from CPA911 Publishing (www.cpa911publishing.com). This book teaches how to adapt QuickBooks for nonprofit needs. The book is available at your favorite bookstore.

To create a new company, choose File | New Company from the QuickBooks menu bar. This opens the EasyStep Interview you saw the first time you used QuickBooks (if you didn't update an existing company file from a previous version). You can go through the EasyStep Interview (it's a wizard) to create the new company by clicking the button labeled Start Interview.

If you don't want to go through the interview process, you can create the company manually by clicking the button labeled Skip Interview. This provides a shortcut method of creating a company, and it begins with the Creating New Company window, shown in Figure 21-1.

Fill in the data and click Next to see a list of company types. In the left pane, select the industry that comes closest to your company's mission. QuickBooks uses this information to create a chart of accounts for the company (the right pane displays the accounts for the selected company type).

Click Next to save the information in a company file. QuickBooks suggests a filename based on your company name, but you can invent your own filename if you wish. Click Save to make this company a file in your QuickBooks system.

QuickBooks loads the new company as the current company, and you can start setting preferences, entering data, and doing all the other tasks involved in creating a company.

Deleting Company Files

Sometimes you have a valid reason to get rid of a company file. Perhaps you created a company to experiment with and you no longer use it, or you sent a copy of the local community association's file to another QuickBooks user who is taking over your job as treasurer.

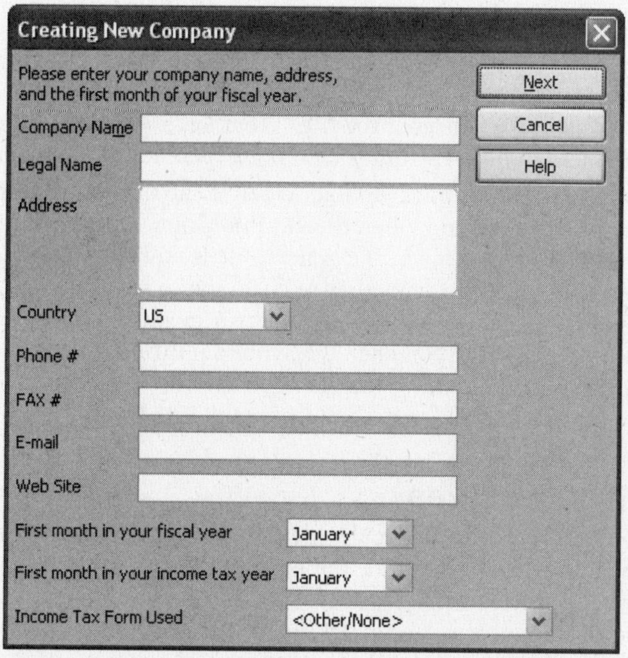

FIGURE 21-1   Fill in the data to create a new company file quickly.

So, how do you delete a company file? In an amazing display of convoluted logic, QuickBooks, the only accounting software I've ever worked with that lets users delete transactions (a dangerous thing to do), has no provision for deleting unwanted company files.

There's a workaround, of course (I wouldn't mention this topic if I didn't have a workaround to offer), but you must use it carefully and pay attention to the order in which you perform tasks.

You've probably guessed the basic workaround: delete the file from Windows Explorer or My Computer. However, before you click the file's listing and press the DELETE key, read on so you don't encounter a problem when you next open QuickBooks.

How QuickBooks Loads Company Files

QuickBooks automatically opens the company file that was loaded when you last exited the software. If it can't find that file it gets confused, and when software gets confused it sometimes slows down or stops working properly. Even if QuickBooks accepts the fact that the file it's trying to open is missing and displays the No Company Open dialog, it's cleaner to make sure you don't have the about-to-be-deleted company file loaded when you close QuickBooks. Use File | Open Company or File | Open Previous Company to select another company file.

I can hear you saying, "Why would I have that file open if I no longer use it?" The answer is, "Because almost every user who has called me for help in this situation opened the file to make sure it didn't contain anything important, closed QuickBooks, and then deleted the file." That last-minute check to make sure it's okay to delete the file is the quicksand many people wander into.

It takes QuickBooks longer to load when it can't find the last-used company file (the one you deleted), and when the No File Open dialog appears to ask you to select a company file to open, the deleted file is still listed. For some reason, many people select that file (perhaps they're checking to see if they really did delete the file—they did). QuickBooks displays an error message explaining that the file could not be found, and when you click OK, you're returned to the No File Open dialog. Open another file. (To remove the listing in the No File Open dialog, see the section "Eliminating Deleted Files from the Company File List.")

Deleting the Files

To delete a company, just delete the file *companyname*.QBW. By default, QuickBooks stores company files in the same folder that holds the QuickBooks software, but you may have opted to create a subfolder to store your files. If you've created an accountant's copy of your company file, you might as well delete that also; it has the filename *companyname*.QBX. If you saved a backup to your hard drive (not a good idea, but some people do this), you can delete that also—look for the file *companyname*.QBB.

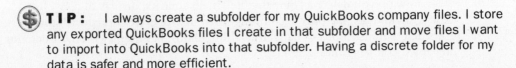 **TIP:**   I always create a subfolder for my QuickBooks company files. I store any exported QuickBooks files I create in that subfolder and move files I want to import into QuickBooks into that subfolder. Having a discrete folder for my data is safer and more efficient.

Eliminating Deleted Files from the Company File List

QuickBooks tracks the company files you've opened and lists the most recently opened files on the File menu to make it easier to open those files. You don't have to open a dialog to select one of those files, you just point to the appropriate listing on the submenu under the File | Open Previous Company command. The submenu lists the company files you've opened starting with the most recent (it's a duplicate of the listing displayed in the No Company Open dialog).

After you delete a company file, if its listing appears on the submenu, or in the No Company Open dialog, a user could inadvertently select it, which produces a delay followed by an error message.

To eliminate this possibility, open another company file and use the following steps to remove the file from the list:

❶ Choose File | Open Previous Company | Set Number Of Previous Companies.

② Change the data for the number of companies to list from 4 (the default) to 1, and click OK.

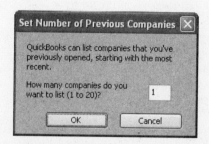

This changes the company files that are listed in the Open Previous Company menu and in the No Company Open dialog to the current company file only. The next time you open QuickBooks, repeat these steps and change the number back to 4, or to any other number that's efficient (depending on the number of companies you work with). QuickBooks begins tracking your work to rebuild the list.

Backing Up and Restoring Files

Backing up your QuickBooks data is an incredibly important task and should be done on a daily basis. When QuickBooks performs a backup, it doesn't make an exact copy of your company file; instead, the data in the file is compressed, making the resulting file much smaller than your original company file.

Backing Up

To create a backup of the current company, choose File | Back Up from the menu bar to open the Back Up Company File tab of the QuickBooks Backup dialog seen in Figure 21-2.

Before opening the Backup dialog, QuickBooks might display a message about using a portable company file to send files to another computer. See the section "Using a Portable Company File," later in this chapter, for more information.

Choose a Location

Choose a location for the backup file. QuickBooks names the backup file for you, which you can change if you wish (but there's rarely a good reason to do so). The default filename is the same as your company filename, with the extension .QBB.

💲 **CAUTION:**   If you've previously restored a backup, when you back up any company file, QuickBooks uses the name of the backup file you restored. Be sure to change the name to match the name of the company file you're backing up.

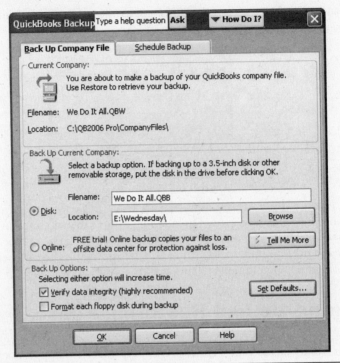

FIGURE 21-2   Back up your company file every day.

If you're on a network, you can back up to a remote folder by clicking Browse, selecting Network Neighborhood or My Network Places, and choosing the shared folder that's been set up for your backups. It's better and faster, however, to map a drive to the remote backup location and enter the mapped drive letter in the Location field of the Backup dialog. (See the Windows Help files to learn how to map drives to a shared folder on another network computer.)

Don't back up onto your local hard drive. Use removable media, such as a USB drive, a Zip drive, an external hard drive, or a network drive (if you're on a network), because the point of backing up is to be able to get back to work in case of a hard-drive or computer failure. QuickBooks also supports backing up to floppy drives, but that method is so time-consuming (it takes many floppy disks), that most users will find excuses to skip backing up.

Don't back up on top of the last backup, because if something happens during the backup procedure, you won't have a good backup file to restore. If you're using expensive media, such as a Zip drive, and you don't want to purchase that many disks, have one disk for odd days and another for even days. If you're using a USB or other external drive with a larger capacity than a Zip drive, create a folder for each day of the week.

When you use a disk that's already received a backup file, QuickBooks will ask if you want to replace the existing file with the new one. Click Yes, because the current backup file is newer and has up-to-the-minute data. The old file is at least two days old, and perhaps a week old, depending on the way you're rotating media.

Periodically (once a week is best, but once a month is essential), make a second backup copy on a different disk and store it off site (a CD is best). Then, if there's a catastrophe (fire or flood), you can buy, rent, or borrow a computer, install QuickBooks, and restore the data (which escaped the catastrophe by being stored elsewhere).

 NOTE: You can also back up to an Internet server. QuickBooks offers an online backup service (click Tell Me More on the QuickBooks Backup dialog to learn about it), and other online backup services exist.

Choose Options

The Backup dialog offers two options for the backup process:

- Verify Data Integrity
- Format Each Floppy Disk During Backup

Verifying data is a process that QuickBooks runs against the current data file (your company file) to make sure its structure is valid. Data verification features can detect corrupt files or corrupt portions of files. However, if you choose the option to verify the data during the backup procedure, the time it takes to back up your file is substantially longer. The feature is enabled by default, so you have to remember to deselect it before starting a backup. The Verify Data command is available on the QuickBooks menu system (choose File | Utilities | Verify Data), so you can check the condition of your file periodically—it's not necessary to run it on a regular basis such as a daily backup.

The option to format the floppy disk(s) you're using for the backup is a way to make sure the disk is "clean." When you buy floppy disks, they're preformatted, but if they've been used and files have been written and deleted, it's probably a good idea to format them once in a while. Formatting destroys all data on a disk, so make sure the disk doesn't contain any important information before taking this step.

Set Defaults

Click Set Defaults to open a dialog in which you can establish default settings for your backups.

Set Defaults	
☑ Remind me to back up when closing the data file every **4** times.	
Default Backup Location: **E:|**	Browse...
☐ Append date and timestamp to the name of this backup file	
☑ Use Windows CD Writing Wizard	
OK	Cancel	Help

Use the following guidelines to set these defaults:

- If you want to be reminded to perform a manual backup, select the option for reminders and enter the frequency specification for the reminder. The frequency is linked to the number of times you close your QuickBooks company file; it's not a specification for elapsed days. If you open and close your QuickBooks files numerous times during the day and you specify a small number, you'll see the reminder at least once every day (not a bad thing).
- If you're using a floppy drive for backups, you cannot set the default unless a disk is in the floppy drive. It doesn't have to be a backup disk (you're just setting defaults; you're not backing up), but QuickBooks checks the drive when you click OK in the Set Defaults dialog.
- Select a default location, which can be an external drive, such as a floppy drive or a Zip drive, or a mapped drive to a shared folder on another computer on your network.
- If you select the option to append a date/timestamp to the filename, the backup filename contains the date and time information for the backup. This means you can tell at a glance when the latest backup was performed, instead of changing your view settings to display the date/time in Windows Explorer or My Computer.
- If you're running QuickBooks on Windows XP, the option Use Windows CD Writing Wizard appears. See the sections "Backing Up to a CD-ROM" and the sidebar "Bypassing the Windows XP CD Writing Wizard" for more information about backing up to a CD.

Automatic Backups

QuickBooks lets you schedule automatic backups. To configure the feature, click the Schedule Backup tab on the Backup dialog (see Figure 21-3).

This dialog offers two types of automatic backups:

- Automated backup when closing a company file
- Scheduled backup at a time you specify

You can configure either or both, using the guidelines presented here.

Automated Backup When Closing Files

The Automatic Backup section of the Backup dialog presents an option to back up your company data file every X times you close that file (substitute a number for X). The word "close" is literal, so an automated backup takes place under either of the following conditions:

- While working in QuickBooks, you open a different company file or choose File | Close.
- You exit QuickBooks.

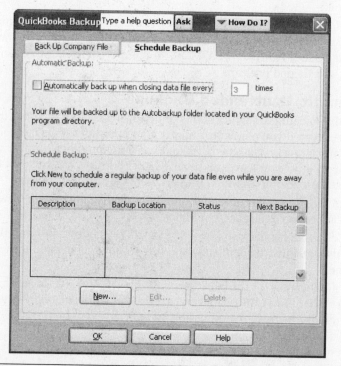

FIGURE 21-3 Use automatic backups to make sure your files are always backed up.

The backup takes place, and the backup file is located in the subfolder named Autobackup under the folder in which you installed QuickBooks. This means your backups are on your hard drive, which isn't a good idea. Copy the backup file to an external drive, a computer on another network, or to a CD.

QuickBooks maintains three discrete automated backup files:

- The first time the automated backup runs, the filename is ABU_0_<*Company Filename*><*TimeStamp*>.QBB.
- The second time the automated backup runs, the file that starts with ABU_0 is copied to a file named ABU_1_<*CompanyFilename*><*TimeStamp*>.QBB, and the latest backup becomes ABU_0.
- The third time the automated backup runs, the pattern continues, as previous files are copied to the next highest number and the most recent backup file starts with ABU_0.

$ NOTE: As an example of the filename structure, my company backup filename is ABU_0_We Do It All Aug 09,2006 06 34 PM.QBB.

If you have some reason to think your current file is corrupt, you can go back to a previous backup instead of restoring the latest backup (which may be a backup of corrupted data). However, you'll have to re-enter all the transactions that aren't in the last-saved good backup.

Automatic Unattended Backups

You can also configure QuickBooks to perform a backup of your company files at any time, even if you're not working at your computer. This is a cool feature, but it doesn't work unless you remember to leave your computer running when you leave the office. Before you leave, make sure QuickBooks is closed so all the files are available for backing up (open files are skipped during a backup).

To create the configuration for an unattended backup, click New to open the Schedule Backup dialog seen in Figure 21-4.

You can give the backup a descriptive name (it's optional), but if you're going to create multiple unattended backup configurations, it's a good idea to identify each by name.

Enter a location for the backup file. In Figure 21-4, the location is a mapped network drive. You can use an external drive if you have one. This won't work with a floppy drive because it's impossible to fit your QuickBooks 2005 file onto a single floppy disk.

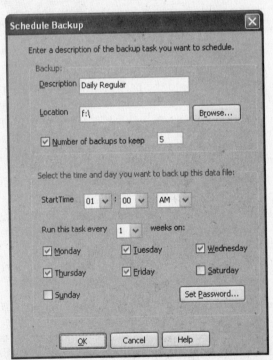

FIGURE 21-4   Configure the specifications for a backup that runs automatically.

$ CAUTION: Be sure the target drive is available—insert the Zip, USB, or other removable drive before leaving the computer; or, be sure the remote network computer you're using for backup storage isn't shut down.

If you don't want to overwrite the last backup file every time a new backup file is created, select the option Number Of Backups To Keep, and specify the number. QuickBooks saves as many discrete backup files as you specify, each time replacing the first file with the most recent backup and copying older files to the next highest number in the filename, which always begins with SBU_0.

$ NOTE: Unattended backup files are saved with the filename pattern SBU_0_<*CompanyFilename*><*Date/TimeStamp*>. If you specify two backup files in the Number Of Backups To Keep field, the second filename starts with SBU_1_. This pattern continues for the number of backups you specified.

Create a schedule for this unattended backup by selecting a time and a frequency. For this example, I created a daily schedule (weekdays) to make sure the backup occurs every day.

If you're on a network, QuickBooks displays the Set Password dialog. The password in question is not to your QuickBooks user and password configuration; it's your Windows network password, and it's quite possible you don't have to use this function. The username and password you enter into the dialog are for a Windows logon name and password, and it's needed only if you're running Windows with permissions and rights configured under NTFS (the secure file system available in Windows NT/2000/XP/2003 Server).

$ TIP: If you're using Windows 2000/XP/2003 Server, and you're familiar with the RunAs feature, this Set Password dialog works similarly.

You can create multiple unattended backups and configure them for special circumstances. For instance, in addition to a nightly backup, you may want to configure a backup every four weeks on a Saturday or Sunday (or during your lunch hour on a weekday) on a removable drive that is earmarked for off-site storage. Be sure to bring the office backup media to the office on that day and take it back to the off-site location when the backup is finished.

I'm a backup freak (my entire professional life is on my computers), so in addition to the nightly backup that runs at 11:00 P.M., I have a second unattended backup running at 1:00 A.M. to a different mapped drive (on a different network computer). A third backup is configured for Fridays at 3:00 A.M., and its target is a USB drive (that's my off-site backup). On Fridays, before I leave the computer, I insert the USB drive into the USB port, confident that all three backups will run while I'm gone. On Monday, I take the removable media off site. In fact, I alternate between two removable media disks, so I'm never backing up over the only existing removable backup.

Backing Up to a CD-ROM

If you're running Windows XP or Windows Server 2003, you can back up to a CD from within QuickBooks. If you're running an earlier version of Windows, you can back up to a CD outside of QuickBooks. A CD is a good media choice for a weekly or monthly backup that is taken off site. Of course, I'm assuming you have a CD-R or CD-RW drive.

If you're not using Windows XP/Windows Server 2003, periodically use your CD-burning software to copy your QuickBooks company files (all of them, if you're running multiple companies). You can copy the company file directly to the CD; you don't have to make a backup first. If you have to restore from this file, you can copy the file back to your QuickBooks folder; you don't have to use the Restore command.

In Windows XP, which has built-in CD writing features, QuickBooks supports backups to CD-ROM. Before you begin make sure you put a blank CD in the drive.

Now use the following steps to back up to CD:

1. Choose File | Back Up.
2. In the Location field of the QuickBooks Backup dialog, enter x: (substitute the drive letter of your CD-R or CD-RW drive for x).
3. Click OK to start the process.
4. When QuickBooks displays a message warning you that backing up to your hard drive isn't a good idea and asking if you're sure if you want to back up to your hard drive, click Yes. (The message appears because the way Windows XP writes to your CD is to write the file to the hard drive before burning the CD.)
5. When the backup file has been written to the hard drive, QuickBooks displays a message telling you your data has been backed up successfully. A balloon appears over the notification area of your taskbar, telling you that files are waiting to be written to the CD. Click the balloon body, not the x, to close the balloon.
6. The folder window for the CD drive opens, displaying a listing for your backup file. Select the file.

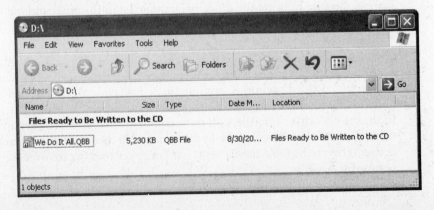

7 Choose File | Write These Files To CD (if you're not displaying the left pane of this window), or, if you display the left pane, click Write These Files To CD.

8 Follow the prompts in the Windows XP CD Burning Wizard to transfer the file to the CD.

The next time you select the Backup command, the location for the backup file is automatically set to the folder that Windows XP uses to store files that are going to be transferred to a CD, to wit: C:\Documents and Settings*YourUserName*\Local Settings\Application Data\ Microsoft\CD Burning\.

You could have entered that location in the Backup dialog the first time, but why type all those characters? Windows XP understood what you were doing and adapted the data appropriately, which is pretty nifty. In addition, the next time you perform this task, you won't see the warning about backing up to your hard drive, because by then, both QuickBooks and Windows XP will have figured out what you're doing.

Restoring a Backup

You just turned on your computer and it sounds different—noisier. In fact, there's a grinding noise. You wait and wait, but the usual startup of the operating system fails to appear. Eventually, an error message about a missing boot sector appears (or some other equally chilling message). Your hard drive has gone to hard-drive heaven. You have invoices to send out, checks to write, and tons of things to do, and if you can't accomplish those tasks, your income suffers.

➡ FYI

Bypassing the Windows XP CD Writing Wizard

If you're running Windows XP, you can back up to a CD without using the wizard and the built-in CD burning features of Windows XP. Instead, you can write your backup file to the CD immediately, omitting the step of manually moving the file from your hard drive to the CD. This means you can write your backup file to a CD during an automated, unattended QuickBooks backup.

In order to accomplish this you must have packet-writing software, such as Roxio's DirectCD or Nero's InCD (not Nero's Burning ROM) installed on your Windows XP computer, and the software must be configured to launch during startup so it's always available (which is the default configuration).

In QuickBooks, configure the backup feature to bypass the Windows XP wizard by clicking the Set Defaults button on the QuickBooks Backup dialog. In the Set Defaults dialog, clear the check mark in the check box for the option Use Windows CD Writing Wizard. (This option is only on the Set Defaults dialog if QuickBooks is installed on a computer running Windows XP.) QuickBooks will use your packet-writing software to write the backup file to the CD.

Don't panic; get another hard drive or another computer (the new one will probably cost less than the one that died because computer prices keep dropping). If you buy a new hard drive, it will take some time to install your operating system. If you buy a new computer, it probably comes with an operating system installed.

If you're running on a network (and you were backing up your QuickBooks files to a network drive), create the mapped drive to the shared folder that holds your backup. Then install your QuickBooks software.

Sometimes it's only your QuickBooks file or your QuickBooks software that experiences a disaster, and your computer is fine. QuickBooks won't open, or QuickBooks opens but reports a corruption error when it tries to open your file. In this case, you don't have all the work of rebuilding hardware. If QuickBooks won't open or opens with error messages about a software problem, reinstall QuickBooks. If the new installation of QuickBooks opens but your company file won't open, restore your backup.

Here's how to restore a backup file:

1. Start QuickBooks. If the opening window tells you there's no company open and suggests you create one, ignore that message.

2. If you backed up to removable media, put the disk that contains your last backup into its drive. If you backed up to a network share, be sure the remote computer is running. If you purchased the QuickBooks Online backup service, be sure you've configured your Internet connection.

3. Choose File | Restore from the QuickBooks menu bar. When the Restore Company Backup window appears (see Figure 21-5), change any settings that are incorrect.

4. Click Restore. If your backup occupies multiple floppy disks, you'll be prompted to insert disks.

5. If you're restoring to an existing company (because the problem was a corrupt data file), you receive a warning that you're about to overwrite the existing file. That's fine; it's what you want to do, so type **Yes** in the dialog.

QuickBooks displays a message that your data files have been restored successfully. You did it! Aren't you glad you back up regularly? Click OK and go to work!

(\$) TIP: If this backup wasn't saved yesterday, you must re-create every transaction you made between the time of this backup and the last time you used QuickBooks.

Using a Portable Company File

QuickBooks 2006 introduces a new feature called a *portable company file*, which is a copy of your QuickBooks company file that has been condensed to save disk space. Portable files not only take up less room on a disk, they also save download time if you need to attach the file to an e-mail message.

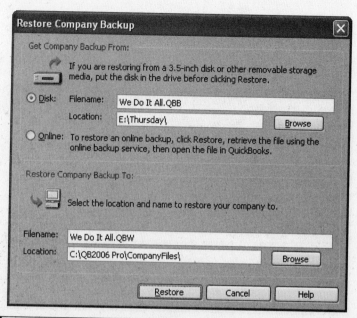

FIGURE 21-5 Tell QuickBooks where to find your backup file, and where to restore it.

You can also use a portable company file to move data between computers (such as your home computer and your office computer), so you can work at home, and then bring the updated file back to the office. You could also send the file to your accountant.

A portable file is not a backup; it's a smaller version of your company file (the smaller size is the result of the condensing process). The portable filename has the extension .QBM.

Creating a Portable Company File

To create a portable company file, choose File | Portable Company File | Create File. QuickBooks displays a message telling you it must close all QuickBooks windows to perform this task. Click OK.

In the Create Portable Company File dialog (see Figure 21-6), select a name for the file. By default, QuickBooks uses the company filename (changing the extension to .QBM), and there's usually no reason to change it.

Select a location for the file (by default, QuickBooks chooses the folder or subfolder in which you store the company file). It's best to select a Zip or USB drive, and take it with you so you can install it on another computer. Or, leave the default location, and then send the file to yourself (or your accountant) via e-mail. When you've set the location, click Save. It takes a while to create the file, and when it's done, QuickBooks issues a success message.

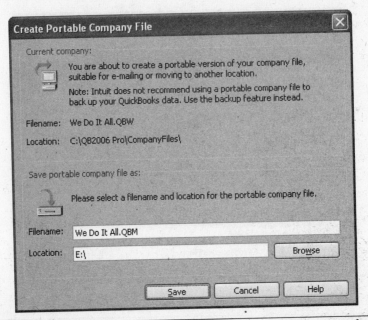

FIGURE 21-6   Locate your portable file in a convenient place, so you can transfer it to another computer or user.

Installing a Portable Company File

To install a portable company file, either on your home computer or on the office computer after you've worked on the file at home and saved it as a portable file, choose File | Portable Company File | Open File.

In the top section of the Import From Portable Company File dialog, click the Browse button to find and select the filename and location of the portable company file you want to install (it has a .QBM extension).

In the bottom section of the dialog, enter the filename and location of the regular QuickBooks company file you want to create. The first time you do this, the company file doesn't exist. After that, replace your existing company file with this portable company file because it's up-to-date.

If the company file already exists on your computer, QuickBooks issues a warning that you are about to overwrite an existing file. Click Yes to confirm the replacement. Then, QuickBooks issues another warning, telling you that you're going to delete the existing file. Type yes, and click OK, to confirm that you want to replace the existing file with the contents of the portable company file.

If deleting and replacing an existing company file makes you nervous (an understandable reaction), before you perform this task, open My Computer or

Windows Explorer and copy your company file (the one with the .QBW extension, that predates the portable company file and its modifications) to another location on your hard drive. Of course, since you back up every day, you have the last backup as another safety measure.

After the portable company file is uncompressed and loaded, QuickBooks issues a dialog suggesting that you back up this file immediately. When you click OK, QuickBooks opens the Backup dialog.

Cleaning Up Data

QuickBooks provides a feature that enables you to remove certain data in your company file in order to make your file smaller. You can use it to make loading your company file faster (and, because the condensed file is smaller, it makes backing up faster). While this seems to be a handy feature, it carries some significant side effects in the loss of details about transactions. Before using this feature, consider other ways to survive with a very large file.

 TIP: If you updated to QuickBooks 2006 from a previous version, this is the utility that used to be called Archive and Condense Data.

Understanding the Data Removal Procedure

This process deletes closed transactions and replaces them with a journal entry that shows totals posted to accounts. (If you subscribe to any QuickBooks payroll services, no current year transactions are condensed.) Open transactions (such as unpaid invoices and bills, and estimates that are not marked "Closed") are not removed. Before removing the data, QuickBooks creates an archive copy of your company file. You should back up that file and restore it if you need to see the original transactions that were removed.

Consider this solution only after you've been using QuickBooks for more than a year or so, because you don't want to lose the details for the current year's transactions (in case you have to have a conversation with a customer or vendor that involves details about a particular transaction).

Choosing a Date

QuickBooks asks you for the date you want to use as the cutoff date. Everything you no longer need before that date is removed. No open transactions are removed; only those data items that are completed, finished, and safe to remove are targeted. Also, any transactions before the cutoff date that affect current transactions are skipped, and the details are maintained in the file.

Understanding Summary Transactions

The transactions that fall within the parameters of the condensing date are deleted and replaced with summary transactions. Summary transactions are nothing but journal entry transactions that show the totals for the removed transactions, one for each month. The account balances are not changed by removing data, because the summary transactions maintain those totals.

Understanding the Aftereffects

After you clean up the file, you won't be able to run detail reports for those periods before the cutoff date. However, summary reports will be perfectly accurate in their financial totals. You will be able to recognize the summary transactions in the account registers because they will be marked with a transaction type GENJRNL. You can restore the archived file if you need to see the original transaction details.

Running the File Cleanup Utility

Cleaning your QuickBooks file is very simple, because a wizard walks you through the process. To start, choose File | Utilities | Clean Up Company Data to open the Clean Up Company Data window seen in Figure 21-7.

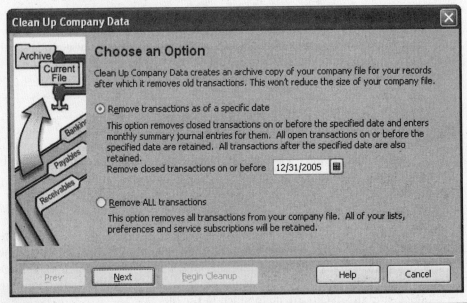

FIGURE 21-7   Select the option you want to use for the cleanup process.

N O T E :   You may see a warning about losing your budget data when your file is condensed (because some budgets are based on detailed postings). Read Chapter 13 to learn how to export your budgets and import them back into QuickBooks.

The wizard offers two choices for proceeding: Remove Transactions As Of A Specific Date (which you choose), or Remove ALL Transactions. QuickBooks automatically displays the last day of the previous year as the condensing date for the first option. You can use this date or choose an earlier date (a date long past, so you won't care if you lose the transaction details). Be sure to choose the last day of a month, quarter, or year.

The other option, Remove ALL Transactions, is really an option to wipe all your data in order to create a new (empty) company file with the same name. It's unusual to do this, but be sure you have a full backup of the original company file in case you change your mind.

Click Next to see a list of the transaction types that are not removed (Figure 21-8). You can select any of them to include them in the "to be removed" list, if you know you don't need to keep details about those transaction types.

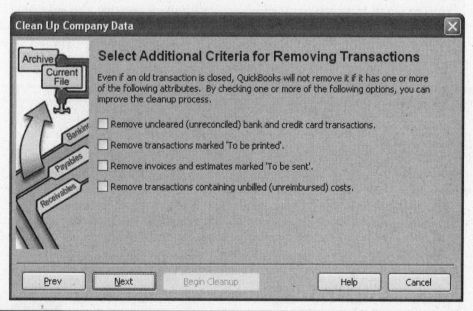

FIGURE 21-8   You can remove transactions that QuickBooks would normally keep, but do so carefully.

Click Next and select the lists (accounts, customers, vendors, and so on) you want QuickBooks to empty of unused items.

Click Next to see an informational window in which the cleanup process is explained. Click Begin Cleanup to start the process. QuickBooks displays a message telling you that first your data file needs to be backed up. This is not an everyday backup; it's the last backup of a full data file before information is removed. Therefore, use new disks for this backup (if you use floppy disks). Additionally, add text to the name of the backup file to indicate that it's special (for instance, MyCompanyFile-Cleaned.QBB). Click OK to begin the backup.

As soon as QuickBooks finishes backing up, it starts removing data. You'll see progress bars on your screen as each step completes. When the job is complete, you're given the name of the archive copy of your data file (which is intact, so you can open it if you need to see transaction details).

Using the Audit Trail

QuickBooks automatically tracks all the additions, deletions, and modifications of transactions in your data file. This record is called an *audit trail*, and it lets you keep an eye on the activity in your data file. You can view the report by choosing Reports | Accountant & Taxes | Audit Trail.

The report lists each transaction, along with the action that affected that transaction, the user who performed the action (if you enabled user login), and the financial information. The transaction action is displayed in bold type, for example, **Deleted Invoice, ID#643.** (The ID# is an internal QuickBooks number.)

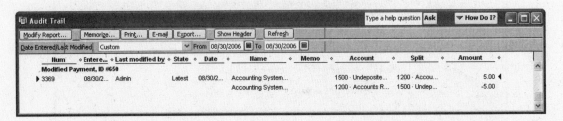

After you perform a file cleanup, all audit-trail data for removed transactions is removed. Note that unlike previous versions of QuickBooks, you cannot turn off the audit trail.

Updating QuickBooks

QuickBooks provides an automatic update service you can use to make sure your QuickBooks software is up-to-date and trouble-free. This service provides you with any maintenance releases of QuickBooks that have been created since you purchased and installed your copy of the software. A maintenance release is distributed when a problem is discovered and fixed. This is sometimes necessary, because it's almost impossible to distribute a program that is totally bug-free (although my experience has been that QuickBooks generally releases without any major bugs, since Intuit does a thorough job of testing).

The Update QuickBooks service also provides notes and news from Intuit so you can keep up with new features and information for QuickBooks.

 N O T E :   This service does not provide upgrades to a new version; it just provides updates to your current version.

The Update QuickBooks service is an online service, so you must have configured QuickBooks for online access (see Chapter 16). When you want to check for updated information, choose Help | Update QuickBooks from the menu bar to open the Update QuickBooks window shown in Figure 21-9.

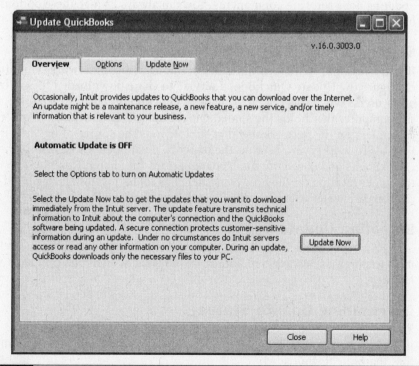

FIGURE 21-9   Use the Update QuickBooks dialog to configure update options, or to download an update.

Automatic Updates

You can take advantage of automatic updates, which allow QuickBooks to check the Intuit update site on the Internet periodically while you're connected to the Internet. QuickBooks doesn't have to be running for this function to occur.

If new information is found, it's downloaded to your hard drive without notifying you. If you happen to disconnect from the Internet while updates are being downloaded, the next time you connect to the Internet, QuickBooks will pick up where it left off.

Manual Updates

If you turn off automatic updates, you should periodically check for new software files manually. Click the Update Now button in the Update QuickBooks window to select and download updated files.

Configuring QuickBooks Update Service

Click the Options tab to configure the Update feature. You have several choices for updating your software components. You can always change these options in the future.

Sharing Updates on a Network

If you're using QuickBooks in multiuser mode across a network, you must configure the Update QuickBooks service to share downloaded files with other users. When this option is enabled, QuickBooks creates a subfolder on the computer that holds the shared QuickBooks data files, and the other computers on the network use that subfolder as the source of updated files. For this to work, every user on the network must open his or her copy of QuickBooks and configure the Update options for Shared Download to reflect the folder location on the host computer. The folder location is displayed on the Options tab when you select the Shared Download option.

Selecting Update Types

Select the types of files you want QuickBooks to download when you update. The most important selection is Maintenance Releases, which fixes problems and adds features.

Determining Update Status

The Update Now tab displays information about the current status of the service, including the last date that QuickBooks checked for updates and the names of any files that were downloaded.

Click the check boxes next to each specific type of update to select/deselect those file types. Then click Get Updates to tell QuickBooks to check the Internet immediately and bring back any files. After files are downloaded, click the listing to see more information about that download. Most of the time, the files are automatically integrated into your system. Sometimes an information box appears to tell you that the files will be integrated the next time you open QuickBooks.

Part Five

Appendices

This custom edition of *QuickBooks 2006: The Official Guide* covers QuickBooks Pro. However, we've included two appendices that cover an overview of features that are not available in that edition, but are, instead, included in the following QuickBooks editions:

- QuickBooks Premier Accountant Edition
- QuickBooks Enterprise Solutions (all editions)

Appendix A explains how Fixed Asset Manager can help you track assets and depreciation. Appendix B is an overview of the powerful Financial Statement Designer, which lets you put together detailed, slick, financial statements.

Fixed Asset Manager

The values of fixed assets decline over time, and calculating the decline is a thorny undertaking. The calculations for depreciation or amortization are extremely complicated, mostly due to the vast number of IRS regulations on the subject. To make it worse, the regulations change frequently, so keeping up with current rules is a complicated task.

In addition to making sure your depreciation calculations don't cause a problem with the IRS, the amounts involved in depreciation transactions have a direct effect on your business:

- The amount by which an asset is depreciated affects the worth of a business because the net (reduced) current value is used on the balance sheet
- The depreciation amount affects the business' tax bill (depreciation is deductible)

The QuickBooks Fixed Asset Manager makes it easier to track and depreciate assets, and enter the resulting calculations in both the tax return and the QuickBooks company file.

 N O T E :   The Fixed Asset Manager is included in QuickBooks Premier Accountant Edition and in all editions of QuickBooks Enterprise Solutions.

Overview of Fixed Asset Manager

Fixed Asset Manager is a robust, complex program, and I think it's a good idea to help you learn to use it by providing an overview of its features. Here's a laundry list that should help you find your way as you discover all sorts of innovative ways to use the program's power:

- A detailed asset entry screen that you can customize
- Up to five user-defined classifications for tracking assets
- Six depreciation bases (Book, State, Federal, Other, AMT, and ACE)
- Projected depreciation calculations
- Disposition tracking
- On-screen queries and custom sorting options for the asset list
- Full calculation overrides (also applies when linking to Pro Series)
- A report list feature that allows you to group commonly-used reports for easy access and printing
- An export feature that allows you to transfer asset information into ProSeries federal tax products
- A desktop workspace you can customize
- A toolbar for quick access to common tasks

QuickBooks Files and Fixed Asset Manager

When you open Fixed Asset Manager in QuickBooks (choose Accountant | Manage Fixed Assets), the currently loaded QuickBooks company file links to the Fixed Asset Manager. You can create a new Fixed Asset Manager client file for this company, transfer prior year clients from QuickBooks Fixed Asset Manager or ProSeries Fixed Asset Manager to the current year, reconnect Accountant's Review Copy with Fixed Asset Manager or restore a previous QuickBooks Fixed Asset Manager file from a backup.

QuickBooks Company Information

Fixed Asset Manager must know the type of tax form this business files. To make sure the right tax form is configured for the company file (or, for that matter, to make sure the tax form information isn't blank, which is often the case), choose Company | Company Information and check the data in the dialog box.

Fixed Asset Manager uses other company information (such as the address, EIN or Social Security number, and so on) when it creates the Fixed Asset Manager file, and you can view that information within Fixed Asset Manager. However, you can't edit the information in Fixed Asset Manager, so you must make sure the data is correct in the Company Information dialog box.

Company Fixed Assets List

QuickBooks provides a Fixed Asset Item list, which tracks the purchase date, the description, and the cost of each fixed asset the company owns. When your clients use this list within QuickBooks, the list is inert; that is, it performs no calculations and is not automatically linked to transaction data entry in QuickBooks. When clients purchase or sell a fixed asset, and create the appropriate transaction entry (a check, a loan, or a cash receipt), the information is not automatically transferred to the Fixed Asset Item list.

Even though the Fixed Asset Item list is nothing more than a list, with no ability to interact with standard QuickBooks software calculations, Fixed Asset Manager can read (import) this list. If the Fixed Asset Item list exists in the company file, your work in Fixed Asset Manager is faster and easier. Another advantage of using the Fixed Asset Item list in QuickBooks is that assets in the list are linked to a Fixed Asset account. In a roundabout way, this ensures the QuickBooks company file has one or more Fixed Asset accounts. Fixed Asset Manager can use that account information, which is another efficient time saver.

Fixed Asset Manager Client File Setup

You must create a Fixed Asset Manager client file for each company, and if no file exists for the currently loaded company when you open Fixed Asset Manager, the process of creating the file begins automatically.

If you'd previously set up a Fixed Asset Manager client file for this company, but the currently open company file is an Accountant's Copy, select the option to reconnect the Accountant's Review Copy to Fixed Asset, and a wizard walks you through the task of opening the file.

When you choose to create a new client, the Fixed Asset Manager New Client Wizard launches, and you click Next to move through each wizard window. The first wizard windows display the company information for the client, and you cannot edit that information (see the previous sections on making sure the company information is correct before running Fixed Asset Manager). The wizard then asks you to respond to queries about the following data:

- Current fiscal year
- Prior short years
- Qualification for the "small corporation" exemption from AMT
- Depreciation bases
- Default depreciation method for each selected basis

The wizard offers the chance to import the fixed assets for this company automatically, using the information in the Fixed Asset Item list in the company file. You can also enter the fixed assets manually.

A client summary is displayed on the last wizard window—click Finish to end the client set up and begin using Fixed Asset Manager. (If you automatically synchronized the fixed assets from the client company Fixed Asset Item list, a log appears to report the fixed assets that were imported.)

When you opt to transfer information from client files for the prior-year version of QuickBooks Fixed Asset Manager, or from ProSeries Fixed Asset Manager, into this year's version, the Transfer Client Wizard launches. Click Next to move through each wizard window. Select the client you want to transfer on the first wizard window that appears. The wizard then asks you to respond to the queries about the following data:

- Calculation options
- Qualification for the "small corporation" exemption from AMT
- QuickBooks Asset Synchronization

When a client summary appears on the last wizard window, click Finish to complete the transfer and begin using Fixed Asset Manager.

Importing Data from Other Software

If you've been keeping depreciation records in another software application, you can import client data to Fixed Asset Manager. Once your Fixed Asset Manager client file is set up, the software can import data from a Comma Separated Value (CSV) format file. You must map the fields in the import file to the fields in Fixed Asset Manager. Fixed Asset Manager provides help for this task during the import.

If the other program can't save to a file in CSV format, but can save data in a file format that is readable by Microsoft Excel, open the file in Excel, and then save the file in CSV format.

If you've been managing fixed assets in ProSeries tax software, you can import data directly from that software to Fixed Asset Manager.

Working in Fixed Asset Manager

After the client file is set up, the Fixed Asset Manager software window opens so you can begin your work. By default, the software window opens with the Schedule tab selected. The tabs at the bottom of the window represent the bases you selected for depreciation. Select the Schedule Tab, and as you select each basis tab the data changes appropriately.

Schedule Tab

In the Schedule tab, Fixed Asset Manager identifies the assets using the text in the Purchase Description field of the QuickBooks Fixed Asset Item list—not the text in the Name field. In fact, Fixed Asset Manager doesn't even import the name field from the QuickBooks Fixed Asset Item list.

Fixed Asset Manager assigns a number to each asset, and that number becomes the asset's name (you can think of it as a code) in the Fixed Asset Manager client file. To arrive at the number (code), Fixed Asset Manager reads the text in the Purchase Description field and appends a hyphen surrounded by spaces, followed by the next available number. For example, if the Description text is Workstation Computer, the Fixed Asset Manager name becomes "Workstation Computer - 1". If another asset has the same description (in QuickBooks, only the Name must be unique, and the Name field isn't used by Fixed Asset Manager, so duplicates can occur when synchronizing with Fixed Asset Manager), the next number is appended to the text ("Workstation Computer - 2"). Asset numbers are appended in the order in which they are sorted in the Fixed Asset Item List in QuickBooks (which sorts on the QuickBooks Name field).

You can sort assets differently by changing the criteria in the sort set. In addition, you can choose to edit an existing sort set or create a custom sort set. You can also change the asset list and the columns in the Schedule tab using the View Column Set, Sort Assets By and Apply Query Criteria controls on the Asset toolbar. To view amounts for any basis supported in a client's file, click the corresponding tab at the bottom of the Schedule tab. The Schedule tab lists all the assets in the Fixed Asset Manager client file. The asset that's currently selected is the asset used when you visit any of the other tabs at the top of the software window.

Asset Tab

Use the Asset tab to enter information about tax forms, the QuickBooks chart of accounts, and other items for the asset you selected in the Schedule tab.

The upper section of the tab is the place to enter general information for the selected asset, including any classification fields. The bottom section of the Asset tab is the Basis Detail section. Enter the cost, date acquired, tax system, depreciation method, recovery period, and other information needed to calculate the asset's depreciation. You can also configure Section 179 deductions here, if appropriate for this asset.

Disposal Tab

Use the disposal tab to dispose of assets. Fixed Asset Manager displays the cost basis, and any Section 179 deductions. Enter the sales price, the expense of sale, and any other relevant information about the Disposal.

Select a property type from the drop-down list to determine where the disposal information will appear on Form 4797, Sales of Business Property (for ProSeries client file exports).

Projection Tab

Use the Projection tab to determine the best depreciation method for the selected asset by reviewing its projected depreciation. Use the Bases tabs at the bottom of the window to see the projections.

 T I P :   You can change information in the Asset tab to alter the projections available in the Projection tab.

 N O T E :   The other tabs on the Fixed Asset Manager window are informational. The Notes tab is a blank window where you can write notes and reminders. The Calendar tab displays information about an asset on the selected date (select date acquired, date of disposal, or both).

Using the Section 179/40% Test

To determine whether the Section 179 deductions claimed for the current year are within allowed limits, or to calculate the percentage of assets acquired in the last three months of the year, use the Section 179/40% test. Perform these diagnostics after you enter client asset information and before you print reports or link the file to the client's tax return. To perform these tests, choose Tools | 179/40% Test. Review the Section 179 test, then click the 40% test tab to review mid-quarter totals.

Reviewing Section 179 Limitations

The Section 179 test determines the total cost of all eligible Section 179 property, the total Section 179 expense deduction made, and how much of the deduction exceeds federal limits for the active year.

Reviewing the Mid-quarter 40% Test

Fixed Asset Manager totals the cost of all assets purchased in the active year and all assets purchased in the last quarter of the active year. If the percentage of assets purchased in the last quarter is greater than 40%, you can convert these assets to the mid-quarter convention.

Using the Client Totals Summary

Use the Client Totals Summary to review the accumulated cost and depreciation before and after current-year calculations for each basis supported in a client file. To see the Client Totals Summary, choose View | Client Totals.

Calculating Depreciation

When the selected asset is properly configured, go to the Asset tab and choose Asset | Calculate Asset. If the command is grayed out, Fixed Asset Manager does not have all the information it needs to perform the calculation. Check all the fields to make sure you've entered the required information about this asset.

You can set Fixed Asset Manager to automatically calculate assets after making modifications using the Program Options window. To select this setting, choose Tools | Program Options. Select the Automatically Calculate Assets option, and click OK to save the change.

Posting the Journal Entry to QuickBooks

Fixed Asset Manager automates the process of creating a journal entry for depreciation expense and/or accumulated depreciation. Choose QuickBooks | Post Journal Entry to QuickBooks, and then enter the appropriate information.

Producing Reports

Fixed Asset Manager provides a variety of report options, including pre-configured report templates. You can sort and select the information you want to print, and the order in which you print it. Table A-1 describes the purpose of each predefined report.

You can select the reports you want to associate with your client using the Report List Organizer and create a custom report list. Having a custom report list allows you to batch print reports. To organize a report list, choose Reports | Report List Organizer.

Use this report	For this purpose
ACE Adjustment Calculation	To determine the total ACE adjustment needed to compute a tax return for a corporation. Assets are grouped by category and sorted by asset number within each group.
Amortization Schedule by G/L Account Number	To see a summary of the activity of the amortized assets. Assets are grouped by general ledger account number and sorted by asset number within each group.
Amortization Schedule by User Defined 1 to 5	To see a summary of the activity of the amortized assets, grouped by one user-defined classification. (There is a report for each user-defined field that you use.) Assets are grouped by the user-defined field and sorted by asset number within each group.
AMT Adjustment Calculation	To print the necessary information for AMT depreciation adjustment reporting (Federal depreciation - AMT depreciation = AMT adjustment). Assets are grouped by category and sorted by asset number within each group.
Asset Disposition by Asset Sale Description	To see a summary of disposition information according to the sale description assigned to each asset. Assets are grouped by asset sale description and sorted by asset number within each group.
Asset, Basis and Disposal Detail Report	To print the asset details for each asset in the Asset and Disposal tabs that you see on-screen.
Assets Acquired in the Current Year	To see a summary of each asset purchased in the current year. Assets are grouped by general ledger account number and sorted by acquisition date within each group.
Depreciation Schedule by G/L Account Number	To see an activity summary for each asset, grouped by general ledger account number. Assets are sorted by acquisition date within each group.
Depreciation Schedule by User Defined (1 to 5)	To see an activity summary for each asset, grouped by one user-defined category. (There is a report for each user-defined field that you use.) Assets are sorted by asset number within each group.
Lead Schedule by Category	To see an activity summary for each asset, grouped by category, in a traditional lead schedule format. Assets are sorted by asset number within each group.
Lead Schedule by G/L Asset Account	To see an activity summary for each asset, grouped by general ledger account number, in a traditional lead schedule format. Assets are sorted by asset number within each group.

TABLE A-1   Description of the predefined reports

Use this report	For this purpose
Lead Schedule by Location	To see an activity summary for each asset, grouped by location, in a traditional lead schedule format. Assets are sorted by asset number within each group.
Lead Schedule by Tax Form and Property Description	To see an activity summary for each asset, grouped by tax form and property description, in a traditional lead schedule format. Assets are sorted by asset number within each group.
Monthly G/L Accumulated Account Summary	To see the total monthly cost additions and deletions and their beginning and ending balances. This report is grouped by General Ledger Asset Account. Assets without assigned account numbers are grouped by "No Account Number."
Monthly G/L Asset Account Summary	To see the total monthly accumulated depreciation/ amortization additions, and deletions and their beginning and ending balances. This report is grouped by General Ledger Accumulated Depreciation and Amortization account. Assets without assigned account numbers are grouped by "No Account Number."
Monthly G/L Expense Account Summary	To see the total monthly depreciation/amortization expense additions and deletions, and beginning and ending accumulated depreciation and amortization balances. This report is grouped by General Ledger Depreciation and Amortization Expense account. Assets without assigned account numbers are grouped by "No Account Number."
Personal Property Schedule by Year of Acquisition	To see a summary of depreciation amounts for assets that you marked as personal property. Assets are grouped by the year each asset was placed in service, and sorted by acquisition date within each group.
Projection by Category	To see a five-year projection for each asset. Assets are grouped by category, and sorted by asset number within each group.
Remaining Basis Over Remaining Life Report	To identify assets that were not fully depreciated. Assets within this report are grouped and subtotaled by category.

TABLE A-1   Description of the predefined reports *(continued)*

Exporting Depreciation Data

Fixed Asset Manager has built-in tools for exporting depreciation data. The export file you create is imported to the appropriate software. The following file formats are supported:

- ProSeries
- Microsoft Word
- Microsoft Excel
- ASCII (text) file
- CSV file

Tax Worksheets

Fixed Asset Manager provides the following tax worksheets that can help you complete the depreciation-related portions of your clients' returns:

- Form 4562 Part I — Section 179 Summary Copy
- Form 4562 Part II & III — Lines 15, 16, and 17
- Form 4562 Part III — Lines 19 and 20
- Form 4562 Part IV — Summary
- Form 4562 Part V — Listed Property
- Form 4562 Part VI — Amortization
- Form 4797 Part I — Property Held More Than One Year
- Form 4797 Part II — Ordinary Gains and Losses
- Form 4797 Part III — Gains from Disposition of Depreciable Property
- Form 4626 — Depreciation Adjustments and Tax Preferences
- Form 4626 — ACE Worksheet
- Form 4626 — Gain/Loss Adjustments

Fixed Asset Manager completes each worksheet automatically using the information in the client's file.

Financial Statement Designer

The Financial Statement Designer (FSD) gives you the power to customize financial statements that are directly linked to a client's QuickBooks data. You don't have to export the data to other programs to create a customized statement; instead, you can produce exactly what you want immediately.

QuickBooks includes FSD with the Premier Accountant Edition and in all editions of QuickBooks Enterprise Solutions.

Overview of Features

The Financial Statement Designer includes the following features, all of which provide more control of your financial statements than is provided with standard QuickBooks reports.

- Includes over 30 predefined templates
- Customize statements by inserting columns or rows to show prior year balances, show percentages and variances between other columns, subtotals and more
- Use your customized statement for any client
- Use the Supporting Document Editor to prepare your title pages, notes to financial statements and compilation letters
- Format the statement anyway you want using familiar spreadsheet-like tools
- Save your financial statements and supporting documents for each client to separate file locations
- Insert rows for subtotals, to group accounts in any way that you want, or even add blank rows for spacing
- Update your client's statement for the following period in seconds
- Print a complete set of financial statements and supporting documents by choosing which items you want to print, in the order you want
- Save as a PDF file
- Export to Excel

 NOTE   With the Financial Statement Designer you can create a standard set of financial statements that are in accordance with Generally Accepted Accounting Principles (GAAP).

FSD and QuickBooks Data Files

As a built-in program, FSD opens from within QuickBooks, by choosing Reports | Financial Statement Designer. The data in the currently open QuickBooks company file is automatically connected to FSD, so open the client company file you want to work with before you launch FSD. When you open Financial Statement Designer in QuickBooks, you can either create a new Financial Statement Designer client file for this company, or work on an existing client file you previously created.

Your client's statement data is always connected to the source. This means updating financial statements is easy and efficient, because the balances update automatically. While you're viewing an FSD financial statement, if you use the QuickZoom feature to edit a source transaction, when you return to the financial statement, you'll see that FSD refreshes the statement with the new account balances automatically.

FSD Components

The power of FSD comes from its three main components:

- Financial Statement Organizer
- Financial Statement Editor
- Supporting Document Editor

Using these three components, you can create professional financial statements including supporting schedules, title pages, and compilation letters.

Financial Statement Organizer

The Financial Statement Organizer sets up and configures your FSD documents. Essentially, this is the "front end" of your FSD software. You use the Financial Statement Organizer for the following tasks:

- Create a new set of financial statements and supporting documents
- Select a period for which a statement needs to be generated
- Set the statement basis
- Select a template for the new financial statement (see the section "FSD Templates", later in this appendix)
- View the list of saved financial statements and supporting documents
- Edit saved financial statements and supporting documents
- Create folders to organize your statements and documents
- Print financial statements and supporting documents in any order you prefer
- Save statements and supporting documents as PDF files

To change the location where you save financial statements and supporting documents for the current QuickBooks client, choose Tools | Select File Locations, and select a new location. The new location of the financial statements and documents appears in the Details column in the Saved Financial Statements and Supporting Documents section. You can choose a discrete location for each client file.

Financial Statement Editor

The Financial Statement Editor is the component you use to design financial statements. The Editor uses spreadsheet-like tools to insert rows and columns, add accounts and formulas, and change the formatting of your financial statements to fit your needs and preferences.

To access the Financial Statement Editor, double-click a financial statement from the Financial Statement Organizer window, or select a financial statement, and choose File | Open Selected.

Editor Toolbars

The Financial Statement Editor includes three toolbars, and if you've been using Windows software you'll be comfortable with their functions instantly, because they provide standard Windows toolbar functions.

The standard toolbar provides the normal file operation functions, such as New, Open, Cut, Copy, Paste, Save, Print, Print Preview, Undo, and Redo. In addition to these familiar icons, the Standard toolbar offers a Refresh icon (to refresh the data in your financial statement). The Format toolbar is similar to the Formatting toolbar in a Windows spreadsheet application such as Excel. Use the icons to apply fonts, font color, indentations, alignments, cell underlines, formats (for decimals, percentage, and currency), and AutoSum functions.

Just like the familiar formula bar you use in spreadsheet software, the Financial Statement Editor's Formula bar identifies the current location of the cursor, and provides a text box for entering formulas into cells.

 TIP   You can display or hide the toolbars by choosing View | Toolbars, and selecting or deselecting the appropriate toolbar.

Properties Panel

The Properties panel appears to the left of the Design Grid in the Financial Statement Editor. This panel consists of four different sections: Column Properties, Row Properties, Cell Properties, and Statement Properties. You can use the Properties panel to quickly view or change the properties for a particular area of the financial statement. If the properties you want to view do not appear in the Properties panel, click the arrows to expand the section. To show and hide the Properties panel, choose View | Properties Panel. If the Properties panel is hidden, you can still access the properties by using the shortcut menus, or selecting the properties area you want to change from the Format menu.

Use the Column Properties to set the date range for account balances. For example, you can configure one column for the prior period balances, and the next column for the current period balances.

Depending on the area selected in the Design Grid, you can use the Row Properties to repeat column headers on every page, change the account description that appears on the financial statement, quickly add and remove accounts for a combined account row, reverse the sign of an account balance, and print the account row on the printed financial statement even if the account balance is zero.

The Cell Properties let you override the column's date range. (Changing the properties using the Cell Properties section only affects the selected cell.)

The Statement Properties allow you to set the column spacing.

Design Grid

The Design Grid displays the account descriptions, balances, report headers and footers, column headers, and the results of the formulas you've entered. This lets you customize statements by inserting columns or rows to show prior year balances, percentages, and variances between other columns and subtotals. You can also insert rows for subtotals to group accounts in any way you prefer, or add blank rows for spacing.

You can also add more information to a financial statement or document by inserting the following fields:

- **Page Break**   Inserts a page break at the location of the cursor.
- **Page Number**   Prints the correct page number.
- **Current Date and Time**   This selection is actually two separate fields; you must insert both fields to print both on the report.
- **Statement Date**   Prints the statement ending date.
- **Statement Basis**   Prints the statement basis (cash or accrual).
- **Client Information**   Prints the selected field from the Client Information window; includes such fields as company name, e-mail address, URL for the company's web site, and so on.
- **Accountant Information**   Prints the selected field from the Accountant Information window; includes such fields as firm name, e-mail address, URL for the accounting firm's web site, and so on.

FSD Templates

FSD comes with a large selection of customizable financial statement templates. Choose from a wide variety of balance sheets, income statements, statements of cash flows, statements of retained earnings, and financial ratio calculations.

While you can easily create a financial statement from scratch, it's quicker to use one of the financial statement templates as your starting point. You can easily make changes to the template to customize it for your client's needs, or your own preferences. Give your altered template a new name so you can use it in the future.

Supporting Document Editor

The Supporting Document Editor works like a word processing tool with simple text editing and formatting functions. Use this tool to design documents such as the title page, compilation letters, and audit reports. Templates are available, and you can change those templates to suit your own purposes.

To access the Supporting Document Editor, double-click a document from the Financial Statement Organizer window, or select a document, and choose File | Open Selected.

Previewing and Printing Financial Statements and Documents

You can preview and print a complete set of financials statements and supporting documents. You can export and e-mail the documents, and even save them as PDF files. Previewing financial statements and documents lets you see how they will look when they're printed, giving you a chance to make sure they're formatted correctly. To print a period's financial statement set, access the Financial Statement Designer. Then, enter the statement date, and choose File | Print.

The Options tab on the Print window includes selections that apply to financial statements. You can configure the way account balances appear on the financial statements as follows:

- Divide by 1000
- Use whole numbers (numbers are rounded to the nearest dollar)

If you select the option to use whole numbers, you can select the account to which rounding errors are posted from the drop-down list on the Print dialog.

You can also suppress the printing of accounts with a zero balance.

 NOTE   The settings on the Options tab of the Print window can also be accessed in the Options window of the Financial Statement Editor (choose Tools | Options).

Export Financial Statements and Supporting Documents

You can export your financial statements to an FST file format, which is the format used by the Financial Statement Editor. You can then import the FST files into another client's company so statements provided by your firm are all using the same professional organization and appearance.

You can export your financial statements to ASCII and tab-delimited text (TXT), comma-delimited (CSV), and Excel (XLS) formats.

You can export your supporting documents to RTF, ASCII and tab-delimited text (TXT), and comma-delimited (CSV) formats.

Save Financial Statements and Documents as PDF Files

You can save your financial statements and supporting documents to PDF files. These files preserve the text formatting of your financial statements and can be viewed using Adobe Acrobat Reader (which can be downloaded from the Adobe web site at http://www.adobe.com).

Of course, like all PDF files, they print beautifully, maintaining the formatting, design, and layout you want.

E-mailing Financial Statements and Supporting Documents

You have the convenience of e-mailing financial statements and supporting documents to another accountant from the Financial Statement Organizer window or the editors. When the recipient accountant receives the email, he or she can save the FST or RTF file to a specified location, and then import the statement or document into the Financial Statement Designer.

If you need to e-mail a financial statement or supporting document to a client, save the item as a PDF file that you can attach to your e-mail message.

Index